Defense Positioning and Geometry

RAJ GUPTA

Defense Positioning and Geometry

Rules for a World with Low Force Levels

THE BROOKINGS INSTITUTION
Washington, D.C.

Library of Congress Cataloging-in-Publication data.
Gupta, Raj.
    Defense positioning and geometry: rules for a world with
low force levels / Raj Gupta.
          p.   cm.
    Includes bibliographical references.
    ISBN 0-8157-3312-7
    1. Defensive (Military strategy)—Mathematical models.
    2. Armed Forces—Mathematical models. I. Title.
    U162.G86 1992
    355.4'5'0151—dc20   92-11039 CIP

9 8 7 6 5 4 3 2 1

For my parents

Foreword

IMAGINE THE DEFENDER of a 500-kilometer-long front armed with ten force divisions confronted by an attacker also possessing ten divisions. The aggressor wishes to gain control over the defender's territory, and the defender's aim is to meet and defeat the attacker as close to the front as possible without being compelled to dispatch its forces across the border into enemy territory. Where should the ten defending units be located? How does the optimal geometry of the defending units change if an arms control treaty reduces both sides to five units? Is there a minimum force-to-space density that every defender must field to prevent breakthroughs?

In this book, Raj Gupta gives answers to such questions about the geometry and density of conventional forces, especially at low force levels. He explains the laws of force positioning and local concentration that all force structures must observe to field an effective defense. He shows how these laws can be exploited to assess the stability of a given conventional force balance and to design arms control treaties that make very deep cuts.

The theory of force positioning developed in the book is general and independent of any specific combat model. It can be applied to formulate military strategy in the Persian Gulf against Iraq, in Somalia, in Yugoslavia, in Afghanistan, or anywhere else where the deployment of force is utilized in the quest for peace. However, the book applies most cogently to such contemporary issues as the minimum threshold to which nations in Eastern and Western Europe can reduce their forces while retaining an effective defense, and the optimal structure of the arms control agreements needed to enforce peace in Bosnia and the fragments of the former Soviet Union. It also provides a framework for assessing whether the current military balance in the Middle East is stable and for visualizing how deep force cuts could go if all sides in the Middle East were to adopt a doctrine of defense sufficiency.

The first draft of this book was completed in the summer of 1989. As regimes fell and wars were fought, the author was constantly forced to rename regions and countries in the manuscript—the Soviet Union became the Commonwealth of Independent States, the Baltics and the Warsaw Pact ceased to exist. Fortunately none of the concepts and ideas presented in the book were buried under the avalanche of change.

The author is grateful to Joshua Epstein of Brookings, Hal Feiveson of Princeton University, and John Steinbruner, director of Foreign Policy Studies at Brookings, for their ideas, suggestions, encouragement, and inspiration. The author thanks the Center for Energy and Environmental Studies at Princeton University for funding his work at Brookings in the summer of 1989. The mathematics that pervades the manuscript was scrupulously checked by Robert Axtell. The author thanks Patricia Dewey, Roz Coleman, and the publishing staff at Brookings for their editing and patience. Finally, the author owes a debt of gratitude to Kin Chan and Brendon Kim for solving some knotty computer problems.

The Brookings Institution is grateful to the Carnegie Corporation of America and the John D. and Catherine T. MacArthur Foundation for partial funding of this project. The views expressed in this book are those of the author and should not be ascribed to the persons or institutions whose assistance is acknowledged above, or to the trustees, officers, or staff members of the Brookings Institution.

Bruce K. MacLaury
President

July 1993
Washington, D.C.

Contents

Introduction

THE FLQW OF FLUIDS in the earth's atmosphere is extremely complicated. In the language of physics, it is turbulent, rotational, compressible and viscous. No foreseeable advance in theory or computational ability will *ever* enable us to model or predict all the complexities of fluid flow in the real atmosphere. Yet, despite this seemingly insurmountable obstacle, weather prediction has evolved into a very reliable and precise science over the last few decades. One way to attack the problem of weather prediction is to·start with a very simplified and streamlined conceptual model of a fluid in motion and examine how such a fluid should behave. This was the approach adopted by Daniel Bernoulli (1700–82) in formulating his basic equation describing the pressure, velocity, and density of an idealized incompressible and nonviscous fluid in steady motion. Bernoulli's Law, which is one of the basic principles of fluid dynamics, was first presented in Bernoulli's *Hydrodynamica* in 1738. From these humble beginnings more than 250 years ago, the theory of fluid dynamics has developed to a point where, when combined with several decades of historical records on the atmosphere and powerful computers for calculation, we can predict the large-scale motion of weather formations with sufficient reliability for most practical purposes.

This book is about the geometry and density of conventional forces especially at low force levels. It attempts to do for conventional defense and conventional warfare what the equations of fluid flow did for weather prediction. In other words, this book lays out the laws of force positioning and concentration that all defending force structures must abide by to field an effective defense. This book uncovers certain spatial relationships that contribute to a successful defense and shows how they can be exploited to construct stable military balances and to reduce forces to minimum levels. Of course, predicting the precise outcome of a war between two existing power blocs is akin to predicting the

1

day-to-day weather in New York City or the likelihood of tornadoes in Oklahoma. The level of discussion in this book is far more basic—closer to the equations of fluid dynamics than to the weather prediction models that are founded on these equations. Thus, in terms of weather prediction, the first step must be to understand how an idealized fluid in motion behaves and what factors determine its properties. Subsequent steps can fruitfully extend the idealized model to incorporate real-world complexities, such as the uneven absorption of solar radiation over the earth's surface, and ultimately combine empirical data with a richly developed theoretical framework to identify wind patterns and issue storm warnings. In terms of a military defense, this means that without first understanding how a model defense should be structured, there is little hope of *confidently* ascertaining whether a real-world defense is optimal, let alone of answering more complex queries such as whether a symmetrical reduction in arms by two nations will enhance defensive capability or what is the least common denominator to which two nations can reduce their forces by mutual consent and collaboration.

The Political Context

The dissolution of the Warsaw Pact in Europe is raising a whole different set of questions from those that preoccupied military analysts throughout the 1980s. The key question is no longer whether NATO has sufficient forces to withstand a Warsaw Pact invasion. The overriding issue now is the minimum threshold to which nations in Europe may reduce their force levels and still retain a meaningful defense. The end of the Cold War has removed many of the political and ideological obstacles to minimizing force levels. North and South Korea appear to be only a step behind Europe along the path of dismantling their redundant military apparatus. In the Middle East there persist onerous political obstacles to regional disarmament but it is not too early to start visualizing how deep force cuts could go if all sides agreed to adopt a doctrine of defense sufficiency. Other regional power balances where disarmament could become a reality are the China–India–Pakistan axis and South Africa. As force levels are reduced across nations, the thinning out of deployed units over the defended terrain makes the spatial configuration of the remaining divisions very critical.

To establish a new order characterized by low force levels a number of questions must be answered:

1. What is the absolute minimum force density necessary for a coherent and robust defense? How deep can mutual cuts go without irreparably damaging defensive capability and upsetting conventional stability? Is there a minimum force-to-space density that every nation must field below which the defense cannot repel an invader?

2. Imagine the defender of a 500 kilometer front armed with ten force divisions and confronted by an attacker who also has ten divisions. The aggressor wishes to conquer the defender's territory, and the defender's aim is to mini-

mize the invader's penetration. The defender wants to defeat the attacker as close to the front as possible without being compelled to dispatch forces across the border into enemy territory. Where should the ten defending units be located? How does the optimal geometry of the defending units change if an arms control treaty reduces both sides to five units?

3. How should an arms control treaty that reduces deployed forces to the minimum needed for defense be structured? What principles should be embodied in mutual agreements to enhance conventional stability but still make very deep weapon cuts?

4. Are there force structures that are inherently defensive and minimize the use of manpower? What is the most effective configuration for these ideal force structures? How can these structures be integrated into the traditional army infrastructure of infantry and artillery brigades, close air support and tank battalions?

Knowledge of the optimal geometry for a defense is directly applicable on the battlefield—in the civil wars raging in Yugoslavia and the Commonwealth of Independent States, in the Iraqi invasion of Kuwait and the subsequent allied response and in all situations where belligerents resort to arms. However, the goal must remain to deter war by fielding "unassailable" defenses rather than by testing the quality of a defense in combat.

What is needed are *general, universally applicable principles* that dictate how conventional forces should be structured to maximize defensive and deterrent capabilities. In the next step, these principles can be used to dictate the ideal force geometry if all sides undergo a substantial force cut, such as a fifty percent reduction, and the cooperative arms control rules that are necessary to plug any holes exposed by the deep cuts.

The Approach

To derive the fundamental rules of force positioning one has no choice but to abstract from the tremendous complexities of real battlefields and war situations. Without some degree of idealization and abstraction from idiosyncratic circumstances, any attempt to decipher the principles of force geometry underlying today's complex weapon structures risks mistaking the proverbial chaff for the wheat. Critical in the process of idealization is maintaining a balance between reducing the problem to a tautology and retaining far too many degrees of freedom. The discussion in this book is mindful throughout of this delicate balance. It is also important to remember that the abstraction needed to generate a successful model leaves out one significant dimension of war—the tremendous human suffering it inflicts. While this book attempts a formal theoretical analysis, its underlying purpose throughout is a stable world where the threat to human life is minimized.

This book examines two forms of defense. For each, the book extracts the essential features and behavior of the defensive units. The first form of defense

(Type I defense) mimics infantry and armored fighting units engaged in ground warfare equipped with artillery, armored personnel carriers, tanks and reconnaissance vehicles and accompanied by close air support bombardment of hostile encampments. It can also be applied to destroyers and frigates in naval conflict. The fundamental units of war are independent firepower concentrations that actively seek out and engage enemy formations and can travel far and wide in the fulfillment of strategic objectives. The principal object of a Type I defense is to restrict the amount of territory captured by the enemy. In addition, the defending divisions are *unwilling* to encroach upon the attacker's homeland or launch a counterattack into the aggressor's territory.[1] The constituent units of this type of defense confront enemy forces directly once the enemy units have trespassed onto the defender's terrain and attempt to physically turn back the advance. In fulfilling their central goal of keeping offensive penetration to a minimum, the defending units are constrained to inflict at least one-for-one casualties on the foe. In other words, a defense that minimizes the attacker's encroachment into defense territory but in so doing loses all its units while only incapacitating half the attacking force is a failure. There must be parity between offensive and defensive force losses.

The second form of defense (Type II defense) imitates an air defense system armed with rapid acceleration surface-to-air (SAM) missiles, an anti-submarine warfare system equipped with depth charges or a "Star Wars"–style ballistic missile defense with x-ray lasers to destroy intercontinental ballistic missiles. In addition, two systems not prevalent in existing force structures but of special relevance because they are the potential defensive technologies most likely to proliferate in the future also belong to the Type II defense category. The first of these very promising defense strategies involves remote-controlled or self-regulating machine guns and anti-tank weapons located in sheltered, stationary bunkers along the border between two combatants. The second consists of small, rapidly mobilized fighting squads manned by trained residents of border districts and armed with light weaponry; these squads race to the scene of an invasion and delay the advancing enemy until the arrival of armored fighting units. Some realizations of Type II defenses are quite attractive in that they are inherently incapable of being used to conduct an invasion and are therefore intrinsically nonoffensive. The bunker defense and border patrol defense are two such examples. To a lesser extent air defense and anti-submarine warfare also

---

[1] This book does not consider counteroffense as a principal goal of the defense. Ideally each side would like to possess a defensive structure such that any offensive attempt by the opponent can be vanquished without having to engage in a counteroffensive invasion of the enemy's territory. Any defender should prefer not losing any defense territory to gaining equal amounts of the enemy's terrain. Besides, if the only means of effective defense available to the side threatened by an invasion is to preempt or to launch a counterattack, a highly unstable situation is created in which each adversary is prompted to initiate the attack.

exhibit a predominantly defensive character. Force structures that possess this inherent defensive quality are collectively addressed under the rubric of passive defense systems. Passive defense does not demand inaction or stasis from the defending nation; however, it does imply limited ability to spearhead an attack. Passive defense systems are constrained in their mobility, maneuverability, range of translocation, concentration, realizable firepower-to-space density, rapidity of deployment and counteroffensive capability but are not restricted in their capacity to effect a devastating defense. In addition, some passive defense organizations, such as a remote-controlled or self-triggered bunker defense or an air defense, make sparing use of human lives limiting the human cost of war for the defender. The driving goal behind this second type of defense is to destroy as much of the enemy's lethality as possible. Put differently, this form of defense seeks to maximize the attrition imposed on offensive forces. At the same time, Type II defenses must not yield vast tracts of defense terrain in achieving this end.

Thus Type I defenses seek to *minimize* offensive penetration while satisfying a constraint of one-for-one attrition with the opponent. In contrast, Type II defenses seek to *maximize* offensive attrition while satisfying a constraint of permitting only *limited* penetration by the foe. In this sense, the two types of defenses are structurally orthogonal.

Idealizing Conventional and Passive Defenses

To analyze what drives the effectiveness of conventional and passive defenses we create simple, conceptual worlds in which these defense types operate and use mathematical analogies to model their behavior. The environment for Type I defenses consists of two nations that share a contiguous frontier of length M kilometers, which serves as the front between the two adversaries. Each side has N units of force. Each force unit is an amalgamation of diverse weapons and personnel working together as a single entity. This hypothetical unit could be the equivalent of a brigade or an Armored Division Equivalent (ADE). Commanders prefer not to break up units or split a single unit among several bases. The N units of the defending side must intercept and destroy the N invading units of the offensive side as close to the front as possible without venturing into the attacker's homeland. In the preliminary stages of our analysis of the optimal geometry for a conventional defense, we adopt simplistic but intuitively appealing assumptions about prevailing conditions. For example, we assume it takes *one* defensive unit to destroy *one* offensive unit; each side has perfect information on all occurrences within its territory but no knowledge of events on the enemy's terrain; the battle terrain is isotropic parallel to the front; and the attacker and the defender transport forces with equal speeds. Under these rather restrictive assumptions we use probability theory to derive the optimal spatial configuration for the N defending units. Subsequently the assumptions are relaxed one by one and their effect on the optimal geometry is studied. In this way we can answer questions such as how much more effective is a defense that can move 1.5 times as fast as the offense? Twice as fast as the invader? What is the wisest strategy for a defender who has no intelligence about the forces of its inimical neighbor but is aware that the enemy fully knows its own positioning? What is the benefit to a defender who can swiftly and surreptitiously transport forces *parallel* to the front? How does the presence of a mountain range or a river across an otherwise contiguous front affect martial strategy?

Finding the ideal spatial configuration for a passive defense requires modeling passive defenses as detect-allocate-intercept systems. Each detect-allocate-intercept system is equipped with a finite number of interceptors and is assigned to protect a certain region of defense territory. The system attempts to detect all aliens that trespass into the space guarded by the system. It allocates available interceptors among all detected aliens. The effectiveness of the passive defense can be measured in terms of the percentage of intruders destroyed by the passive defense. It is straightforward to establish the relationship linking the proportion of incoming aliens destroyed by the defense to the probability that an individual interceptor will kill its target with a single shot, the total interceptor load available to the passive defense and the detection capability of the passive defense. Moreover, using systems theory, passive defense systems with parallel and cascade architecture can be compared analytically and the ideal configuration for passive defenses isolated. In the initial stage of analyzing Type II defenses simple assumptions are again made. For instance, it is implicitly assumed that the passive defense elements are not subject to direct attack by the intruders. As these assumptions are subsequently relaxed, significant insights emerge. Our analysis of passive defenses unearths the relationship between force dispersion and defense effectiveness. We discover how an objective of maximizing offensive attrition imposes upon the defender a slower response time to the invader's penetration. We find how counterattack by the intruders can severely limit the diffusion of defense lethality and compel its concentration at a few locations.

Throughout this book the challenge is to get as far as possible without making any assumptions about the nature of combat or the laws, Lanchester, adaptive or whatever, by which firepower and casualties are exchanged between two combatants. As far as possible our theory of force structure is developed independently of what happens in actual combat. Ideally, we would like to present a complete model of combat, which would formalize mathematically the process by which two adversaries engage in battle. We would like to know how the duration of an engagement and the casualty exchange ratio are determined, what is the fundamental nature of the attrition process in battle, what causes the movement of the front between two sides and how do circumstantial factors such as terrain, defense fortification and the defender's home advantage influence war. However, though progress has been made in recent years in formalizing the principles of attrition, withdrawal and victory that govern the mechanics of battle, a reliable model of combat remains elusive. The main reason for our lack of confidence in any specific model of combat is the unavailability of detailed data on battlefield conditions during historical conflicts. The absence of numerical real world values for variables involved in combat modeling makes it impossible to verify any theory of force-on-force attrition; and a battle model is a faithful representation of reality only to the extent to which the majority is willing to believe in its accuracy. In light of these caveats, our theory of optimal force structure is advanced with only the broadest assumptions about the nature of combat. At an advanced stage in our exposition we are compelled to think about how to determine the duration of a battle and the attacker-to-defender casualty exchange ratio observed in battle. We adopt a minimalist approach, making parsimonious assumptions about the fundamental nature of combat, relating battle duration and casualty exchange only to the force ratio between the two sides at the start of the battle and taking care to express even this sparse relationship in very general terms. It is a pleasant surprise that questions such as whether there is a minimum force-to-space density necessary to prevent breakthroughs, what is the consequence of deep force cuts on defense robustness and stability and how should practical arms control treaties be designed to drastically reduce force levels can be substantially answered without making our conclusions at all sensitive to the exact nature of the combat process.

Conclusions about Conventional Defenses

Studied first is the optimal force geometry for a defense composed of traditional infantry and armored fighting units. Consider two opposing nations separated by a continuous border of length M kilometers, referred to as the length-M front. The nations possess equal overall force levels and equal speed in transporting force. Opponents on either side of the length-M front have perfect information on all occurrences within their own domain but have no knowledge of events on the other side of the front. Thus each side has perfect information on any enemy troops that encroach upon its territory but is unaware of the location or movements of enemy forces as long as the adversary remains within its own territory. One side wishing to conquer the lands of its neighbor launches an invasion and dispatches its troops into the other side's terrain at various locations along the border as depicted in Figure I-1.

The defending side seeks to match the attacking forces unit for unit at each point of penetration. The defender's goal is to meet and defeat the invader as far forward as possible without venturing into the attacker's territory. In effect, the defender wants to minimize the depth to which the attacking troops can infiltrate without encountering any opposition from defending forces. Where should the defending units be stationed before the start of the invasion to be assured of minimizing the unopposed infiltration by the aggressor? The answer depends on where the defender believes the attacker is likely to cross over the front. The probability that the attacker will choose a particular location along the front as a focus of infiltration depends on such factors as the extent to

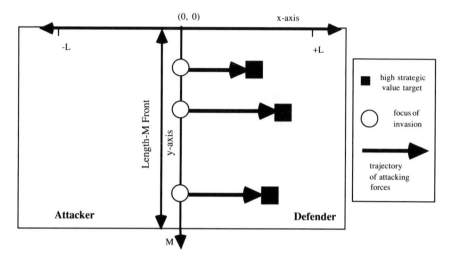

Figure I-1 Conceptualization of a Length-M Front. The invader penetrates the border between the two sides at various points along the front and proceeds directly toward targets of high strategic value on defense territory.

which the surrounding terrain facilitates large-scale mechanized and armored vehicle maneuvers, the proximity of the axis of penetration to targets of high strategic value to the invader, the likelihood of encountering large defensive force concentrations near the infiltration point and the degree of natural cover provided by the adjacent terrain once the no man's land between the two nations has been breached. Consequently, an attacker will tend to prefer certain points along the length-M front for launching its attack. The defender will doubtless formulate its own expectations of where invasion would most likely occur. In terms of probability theory, the defender can attribute a certain probability of assault to each point along the length-M front, giving rise to a probability density function of attack as shown in Figure I-2.

The Basic Optimal Defense

The height of the probability density function at each location along the border denotes the defender's beliefs about the likelihood of that location becoming the point of attack.

For an arbitrary probability density function of attack, all defending units must base themselves at a single location distance μ along the length-M front and distance σ inward from the border (σ–μ Theorem) in order to meet and defeat the invading forces as close to the front as possible. In terms of the rectangular coordinate system established in Figures I-1 and I-2, all defense lethality should be positioned at the point (σ, μ). Point μ is the mean and σ is the stan-

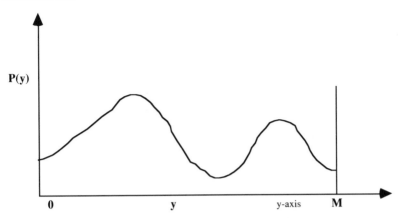

Figure I-2 Probability Density Function of Attack. P(y) denotes the probability that point y along the length-M front will be chosen by the attacker as the focus of a penetration into defense terrain. The sum of the area under the curve P(y) must equal 1.

dard deviation of the probability density function of attack that the defense expects the would-be conqueror to follow. The μ of the σ–μ Theorem arises because the defender is required to position all defending lethality diametrically opposite the point along the front where the invader is *expected* to infiltrate as denoted by the mean of the probability distribution of attack. What is more intriguing is the σ portion of the theorem. The σ measures the spread of the probability distribution of attack along the front. However, when applied to the determination of the optimal defense posture, σ is transformed to a depth perpendicular to the front. A measure determined parallel to the front is exactly transformed into the inward displacement of the defending base orthogonal to the front. The rationale for this is clear: the greater the variance associated with the universe of possible attacks, that is, the larger the spread of potential infiltration points along the front, the farther removed from the front the defender must be to minimize the aggressor's incursion. It is striking how the optimal geometry for the defense depends only and exactly on the first two moments of the probability density function of attack. For the situation where there is an even chance that any point along the length-M front could be chosen as the focus of invasion, that is, there is a uniform probability of attack along the front, all defending units must position themselves halfway along the front and $M/\sqrt{12} = 0.29M$ orthogonally inward from the front.[2] Thus the optimal position for the defending troops is not along the front but at a nonzero distance

---

[2] $M/2$ is the mean, while $M/\sqrt{12}$ is the standard deviation of the uniform probability distribution of attack.

behind the front. Another interesting discovery is that *all* defending units should optimally be concentrated at the *same* location.

Closely linked to the σ–μ Theorem is the concept of a defense locus. The defense locus is the set of points where the defending forces, if optimally positioned, are first able to confront the attacker. For the uniform probability distribution of attack, where the attacker is equally likely to launch an invasion at any location along the border, the defense locus ranges from $M/2\sqrt{12} = 0.14M$ for an attack launched directly opposite the peacetime defense encampment to $2M/\sqrt{12} = 0.58M$ for an attack launched at either extremity of the length-M front as shown in Figure I-3.

Therefore if the front was 100 kilometers long, the defense locus indicates that the invader could "walk over" 14 to 58 kilometers of defense terrain without encountering the defender's armored fighting units. The defense locus thus represents the minimum inward penetration inevitably achieved by the offense and, consequently, is a measure of stability. The closer the defense locus is to the frontier, the smaller is the portion of defense terrain vulnerable to preemptive capture by the enemy and the lower is the award for a first strike by the adversary. In other words, the defense locus provides a quantifiable and directly observable measure of the stability of a conventional balance. Maximizing conventional stability can be translated into the objective goal of moving the defense loci of both adversaries as close to the front as possible.

If the assumption that both sides shift forces with equal velocity is dropped, it is easily demonstrated that for enhancing conventional stability the absolute speed of transporting force is irrelevant. Outcomes depend only on the ratio of attacking-to-defending velocity. The defense loci of both sides are pressed closer to the front if each side is capable of outstripping the aggressor in force mobility when subjected to an invasion and, in turn, is surpassed by the defender when initiating the attack. A second point is that the farther the defender's peacetime encampment is from the demarcation line, the deeper is the incursion allowed by the defense locus. However, because the displacement of the optimal defensive base inward from the frontier is equal to the standard deviation of the adversary's probability density function of attack, the two sides should try to reduce the dispersion of the points along the front that can be transformed into foci of infiltration in order to enhance stability.

Defining the Effective Front Length and Asymmetric Information

A nation's borders with its neighbors can be divided into discrete segments such that the nation is always cognizant of the total number of enemy units behind each segment, and the transfer of hostile forces between segments is easily discernible, though the nation is perfectly blind to intrasegment force mobility. Each such segment constitutes a length-M front. Any two regions of a border separated by a natural barrier, such as a river or a mountain range, or an institu-

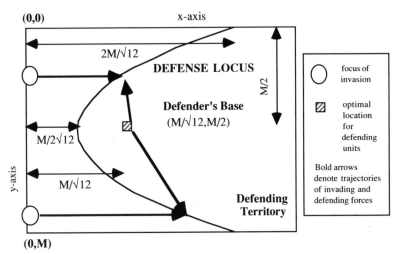

Figure I-3 Defense Locus for a Uniform Probability of Attack along the Length-M Front. The defense locus is the set of points where the defending forces, if optimally positioned, are first able to confront the attacker.

tional or man-made obstacle that restricts the transfer of force from one region to the other, should be treated as two distinct length-M fronts. The goal of each country is to be able to divide the border regions it faces into several small length-M fronts, while compelling its neighbors to define a few, large length-M fronts from its own border terrain. As a consequence, the fortunate country can position its forces close to the frontier and decrease the amount of its territory vulnerable to capture while simultaneously forcing its adversaries to locate their troops farther away from the common frontier. A country can increase the length of the length-M front constituted by its border with another nation by developing the ability to fluidly and unobtrusively transport force parallel to the front. On the other hand, a state can partition the borders of its neighbors into smaller length-M fronts by obtaining better information on the enemy's force distribution. Better intelligence also imbues the defender with confidence in forming an expectation of the probability distribution of attack. The beneficial effects of improved mobility parallel to the front, stealth in conducting maneuvers and better surveillance and reconnaissance of enemy terrain can be measured by the changes in the effective length of the length-M fronts along the border.

An interesting situation of asymmetric information arises when the potential aggressor can "see" into defense territory, but the defender is blind to the aggressor's position, troop movements and martial designs. If the defender is aware that the attacker can pinpoint the peacetime defensive base before hostilities commence, the wisest course of action for the defender is to base all de-

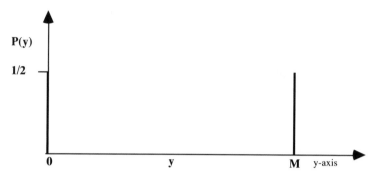

Figure I-4 The Double Foci of Penetration Probability Density Function of Attack. This probability distribution displays the maximum variance of any well-behaved attack function.

fending units at the location (M/2, M/2). This defense geometry of positioning all divisions midway along the front and 0.5M inward from the front corresponds to a probability density function of attack with an even chance of a penetration at either extremity of the length-M front and zero likelihood of an invasion at any point in between (Figure I-4).

Such a probability density function displays the largest variance of any well-behaved attack function that can be defined on the length-M front. It is intuitively clear that in a scenario where the offense has perfect information on the defense while the defense is blind to whatever transpires in the invader's country, the defense is compelled to adopt the worst-case geometry, namely one that corresponds to the probability distribution of attack with the *largest* standard deviation forcing the *greatest* inward recession of the defender's base from the frontier.

The defender's displacement inward from the frontier thus depends on two factors:

1. The absolute length of the length-M front. The larger the value of M the farther away from the front is the base in absolute terms.

2. The variance of the probability density function of attack from which the defender expects the aggressor to derive its plan of invasion. As per the σ–μ Theorem, the defender's forces must be based at a distance equal to the standard deviation of the probability distribution of attack inward from the front.

To minimize the ground exposed to infiltration and occupation by the enemy, the defense must be based as close to the frontier as possible. The defender's vulnerability may be reduced and stability enhanced by defining shorter length-M fronts. Shorter length-M fronts reduce the absolute displacement of the defensive peacetime base from the border; after all, the farthest back the defensive forces can be from the demarcation line is M/2. In addition, shorter fronts imply smaller standard deviations of the probability distribution of attack, since the standard deviation is ultimately expressed in units of M. Also, and not so patently obvious, shorter fronts do not penalize the defender as heavily for errors in the determination of the true probability density of attack; the defender can make significant erroneous assumptions about the attacker's likelihood of assault at each point along the length-M front without disastrous consequences in terms of territory lost.

Constraining the Basic Optimal Defense

The solution to the basic defense positioning problem as advanced has two drawbacks. First, it concentrates all defending forces at a single location which poses an alluring target for raids by deep interdiction aircraft and for C^3I strikes and suffers from the fallacy of putting all the defender's eggs in one basket. Second, for an invasion conducted over urbanized and densely populated tracts of land, the unopposed incursions of 0.14M to 0.58M permitted by the defense locus for a uniform probability of attack could be disastrous unless M is very small. The fact that the loss of terrain allowed by the defense locus can be fatal if M is large can be easily brought home by considering actual fronts such as those between North and South Korea and between Iran and Iraq.

The problems of local force concentration and too permissive defense loci can be dealt with simultaneously by dividing the defensive forces among K distinct force centers and partitioning the length-M front into K length-(M/K) subfronts. Each force center is assigned to guard a specific subfront. This partitioning of a border differs from that due to natural or man-made barriers because the defense is not aware of the number of enemy units behind any individual length-(M/K) subfront and the adversary can freely transfer lethality from one length-M/K subfront to another without alerting the defense. All the defense can be certain of is the total number of enemy units behind all K length-(M/K) subfronts put together. Consequently there could be far more offensive units conducting an invasion through a particular length-(M/K) subfront then the number of defensive units assigned to protect that sector of the length-M front. For a uniform probability distribution of attack, the total number of defending units would be equally divided among the K force centers, and each force center would be located at the midpoint of its corresponding subfront at a distance of $M/K\sqrt{12} = 0.29M/K$ inward from the border. Each "such force" geometry is referred to as a K-constrained positioning since the total defending lethality is constrained to be divided among K bases, and the length-M front is constrained to be sliced into K length-(M/K) subfronts. Associated with each K-constrained geometry is a defense locus. The defense loci indicate where the invading legions will first encounter defensive opposition in a sector. Thus for K=2, the length-M front is split into two subfronts, each M/2 in length. Half the defending lethality is located at $(M/2\sqrt{12}, M/4)$ while the other half is based at

$(M/2\sqrt{12}, 3M/4)$, constituting a 2-constrained force geometry. The defense locus for this 2-constrained defense shown in Figure I-5 indicates that the maximum distance to which invading forces can penetrate before being intercepted by the defense is $M/\sqrt{12} = 0.29M$.

Similarly a 5-constrained force geometry would divide the length-M front into five subfronts of equal length. Each subfront would be guarded by one-fifth of the total defending army. In peacetime, the five defense contingents would be stationed opposite the mid-points of their respective subfronts and at a distance $M/5\sqrt{12} = 0.058M$ behind the border. Figure I-6 highlights the defense locus for the 5-constrained defense.

The maximum distance to which infiltrating forces can advance against a 5-constrained defense without being challenged is $2M/5\sqrt{12} = 0.115M$. The 1-constrained, or $K = 1$, case corresponds to the unconstrained solution, which bases all defensive lethality at a single location, namely $(M/\sqrt{12}, M/2)$, and does not partition the length-M front or distribute defending divisions among multiple bases (note Figure I-3). It might be recalled that the 1-constrained or unconstrained defense allows invading divisions to infiltrate up to a maximum distance of $2M/\sqrt{12} = 0.58M$ without encountering defensive opposition.

For a 100-kilometer front and a defending army divided among five bases, the maximum unopposed penetration is limited to 11.5 kilometers—a far more bearable outcome than the 58 kilometers allowed by an unconstrained defense. However, with the adoption of a K-constrained geometry with K>1, the defense is no longer able to match the invader unit for unit at each focus of penetration as is guaranteed by an unconstrained force deployment. More generally, in any sector of length M/K, the 1/Kth of the defender's total lethality entrusted with that particular subfront must be prepared to battle a hostile strength that could be K times as large. The artificially imposed partitioning of an otherwise contiguous length-M front into K subfronts reduces the maximum distance to which infiltrating forces can advance without being challenged by the defense by 1/K (from $2M\sqrt{12}$ to $2M/K\sqrt{12}$) but simultaneously exposes the defending contingent in charge of protecting a particular subfront to an invading force concentration that could be K times more lethal than the local defense. *There is a fundamental trade-off between force dispersion and forward displacement on the one hand and perfect counterconcentration on the other.* The defense can trade off its capacity to match the opponent unit for unit at each point of conflict in exchange for the option to disperse forces and meet the invader closer to the border. The further forward the defensive armies are stationed the poorer is the counterconcentration ability of the defense.

The Dynamic Conditions for a Robust K-constrained Defense

As a result of imperfect counterconcentration the defender must move divisions from sectors that are not the subject of an onslaught to aid in the defense of sectors under the heaviest enemy fire. The offensive force that penetrates a particu-

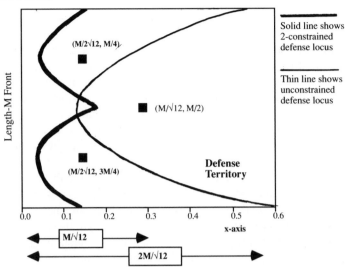

Figure I-5 The 2-constrained Defense Locus. The x-axis is calibrated in units of M.

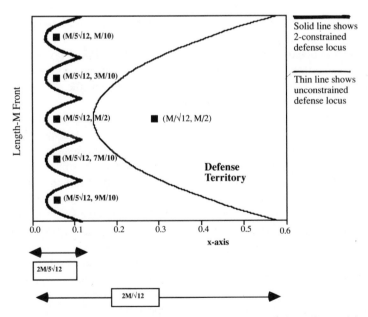

Figure I-6 The 5-constrained Defense Locus. The x-axis is calibrated in terms of M. Dividing defending forces among five bases limits the maximum unopposed penetration achievable by the offense to $2M/5\sqrt{12} = 0.12M$ as compared with $2M/\sqrt{12} = 0.58M$ for a single defense base.

lar length (M/K) subfront is confronted by the defending units assigned to protect that specific subfront. The initial point of contact is determined by the defense locus associated with the K-constrained force geometry adopted by the defense. Now if the invading spearhead far outnumbers the 1/Kth of total defense lethality attempting to block its advance, it is plausible that after a short battle the first defensive wave will be annihilated leaving the attrited forces of the aggressor in control of the arena. However, the battle does impede the advance of the invading units and if waged effectively by the defense can hold up the adversary for a considerable length of time. While the two sides are engaged in combat, the defensive encampments adjacent to the one under fire have the option, if not under attack, to mobilize to the aid of the defense contingent under attack. The duration of the battle between the offense and the initial defense wave can be used by neighboring defense encampments to reinforce the stricken subfront. To prevent a strategic breakthrough, these reinforcements must arrive in time to restrict the attacker's advance to the initial point of contact. Only then will the defending army succeed in containing an invasion to the new forward defense locus associated with the K-constrained defense. This condition implies that defensive reinforcements must always arrive at the scene of battle before the close of the previous engagement. For example, the second defending contingent must arrive before the invading force defeats the first defensive force element. Similarly, the third defense contingent must arrive on the battlefield before the second defending contingent is destroyed and so on. This process of dispatching waves of defending reinforcements must continue until the last of the invading lethality has succumbed at the initial point of contact. Since this condition on robust defense performance depends on the duration of successive engagements between the attacking units and the defending echelons, it can be termed the *Duration Condition.*

In addition to satisfying the Duration Condition, the defense must also ensure that destroying the attacking lethality along a given axis of invasion does not consume more defending force than offensive ones. For instance, if the attacker dispatched J offensive units out of a total force of N, all J invading units must be annihilated by *at most* J defending units at the close of their last encounter. For if the defense utilizes more units to neutralize the offense than the offense has allocated to a particular axis of infiltration, then after the aggressor's forces along that axis have been destroyed, the defender will be confronted with a fundamental inequality in forces along the rest of the front. Since this requirement for a robust defense depends on the ratio at which casualties are exchanged by the combatants it can be called the *Casualty Exchange Condition.*

For an unconstrained defense, the campaign plan of the attacker is irrelevant. Irrespective of the attacker's choices, an unconstrained defense always matches the invader unit for unit at each focus of infiltration and minimizes total offensive penetration. In contrast, the performance of a dispersed defensive structure is vastly influenced by the specific campaign plan adopted by the attacker.

Whether or not the invader achieves a strategic breakthrough depends on the points along the length-M front chosen for the onslaught, the amount of lethality allocated to each focus of infiltration and the times at which individual penetrations occur. Therefore a defense is robust only if it satisfies the Duration and Casualty Exchange Conditions for the entire universe of campaign plans of attack, a condition that shall be called the *Completeness Condition*. If any of these three conditions on defense robustness is violated by a K-constrained force geometry, the offense is capable of achieving a strategic breakthrough against the K-constrained defense.

The defense positioning problem may thus be generalized as follows. What is the most dispersed forward position that the defending forces can adopt while satisfying the Duration, Casualty Exchange and Completeness Conditions? In other words, for a defender with N units, which of the { 1-constrained, 2-constrained, 3-constrained, ..., K-constrained, ..., N-constrained} set of geometries satisfies the three conditions for defense robustness *and* has the highest value of K? So far all results have been derived without any reference to the nature of combat or to any assumptions about the process of firepower exchange. However, to determine whether a particular dispersed and forward positioned defense geometry can contain all offensive incursions, it is necessary to know the duration of each battle and the average attacker-to-defender casualty exchange ratio between offense and defense in each encounter. Both duration and casualty exchange are expressed as general functions of the initial force ratio between the two sides at the start of each engagement. The initial force ratio between the two adversaries is used as the primary explanatory variable because it is easily measured, is the variable that changes the most when comparing the responses of diverse defense configurations to various attack plans, has a massive impact on the ultimate resolution of the encounter and is the variable sought to be manipulated by most arms control agreements. Once battle duration and casualty exchange have been specified as functions of the initial force ratio, the task of solving the generalized defense positioning problem for the geometry with the largest K value to satisfy the Duration, Casualty Exchange and Completeness Conditions is straightforward, and a step-by-step algorithm for this purpose is outlined at the end of Part One.

It is worth reemphasizing that a defense philosophy of basing all units as far forward as possible is almost certainly not optimal. The most forward configuration for the defense involves positioning all N defending divisions at equal distances from each other at the frontal edge of the demarcation line as depicted in Figure I-7. Basing defending units as close to the front as possible does not minimize infiltration; all it minimizes is the physical displacement of the defending units from the front. The extremely poor counterconcentration capability inevitable in such a forward deployed defense could easily overwhelm the defense effort of containing offensive incursion. It is a blind hope that placing men forward will somehow defeat the invader at the border.

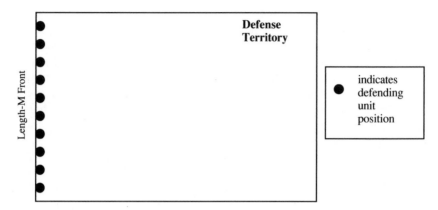

Figure I-7 The Most Forward Deployed Force Geometry for a Defender with 10 Divisions.

Conclusions about Passive Defenses

Examined next is the optimal geometry for passive defenses and how they can be combined with conventional mobile military units to improve defense efficacy. The simplest conceptualization of a passive defense is a detect-allocate-intercept system armed with a detection mechanism and interception vehicles. The detection mechanism identifies alien entities that intrude into the space protected by the system, an allocation routine divides available interception vehicles among the detected aliens and finally the interceptors are dispatched on a collision path with the foreign bodies. The whole detect-allocate-intercept cycle is repeated once the interceptor pods or launchers have been reloaded. An obvious example of a passive defense is an air defense system that uses radar and satellite surveillance to detect incoming enemy aircraft and cruise missiles and then dispatches rapid acceleration surface-to-air (SAM) missiles in pursuit of the intruders. Another example is a ballistic missile defense that uses satellite and airborne reconnaissance to detect ballistic missiles and uses x-ray lasers for interception. A less commonly encountered example is a bunker defense. The bunker defense could comprise machine guns and anti-tank weapons housed in hardened bunkers along the border between two adversaries. The machine guns and anti-tank weaponry would engage all detected enemy tanks and armored fighting vehicles trespassing within shooting range of the particular bunker. The allocation algorithm—in this case, of assigning rounds of machine gun fire or anti-tank shells—to all detected disruptions of the security network could be remote-controlled or even self-regulated, thus minimizing human involvement and loss of life. Finally the detection web for such a passive ground defense could be a symbiotic network of electronic tripwires, remotely piloted vehicles or drones and satellite and airborne reconnaissance. A bunker defense is almost

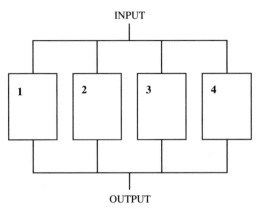

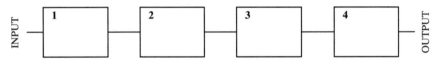

Figure I-8.1 Parallel System Interconnection. Blocks denote individual system modules.

Figure I-8.2 Cascade System Interconnection. Blocks denote individual system modules.

exclusively nonoffensive since the lethality contained in the bunkers cannot ordinarily be used to conduct an offensive maneuver into enemy territory.

Consider a passive defense equipped with a total of I interceptors confronted by an invasive barrage of A aliens. The goal of the passive defense is to incapacitate as many of the intruders as possible. The passive defense may be split into two subsystems armed with I_1 and $I_2 = I - I_1$ interceptors, respectively. To target the intruders the passive defense can assume two possible arrangements: a parallel connection of the two subsystems or a cascade interconnection. In parallel alignment, systems are linked so that all subsystems simultaneously access the incoming signal and process it concomitantly. The net result of the parallel processing is the sum of the outputs generated by each individual component. In contrast, for systems implemented in a cascade format, the input signal or trigger is processed sequentially by each individual module; the subsystems are linked end to end, and the input is initially fed to the foremost subsystem along the chain. The output of the first subsystem is the input to the subsystem second-in-line, whose output, in turn, constitutes the input for the third subsystem and so on. The net result of the cascade processing is identical to the output of the last subprocessor in the hierarchy. Figures I-8.1 and I-8.2 are a visualization of parallel and cascade systems.

For a passive defense, a parallel system detects the incoming intruders, allocates all I interceptors among the detected aliens, and dispatches the total interceptor load against the enemy in a single shot. Linking the passive defense through a cascade system requires identifying foreign intruders, allocating I_1 interception vehicles among the detected trespassers and dispatching I_1 interceptors on a collision path with the intruders *and then* redetecting the location of the intruders that survive the first stage of the cascade and allocating and dispatching the remaining I_2 interceptors. By interposing detection and allocation between phases of interception, the cascade interconnection ensures that no interceptors are dispatched in vain in pursuit of infiltrators that have already been destroyed at an earlier point. To increase the percentage attrition of the invading force, the total number of interceptors must be divided into two equal groups, and the two groups should target the intruders in strict succession, that is, the two groups should be hitched together in cascade. Carrying the argument one step further, to maximize the percentage attrition of the intruders, each individual interceptor should function as an independent passive defense subsystem, and the overall passive defense should link I interceptors together in cascade. When applied to ground warfare, cascade implementation is an argument for the maximum dispersion of passive defense lethality and its deployment in depth. As shown in Figures I-9.1 and I-9.2, a cascade interconnection of a bunker defense distributes the total lethality among as large a number of bunkers as is economically and technologically feasible and spreads bunkers in a straight line stretching as far inward from the frontier as possible. A parallel, or single-layer, geometry is wasteful in its use of interceptors and does not impose the greatest attrition on the invading forces. Thus the optimal configuration for a passive defense involves maximum dispersion of lethality and deployment in depth. Earlier it was demonstrated that for a force structure consisting of traditional infantry and armored fighting units basing defending troops as close to the front as possible does not minimize the infiltration of the aggressor into defense terrain. Once again it is apparent that for passive defenses parallel design or the physical forward basing of lethality is a misguided approach to the optimal utilization of defensive force.

Three Weaknesses of Cascaded Passive Defenses

Of course, a dark cloud accompanies every silver lining and cascade interconnection is no exception. There are three shortcomings of the cascade structure for a detect-allocate-intercept defense. First, cascade interconnection poses detection and allocation phases between interception routines. The number of detection-allocation elements increases linearly with the length of the cascade increasing the procurement and maintenance cost of the passive defense system. Second, each detection-allocation cycle requires a finite amount of processing time adding to the lag in defense response and allowing the intruders to pene-

Figure I-9.1 Parallel Realization of a Bunker Defense. The large shaded circles represent the range of the deployed interceptors. The number at the center of each circle indicates the quantity of interceptors deployed at the point. To cover the length of the front the distance between bunkers measured parallel to the front cannot exceed twice the range of an interceptor. This minimum front coverage requirement holds for both parallel and cascade bunker defenses. In a parallel implementation, all interceptors are based as far forward as possible.

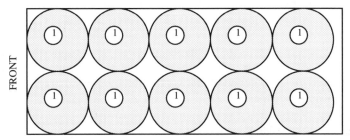

Figure I-9.2 Cascade Realization of a Bunker Defense. Each bunker is armed with a single interceptor. Bunkers are positioned one behind the other orthogonally inward from the front. A cascade implementation produces maximum dispersion and inward displacement of the interceptor defense.

trate further into the defender's space. Because of its lower upfront interceptor density, a cascade implementation, while imposing greater cumulative attrition on the offense, permits invading forces to accomplish greater inroads into defense territory when compared with a parallel systems design. The deeper infiltration allowed by a cascade system might be fatal if the strategic objective of the invader is simply to gain a limited penetration into the enemy's territory. For example, a bombing air raid not destroyed or rebuffed by the air defense before it reaches its target will render the defense a failure irrespective of how many enemy aircraft are shot down by the defense on the aggressor's return sortie from a successful raid. There exists a basic trade-off between the ability of an interceptor defense to maximize the percentage of incoming aliens destroyed and the lag in defense response to the invasion. The greater the proportion of intruders to be annihilated by a passive defense, the deeper is the distance to which large portions of the offensive force might penetrate into the defender's homeland. The third potential drawback of cascade design is that it does not allow for the fact that some forms of passive defense might be susceptible to counterattack by the offense. If combat between the passive defense elements and the invading force displays Lanchester Square-type quality, that is, the casualties suffered in battle per unit time by each side are proportional to the local force concentration of the foe, it might be unwise for the defense to disperse lethality across a large number of cascaded layers. The diminutive force of a single layer of the cascade would be cheaply eliminated by the numerically superior might of the offense.

The disastrous consequences of counterattack on a distributed passive defense can be appreciated by imagining a concerted onslaught by armored divisions and close air support on a border patrol passive defense. The border patrol defense is manned by trained reserves, normally inhabitants of the border districts, who may have the misfortune of waking up one morning to find a full-fledged incursionary expedition in their backyard. The reservists would race to the site where the enemy has penetrated the defender's homeland and attempt to slow the advancing columns in anticipation of the defender's armored brigades. The reservists possess lightly armored, improvised means of ground transport, and their arms would be no match for the heavy weaponry of the foe. These border civilians do not enjoy the luxury of minimum counterattrition and quite likely would be wiped out in the early stages of the engagement. For such a border patrol defense it is a critical question whether the effectiveness of the defense is aided or hindered by adopting the dispersed structure advocated by a cascade design. The answer depends on the relationship between the attacker-to-defender casualty exchange ratio and the size of the engaged defensive lethality. If concentrating defending troops increases defensive vulnerability and reduces the number of attacking casualties for each defending warrior put out of action, the defense should disperse its lethality into as large a number of units as possible and dispatch these units one by one to engage the invader. On the other hand, if the attacker-to-defender casualty exchange ratio increases with increasing engaged defensive lethality, the defense can afford the luxury of force dispersal only if the defense has superior overall effective lethality. In this case, to the extent that the defender chooses to disperse its forces, it relinquishes its ability to retain residual military strength after the destruction of the last of the attacker's lethality. In addition, there is an upper bound on the number of independent fighting units into which the superior side may divide its firepower. For passive defenses where counterattack is significant, cascade-type force diffusion cannot be advocated without probing the dynamics of casualty exchange likely between the two parties.

To summarize, passive defenses are best structured as linear cascades of maximum length. When applied to ground forces, this is an argument for the maximum dispersion of passive defense lethality and its deployment in depth.

In practice, the degree of force diffusion is limited by the cost of additional detection and allocation layers, the risk associated with permitting a large fragment of the invading force to penetrate deep into defense terrain and the functional nature of the casualty exchange ratio observed in combat.

Why Passive Defenses Are the Force Structure of the Future

Passive defenses are the force structure of the future and are extremely desirable as complements or even substitutes for more conventional armored and infantry divisions for the following reasons.

1. Passive defenses, such as an unmanned, remote-controlled bunker defense with hardened, stationary bunkers each housing limited weaponry distributed over a large region, are intrinsically nonoffensive. They cannot be used to lead an invasion of a neighbor's home territory.

2. The biggest virtue of passive defenses is that they spare human life, the most scarce and valuable resource of the defender.

3. Passive defenses can curb the attacker's mobility without impairing defense mobility, creating a wedge between the aggressor's velocity, v_a, and the defender's speed, v_d. As v_d increases relative to v_a, the defense locus is displaced outward toward the front, thus exposing a smaller region of defense terrain to unopposed capture by the attacker and enhancing conventional stability.

4. Passive defenses can take a big bite out of an aggressor's lethality by imposing heavy attrition on its forces.

5. The feedback from deployed passive defense systems is conveniently available, accurate and reliable intelligence on the progress of invading columns.

6. A passive defense perched on the border between two nations can be used as a political signaling tool. Each combatant can forcefully assert that any violation of its outlying passive defense would signify an act of war and lead to full-scale retaliation. Any incursion into a region protected by a passive defense would be highly visible and would provide legitimacy to the martial preparations of the defender in the eyes of the international community.

Combining Passive and K-constrained Defenses

How should passive defenses be combined with the K-constrained force geometries for traditional defense units discussed earlier? A defender who is outpaced and outnumbered by its enemy along any subfront of the length-M front should deploy a hardened bunker passive defense system along that subfront as shown in Figure I-10.

The passive defense slows down the attacking force concentration, reducing the disparity between v_a and v_d and propelling the defense locus forward. The passive defense elements should be based only in the region between the

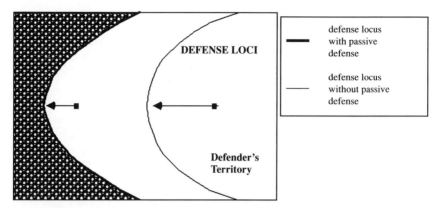

Figure I-10 Improvement in the Defense Locus with a Passive Defense. The passive defense is deployed in the shaded area between the front and the new defense locus. The passive defense decreases the attacker's velocity and causes the defense locus to be displaced forward reducing unopposed infiltration.

length-M front and the new, or postbunker, defense locus. Locating bunkers behind the new defense locus can impede defensive mobility if the passive defense does not differentiate between friendly and hostile aliens. Another benefit of the passive defense is to impose heavy attrition on the invading legions, countering the imbalance between the numerically superior offense and the weak conventional defense. The new defense locus and optimal force geometry is determined by solving the generalized defense positioning problem adjusting for the reduction in the attacker-to-defender velocity ratio, v_a/v_d, and for the attrition of the invading troops caused by the passive defense.

There are two choices for the density of the passive defense elements in the region between the front and the new defense locus:

1. The total interceptor population can be uniformly deployed over the entire area between the length-M front and the new defense locus. This depresses the speed of the invading columns uniformly, since the bunker density is identical at each point along the frontier. However the percentage of offensive firepower that survives the passage through the passive defense differs from point to point along the defense locus since there are fewer cascade layers where the defense locus is closer to the front and many more layers in the areas where the defense locus is distant from the front.

2. A second option is to position the same number of cascade layers between each point along the length-M front and the defense locus. Consequently, the density of deployed bunkers is much greater in regions where the defense locus is close to the front while bunkers are spaced relatively further apart in areas where the defense locus is distant from the border. Since all intruders must navigate the same number of interceptor layers to get to the defense locus, the

proportion of offensive lethality that survives the passage through the passive defense is identical at each point along the defense locus and is independent of the focus of infiltration. However, the velocity of the aggressor's forces will be higher in regions of low bunker density and lower in areas of high bunker density. Since the bunker density is not uniform along the front, the attacker's velocity, v_a, will be a function of the point along the border chosen as a focus of penetration.

A second benefit from the combination of passive defense systems with K-constrained force geometries is in solving the quandary of a country that is bordered by more than one nation, with some neighbors friendly and others hostile. The defender's nightmare is that an inimical neighbor will seize control of a friendly adjacent nation and launch an invasion across the previously amicable neighbor's border. Because it might be logistically and politically impossible for the defense to maintain a standing, battle-ready army along the front with its friendly neighbor, a compromise solution is to deploy an extensive passive defense in the region. In peacetime, the inherently nonoffensive posture of a bunker-type defense can allay any fears of aggression invoked in the friendly neighbor. In war, the passive defense can block an advancing aggressor and thus provide the defense with the time needed to transfer lethality to the new front.

A third opportunity for combining passive defense systems with K-constrained force geometries is in situations where the defender expects a nonuniform probability distribution of attack. For skewed probability distributions of attack, the optimal positioning of defensive units can be significantly different from the usual 1-constrained position. For instance, if the defender is convinced that the enemy will very likely invade in the upper third of the length-M front, then the unconstrained solution to the generalized defense positioning problem will require all defending lethality to be based opposite to the upper third segment of the frontier. The adoption of this defense exposes a large portion of territory adjoining the lower two-thirds of the length-M front to uncontested conquest by the offense. Reinforcing this area with passive defense systems as depicted in Figure I-11 arrests the inward shift of the defense locus and could slow down the attacking forces should a campaign be launched through the lower part of the border providing the defense with more time to transport forces from the misguided peacetime base to the relevant front. Thus the defender is hedged against the occurrence of improbable attack sequences or gross miscalculations of the expected probability density function of attack.

Implications of the Optimal Defense Geometry for Deep Force Cuts and Arms Control

At this juncture we understand what determines the optimal spatial configuration both for "traditional" conventional defense forces such as infantry and armored fighting brigades and for "nouveau" passive defenses such as a hard-

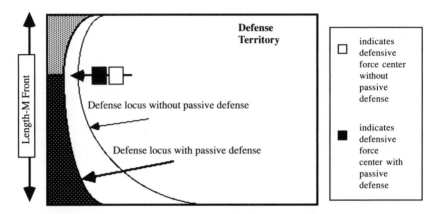

Figure I-11 Improvement in Defense Response to a Nonuniform Probability Distribution of Attack. The lightly shaded area indicates a low-density passive defense deployment, while the heavily shaded region is the home of a high-density passive defense. Most of the mass of the probability distribution of attack is concentrated in the upper third region of the length-M front.

ened-bunker defense with remote-controlled machine guns. We have explored how these two forms of defense may be united to defeat the aggressor on the defender's home ground without encroaching upon the attacker's own home territory. With this powerful framework for analyzing defense geometry and efficacy, we can address three extremely important questions: How do deep force cuts, such as a fifty percent reduction in deployed lethality, affect the optimal geometry of defensive forces? Is there a minimum force-to-space density below which the defense cannot prevent an invader from routing all defending units? How should cooperative arms control agreements that implement deep cuts be structured to maximize stability and make aggression prohibitively expensive and futile? Addressed first is the issue of deep force cuts and their impact on defensive force positioning.

The loss in defensive firepower caused by deep force cuts can be diminished through the deployment of hardened bunker-type passive defenses, which are limited in their mobility and counteroffensive capability and are therefore stabilizing. However the major burden of the reduction in lethality must be borne by the traditional infantry and armored divisions of both sides. Consider an N-strong defender confronted by an opponent also armed with N units. The defending units are positioned in a U-constrained geometry prior to the enactment of an arms control treaty that reduces the aggregate lethality of both sides by k percent. The restrictions on defensive force positioning imposed by the arms control regime depend on how forward and dispersed is the pre-reduction U-constrained lethality matrix and on how deep are the mandated force cuts (see following table). In a world where all parties are equipped with comparable firepower and are able and willing to adopt the optimal *unconstrained* defen-

Pre-reduction Force Geometry	Postreduction Optimal Defensive Force Positioning Options
Unconstrained with all N units at a single base	Unconstrained with all N(1 − k) units at the same base. The unconstrained defensive force geometry is based on parity in overall might between the two opponents and does not depend on absolute force levels. Whether each side has N or N(1 − k) units is irrelevant.
U-constrained with N(1 − k) >= U	No change in defensive force geometry necessary. Apply the k percent reductions uniformly to each base in the pre-reduction defensive force geometry.
U-constrained with N(1 − k) < U	The defender is limited to the universe [1-constrained, 2-constrained, . . . , N(1 − k)-constrained] with N(1 − k) less than U. To determine which of the N(1 − k) geometries is optimal the defender must resolve the generalized defense positioning problem with N(1 − k) units as the input. Since the most dispersed geometry available to the defense is limited to N(1 − k)-constrained, the defense is compelled to adopt a less forward positioned force geometry permitting the invader to achieve greater unchallenged incursions into defense territory. Besides even the deployment of a N(1 − k)-constrained geometry might not be feasible because of the diminution in the defender's vertical force-to-space density parallel to the front.

sive posture, there is no militarily justifiable limit on the level to which the nation-states may reduce their deployed forces by mutual agreement as long as parity in overall lethality is maintained. However, if the defense posture before reductions is highly dispersed and in an extreme forward position or the level of force cuts is very deep, an arms control treaty could compel the relocation of defensive firepower to a position well behind its pre-reduction spot.

Battle Duration and Casualty Exchange under Deep Force Cuts

By examining the impact of deep force cuts on the defender's ability to satisfy the Duration and Casualty Exchange Conditions, much more can be inferred about which of the N(1–k) geometries available to a defender, for whom

$N(1-k)$ is less than U, is the ideal spatial configuration in the new world of low force levels. Concomitant with the increased inward displacement of defending units caused by deep force cuts is the thinning out of defensive forces along the front. For instance, while the average separation between adjacent defending units in a N-constrained geometry is M/N, the intervening distance between successive units doubles to 2M/N for a (N/2)-constrained defense. As a consequence of this vertical diminution in force-to-space density parallel to the front, reinforcing defense echelons are forced to travel greater distances in the postreduction environment in order to engage an invading spearhead. If the reinforcing echelons are to satisfy the Duration Condition and intercept attacking forces before the previous engagement has ended, battle durations in the postreduction world must increase to accommodate the longer distances traversed by the secondary and tertiary waves of defense units. The required increase in battle duration is easily calculated. If the defender possesses an N_1-constrained defense before a cut of $(N_1-N_2)/N_1$ percent and the defender positions its N_2 units post reduction in a N_2-constrained force geometry, the postreduction geometry will satisfy the Duration Condition only if the length of all battles increases by the factor N_1/N_2.

How is this increase in battle duration achieved? A reduction in force levels uniformly applied to both sides lowers the maximum imbalance the aggressor can hope to achieve at the commencement of any single encounter with the defending units. For instance, in a N-unit world, the attacker can aspire to an initial force ratio of N-to-1, but after a k percent force cut the maximum initial imbalance is reduced to N(1–k)-to-1. Thus, a reduction in deployed forces translates to a lower initial force ratio, γ. Recollect that battle duration must be specified as a function of the initial force ratio to determine whether a given K-constrained geometry satisfies the three conditions for robustness. The battle duration curve as a function of the initial force ratio could have two possible forms as indicated in Figures I-12.1 and I-12.2.

In either case lowering the initial force ratio increases battle duration. If the duration of an individual engagement is to increase in proportion to the reduction in γ, the battle duration curve must be relatively steep (Figure I-12.1). If the battle duration curve is flat instead as in Figure I-12.2, there will be little or no increase in battle length, with decreasing initial force ratio, making it very difficult for reinforcing echelons to travel the greater distances between units in a postreduction situation and arrive in time to prevent the offense from accomplishing a breakthrough. How steep should the curve of battle duration versus the initial attacker-to-defender force ratio be to permit force dispersion and forward emplacement under low force levels? A *sufficient but not necessary* condition on steepness is that the percentage increase in battle length that accompanies a reduction in the initial force ratio must be equal to or greater than the percentage decrease in the initial force ratio that caused the rise in battle duration. Battle duration must be an *elastic* function of the initial force ratio to facilitate deep force cuts.

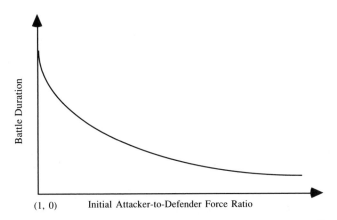

Figure I-12.1 A Steep-sloped Battle Duration Curve. The duration of a battle is expressed as a function of the attacker-to-defender force ratio at the start of the battle.

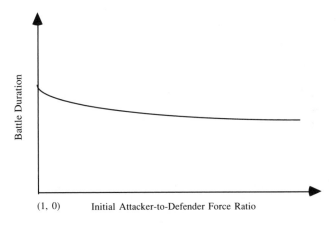

Figure I-12.2 A Flat Battle Duration Curve.

Along any axis of infiltration there will, in general, be a series of encounters between the offensive forces and successive defending echelons. The Casualty Exchange Condition will be satisfied provided the J offensive units dispatched along a particular invasion axis are destroyed by J or less defending units. To assess whether a specific K-constrained geometry satisfies the Casualty Exchange Condition, one must specify the attacker-to-defender casualty exchange ratio observed in battle as a function of the initial force ratio. As graphed in Figures I-13.1 and I-13.2 this functional relationship can take one of two forms.

In either case the attacker-to-defender casualty exchange ratio rises with

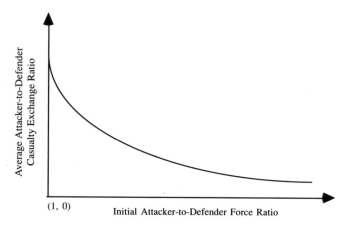

Figure I-13.1 A Steep-sloped Casualty Exchange Curve. The average number of attackers destroyed per defender killed during a battle is expressed as a function of the attacker-to-defender force ratio at the start of the battle.

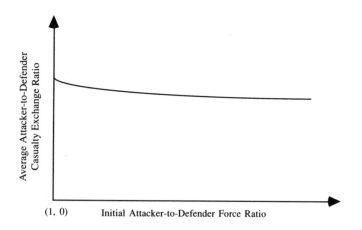

Figure I-13.2 A Flat Casualty Exchange Curve.

falling initial force ratios. As discussed above, equal force reductions on both sides reduce initial attacker-to-defender force ratios since the maximum imbalance is lowered from N-to-1 to N (1 − k)-to-1. Lower initial force ratios mean higher exchange ratios because of the downward sloping nature of the casualty exchange function. Hence irrespective of the steepness or flatness of the casualty exchange function, the newly constituted defense in a force-reduced world will be at least as efficient as its ante-reduction precursor in annihilating the total offensive lethality along each axis of invasion. While the steepness of the

casualty exchange curve has no direct effect on the defender's ability to undergo deep force cuts, it does play a critical role in determining how much dispersion a defending army can tolerate under any overall ceiling on force deployments. A flat casualty exchange function, such as in Figure I-13.2, permits
extensive dispersion and forward basing of defensive divisions, while a steeply
downward-sloping casualty exchange curve as in Figure I-13.1, may severely
limit defensive dispersion.

To summarize, the capability of the defense to prevent offensive breakthroughs and protect its homeland without invading the enemy's territory is
strengthened by steep battle duration curves and flat casualty exchange functions. Steep battle duration curves allow deep force cuts, while flat casualty exchange functions permit highly dispersed and forward-positioned defensive
force geometries.

The Muddle over Force-to-space Ratios

Next we examine the muddle over minimum force-to-space ratios. Many
prominent analysts in the field of conventional force planning have argued that
there are restrictions on the length of front that can be defended by a unit of
force. For example, Jack Snyder and Barry Posen advance the view that
"roughly one ADE (Armored Division Equivalent) is required to hold every
twenty-five kilometers of front."[3] John Mearsheimer has formulated his constraint on force to space in terms of brigades. He has popularized the view that
"a brigade can hold a front approximately seven to fifteen kilometers long."[4]
According to the force-to-space proponents, the defense must deploy this minimum force-to-space density along the entire length of the front to prevent enemy breakthroughs. In its strictest form, the doctrine of force-to-space espouses
that the required force-to-space threshold is not altered by any changes in the
size, composition or potency of the enemy forces. The force-to-space argument
was primarily used before the collapse of the Warsaw Pact to justify NATO's
inability to make any cuts in deployed lethality in Central Europe.

There are several fatal flaws in the logic behind force-to-space:

1. Under the assumptions of a uniform probability distribution of attack and
equal offensive and defensive velocities of transporting force on defense terrain, a defense geometry that bases all units at $(M/\sqrt{12}, M/2)$ minimizes unop-

---

[3]Barry R. Posen, "Measuring the European Conventional Balance," in Steven E. Miller,
ed., *Conventional Forces and American Defense Policy* (Princeton University Press,
1986), p. 106, and Jack Snyder, "Limiting Offensive Conventional Forces," *International Security*, vol. 12 (Spring 1988), p. 66.

[4]John J. Mearsheimer, *Conventional Deterrence* (Cornell University Press, 1983), p.
181.

posed offensive infiltration and possesses perfect counterconcentration capability. For the 1-constrained force geometry there are no restrictions of any kind on how large M can be. Depending upon its distance from the border, the same unit can *optimally* defend a front 25 kilometers long, 50 kilometers long or 1,000 kilometers long. However as the length of the front defended by the unit increases, so does the inward displacement of the unit. As M increases, the defense locus is pushed inward permitting the opponent to seize larger tracts of defense terrain unchallenged and increasing the enemy's reward for a first strike. Thus it might be prudent to prescribe a specific numerical threshold on the invader's infiltration *orthogonal* to the front but without solving the defense positioning problem there is no way to come up with a minimum force-to-space density *parallel* to the front.

2. In requiring a minimum density of force along the front no account is taken of the probability distribution of attack. The density of defensive forces at a location along the front must represent the defender's expectations of the likelihood of attack at that point and cannot be independent of the probability of penetration.

3. The force-to-space approach does not recognize or incorporate any differences in the intelligence, reconnaissance and surveillance capabilities of the two sides in determining the one ADE per 25 kilometers rule.

4. There is no mechanism for adjusting the force-to-space rule for the different relative speeds at which the offense and defense can mobilize and transport units.

5. It is impossible from the force-to-space rule to infer the strategic goals of the defense. Is the defender minimizing offensive infiltration, maximizing offensive casualties, maximizing the ratio of offensive casualties to offensive penetration or maximizing the ratio of offensive casualties to defensive casualties? It is not clear in what sense the force-to-space rule is optimal.

6. Stationing units in accordance with the force-to-space rule is a static procedure. No dynamic analysis is conducted to demonstrate that at least under a simulated invasion, the one ADE per 25 kilometers defense does indeed succeed in preventing offensive breakthroughs for the universe of possible attack plans. There is no analogue of the Duration, Casualty Exchange and Completeness Conditions and no sensitivity analysis of defensive response to different infiltration scenarios is deemed necessary by the force-to-space adherents.

7. Postulating a minimum force-to-space density has the effect of making a country's armament level proportional to the length of its borders with adjoining states and independent of the quantity of lethality possessed by its neighbors. The correct method of determining optimal force geometries is to solve the generalized defense positioning problem. Reducing the science of defense positioning to a universally applicable one ADE per 25 kilometers rule is misleading and could be extremely dangerous. Territory comes with two dimensions, and the dimension orthogonal to the front cannot be ignored.

Potential Schema for Arms Control

Weapon reductions compel the defense to abandon its pre-reduction force geometry and accept a less forward and less dispersed position if either the defense posture before reductions is *highly* dispersed and *extremely* forward or the level of mandated force cuts is *very deep*, or both. The inward displacement of the defense locus resulting from a less forward force geometry is destabilizing and raises the reward for first strike. A second concern is the concomitant decrease in defensive force dispersal and the consequent increased vulnerability of defensive force concentrations to decapitation. These obstacles in the path of deep force reductions can be overcome by structuring disarmament protocols in an innovative fashion, keeping in mind what we have learned about the optimal force geometry for the defense. A few arms control regimes that facilitate deep cuts are described below.

Horizontal Lines of Arms Control

If the adversary can fluidly transfer force along the entire front without alerting the defender, then the defender is compelled to treat the full length of the border between the two states as a single length-M front. In this situation the only path open to a defender who wishes to disperse forces and base units forward is to adopt a suboptimal constrained defense and trade off counterconcentration capability against dispersion and forward emplacement. Such a suboptimal defense is risky and testing its robustness is difficult and based on assumptions about the nature of combat. However if the long border tract can somehow be partitioned into several, smaller length-M fronts, the defense can adopt an optimal unconstrained geometry along each front segment. Such a border partitioning can be accomplished if both sides agree to construct horizontal lines of arms control, that is, lines constructed perpendicular to the front, as shown in Figure I-14, such that each side is always aware of the opponent's *total* lethality in each region bounded by adjacent horizontal arms control lines.

Each side can easily and reliably detect any of its neighbor's force transfers across the horizontal segments and can match the transfer so that the same number of offensive and defensive units are always deployed along each front segment. Within a region bounded by the horizontal lines, the defender is free to base all units assigned to that sector at the 1-constrained location because of the relatively small length of the front segment. The separation between the horizontal lines should be based on the maximum infiltration either side is willing to suffer. For a front with a uniform probability of attack, the distance between the horizontal lines should be $\sqrt{3}I_{MAX} = 1.73I_{MAX}$, where I_{MAX} is the maximum unopposed infiltration either side is willing to tolerate.

Horizontal arms control lines enable both sides to deploy units close to the border without any sacrifice in the capability to counterconcentrate perfectly. A

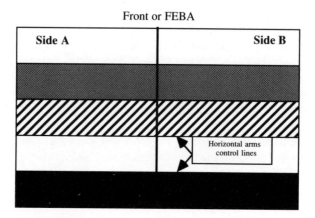

Figure I-14 Horizontal Lines of Arms Control. The border is divided into segments by the arms control lines. Any two segments with identical shading must contain the same number of deployed units for stability. Each segment constitutes a mini-length-M front.

horizontal arms control regime also allows both sides the luxury of misjudging the expected probability distribution of attack without any disastrous consequences. Since the segment of the front defined by the horizontal arms control lines is small in absolute terms, the defense can grossly miscalculate the expected probability density function of invasion and still find its peacetime base only a few kilometers away from the true optimal position.

Vertical Lines of Arms Control

The vertical analogue of horizontal arms control lines is to specify zones *parallel* to the length-M front and limit the total lethality that can be fielded in each zone. Interzonal force transfers across vertical lines are easily discernible. A vertical arms control regime is displayed in Figure I-15. Under vertical arms control lines, if the attacker wishes to preserve the advantage of strategic surprise, it is compelled to initiate the invasion using only the units allowed in the zone nearest the frontier. Therefore the maximum imbalance that can be experienced by the defense when confronting the first attack wave, is lowered from N-to-1 to F_1-to-1, where F_1 is the force ceiling on the zone nearest the front. Alternatively, if the attacker wishes to transport forces from zones well behind the front to locations closer to the border before making the incursion into defense terrain, the defending commander is provided with advance warning of at least W_1/v_{aa}, where W_1 is the width of the zone closest to the front and v_{aa} is the attacker's speed of transporting force across this zone to prepare for an onslaught by the additional offensive units from Zones 2 and beyond. As the

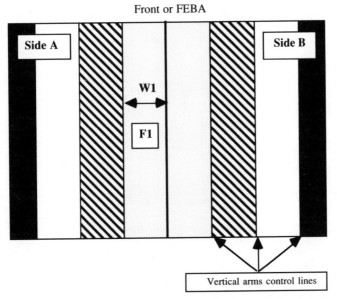

Figure I-15 Vertical Lines of Arms Control. The territory on each side of the front is divided into vertical zones by the arms control lines. Any two zones with identical shading have the same ceiling on the number of force units that may be deployed within the zones.

attacker attempts to achieve higher and higher values of the initial attacker-to-defender ratio, the defense is automatically provided with earlier and earlier notification of the impending invasion. The vertical arms control regime thus compels the side with aggressive intents to sacrifice the element of strategic surprise.

The lethality cap on and the width of each zone parallel to the front should be determined so as to allow both sides to deploy a force geometry that solves the most general formulation of the defense positioning problem that permits the assignment of a single-front segment to multiple defending bases. What vertical arms control does is to leave each side with no choice but to position troops according to the optimal *defensive* force structure determined by solving the most general form of the defense positioning problem. In other words, the primary objective of vertical arms control lines is to compel both sides to disperse firepower inward from the front and adopt a defensive posture. Since the placement of and force limitations on the vertical zones correspond to an optimal defensive force geometry, by obeying the arms control regime each side automatically ends up with an optimal or close to optimal defensive configuration.

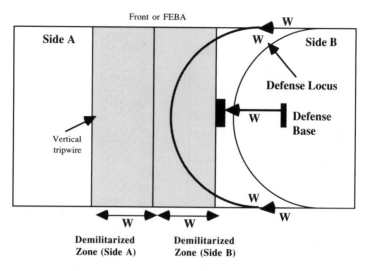

Figure I-16 Demilitarized Zones. Shaded region indicates demilitarized zones. Arrows depict forward displacement of Side B's defense locus and defense base as a consequence of Side A's demilitarized zone. The thick curve is Side B's new defense locus after the vertical tripwire is put in place.

Demilitarized Zones

Demilitarized zones can be visualized as regions immediately adjacent to the border where neither side can position armored, mechanized or infantry divisions and where total deployed lethality is highly restricted. Further the intelligence capabilities of each side no longer fall off at the front but extend into the demilitarized zone of its neighbor. Each side can observe all events in its neighbor's demilitarized zone but cannot see past the zone boundary. Thus the instant the opponent's heavy firepower crosses the vertical tripwire (the edge of the demilitarized zone) on the side of the length-M front away from the defense, the defender is alerted and can dispatch forces into the adversary's demilitarized zone to contain the advancing spearhead. A demilitarized zone of width W on either side of a length-M front propels the defense locus forward by a distance W as pictured in Figure I-16 and allows the defense to move all defensive encampments distance W toward the front thereby reducing considerably the amount of territory open to uncontested conquest by the enemy.

Comparison between Horizontal Arms Control Lines and Demilitarized Zones

An increase of ΔW in the width of the demilitarized zones on either side of the length-M front allows each side to move forces a distance ΔW closer to the front. In contrast, reducing the distance between horizontal arms control lines by ΔM allows force units on either side to approach closer to the border by a distance of approximately $\Delta M/\sqrt{12} = 0.29\Delta M$ only. However there are two drawbacks associated with the concept of demilitarized zones. First, there is a limit to how far back the demilitarized zones can extend from the front. For a border with an arbitrary probability density function of infiltration, the closest an unconstrained defense can approach the front through a demilitarized zone is $\sigma/2$ as compared with its normal distance of σ from the front. A proximity of $\sigma/2$ to the frontier can be gained by the construction of a single horizontal arms control line at $M/2$. Second, the trade-off between force dispersion and perfect counterconcentration is not eliminated by the adoption of demilitarized zones. Note that to truly contrast the effectiveness of horizontal lines with demilitarized zones one must assume that the defense deploys an unconstrained defense in the demilitarized zone scenario since the force geometries protecting each segment of the length-M front in the horizontal arms control scenario are also unconstrained. However while total defending lethality is divided among the various segments defined by the horizontal lines, the entire defending force in the demilitarized zone scenario must be based at a single location to provide the same kind of perfect counterconcentration available with horizontal lines. In conclusion, if the two combatants are willing to partition the length-M front into more than two horizontal zones, each side can achieve greater dispersion and forward emplacement of forces through horizontal arms control lines than through demilitarized zones.

Velocity Differentials

The introduction of a velocity differential in favor of the defense makes room for the forward basing of forces. Arms control accords should seek by mutual consent to structure forces, equipment and terrain in a manner that ensures the defense unequivocal superiority in locomotion over home territory. Each side must be capable of outstripping the attacking forces when subject to an invasion and, in turn, must be surpassed by the opponent when initiating the attack. Increasing the differential between defense velocity, v_d, and the attacker's speed over defense territory, v_a, moves forward both the optimal defensive location and the defense locus as shown in Figure I-17.

Functionally, the goal of $v_d > v_a$ might be accomplished by deploying along the border a network of barriers and mine fields or a remote-controlled, hardened-bunker passive defense system and policing the air with short-range close air support aircraft to slow down the invader.

Mobility Constraints and Passive Defenses

Arms control agreements must force the transfer of lethality from conventional basing modes to modes with limited mobility and minimal offensive potential.

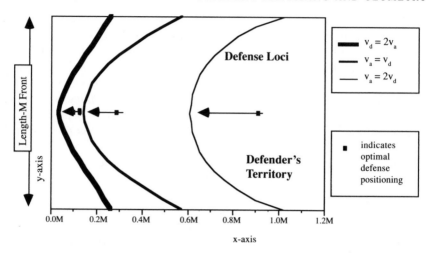

Figure I-17 Defense Loci for $v_d = 2v_a$, $v_a = v_d$ and $v_a = 2v_d$. The x-axis is calibrated in terms of the length of the front.

One method may be to mandate mobility constraints on each side's residual lethality after outright k percent cuts. For example, if Side A has N(1–k) lethality units after an arms reduction treaty, mobility constraints would require one-tenth of the N(1–k) units to be structured so that their maximum mobility is 5 kilometers. Thus one-tenth of Side A's lethality must remain within 5 kilometers of the home bases designated for this fraction of Side A's army. Another tenth of Side A's units must remain within a circle of radius 15 kilometers. Further, another fifteen percent cannot be transported outside a 25 kilometer radius, while another fifteen percent are limited to 50 kilometers. For the remaining fifty percent, there are no constraints on mobility. Note that the mobility constraints on the placement of firing platforms must also include restrictions on the range of the projectiles launched by the firing platforms to truly limit the offensive potential of the mobility constrained units.

One effective way to structure mobility constrained lethality is to deploy it in the region adjacent to the front as an unmanned, remote-controlled bunker-type passive defense armed with machine guns, anti-tank missiles, anti-aircraft guns and anti-missile missiles. Since the passive defense would not demand much manpower to operate, it can afford to be quite large and can run the entire length of the border, thus preventing the adversary from outflanking the stationary elements of the passive defense system.

Traditionally military commanders have been extremely reluctant to limit the mobility of their forces. Immobility has been considered synonymous with weakness and vulnerability. Elsewhere we have demonstrated the advantages that flow to the defense from an agility and fluidity in transporting forces both orthogonal to and parallel to the front. However it should be emphatically clear that we are advocating that only a small but significant minority of the total forces of *both* sides be structured as a dispersed passive defense with limited mobility. Furthermore, such a nonthreatening arrangement should be forced upon both sides only as part of a comprehensive arms control agreement whose paramount objective is first and foremost to reduce the aggregate war-waging capacity of both sides by a third or a half. Besides, if all parties to an accord willingly agree to base roughly the same proportion of their total permitted lethality as a bunker-type or other passive defense system, no side has any advantage relative to its neighbors in its flexibility to relocate divisions.

Nuclear Decoupling

One source of pressure for the dispersal of defending lethality is generated by the possibility of nuclear bombardment of local force concentrations. The consequent need to more widely distribute forces leads to the relinquishment of optimal force geometries which concentrate defensive forces at a few locations. The nuclear threat against local concentration can be alleviated by adopting a policy of no first-use of nuclear weapons by both sides, by decoupling the nuclear command and control structure and the capacity to employ nuclear warheads from conventional force authority and, if both sides are amenable, eliminating tactical and, perhaps, all nuclear weapons from the theater of war.

Relaxing the Information Functions

In deriving the optimal spatial configuration for defending forces it was assumed that neither side has any information about events that occur on its neighbor's home territory. In other words, the information functions of both sides switch off at the length-M front. If the means for executing a deep attack can be eliminated, each side may permit its opponent to gather information within its territory and to relax the steepness of the information functions confronting the nations and extend them beyond the front into hostile terrain. The extended knowledge of force deployments and mutual intentions that comes with relaxed information functions can enhance the optimization of defensive force positioning for both sides. However, this knowledge can only be exchanged if each nation is guaranteed that the information will not be used against its armed forces in a preemptive attack. One way to guard against such abuses is to ban deep interdiction aircraft and fighters and long-range precision guided munitions from the theater of war. Ideally, if the defensive force structure is truly robust, the defense only needs information on the intentions of the attacker; there is really no imperative for retaining the capability to engage hostile forces on enemy territory. Further, if each side can convince the other of the optimality and robustness of its defense and the extreme unlikelihood of success in attempting a conquest, war should hold little interest for either side.

Complementary Use of Arms Control Regimes

While some of the seven schemes for structuring arms control agreements illustrated above are mutually exclusive, most of the schemes complement each other very well to create an atmosphere conducive to achieving deep weapon cuts. As an example, two sides could agree to create horizontal lines of arms control spaced 50 kilometers apart. Within each horizontal region, the two sides could create demilitarized regions extending for a distance of 6 kilometers on either side of the border. Further, twenty-five percent of each side's total lethality could be constrained in its mobility and could be structured as a passive defense in each horizontal zone. The two treaty signatories could limit deep interdiction aircraft and long-range missiles and grant the opponent inspection rights and air rights for a specified number of drones up to a distance of 100 kilometers inward from the front. Such a combination of concrete concessions and confidence-building measures might allow both sides to become comfortable with a fifty percent cut in overall force levels. The precise nature of the weapons reduction regime most suitable for a specific region will obviously depend on factors such as topography, the kinds of weapons possessed by the adversaries, the risk tolerance of the involved nations, the economic, human and psychological costs of negotiating, implementing, monitoring and enforcing the chosen arms control treaty and the extent to which the arms control agreement would disrupt the normal way of life of each country's citizens. The power of the different approaches to arms control outlined above lies in the fact that when conjoined, their ability to encourage very deep reductions and foster worlds with low force levels is multiplicative rather than additive.

PART ONE

Positioning a Conventional Defense

THE CONVENTIONAL MILITARY BALANCE between two nations is stable if and only if the defender is always assured of victory. Each side must prevail if subjected to an invasion by an adversary and, in turn, must be soundly defeated if it initiates the attack. In a situation where the odds overwhelmingly favor the defense neither opponent has any incentive to commence an attack. This discussion of offense and defense raises some fundamental questions: Who is the attacker? Conceive of the attacker simply as the entity that launches an uninvited armed invasion of a sovereign state. What is the attacker's goal in initiating such an incursion? There is a whole universe of objectives from which the aggressor is free to choose. The invader may wish to maximize the territory under its control, that is, Max [Territory Controlled]. Or the attacker may seek to maximize territory gained while minimizing the attrition of its forces, namely, Max [Territory Controlled/Attacker Attrition]. A third possibility is for the offense to prolong the conflict for as long as possible to wear down the defending forces, that is, Max [Duration]. Other possible choices for the ultimate objective sought by the invader are Max [Defender Attrition], Max [Defender Attrition/Attacker Attrition], capture control of a specific target such as an oil or natural gas field or a strategic inland waterway, Max [Territory Controlled/Duration] or Max [Territory Controlled x Defender Attrition/Attacker Attrition x Duration].

The singular and salient objective of the prototypical attacker considered in this book is to conquer as much territory as possible, that is, Max [Territory Controlled]. There are several reasons why we choose territorial conquest as the primary goal of our invader. First, historically, most military commanders have associated victory in battle with gaining control over the enemy's lands. Germany was not defeated in the Second World War until the allies occupied Berlin. Iraq was not vanquished in the 1991 conflict until Kuwait was recaptured and the United States and its allies held sway over southern Iraq. Second, many wars *begin* because of territorial disagreements and boundary disputes among nations. A recent instance is the British war with Argentina over the Falkland Islands. Third, battle goals such as the maximization or minimization of enemy attrition, friendly losses, or battle duration are usually secondary aims in any conflict and are more accurately treated as *constraints* applied to the fundamental objective of gaining territory. Fourth, our primary concern throughout this book is the optimal spatial geometry for configuring conventional forces. We want to understand where the defender's divisions should be positioned and why certain geometries for locating forces are optimal while others are not. Since we want to know how defensive firepower should be physically distributed over defense terrain and what determines the ideal density of defensive lethality at each location, the attacker's ambition of maximizing territorial domination is appropriate. Finally, if the duration of the confrontation or the attrition of the two sides is included in defining the strategic goal of the aggressor, we are compelled to anchor our entire analysis on assumptions about the laws of combat and the nature of the attrition and withdrawal process in battle. In the absence of sufficient historical data it is impossible to empirically test the validity of any model of combat and fire exchange. To the extent that robust defensive force structures can be identified without any dependence on unverifiable theories of the attrition process in combat, we would prefer to avoid basing any portion of our conceptual framework and its results on battle duration or attrition.

What about the character and role of the defender? The defender is the party subjected to an unsolicited invasion by enemy troops. To defeat the invasion, the defense pursues the exact mirror image of the attacker's goal; the defender seeks to minimize territory conceded to the offense, that is, Min [Territory Lost]. Again note that minimizing the loss of defense terrain is not the only possible doctrine that may be pursued by the defense. The defender may choose to match or exceed the invader's conquest of the defender's homelands by launching a counterattack into the enemy's home terrain. Alternatively the defender may decide to maximize the attacker's loss of human life or threaten the attacker with vertical or horizontal escalation. We choose the simplest aim for the defense of minimizing offensive penetration into defense terrain for all the same reasons mentioned above to justify the attacker's choice of Max [Territory Controlled] as the primary objective of aggression. The simplest and most effective defense is one that can defeat the enemy on defense territory without being forced to counterattack or escalate. It is just such a strategy and force posture that is truly defensive and stability enhancing; as long as a defender has to rely on counteroffense or escalation to protect sovereignty it can never be unequivocal to its neighbors that the defender will not launch a first strike. Where the military intentions of nations are ambiguous, distrust and misinterpretations among the countries will grow, leading inevitably to dangerous and expensive arms races as each state tries to match its perceived opponents in firepower. If all countries could adopt geometries that enabled them to beat their adversary on defense terrain for any realizable campaign plan of invasion, there would be little necessity for them to anchor their force structure on a philosophy of counterattack, preemption or escalation and little incentive for would-be conquerors to embark on a course of aggression. The defense objective of Min [Territory Lost] is a concise and precise expression for the broader defense goal of defeating the invader on defense terrain.

An efficient and effective defense is that geometrical configuration of defensive force that minimizes territory lost to the enemy. To set up and solve the minimization problem faced by the defender we need to construct a mathematical abstraction of the process of invasion and occupation of territory. This mathematical approach is later rewarded by significant conclusions not just on optimal defense positioning but on a host of issues intrinsic to conventional warfare. To answer the question of what constitutes the optimal force geometry we begin by abstracting the concept of the border between two nations as a contiguous front of length M. Next we assume that the physical features of the terrain on either side of the front exhibit fairly uniform characteristics at the same orthogonal distance from the front. We add on assumptions about each side's ability to obtain information concerning the force deployment and disposition of the enemy. Based on these bare-bone assumptions we are able to uniquely determine the trajectory of the attacking units once they penetrate defense territory. We examine from the defender's point of view what is the probability that any particular location along the length-M front will be chosen as the focus of infiltration by the invader. Initially we assume that the probability of attack is the same at all points along the border. We codify the defender's goals as seeking to meet and defeat the invader as far forward as possible. Meeting the invader as close to the front as possible is mathematically equivalent to minimizing the attacker's unopposed infiltration into defense terrain. Defeating the invader is equivalent to matching the aggressor unit for unit at each focus of penetration. Since attacker and defender are assumed to possess parity in aggregate lethality, the defense must simply meet the offense at each point of interception with the same quantum of firepower as that dispatched by the offense along that particular line of invasion.

We proceed to determine what geometrical positioning of defensive lethality will satisfy the aims of meeting and defeating the invader as far forward as possible. We first consider the case where both adversaries have one force unit each and derive the optimal location of the defensive unit given three different cases of defensive velocity: (1) the defense can transport force over defense terrain as fast as the offense, (2) faster than the offense and (3) slower than the offense. We discover the extremely useful concept of the defense locus, which indicates the minimum inward incursion inevitably achieved by the offense. We find that the optimal position for a defending unit is not along the front but at a nonzero distance behind the front. We examine in greater depth the relationship between stability as measured by the defense locus and the relative velocity of the forces of the two sides. The next step is to demolish one by one the assumptions made at the beginning of the discussion. We first relax the uniform probability of attack assumption and allow arbitrary probabilities of attack at each point along the front. We generalize the solution to the defense positioning problem to the scenario where each side has more than one force unit. We expand the concept of a length-M front to account for natural barriers such as rivers and mountain ranges as well as for institutional or man-made barriers along the border between a state and its neighbors. We show how the value of superior information can be measured by observing its effect on the size of the length-M front.

Next we examine any potential drawbacks of our approach to positioning defensive forces. Unfortunately we discover two problems with our optimal force geometry: it concentrates forces too heavily and it still allows dangerously deep incursions by the aggressor. These problems are illustrated with real-world examples from South Korea and Iraq. These two shortcomings can be overcome by trading off the defender's perfect counterconcentration capability against dispersion and forward emplacement of defensive forces. Depending upon the degree of dispersal and forward positioning of troops desired by the defense, there are a large number of defensive force geometries that can potentially be optimal. Earlier we assumed that perfect counterconcentration, or the ability to match the invader unit for unit at each point of penetration, was a prerequisite for the force geometry chosen by the defense. Under this assumption of perfect force-matching ability there is only one solution to the problem of locating defensive forces. However, if less than perfect counterconcentration is acceptable to the defending commander, a very large number of force geometries can be optimal. We limit consideration of force geometries to those that do not allow the assignment of a single segment of the length-M front to more than one defense subgroup. Under this constraint of no overlap in the designating of front segments to defending divisions, we demonstrate that a defender with N units can position its troops in N distinct configurations. In N - 1 of these configurations the defense fails to match the offense unit for unit at all points of penetration along the border. We study how the loss of perfect counterconcentration can lead to strategic breakthroughs by the attacker and identify precisely the three conditions that must be met by a defense geometry to guarantee the defender's ability to prevent breakthroughs.

Among the N configurations available to the defender, the optimal force geometry is that configuration which distributes units over the largest area and locates divisions closest to the front while fulfilling the three conditions essential for preventing offensive breakthroughs. Determining whether a particular force geometry satisfies the three conditions for robustness involves predicting the duration of and the attacker-to-defender casualty exchange ratio observed in each encounter between the two adversaries. Consequently for the case of a defender who wishes to disperse its units and position them as far forward as possible, we develop an extremely skeletal and threadbare framework for predicting duration and casualty exchange ratios based on the force ratio between two opponents at the start of the battle. We adopt a minimalist approach to modeling combat because in the absence of sufficiently detailed historical data for testing we can have no confidence in the predictive ability of any comprehensive or complex model of the process of attrition and withdrawal in battle. Our only assumptions concern the *nature* of the functional relationship between the initial force ratio on the one hand and battle duration and casualty exchange on the other. Our simple assumptions allow for the fact that numerous factors, known and unknown, other than the initial force ratio influence combat duration and the casualty exchange ratio. Armed with our minimalist assumptions concerning combat, we present in the final section a step-by-step algorithm for determining which of the N configurations available to a N-strong defender is successful in restricting the loss of defense territory to tolerable levels while maximizing defensive dispersion and preventing the aggressor from accomplishing a breakthrough. The reader may prefer to first skim the outline at the conclusion of Part One to get a synopsis of all the arguments and revelations presented in this part before starting to read the main text.

Definition of a Length-M Front

Consider a contiguous region or piece of territory that forms the border between two opposing nations. This region constitutes a front, or FEBA (Forward Edge of Battle Area), between the two adversaries along which each side masses its conventional forces. Each country's regime controls the territory on its respective side of the front but is excluded from any participation in events on the other side. This "Iron Curtain" front may be conceptually concretized as in Figure 1-1. The length of the front, M, is defined as the length of the continuous border shared by the two antagonists. To ensure clarity and unambiguity in the discussion to follow, the front of length M, as defined, is referred to as a length-M front.

The On-off Information Assumption

Each side can obtain information concerning the force deployment and disposition of the enemy through means such as reconnaissance, surveillance and espionage. The information available to each side can be formalized mathematically as an information function, r. This term r denotes the quantity of information available to an observer about a specific locale on the battle terrain and is consequently a function of spatial position, (x, y), where x and y are the abscissa and ordinate of a point on the battlefield. This concept of information has a

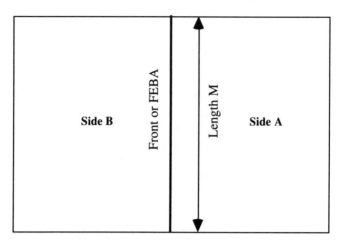

Figure 1-1   Definition of a Length-M Front

classical Newtonian interpretation. If an observer can discern the number and types of enemy divisions in a vicinity, their exact location and their instantaneous speed and direction of motion, the observer has perfect information ($r = 1$) about the enemy's military infrastructure at that point of the battlefield. The other extreme is zero or no information ($r = 0$), in which case the observer is unable to locate the enemy forces, their numbers, their nature or their velocity.[1] It is assumed throughout that each side has perfect information about the physical terrain of the enemy's territory and that each side always possesses complete information on its own military forces. Further each side has some notion of where the targets of high strategic value such as capital cities, industrial centers and government towns of the antagonist are located. Thus the information function, r, describes solely the capacity of a side to monitor the current force structure of the enemy military machine.

Assume that the battlefield is reasonably isotropic parallel to the front. By isotropy we mean that the physical features of the terrain exhibit fairly uniform properties at all points that are at the same perpendicular distance from the

---

[1]A rigorous formulation of the information function would define it as a mapping from R^2 to R^3, since information is a function of two variables (the x and y coordinates of a point on the battlefield) and information itself has three components: the total lethality of enemy forces at a point, which depends on the number and nature of enemy force units; the speed of the opposing forces; and the direction of motion of the antagonistic forces. For our purposes, we assimilate the three components into a single comprehensive information function, r, that is constructed from its components by some appropriate process such as simple or weighted averaging.

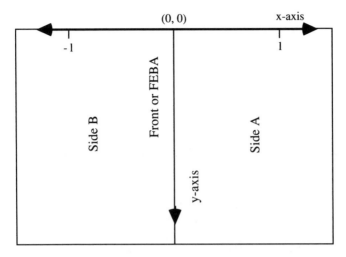

Figure 1-2.1 Setting Up a Rectangular Coordinate System

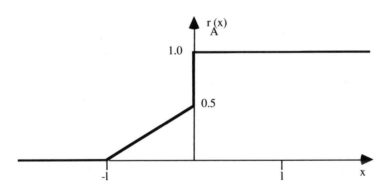

Figure 1-2.2 Information Function for Side A

front. Isotropy of the battle terrain is usually assured in naval warfare (except for the odd intervening island) and is often the case in land battles fought over relatively flat plains. For our conceptual length-M front, the information function, r, for each side, reduces simply to a function of distance measured orthogonally from the front as a consequence of our isotropy assumption. For any set of points parallel to the front, the observer has identical look-ahead capabilities at all points, because of the isotropy of the battlefield parallel to the front. Figures 1-2.1 through 1-2.3 depict possible information functions for a length-M front.

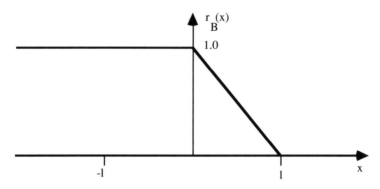

Figure 1-2.3   Information Function for Side B

Side A has very little information about enemy forces at distances deep inside the territory of side B. This is denoted in side A's information function by $r_A(x) = 0$ for $x < -1$. However, with decreasing depth inside B's territory and increasing proximity towards the front, A's reconnaissance capabilities grow and the information function, $r_A(x)$, increases from 0 to 0.5 as x increases from -1 to 0. Finally, for points within the region under A's hegemony, A has perfect information about all events and $r_A(x) = 1$ for $x > 0$. The situation is reversed for the information function of side B, $r_B(x)$, with intelligence capabilities tapering off with increasing distance inside A's territory. Among the infinitude of possible information functions for a length-M front, we assume that the simplest of information functions, the on-off function, holds. In a scenario governed by the on-off information function, each side has perfect information on the disposition of enemy forces for all points within its domain but has no information for positions within the enemy's territory. The on-off information function for sides A and B is represented in Figures 1-3.1 and 1-3.2.

Our adopted premise regarding the nature of the information function for a length-M front is summarized as Assumption I.

ASSUMPTION I: THE ON-OFF INFORMATION FUNCTION. *Opponents on either side of a length-M front have perfect knowledge of military infrastructure for all enemy forces that encroach upon their territory but have no information of the exact location, number, nature, speed or directional motion of antagonistic forces on the opposing side of the front. The information function for each side is switched on within friendly territory and switched off in enemy terrain. Furthermore, the adversaries are cognizant that each side is restricted in its reconnaissance capabilities by the on-off information function.*

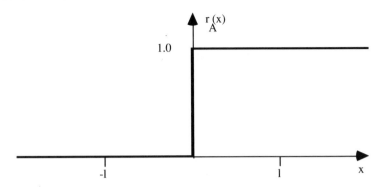

Figure 1-3.1   On-off Information Function for Side A

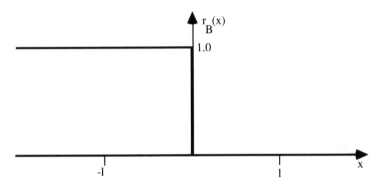

Figure 1-3.2   On-off Information Function for Side B

The Trajectory of Attacking Forces inside Defense Territory

At this juncture, the discussion is aided by discarding the assumed symmetry of purpose between the sides A and B and allocating to side B the role of the attacker, aiming to gain control over the territory of side A. The aggressor possesses three dimensions of choice: the choice of a point (or points) along the front whence to launch the attack, the number of force units committed to each focus of attack and the times at which the incursions will commence at each focus of attack. Once the location of the foci of attack, the distribution of forces among the foci and the time sequence of attack have been settled, the behavior and trajectory of the attacker's forces can be unequivocally determined and are formalized as Theorem I.

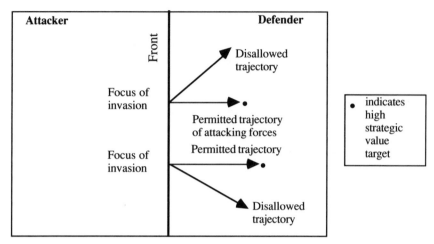

Figure 1-4   Allowed and Disallowed Trajectories of Attacking Forces at Focii of Invasion

THEOREM I: *At each focus of attack, the aggressor's invading forces will proceed into enemy territory with the maximum possible velocity in a direction perpendicular to the length-M front at the point of infiltration.*

Demonstration: Figure 1-4 illustrates the allowed trajectories of the attacker's forces at a focus of invasion once the front has been breached. The attacker is aware that once its forces have ventured across the front into the defender's domain, the defender's perfect reconnaissance capabilities will ensure the defense a steady stream of information on the whereabouts, composition and translational motion of the aggressor's forces. Hence, it is the assailant's overriding priority to minimize the time taken to reach the target of the foray once the incursion into enemy territory has occurred, thus providing the defender with a minimal interval in which to react. Since the attacker's information function switches off inside enemy territory, the attacker has no knowledge of the distribution of the defending forces along the front. Therefore the aggressor will simply choose those points along the front that are closest to targets of the highest strategic value, breach the front at these foci of invasion and proceed from the incursion points at the maximum attainable velocity heading directly towards the strategic centers in order to minimize the time spent travelling to the targets. Under the assumption of an on-off information function, the trajectory of attacking forces once inside enemy territory is always the path that offers the shortest time of travel from the front to the desired objective. If the battlefield terrain is isotropic parallel to the front, the quickest path to the target is orthogonally outward from the front diametrically opposite to the target. The aggressor will thus breach the front at points directly opposite to the desired targets and proceed orthogonally outward from the foci of infiltration at the maximum possible velocity toward the high strategic value centers as shown in Figure 1-4.

The Uniform Probability of Attack Assumption

From the point of view of the defender there is a probability distribution associated with the likelihood that the attacker will infiltrate the front at a designated point. In general, $P(f)$ is the probability that the attacker will choose point f along the front. This probability is determined by such factors as the defender's beliefs about the strategic value attributed by the aggressor to targets located in defense territory and the ease with which the topology of the terrain permits the breaching of the front with large force concentrations at a given point. Since the attacker must breach the front at some point along the front to launch an invasion, it must be true that:

$$\int_{f=0}^{f=M} P(f)df = 1 \qquad \text{(1-1)}$$

Possible probability distribution functions for the likelihood of attack at a point f along the front are illustrated in Figure 1-5.[2] Figure 1-5.1 shows a continuous probability distribution of attack while Figure 1-5.2 depicts a discrete probability distribution.[3]

We adopt the following assumption regarding the likelihood of attack at any point along the front.[4]

ASSUMPTION II: UNIFORM PROBABILITY OF ATTACK. *It is equally likely that any point along the length-M front will be chosen by the attacker as a focus of invasion. Thus the appropriate probability distribution for the likelihood of*

---

[2]The defender can construct a valid probability distribution function by listing in order of decreasing likelihood (that is creating an ordinal sequence of) the points at which the adversary is bound to launch an invasion. A numerical score can then be assigned to each point (that is the ordinal sequence can be used to generate a cardinal mapping) and the scores normalized so that they sum to unity

[3]The terms probability distribution and probability density function are used interchangeably throughout the discussion.

[4]Appendix 1A relaxes this assumption and generalizes the analysis to an arbitrary probability distribution of attack. It is also shown in Appendix 1A why the uniform probability of attack function is the sensible choice for the rational defense planner in charge of defending a fairly isotropic piece of territory.

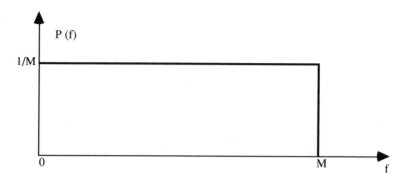

Figure 1-5.1 Continuous Probability Density Function of Attack

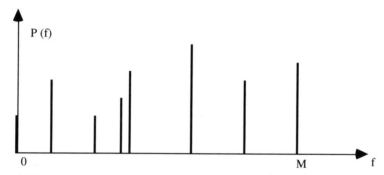

Figure 1-5.2 Discrete Probabilty Density Function of Attack

attack at any point along the front is the uniform probability distribution depicted in Figure 1-5.1.

The uniform probability density function is described by the following equation.

$$P(f) = \begin{cases} \dfrac{1}{M} & 0 \le f \le M \\ 0 & \text{otherwise} \end{cases} \qquad (1\text{-}2)$$

Defining the Goals of the Defense

Once the form of the probability distribution function governing the likelihood of attack at each point along the front has been settled, the defender must decide upon a philosophy of defense—a fundamental ideal or aim that can be used to derive a guiding principle of action. Any conscientious defender, concerned with the welfare of its populace living in border districts, will seek to minimize enemy infiltration and occupation of territory. Besides from a purely military and strategic perspective, permitting the invader to occupy large tracts of territory or achieve deep incursions is an invitation to the aggressor to consolidate control over the surrounding locale and rejuvenate its forces during periods of inaction. In fact, it is not hard to imagine that even if the regions bordering the demarcation line are sparsely populated and undeveloped, their capture by enemy forces could by itself lead to a loss of the defender's political will and public morale, both essential to sustaining the will to fight. This leads us to postulate the following principle of action for the defense.

THE FUNDAMENTAL POSTULATE OF FORWARD DEFENSE: *It is incumbent upon the defending forces to meet and defeat the invader as far forward as possible. The phrase "as far forward as possible" implies that the defending forces engage the aggressor as close to the length-M front as feasible without breaching the front and encroaching upon the attacker's terrain.*

The Fundamental Postulate of Forward Defense states the dynamic, real-war-time goal of the force planners of the defense. In times of peace, any rational force planner will be induced to structure defending forces so as to maximize the probability of attaining desired war-time objectives. This causal relationship between professed wartime aims and the peacetime positioning and structuring of forces must be scrupulously adhered to if the most effective utilization of available force elements is to be achieved. The forward defense imperative—to engage and defeat the assailant as far forward as possible to minimize the infiltration accomplished by the attacker—gives rise to the following implication for force structuring.

FORCE STRUCTURING POSTULATE: *The defensive forces must be positioned, organized and structured to minimize the expected infiltration of the attacker. If the aggressor launches more than one foray into enemy territory, the defending forces must be structured to minimize the expected infiltration of the attacker in each individual foray.*

The Force Matching Constraint

The Forward Defense Postulate requires the defender not only to meet the attacker as close to the demarcation line as possible but also to repulse the invasion at each focus of attack. Repulsing an attacking strength of A units will require from a defending force commitment of D units. The relationship between A and D is determined by the algorithm for the conduct of battle employed by the force planner. Thus in any given set of equations of warfare, we must plug in the condition that the encounter culminate in a stalemate and then determine the initial defending strength required to achieve this objective as a function of various initial attacking force strengths. The simplest assumption would be to require the defense to match the attacker unit for unit at each focus of infiltration.

ASSUMPTION III: FORCE MATCHING CONSTRAINT. *To be ensured of a stalemate, the defender must match the attacking forces unit for unit at each focus of penetration.*

Thus if the aggressor launches invading forays at three positions along the length-M front and allocates 3 units to the first focus of infiltration, 6 units to the second and 2 units to the third, the defender must provide defending units to combat the adversary at the first point of incursion, 6 defending units at the second point and 2 units at the third if the defender is to thwart the invasion.

It follows directly that for a stalemate outcome the total number of defending units must be *at least equal to* the total number of attacking units. Since conceding the defense a greater overall strength than the offense does not lead to any augmentation of explanatory power and disturbs the intrinsic symmetry of the problem, we assume that the total number of defending force units exactly equals the total number of attacking force units.

Optimal Defense Position for the One Force Unit Case

Strengthened by a clear, unequivocal definition of its objectives and constraints, the defender is now in a position to pose the fundamental Defense Positioning Problem:

Where should the defending force units be stationed to minimize the infiltration of attacking forces and match the adversary at each focus of penetration unit for unit?

Suppose the offense and defense each has N force units under its control. With a view to comprehending the dynamics of the problem, we begin by setting N = 1. Thus each side has exactly one force unit to commit to battle. The attacker must select the point f along the length-M front at which the solitary attacking unit will launch its attempt at infiltration. The defending commander must determine the coordinates (x, y) of the single defensive unit. The unopposed infiltration, I, into defense territory achieved by the invader is a function of the particular focus of attack chosen by the attacker and the specific location (x, y) of the defending unit. To derive an explicit expression for I in terms of f, x and y, it is necessary to invoke Theorem I, which is restated here for convenience.

THEOREM I: *At each focus of attack, the aggressor's invading forces will proceed into enemy territory with the maximum possible velocity in a direction perpendicular to the length-M front.*

The campaign plan, as it evolves over time, is depicted in Figure 1-6.

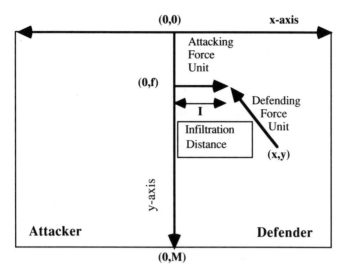

Figure 1-6   Battle Trajectories for the Attacking and Defending Force Units

The attacker launches a foray at point f along the length-M front and commences its infiltration perpendicular to the front. The defending force unit re-
sponds "instantaneously" as the aggressor breaches the common frontier between the two neighbors and, being constantly reinforced by perfect
information on the trajectory of the attacking force unit, the defender directs its
forces along the shortest collision path with the adversary's invading troops. By
the time the two opponents come face to face the attacking force unit has infiltrated a distance I into enemy territory. It must always be true that:

> *The time taken by the attacking force unit to traverse a distance I into enemy*
> *territory = The time required by the defender to transport its forces from*
> *their peacetime base (x, y) to the scene of the conflict (I, f).*

Let v_a be the average velocity of attacking forces when travelling over enemy terrain and v_d be the mean speed of the defender on home ground. Then it
follows that:

$$\frac{I}{v_a} = \frac{\sqrt{(x - I)^2 + (y - f)^2}}{v_d} \tag{1-3}$$

where $\sqrt{(x - I)^2 + (y - f)^2}$ is the distance between the points (x, y) and (I, f).
There arise three scenarios of strategic interest, depending on the relative
speeds of the attacking and defending forces on defense terrain.

Case 1. $v_a = v_d$. The defense and the offense move with equal agility.

Case 2. $v_a < v_d$. The defense can outrun the offense.

Case 3. $v_a > v_d$. The offense outstrips the defense. This scenario can also be used to simulate a defense response that is lackadaisical and slow. Though, once in motion, the defense might be capable of transporting force more rapidly than the attacker, the defense might fail to respond immediately to the offensive invasion and initially lose valuable time, leading to a subdued average defensive force velocity, v_d.

For expository purposes, the mathematical details are worked out here only for the equal velocity case ($v_a = v_d$). However the final results for the cases $v_a < v_d$ and $v_a > v_d$ are included for completeness.[5] For Case 1, $v_a = v_d$, Equation 1–3 reduces to:

$$I = \sqrt{(x - I)^2 + (y - f)^2} \qquad (1\text{-}4)$$

Squaring both sides yields:

$$I^2 = (x - I)^2 + (y - f)^2 \qquad (1\text{-}5)$$

Solving for I, we have:

$$I = (x, y; f) \quad \frac{x^2 + (y - f)^2}{2x} \qquad (1\text{-}6)$$

As before, let P(f) be the probability that the attacker will choose point f along the front as a focus of invasion. Then the expected infiltration of the invading forces into enemy territory is given by:

$$\bar{I}(x, y; f) = \int_0^M P(f) \frac{x^2 + (y - f)^2}{2x} df \qquad (1\text{-}7)$$

The form of P(f) is dictated by Assumption II, the Uniform Probability of Attack Assumption. Thus P(f) is simply the uniform probability distribution defined on the closed real interval [0, M].

$$P(f) = \frac{1}{M} \qquad f \in [0, M] \qquad (1\text{-}8)$$

Hence the expected infiltration reduces to:

$$\bar{I} = \frac{1}{M} \int_0^M \frac{x}{2} + \frac{(y - f)^2}{2x} df \qquad (1\text{-}9)$$

[5]The algebraic derivations for the $v_a < v_d$ and $v_a > v_d$ cases are discussed in Appendix 1B.

The defender must choose his position (x, y) to minimize the expected infiltration.

$$\operatorname*{Min}_{(x,y)} \left[\frac{1}{M} \int_0^M \frac{x}{2} + \frac{(y - f)^2}{2x} \, df \right] \qquad (1\text{-}10)$$

Minimizing the expected infiltration translates mathematically to taking the partial derivatives of $\bar{I}(x, y; f)$ with respect to x and y and setting the derivatives to zero.[6]

$$\frac{\partial}{\partial x} \left[\frac{1}{M} \int_0^M \frac{x}{2} + \frac{(y - f)^2}{2x} \, df \right] = 0$$

$$\text{and} \quad \frac{\partial}{\partial y} \left[\frac{1}{M} \int_0^M \frac{x}{2} + \frac{(y - f)^2}{2x} \, df \right] = 0 \qquad (1\text{-}11)$$

Calling upon the Leibniz Rule for interchanging the order of partial differentiation and integration, we have:[7]

$$\frac{1}{M} \int_0^M \frac{\partial}{\partial x} \left[\frac{x}{2} + \frac{(y - f)^2}{2x} \right] df = 0$$

$$\text{and} \quad \frac{1}{M} \int_0^M \frac{\partial}{\partial y} \left[\frac{x}{2} + \frac{(y - f)^2}{2x} \right] df = 0 \qquad (1\text{-}12)$$

This leaves us with two equations and two unknowns, x and y. Performing the algebraic operations indicated above yields the optimal defensive force placement for the $v_a = v_d$ case.

THEOREM II: *For the equal velocity scenario, the defensive force unit must be stationed halfway along the length-M front and at a distance $M/\sqrt{12}$ behind the demarcation line. Equivalently, in terms of our rectangular coordinate*

---

[6]It can be shown using the usual second-order conditions that the values of x and y determined by taking the first-order derivatives and setting them to zero represent a minimum and not a maximum or a saddle point.

[7]The Leibniz Rule for interchanging the order of differentiation and integration can only be applied under certain conditions on the functional nature of the integrand and the limits of integration. Thus one must be careful in applying the rule in a general setting. Since the rule holds unconditionally in all the specific circumstances under which it is invoked in this study, a compilation of the mathematical constraints on the eligibility of the law is beyond our scope.

system established earlier, the defensive unit must base itself at the point
(M/√12, M/2) to minimize the attacker's hostile incursion.

Proof: From Equation 1-12, the optimal defense position can be determined
by solving the following pair of simultaneous equations.

$$\int_0^M \frac{\partial}{\partial x}\left[\frac{x}{2} + \frac{(y - f)^2}{2x}\right] df = 0$$

and $$\int_0^M \frac{\partial}{\partial y}\left[\frac{x}{2} + \frac{(y - f)^2}{2x}\right] df = 0$$

Thus,

$$\int_0^M \frac{1}{2} - \frac{(y - f)^2}{2x^2}\, df = 0$$

and $$\int_0^M \frac{y - f}{x}\, df = 0$$

$$\frac{f}{2} + \frac{(y - f)^3}{6x^2}\Bigg|_{f=0}^{f=M} = 0$$

and $$-\frac{(y - f)^2}{2x}\Bigg|_{f=0}^{f=M} = 0$$

$$\frac{M}{2} + \frac{(y - M)^3}{6x^2} - \frac{y^3}{6x^2} = 0$$

and $$\frac{y^2}{2x} - \frac{(y - M)^2}{2x} = 0$$

$$y = \frac{M}{2} \quad \text{and} \quad x = \frac{M}{\sqrt{12}}$$

For example, a single unit defending a 100 kilometer front must be stationed
100/2 = 50 kms along the front and 100/√12 = 50/√3 = 28.9 kms behind the
front. Thus the defense will intercept the offense at points (I, f) given by:

$$I^2 = \left(\frac{M}{\sqrt{12}} - I\right)^2 + \left(\frac{M}{2} - f\right)^2 \tag{1-13}$$

Algebraic simplification yields:

$$I = \frac{M\sqrt{3}}{12} + \frac{\sqrt{3}}{M}\left(\frac{M}{2} - f\right)^2 \tag{1-14}$$

This set of points (I, f) is termed the *defense locus* and is pictured in Figure 1-7. The defense locus is the set of points where the defending forces, if optimally positioned, are first able to confront the invader. The defense locus thus indicates the minimum inward penetration of the defender's territory inevitably achieved by the offense. Given the attacker's velocity, v_a, the defense speed, v_d, and the length of the front, M, the defender is inherently incapable of restraining penetration to distances less than those decreed by the defense locus. On the other hand, the defender can rest assured that if it positions its fighting unit optimally, any battle for supremacy will occur along the defense locus. In consequence, positions along the defense locus could be reinforced with barriers or supply depots to increase the defensive force multiplier.

From Figure 1-7, it is evidenced that the infiltration achieved by the offense varies from $M/2\sqrt{12}$ for a foray launched directly opposite the peacetime defensive base to $2M/\sqrt{12}$ for an attack launched at either extremity of the common border. Further, the defense locus is a parabola for the equal velocity case.

Where do the coordinates of the optimal defensive force position, $M/\sqrt{12}$ and M/2, come from? As shown in Appendix 1A, the y coordinate of the optimal defensive base is the *mean* of the probability density function of attack, while the x coordinate is the *standard deviation* of the probability density function. Thus for an arbitrary probability distribution of attack, the defender should

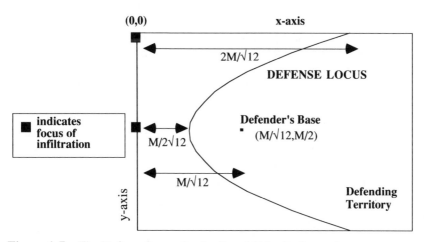

Figure 1-7   The Defense Locus for the Equal Velocity Scenario

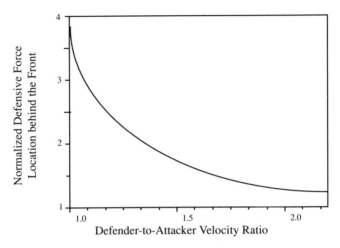

Figure 1-8 Defense Velocity Greater than Attack Velocity. Defensive location behind the front expressed as a fraction of the placement for the equal velocity case.

position its troops at a distance μ along the length-M front and at a displacement σ inward from the frontier. The terms μ and σ are the mean and standard deviation respectively of the general probability distribution of attack. We term this very powerful result the σ–μ Theorem. Under certain reasonable assumptions, all we need to know to determine the optimal force geometry for the defense is the mean and standard deviation of the probability distribution of invasion. For the *uniform* probability density function considered above, the mean is $M/2$ and the standard deviation about the mean is $M/\sqrt{12}$. Hence the defense must locate its unit at $(M/\sqrt{12}, M/2)$ to minimize unopposed offensive incursion.

For the case of defense velocity greater than offense velocity,[8] Case 2 ($v_a <$ v_d), the defending unit must be stationed halfway along the length-M front, that is $y = M/2$. However the inward displacement of the unit from the front, x, is less than the displacement under the equal velocity case. The inward displacement, x, is a decreasing function of the defender-to-attacker velocity ratio and is depicted graphically in Figure 1-8. The independent variable along the x-axis is the defender-to-attacker velocity ratio which is greater than 1 for the $v_a <$ v_d case. The dependent variable along the y-axis is the optimal location of the defending force unit behind the frontier between the two antagonistic states. The positioning of the defending forces is expressed relative to the defensive

---

[8]The mathematics of deriving the optimal defense position for the $v_a < v_d$ case is relegated to Appendix 1B.

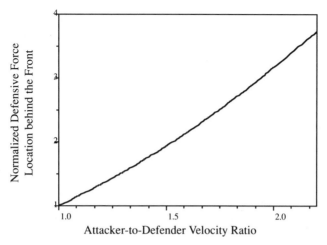

Figure 1-9 Attack Velocity Greater than Defense Velocity. Defensive location behind the front expressed as a multiple of the placement for the equal velocity case.

force location for the case of equal offense and defense speeds. In effect, it is assumed in constructing the graph that the defending force unit would be stationed at unit distance inward from the border if the attacker and the defender were evenly matched in speed.

As defensive force agility begins to eclipse the speed of the invading forces, the defending force unit can be located closer and closer to the front. However there are diminishing marginal returns associated with increasing defense speed; each incremental advance in relative speed corresponds to a progressively smaller movement toward the demarcation line.

The solution to the case of attack velocity exceeding defense velocity (Case 3, $v_a > v_d$)[9] again requires the defending unit to be positioned halfway along the length-M front, that is y = M/2. For the $v_a > v_d$ case, the inward displacement, x, of the defense from the front is greater than that for the equal velocity case and is depicted as a function of the attacker-to-defender velocity ratio in Figure 1-9. Along the x-axis is the ratio of attacker velocity to defense velocity which is greater than 1 for $v_a > v_d$. The y-axis indicates the optimal peacetime displacement of the defense unit behind the front. The ordinate is graduated in units of the distance behind the front of the defensive forces for the scenario of equal offense and defense velocities. Thus a 1 on the y-axis corresponds to a location

---

[9]Appendix 1B contains the algebraic derivation of the optimal defense position for the $v_a > v_d$ scenario. Only the final result is presented here.

behind the border equal to the optimal defense displacement for $v_a = v_d$, a 2 on the y-axis corresponds to twice the optimal distance for the equal velocity case, and so on. It is evident from Figure 1-9 that as the attacker's speed of transporting force exceeds that of the defender's, the defender is compelled to position forces further and further inward from the demarcation line. For attacking force velocities more than twice the average defense speed, the displacement of the defensive unit behind the front escalates sharply.

The Defense Positioning Problem has been solved for the situation where both the offense and the defense possess a single force unit. Assuming that each opponent has perfect information on its side of the length-M front and zero information on the enemy's side, that there is a uniform probability of attack at any point along the common border, and that the defender is required to match the invader unit for unit as far forward as possible, the unopposed infiltration of the attacker is minimized by locating the defensive unit halfway along the front and at a nonzero distance inward from the front. This inward displacement is equal to $M/\sqrt{12}$ for the equal velocity case and is indicated in Figures 1-8 and 1-9 for the scenario of unequal velocities.

In summary, the optimal position for a defending unit is not along the front but at a nonzero distance behind the front. The position is optimal in the sense that the defending unit meets and defeats the attacker as far forward as possible, minimizing the invader's unopposed infiltration. Thus forward defense requires the defending unit to be displaced inward from the front. The word "forward" in the term forward defense does not imply that the defense unit itself be pressed as close to the front as physically feasible. Rather, it is the point where the attacker is confronted and defeated that must be pushed forward towards the front. We shall adopt the phrase "forward-deployed defense" to refer to a defense strategy of basing defensive units as close to the front as possible and shall continue to use the phrase "forward defense" to refer to the notion of meeting and defeating offensive forces as close to the border as possible. We may restate the conclusion of our analysis in this new terminology: Forward-deployed defense is not optimal. It does not minimize the loss of territory to the attacker.[10]

---

[10]We are assuming a uniform probability distribution of attack throughout this argument. There is one form of the probability density function of attack for which a forward defense degenerates into a forward-deployed defense. This is the case where the defender knows with certainty which point along the length-M front will be chosen by the invader for the attack. The probability of attack is unity at this point and zero at all others. In this situation the defender should deploy its entire defensive lethality as close to the length-M front as possible at the point where the attack is certain to occur. In all other cases a forward-deployed defense does not minimize offensive infiltration.

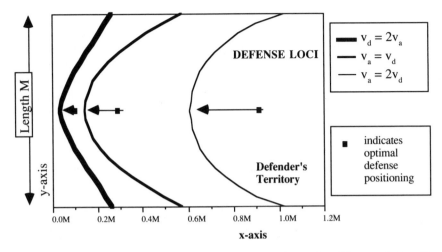

Figure 1-10   Defense Loci for $v_d = 2v_a$, $v_a = v_d$ and $v_a = 2v_d$. The x-axis is calibrated in terms of the length of the front.

Stability and the Relative Attacker-to-Defender Force Velocity

The significance for the defense of maintaining superiority or at least parity in the speed of transporting force is underscored by examining the defense loci for each of the three cases of $v_a = v_d$, $v_a < v_d$ and $v_a > v_d$. Figure 1-10 juxtaposes the defense loci for $v_d = v_a$, $v_d = 2v_a$ and $2v_d = v_a$. Under our assumptions of an on-off information capability for both sides and equal total lethality between the two adversaries, the defense locus is the minimum territory that the optimally positioned defender must relinquish to the invader; it is the guaranteed payoff of launching an attack and serves as an inducement to each side to be the aggressor.

As the defender slows down in mobilizing force across home ground, not only is the defense's optimal peacetime deployment pushed back from the front but the expeditious assailant succeeds in realizing deeper and deeper incursive thrusts into the opposition's territory. While, obviously, in warfare moving faster is better than moving slower, the unavoidable minimum loss of territory as embodied by the defense locus does provide a direct, comparative measure for quantifying the real, war-time benefit of improved mobility.

Another illuminating conclusion that can be drawn from our study of mobility is that outcomes depend only on the *ratio* of invading-to-defending force velocity; from the point of view of enhancing conventional stability the absolute speed of transporting force is essentially irrelevant. Mitigating the rapidity of force mobility equally on both sides does not fundamentally alter the defense locus or the reward to attack. In other words, each side if it chooses to launch an onslaught will enjoy the identical incentives of guaranteed incursion, the only distinguishing feature being the overall slower prosecution of the campaign. An innovative arms control agreement should seek by mutual consent to structure forces, equipment and terrain in a manner that ensures force units unequivocal superiority in speed over home territory. Each side must be capable of outstripping the attacker when subjected to an invasion and, in turn, must be surpassed by the opponent when initiating the attack. More succinctly, stability is enhanced by $v_d > v_a$.[11]

Generalizing the Defense Positioning Problem to the N Force Unit Case

We now generalize the solution to the Defense Positioning Problem to the situation where each side has an arbitrary number of force units, N. Each side possesses an identical complement of N discrete force units. The attacker can launch forays at different times at more than one point along the border. For instance, the aggressor could launch a 2-unit attack at time $t = 0$ at the location $y = M/4$, a subsequent 6-unit attack at time $t = 10$ at $y = M/2$ and a final 2-pronged onslaught at time $t = 20$ with 5 units prosecuting the attack from $y = M/3$ and 5 units launched into defense territory from $y = 2M/3$. The defender has the mandate of minimizing overall penetration achieved by the invading forces. It is logical for the supreme commander of the defense to instruct each individual unit leader to position his or her unit so that the unopposed infiltration of the offense is minimized. The individual unit commanders do not have to concern themselves with the total magnitude of hostile force that penetrates into the defense terrain. They must simply fulfill their individual mandate of engaging the adversary as far forward as feasible. This objective may be accomplished by basing each unit at the position dictated by the solution to the 1-unit Defense Positioning Problem. If the defensive force structure is analyzed unit by unit, it is apparent that each unit commander can be assigned to only one focus of penetration, and this one-on-one dynamic decision rule is unaffected by the amount of offensive lethality at each point of invasion. Viewed in this disaggregated manner, the N-unit Defense Positioning Problem reduces to N 1-unit problems. Thus if the attacker and defender can generate equal speeds across the battle territory, each of the N defending unit commanders will base his or her forces at $(M/\sqrt{12}, M/2)$. Only this location ensures that each defending unit will meet the attacker as close to the border as possible. Since all defending force units are identical, no individual defending unit commander will deviate from our prototypical force unit leader, and the entire defense contin-

---

[11]One possible means for ensuring defensive superiority in velocity is to deploy passive defenses in the region between the defense locus and the front. Part Two describes passive defenses and derives an optimal structure for such defenses.

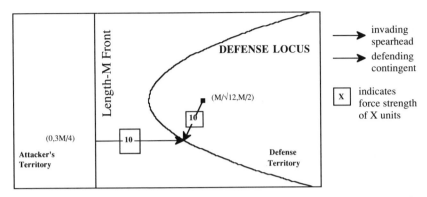

Figure 1-11   Generalizing the Defense Locus. Single offensive incursion for N = 10.

gent of N force units will base itself at the location $(M/\sqrt{12}, M/2)$. If the offensive and defensive force velocities are not equal, the defender's N force units will collectively establish a peacetime base at a position dictated by our earlier analysis for the one-on-one case summarized in Figures 1-8 and 1-9. To keep the discussion simple and concrete, we will assume throughout the succeeding analysis that the defense and the offense possess equal speeds of transporting force across the defense terrain.

Let us convince ourselves that the force positioning envisioned above is indeed optimal for the defense. Consider the most straightforward attack scenario involving a 10-unit onslaught at 3M/4 in a world where the attacker and the defender each possess a total of 10 lethality units. As indicated in Figure 1-11, the defense, in reaction, will mobilize all 10 defensive force units from their peacetime position of $(M/\sqrt{12}, M/2)$ to the front. The defense locus for this rather unimaginative attack scenario is identical to that derived for the one-on-one equal velocity case (Figure 1-7) since all 10 force units on either side function together as a single, cohesive concentration of force.

What is less evident but equally true is that the optimal defense positioning and the defense locus are unaltered for any choice of invasion blueprints. For instance, a less rudimentary onslaught than the one hypothesized above might involve attacking groups of 2 units, 2 units and 3 units, each conducting forays at three distinct places along the length-M front. The defense will respond by designating groups of 2, 2 and 3 force units from the central reserve to plug the incursions of corresponding strength as depicted in Figure 1-12. The residual defensive capacity of 3 force units will remain at the peacetime base of $(M/\sqrt{12}, M/2)$ to deal with the possibility of a further onslaught by the remaining 3 force units of the aggressor.

From the figure, it emerges that the defense locus is unaltered by the increased complexity of the attacker's campaign plan and is identical to the one

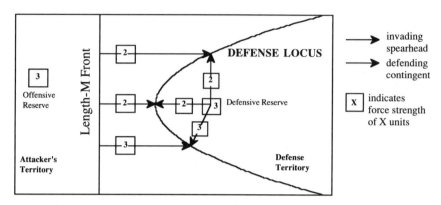

Figure 1-12 Generalizing the Defense Locus. Multiple offensive incursions for N = 10.

in Figure 1-7. The invader's three forays could be launched at different points in time. The defending commander would view each foray as a discrete, independent onslaught. For any one foray, containing the infiltration of each individual attacking unit constitutes a distinct 1-unit Defense Positioning Problem. The N-unit Defense Positioning Problem when analyzed foray by foray, unit by unit, collapses into N 1-unit problems. We have thus demonstrated that if the attacker and defender are evenly matched in force strength and speed across the defense terrain, the defense must concentrate all its force at a distance $M/\sqrt{12}$ behind the demarcation line and halfway along the length-M front to minimize unopposed infiltration.

Refining the Concept of a Length-M Front

When we commenced our discussion of optimal force positioning, we propounded a simple notion of a length-M front as a contiguous boundary of length M between two adversarial countries. Now that the problem of defensive force placement has been solved for the most general case, we may apply the solution to a real-world example and see how the definition of a length-M front must be refined in order to have meaning in an actual situation.

Imagine a fictitious conflict between the United States and Canada with the US-Canadian border as the expected arena of battle. Assume it is the Canadians who seek to invade the United States. If the entirety of the US-Canadian border were treated as a single length-M front by a defense planner, a zealous application of our methodology would set M equal to approximately 3,000 miles. Thus as shown in Figure 1-13 all US forces would be dispatched in anticipation of the invasion to Wichita, Kansas, roughly halfway across the continental landmass of the United States and $3{,}000/\sqrt{12} = 866$ miles inward from the

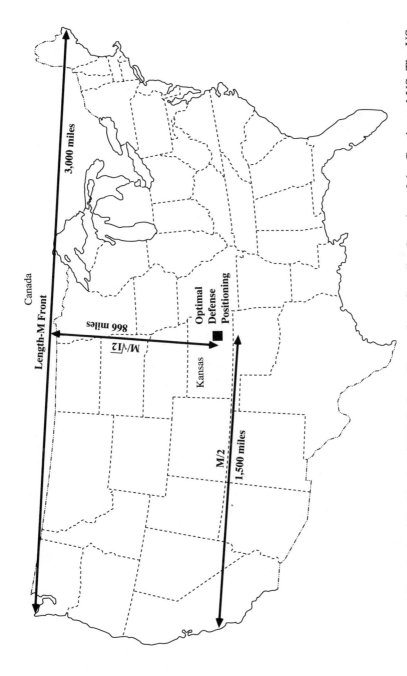

Figure 1-13 Optimal Positioning of US Defense Troops for a Canadian Invasion of the Continental US. The US-Canadian border is treated as a single length-M front.

Canadian border. A defense positioning so removed from the common frontier is excessively conservative and meek and results from an improper definition of the front. In determining the effective length of the front, the force planner must survey the terrain to isolate segments of the contiguous border separated by natural divides or other "insurmountable" obstacles. A length-M front is a disparate, unbroken segment of the line of demarcation that satisfies the following properties:

1. The defender must always be cognizant of the *total* number of enemy force units deployed behind the designated segment.

2. The defender may be utterly ignorant of the distribution of the hostile units along the particular segment, despite its complete knowledge of the overall quantity of force allocated to the segment.

3. Should the opponent import additional force units into the segment or export entrenched units from the segment, defense intelligence must be capable of monitoring the movements and reestimating the total rival contingent stationed on the other side of the segment. Essentially, intrasegment force mobility can be perfectly fluid while intersegment force mobility must be difficult and easily detectable.

4. The terrain adjoining the segment on either side must be reasonably isotropic.

Thus any two segments separated by a modestly unfordable physical barrier, such as a river or a mountain range, could each constitute a length-M front. Defining the length-M front in this manner allows us to assume that the topography of the terrain adjoining each individual length-M front is fairly isotropic parallel to the front. Severe violations of such terrain isotropy should be used to define the barrier between adjacent length-M fronts. Obstacles between segments can also be man-made or institutional. Returning to our Canadian invasion test case, the Canadians could conceivably apportion responsibility for the predominantly English-speaking western half of Canada to English-speaking military formations and use French-speaking regiments to lead the charge from the east. The transmittal of force between these two halves could be so cumbersome and discernible that this rigid, inflexible hierarchy of command would bisect the Canadian frontier into two length-M fronts. As depicted in Figure 1-14, the division of the US-Canadian border into two length-M fronts would permit the United States to position its forces much closer to the demarcation line when compared with the optimal US deployment for a unified Canadian force structure. Each defensive force center would be located 433 miles inward from the front and halfway across its respective frontier. The western half of the United States would be defended out of an encampment situated southeast of the Yellowstone National Park and northeast of Jackson, Wyoming, while the eastern half would be protected by a force concentration near Detroit, Michigan.

Another example of how man-made barriers can vitiate the effectiveness of a military force is that of a United Nations peacekeeping contingent composed of

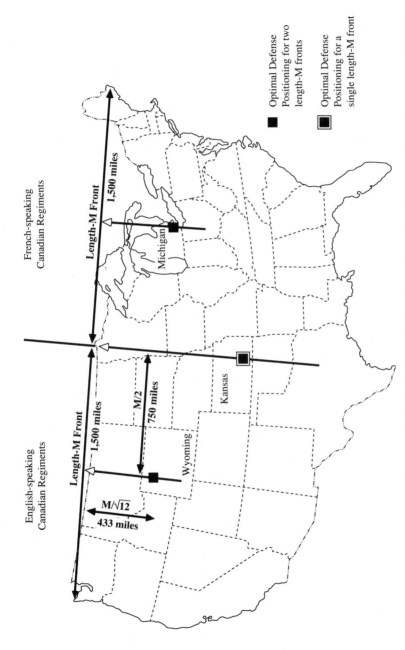

Figure 1-14 Optimal Positioning of US Defending Troops for a Canadian Invasion of the Continental US. The US-Canadian border is treated as two separate length-M fronts.

units from various member countries. If the peacemakers insist on dividing military duties along national lines, thus fragmenting the peacekeeping "front," it becomes extremely difficult to transfer forces rapidly across these nationally constituted boundaries. The line of confrontation is split into numerous length-M fronts, lowering the effectiveness of the peacekeeping regiment and permitting the enemy to encroach closer upon the front.

A final instance of the hierarchical sectioning of an otherwise contiguous front is posed by the post–World War II organization of NATO forces in West Germany as eight corp sectors. Tactical and operational responsibility for the conduct of missions within corp sectors was assigned to the NATO member country in command of the particular sector. This nationality-based distribution of corp sectors inhibited the intersector transmittal of force and the harmonious performance of strategic missions integrating resources from more than one sector.

A further limitation on the size of M is imposed by the on-off information assumption. In a world where both sides possess technologically sophisticated means of surveillance, each party will be completely blind to the opponent's distribution of force along its side of the front for small values of M only. For instance, the on-off information function clearly does not hold for the entire border between Iran and Iraq in Central Asia, and it is therefore misleading to conceive of the 1,000 km long Iran-Iraq border as a single length-M front. Thus in addition to the partitioning of the demarcation line caused by natural and man-made barriers, one must also take into account how reasonable the on-off assumption is in determining the length of the length-M front.

Better intelligence allows us to monitor enemy force movements more closely, permitting us to define smaller length-M fronts. With superior surveillance and reconnaissance webs we can monitor the total enemy strength in progressively smaller regions, creating the ability to define smaller and smaller length-M fronts. The smaller the front, the closer to the front the defense encampment can be located in absolute terms and the smaller is the area exposed by the defense locus to uncontested conquest by the foe.

Examining the definition of a length-M front also offers us an insight into why it is desirable to maintain a capability to rapidly and efficiently transport force parallel to the front. The larger the distance over which a side can fluidly and unobtrusively shift force parallel to the partitioning border, the longer is the length of the length-M front faced by the other side. Consequently, the other side, who is required by considerations of minimizing offensive incursion to locate its forces at a distance $M/\sqrt{12}$ behind the line of conflict, has no alternative but to base its encampment further and further away from the border with increasing M. In addition, should the other side be invaded, it can potentially lose a larger portion of its territory with increased M, as the defense locus recedes inwards in terms of absolute mileage with expanding length of the front. The change in the defense locus of the adversary with changing M serves as an excellent mathematization of the benefits accruing to a side that expends resources to promote force mobility parallel to the front.

To summarize, the effective length of the length-M front is determined by the following factors.

1. The existence of reasonably unfordable physical barriers between two adjacent regions of otherwise contiguous, isotropic topology. Natural formations such as mountain ranges or rivers effectively split the terrain into multiple length-M fronts, lowering the guaranteed reward to the aggressor for first strike as embodied by the defense locus.

2. The existence of man-made or institutional barriers that limit intersegment force mobility. The barriers might be "legislated" through arms control to lower the M of the length-M front and enhance stability.

3. The ability of the enemy to surreptitiously transport forces large distances parallel to the front. The larger the tract over which enemy lethality can be dispatched without detection by the other side, the longer the length of the length-M front constituted by the tract in question and the farther back the defender must be positioned behind the front.

4. The information capabilities of the defense. Superior intelligence about enemy force maneuvers limits the effective size of the length-M front confronting the defender and reduces the defender's vulnerability to preemptive attack.

Why Our Force Positioning Algorithm Might Be Impractical

Thus far we seem to have solved the Defense Positioning Problem. A defense planner should commence defense preparations by studying its frontiers with adjoining nations and isolating the length-M fronts that are vulnerable to conquest. Then halfway along each length-M front and at a distance $M/\sqrt{12}$ inward from the front, the defender should establish a peacetime base manned by a force strength equal to the opponent's force strength in that sector. However there are a number of problems that arise if all the defending force is concentrated in a handful of locations as dictated by our axiom for minimizing offensive incursion:

1. Localized force concentrations are alluring targets for preemptive strike. A small number of deep interdiction aircraft armed with conventional bombloads can wreak havoc over a concentrated defense encampment.

2. If forces are centralized and concentrated locally, it is likely that the associated command and control will also be lashed together into a high density C^3I headquarters. A surreptitious, preemptive, selective air raid could devastate the command and control network leaving behind an acephalous and incoherent local defense.

3. Finally, we have not yet scrutinized the strategic and operational consequences of the loss of territory implied by the defense locus. We have shown

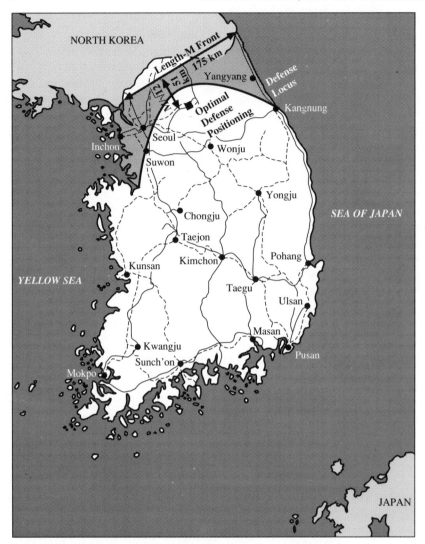

Figure 1-15 North Korean Invasion of South Korea: Optimal Defense Positioning and the Defense Locus.

that if the objective is to match the invader unit for unit at each focus of penetration and simultaneously minimize expected offensive infiltration, the defense locus is the absolute minimum loss of ground that the defender must sustain. However even the implementation of this optimal defense structure might prove fatally harmful to the defending regime because the defense locus permits the attacker to gain up to $2M/\sqrt{12}$ of the defender's territory for forays conducted at either extremity of the length-M front and $M/2\sqrt{12}$ of the defended terrain for a head-on onslaught, launched opposite the peacetime defense encampment. The point can be brought home more forcefully by considering a number of real-world examples.

Visualize a North Korean invasion of South Korea with the principal thrust along the inter-Korean border. The 175 km long demarcation line between the two Koreas—stretching from the Yellow Sea in the west to the Sea of Japan in the east— may be treated as a single length-M front with M equal to 175 kms. If the North Korean and South Korean forces are matched in speed of translation over South Korean terrain, the South Korean contingent will station itself midway between Inchon and Yangyang as shown in Figure 1-15. This peacetime base is approximately halfway along the length-M front and $175/\sqrt{12} = 51$ kms inward from the border. If the North Korean invasion were launched at the western extremity of the front, the North Koreans could capture Seoul without encountering any resistance, since Seoul would fall in the vulnerable strip between the border and the defense locus. The first battle between the armies of the North and South would be waged beyond Suwon, defeating the purpose of the South Korean defense. Similarly, a North Korean infiltration at the eastern extremity of the front could travel up to Kangnung unopposed, facilely yielding the city of Yangyang and possibly Kangnung to the enemy. The South Korean defense, though efficient, is ineffective because, while it minimizes unopposed offensive infiltration and meets the enemy unit for unit at each focus of penetration, it fails in its objective of protecting the South Korean homeland.

Another case-in-point is provided by an Iranian invasion of Iraq with the principal thrust launched into the oil-producing southern region of Iraq. The length-M front for this conflict would be almost a straight line running from Khanaqin in the northwest to Basra and the Persian Gulf in the southeast as shown in Figure 1-16. The length of this front would roughly equal 550 kms, requiring an Iraqi peacetime base 225 kms along the front and $550/\sqrt{12} = 159$ kms inward. Thus the Iraqi troops would be deployed just northeast of Samawa before the outbreak of hostilities. As before, the consequences of infiltrations at either extremity of the front would be cataclysmic for Iraqi security. An Iranian penetration at the northern edge of the front would permit the Iranians to capture Baghdad, the capital of Iraq, with no resistance from Iraqi forces. On the other hand, if the Iranians chose to prosecute their campaign near the southern edge of the front, the Iranian army would capture Basra and conquer almost the

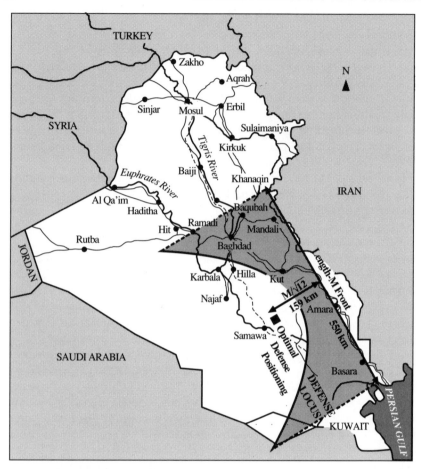

Figure 1-16 Iranian Invasion of Southern Iraq: Optimal Defense Positioning and the Defense Locus.

entire width of Iraq, all the way up to the Saudi Arabian border, without confronting the preponderant portion of the Iraqi military.[12]

The seriousness of the expansive losses of terrain allowed by the defense locus cannot be underscored more emphatically than by contemplating an

---

[12]Of course we are making a rather conservative assumption in deriving this gloomy scenario in the two cases considered above. The on-off information assumption means that South Korea and Iraq have no information about the distribution of North Korean and Iranian forces, respectively, behind the front prior to the start of the campaign. Since the

invasion conducted over territory of high strategic value, such as urbanized and densely populated tracts of land, as exemplified by the three campaigns described above. The problems associated with our force positioning algorithm are twofold: the vulnerability to preemption of any large force localization and the dangerously generous incursions permitted by the defense locus. These problems are a consequence of the fact that our optimization of defensive force location has not imposed any upper bound on the local concentration of forces.

The 2-constrained Solution to the Defense Positioning Problem

The anxiety-ridden defense planner can impose the constraint that total military might must be divided into two or more independent force formations based at different peacetime locations. We begin our investigation of the constrained Defense Positioning Problem by zeroing in on the simplest possible constraint, namely, dividing the defense forces into two equal subgroups. These two independent defense elements must be based at two separate locations and the force analyst's task is to determine these optimal positions. One way to determine these two optimal positions is to divide the length-M front into two length-(M/2) fronts and assign each subfront to one of the two defending force elements. Each defending force formation applies the unconstrained form of the defense optimization algorithm to its respective length-(M/2) front and determines its peacetime location. Thus, the force element in charge of the upper half of the front bases itself at $(M/2\sqrt{12}, M/4)$, while the force responsible for the lower half bases itself at $(M/2\sqrt{12}, 3M/4)$. We shall call this set of positions $\{(M/2\sqrt{12}, M/4), (M/2\sqrt{12}, 3M/4)\}$ the 2-constrained scenario. The 2-constrained scenario is one possible solution we can offer to the defender who wants to divide its forces between two equal subgroups. The defense locus for the 2-constrained scenario is depicted in Figure 1-17.

The defense locus for the 2-constrained scenario limits maximum offensive penetration to $M/\sqrt{12}$ as opposed to $2M/\sqrt{12}$ for the unconstrained defense optimization situation. The defense units under the 2-constrained scenario are based at a distance $M/2\sqrt{12}$ inward from the demarcation line, which is half the

---

defenders do possess some information about the location of enemy force units through means such as espionage and high-flying reconnaissance aircraft, and since the defending commanders can monitor the movement of enemy forces within the regions of North Korea and Iran immediately adjacent to the length-M front, it is inappropriate to consider the entire border from the Yellow Sea to the Sea of Japan in the case of South Korea and from Khanaqin to the Persian Gulf in the case of Iraq as a single length-M front. Rather these sectors of the interstate borders should be considered as a number of discrete length-M fronts depending on the quality and extent of the defense's surveillance capabilities.

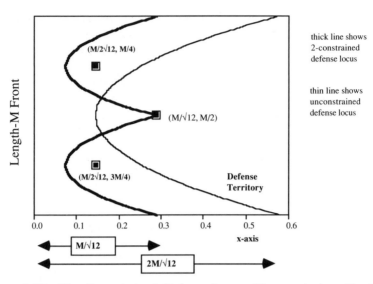

Figure 1-17   The 2-constrained Defense Locus. The x-axis is calibrated in units of M.

distance prescribed by the unconstrained case. It is evident from the figure that each defensive entity independently shoulders the responsibility for defending its section of the total length-M front. This sectioning of the length-M front arising from the need to disperse defensive force and enhance survivability, is fundamentally opposed to the sectioning of a contiguous border into separate length-M fronts based on restrictions on intersegment force transfer of the enemy. While the latter division is based either on physical obstacles that are a natural feature of the intervening terrain, on institutional and hierarchical barriers characteristic of the opposition's organizational structure or on information considerations, and implies that the transfer of force between appropriately constituted, discrete length-M fronts is highly visible if not impossible, there are no such imbedded assumptions in the arbitrary bisection of a length-M front into two length-(M/2) fronts. The enemy can easily transfer force units in total secrecy from one length-(M/2) front to the other, and thus the commander of each defense encampment of N/2 units, entrusted with the safekeeping of a length-(M/2) front, must be prepared to engage in battle with a hostile strength ranging anywhere from 0 to N force units. In the worst case situation, the defense might have to pitch N/2 units in one sector of the length-M front against N invading force units while the N/2 defending units in the other sector remain idle, far removed from the battlefield. We shall adopt the term *overload factor*

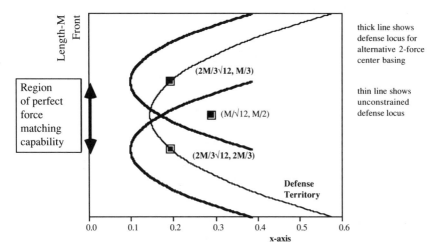

Figure 1-18   An Alternative Basing Scheme for Two Separate Defensive Force Centers. The x-axis is calibrated in units of M.

for the most unfavorable offense-to-defense force ratio that could be impressed upon the defender in any fragment of the length-M front as a consequence of the imposed constraint of force dispersion. For the 2-constrained case, the overload factor is 2 (N: N/2). The dual benefits of improving survivability by splitting the defending forces into two local force concentrations and of pushing the defense locus towards the front, thus lowering expected offensive incursion into defense territory, are attained at the expense of violating the force matching constraint; no longer is the defense capable of matching the adversary unit for unit at each focus of penetration. Effectively, the defense has traded off its capacity for perfect counterconcentration in exchange for force dispersal and reduced offensive incursion.

There are several intermediate possibilities between the two extremes of basing all defensive forces at a distance M/2 along the common border and dividing the forces equally between the centers, at distances M/4 and 3M/4 along the length-M front. For instance, the two force centers could be located at distances M/3 and 2M/3 along the front. The upper force concentration would be responsible for the upper two-thirds of the length-M front while the lower force localization would be responsible for the lower two-thirds of the front. Peacetime bases would be established at $(2M/3\sqrt{12}, M/3)$ and $(2M/3\sqrt{12}, 2M/3)$ as shown in Figure 1-18.

As a consequence of the overlap in defense responsibilities, the defender would enjoy almost perfect counterconcentration capability in the region adjoining the central third of the length-M front. The counterconcentration capability in the central region is still not perfect because the defense units from the two peacetime bases will not arrive simultaneously at the point of initial contact with the adversary. However the gap between the arrival of the two defending echelons at the battlefield will be relatively small for engagements in the domain adjoining the central third of the front. The trade-off against which the improvement in counterconcentration capacity must be weighed is the recession of the defense locus from the partitioning line as compared to that for the basing of forces at distances of M/4 and 3M/4 along the front. Maximum allowed offensive incursion increases to $4M/3\sqrt{12}$ from $M/\sqrt{12}$ for the previous case. Also the dispersion between the two independent force centers as measured by the straight-line distance between the two locations is reduced from M/2 for the defensive basing at M/4 and 3M/4 to M/3 for the current scenario. We emphasize that the defender who wishes to split forces into two equal subgroups can choose either the $\{(M/2\sqrt{12}, M/4), (M/2\sqrt{12}, 3M/4)\}$ configuration or the $\{(2M/3\sqrt{12}, M/3), (2M/3\sqrt{12}, 2M/3)\}$ configuration. The basing at distances of M/4 and 3M/4 along the front which we termed the 2-constrained scenario is only one option among many others available to the defender. However if total defense units are divided equally between the two force centers, the 2-constrained scenario is the optimal null-overlap methodology for partitioning the front. Thus if we require that no section of the front be assigned to more than one defense subgroup, the 2-constrained scenario is the optimal solution to the Defense Positioning Problem modified to include an upper bound of N/2 on local force concentration. Henceforth we shall adhere to a null-overlap methodology for generalizing the dispersion of force; that is, we shall partition the length-M front into nonoverlapping segments and maintain a one-to-one mapping of responsibility between each front segment and corresponding defending force division.

The K-constrained Defense Positioning Problem

Before proceeding to the general K-constrained defense optimization problem under which the N defending force units are grouped into K equal independent entities, we acclimatize the reader to the process of generalization by considering the case where K equals 5. The defense planner, using our null-overlap methodology, partitions the length-M front into 5 length-(M/5) fronts and allocates responsibility for each subfront to a defending force formation of strength N/5. The 5 defending elements base themselves at the locations $(M/5\sqrt{12}, M/10)$, $(M/5\sqrt{12}, 3M/10)$, $(M/5\sqrt{12}, M/2)$, $(M/5\sqrt{12}, 7M/10)$ and $(M/5\sqrt{12}, 9M/10)$. The defense locus for the 5-constrained scenario, graphed in Figure 1-19, shows that maximum offensive incursion is limited to $2M/5\sqrt{12}$; on the other hand, the overload factor is as high as 5 since in any sector of the length-

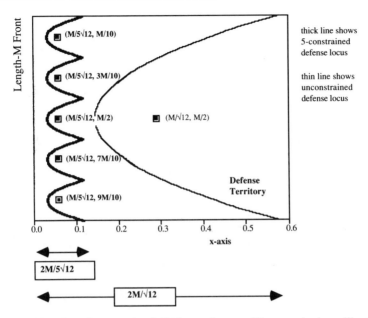

Figure 1-19 The 5-constrained Defense Locus. The x-axis is calibrated in terms of M.

M front the N/5 defense units could be confronted with all N invading force units.

For the general K-constrained case, the defender organizes its forces into K independent force formations, each composed of N/K units. The front is decomposed into K length-(M/K) fronts and each front segment is assigned on a one-on-one basis to defending force entities. The defense elements locate themselves at K separate force centers. Each center is at a distance $M/K\sqrt{12}$ inward from the border between the two countries. The uppermost center is positioned at a distance M/2K along the length-M front. Each succeeding force center is located at a distance of M/K from the force element immediately above it as measured parallel to the front. In terms of our usual coordinate system, the forces are localized at the positions $(M/K\sqrt{12}, M/2K)$, $(M/K\sqrt{12}, 3M/2K)$, $(M/K\sqrt{12}, 5M/2K)$, $(M/K\sqrt{12}, 7M/2K)$, ..., $(M/K\sqrt{12}, [2K-3] M/2K)$ and $(M/K\sqrt{12}, [2K-1] M/2K)$. The defense locus for the K-constrained situation indicates that the maximum unopposed penetration that the invading units can possibly accomplish before encountering defending force units is limited to $2M/K\sqrt{12}$ while the overload factor is equal to K (N offensive force units could hypothetically be deployed against N/K defending force units in the worst case). The results of our analysis of increasing force dispersion are summarized below.

Number of independent defending force formations[1]	Strength of each defending force formation[2]	Length of each segment of length-M front[3]	Distance of defending force formations from front[4]	Maximum unopposed offensive incursion[5]	Overload factor[6]
1	N	M	$M/\sqrt{12}$	2 $M/\sqrt{12}$	1
2	N/2	M/2	1/2 $M/\sqrt{12}$	1 $M/\sqrt{12}$	2
3	N/3	M/3	1/3 $M/\sqrt{12}$	2/3 $M/\sqrt{12}$	3
4	N/4	M/4	1/4 $M/\sqrt{12}$	1/2 $M/\sqrt{12}$	4
5	N/5	M/5	1/5 $M/\sqrt{12}$	2/5 $M/\sqrt{12}$	5
6	N/6	M/6	1/6 $M/\sqrt{12}$	1/3 $M/\sqrt{12}$	6
7	N/7	M/7	1/7 $M/\sqrt{12}$	2/7 $M/\sqrt{12}$	7
8	N/8	M/8	1/8 $M/\sqrt{12}$	1/4 $M/\sqrt{12}$	8
9	N/9	M/9	1/9 $M/\sqrt{12}$	2/9 $M/\sqrt{12}$	9
10	N/10	M/10	1/10 $M/\sqrt{12}$	1/5 $M/\sqrt{12}$	10
20	N/20	M/20	1/20 $M/\sqrt{12}$	1/10 $M/\sqrt{12}$	20
50	N/50	M/50	1/50 $M/\sqrt{12}$	1/25 $M/\sqrt{12}$	50
K	N/K	M/K	1/K $M/\sqrt{12}$	2/K $M/\sqrt{12}$	K
N	1	M/N	1/N $M/\sqrt{12}$	2/N $M/\sqrt{12}$	N

[1]The number of independent defending force formations is a measure of the dispersion of the total defending force.

[2]The strength of each defending force formation measures the aggregate fighting capability of each individual defending force element.

[3]The length of each segment of the length-M front represents the effective front length that each subgroup commander has been assigned to protect.

[4]The distance of the defending force formations from the front indicates how far inward the defensive forces are positioned from the common border.

[5]The maximum unopposed offensive incursion states the distance to which infiltrating forces can advance without being challenged by the defense.

[6]The overload factor is a proxy for the imbalance in the counterconcentration capability of the defense created as a consequence of the partitioning of the front and the forward placement of defending forces.

Thus if we adopt a null-overlap methodology for sectioning the front, the universe of choices for defense positioning is given by the set {unconstrained or 1-constrained, 2-constrained, 3-constrained, ..., K-constrained, ..., N-constrained}.

Imperfect Counterconcentration and a Robust Defense

At first glance, it might appear that the deficiency in counterconcentration capacity that comes with the dispersal of defensive force makes such a military structure ineffective and undesirable. To see if this is true, consider carefully what befalls an invader confronted with a K-constrained defense. The invading forces after penetrating the border sweep inward but are eventually compelled to engage in hostilities with a defense contingent of strength N/K. If the defense is widely dispersed, K is large and we may assume that the invading spearhead is formed by far more than N/K force units and dominates occurrences on the battlefield. Thus we would expect that after a short battle the defense is annihilated leaving the attrited forces of the aggressor in control of the arena. However the battle impedes the advance of the invading units and if waged effectively by the defense can hold up the adversary for a considerable length of time. While the two sides are engaged in combat, the defensive force encampments adjacent to the one under fire have the option, if not under attack, to mobilize to the aid of the engaged contingent.

The invader spends a time of I/v_a making its penetration into defense territory before the initial engagement. In the expression I/v_a, I is the infiltration of the offense orthogonal to the front and v_a is the velocity of the enemy forces over the defender's territory. An additional respite is created by the duration of the battle, τ, between the invading spearhead and the first defense encampment. Thus the total time available to neighboring defensive forces to arrive at the battlefield, T_a, is equal to $I/v_a + \tau$. Let T_d represent the actual time required by the nearest defensive formation to get to the scene of conflict. Then if T_d is less than T_a, the defensive reinforcements will appear in time to engage the attacking forces remaining after the initial defense onslaught. If v_d is the speed of the defending forces over home terrain, then, we must have:

$$T_d = \frac{\lambda}{v_d} \qquad (1\text{-}15)$$

where λ is the distance between the peacetime location of the adjoining defense encampment and the scene of battle.

With $T_d \leq T_a$, the offensive forces, after defeating the first echelon of defending force units, are immediately confronted by the second echelon of defensive forces. If the invading force strength exceeds $2N/K$, then a tertiary and quaternary wave of defending reinforcements might be needed to neutralize the invader. It is clear that if the duration of each successive engagement is greater than the time required by the nearest unoccupied defense element to get to the scene of battle, the invasion will be quelled and the invader gradually attrited to nothingness.

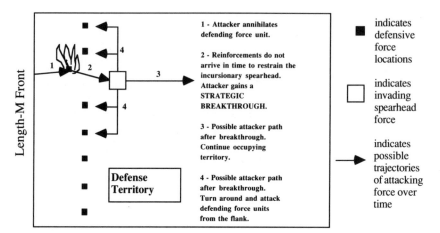

Figure 1-20   Strategic Breakthrough for the Aggressor

Conversely, if $T_d > T_a$, the invading forces will be left unhindered after the defeat of the first echelon of defenders to resume their conquest of the defense terrain. As depicted in Figure 1-20, the aggressor can either choose to forge ahead seeking to aggrandize territorial control or may wheel around, outflank defensive force formations and launch a devastating new attack on the nearby defense entrenchments from their rear.

Stated briefly, the offense will have accomplished a breakthrough; by a breakthrough we are referring to a strategic and operational breakthrough as opposed to a transient tactical advantage gained through maneuvering or momentary superior firepower.[13] One avenue open to the invader for increasing the likelihood of a strategic breakthrough is to pin down the defense encampments immediately adjacent to the main axis of penetration with small, repeated, persistent attacks. This restricts the defending regiments nearest the principal infiltration axis from mobilizing to the aid of the defense contingent exposed to the full force of the invading spearhead. The first wave of reinforcements is therefore compelled to travel two or three times the distance to the main battlefield than those units closest to the central focus of attack would have had to travel, providing the aggressor's forces with breathing space over and above the usual interval of T_d in which to defeat the initial echelon of the defender.

The responsibility of the defense is not limited to ensuring that successive defensive echelons arrive at the scene of battle before the previous engagement ends. The defense must also ensure that destroying the last of the attacking

---

[13]The classic historical instance of the kind of strategic breakthrough we are considering is offered by the decisive infiltration of the French forces by the German spearhead lead by von Rundstedt during the Battle of France in May 1940.

lethality along a given axis of invasion does not require more defending force units than offensive units assigned by the invader to the particular focus of penetration. For instance, if the attacker dispatched J offensive units out of a total force of N, all J invading units must be annihilated by *at most* J defending units. If the defense uses more units to neutralize offensive lethality than was allocated by the invader to a particular axis of infiltration, the defender will be confronted with a fundamental inequality in forces between the two sides after the aggressor's forces along the axis have been destroyed. A situation where the defense suffers heavier casualties than the offense creates a compelling incentive for preemptive aggression and is extremely destabilizing. Thus a defensive force structure is robust if it satisfies the following three performance parameters.

1. Each invading spearhead will be confronted by a defensive force element after an unopposed infiltration, I, into defense territory. This position where the spearhead and the first defense contingent engage in battle will be termed the initial point of contact. A robust defense must pin the intruder to the initial point of contact and prevent any further ingress into defense territory. This condition implies that defensive reinforcements must always arrive at the scene of battle before the close of the previous engagement. For example, the second defending contingent must arrive at the initial point of contact before the invading spearhead defeats the first defensive force element. Similarly the third defense contingent must arrive on the battlefield before the second defending contingent is destroyed and so on. This process of dispatching waves of defending reinforcements must continue until the last of the invading lethality has succumbed at the initial point of contact. Since this condition on robust defense performance depends on the duration of successive engagements between the attacking units and the defending echelons, we shall call it the Duration Condition.

2. Suppose the invader dispatches J attacking units along a particular axis of penetration. All J attacking units must be annihilated by J or less defending units. If the defender requires more than J defending units to defeat the J offensive units, the defense will be left with fewer than N - J units at the conclusion of the campaign, and an imbalance in the overall military strength of the two sides will be created. In brief, the defender must be able to destroy the invading lethality along each axis of invasion with not more than the number of units committed by the aggressor to the particular axis. Since this requirement for a robust defense depends on the ratio at which casualties are exchanged by the sides in combat, we shall call it the Casualty Exchange Condition.

3. For an unconstrained or 1-constrained defense, the campaign plan of the attacker is irrelevant. The attacker can choose the points along the length-M front where the attempts at penetration will be launched, the number of attacking units assigned to each focus of infiltration and the moments in time at which the various invasion attempts will be conducted. Irrespective of what choices are made by the attacker, an unconstrained defense always matches the

invader unit for unit at each focus of infiltration and minimizes total offensive penetration. In contrast, the performance of a dispersed defensive structure depends on the specific campaign plan adopted by the attacker. Consider, for example, Attack Plan A where all N offensive units collectively launch an invasion at (0, 0) along the length-M front and Attack Plan B where N - 2 offensive units launch an invasion at (0, 0), 1 unit attacks at (0, M/N) and 1 unit attacks at (0, 2M/N). Attack Plan B ties down defending units nearest the main axis of penetration, forcing defensive reinforcements to travel a longer distance from their peacetime base to the initial point of contact with the primary attacking spearhead. Thus while a N-constrained defense might be robust when facing Attack Plan A, it might be a disastrous failure when confronting Attack Plan B. Therefore a defense is robust only if it satisfies the Duration and Casualty Exchange Conditions described above for the entire universe of attacking campaign plans. We shall call this third condition on robust defense performance the Completeness Condition since the defense must be robust for the complete set of attack choices.

Earlier we defined a forward defense as a defensive force structure that can meet and defeat offensive forces as close to the front as possible, and we called the problem of finding such force structures the Defense Positioning Problem. The three conditions for a robust defense that we have specified above, namely, the Duration Condition, the Casualty Exchange Condition and the Completeness Condition, are the generalizations of the objective of "meeting and defeating offensive forces as close to the front as possible" that must be adhered to when we disperse defensive units and forgo perfect counterconcentration in order to position defending units closer to the front. Any defensive force structure that satisfies these three conditions is a robust forward defense. We have already found one example of a robust forward defense, namely, the unconstrained positioning of all defending forces at $(M/\sqrt{12}, M/2)$. We now seek other solutions to the Defense Positioning Problem generalized to admit an upper bound on the local concentration of forces. The Force Structuring Postulate may thus be restated to reflect the possibility of dispersing defensive units and basing them forward.

THE GENERALIZED FORCE STRUCTURING POSTULATE: *The defensive forces must be positioned, organized and structured to minimize the expected infiltration of the attacker and to satisfy the Duration, Casualty Exchange and Completeness Conditions. Any defensive force geometry that minimizes offensive incursion and satisfies these three conditions is a robust and efficient defense.*

To proceed further in our quest for solutions to the generalized Defense Positioning Problem, we need to know the answers to two questions:

1. What determines the duration of an engagement between two sides? The

answer to this question is needed to apply the Duration Condition in evaluating the robustness of a defensive force structure.

2. What determines the ratio at which casualties are exchanged by two sides in combat, or the casualty exchange ratio? The answer to this query will help us test whether a given force structure satisfies the Casualty Exchange Condition for robustness.

We thus require a theory of combat or a model of battle that will show us how to determine battle lengths and casualty exchange ratios.

Why We Need a Minimalist Approach to Combat Modeling

Ideally, we would like to present a complete model of combat which will formalize mathematically the process by which the two sides engage in battle. We would like to know not only how the duration of an engagement and the casualty exchange ratio are determined but also what is the fundamental nature of the attrition process in battle, what causes the movement of the front between the two sides and how do circumstantial factors such as terrain, defense fortification and the defender's home advantage influence the war dynamic. However, though progress has been made in recent years in formalizing the principles of attrition, withdrawal and victory that govern the mechanics of battle, we still do not possess a model of combat that we can truly rely on with any substantial degree of certainty. The main reason for our lack of confidence in any specific model of combat is the unavailability of detailed data on the battlefield conditions during actual historical conflicts. The paucity and inadequacy of numerical real-world values for variables involved in combat modeling[14] make it impossible to verify any theory of force-on-force attrition, and a battle model is a faithful representation of reality only to the extent to which the collective majority is willing to believe in its accuracy.

In light of all these caveats, we have thus far advanced our theory of optimal force structure without resorting to any assumptions about the nature of combat. Now that we need a determining relationship for battle duration and casualty exchange to evaluate the robustness of a dispersed forward defense, we shall adopt a minimalist approach—making the fewest possible assumptions about the fundamental nature of battle. We shall strive to establish an intuitive relationship between the duration of battle and the casualty exchange ratio as a

---

[14]In Appendix 1C we undertake a statistical analysis of recorded historical data on battles fought during and after the Second World War but find that the data do not provide any conclusive results. Our brief empirical study of twentieth century warfare does unearth some interesting relationships between various battle parameters and expose avenues for further statistical exploration.

function of the initial force ratio between the two sides at the start of combat. Why use the initial force ratio as the explanatory variable? Chiefly because it is the most easily observed, manipulated and quantifiable input of the battle dynamic. Indeed, all arms control agreements in principle seek to alter the ratio of forces deployed by the two sides on the battlefield.

The Duration of Battle, τ

The duration of an engagement, τ, is the length of time that the two adversaries are engaged in combat, ending when the weaker side withdraws or is annihilated, or in the case of equal offensive and defensive lethalities, when a stalemate is reached. In our discrete representation of conflict, withdrawal or the cession of territory occurs through the unchallenged advance of invading forces and does not occur as a part of combat. Hence we limit the definition of τ to the period required for the superior side to beat its inferior opponent or, in the scenario of equal initial force strengths, to the time needed to produce a stalemate. In other words, τ is the length of time the defending force can hold its position and frustrate the invader's advance.

Let γ represent the attacker-to-defender force ratio at the start of an engagement between the two sides. γ can be conceptualized as a ratio of attacking force strength to defending force strength where the measure of force strength could be manpower on either side, a weighted score-keeping system for aggregating firepower or some other indicator of combat lethality. We set forth the following two assumptions about the duration of the battle.

DURATION POSTULATE I: *The duration of an engagement declines with increasing initial force strength of the superior side, assuming the initial force strength of the weaker side is unchanged. More succinctly:*

$$\frac{\partial \tau}{\partial \gamma} < 0 \qquad\qquad \textbf{(1-16)}$$

Thus, assuming the attacker exceeds the defender in combat lethality, the duration of the battle between the two will decrease with increasing initial attacker-to-defender force ratio. This is a consequence of the greater imbalance prevailing on the battlefield, with increasing offensive superiority causing the early demise of the outnumbered defense.

DURATION POSTULATE II: *While the side with force superiority can shorten the length of the conflict by escalating to higher force levels at the outbreak of hostilities, the decrease in duration achieved for each additional quantum of force decreases with increasing initial force deployment. Again, in symbolic terms:*

$$\frac{\partial^2 \tau}{\partial \gamma^2} > 0 \qquad \text{(1-17)}$$

Duration Postulate II is a statement of the diminishing marginal returns accruing to the stronger opponent with each additional unit of force. Thus though the duration of the battle decreases with increasing lethality of the superior adversary, the rate of decrease falls with increasing force levels. For instance if increasing the initial force ratio from 5 to 6 decreases the period of combat by 1 day, then a subsequent increase in the initial force ratio from 6 to 7 will lower the battle time by less than a day.

If we were to construct a graph of battle duration, τ, as a function of the initial attacker-to-defender force ratio, γ, the slope of τ (γ) would be negative for all γ, as dictated by Duration Postulate I. The magnitude or absolute value of the slope would, in turn, be a strictly monotonic decreasing function of γ, as required by Duration Postulate II. A graph of τ (γ), with the duration of the engagement, τ, along the y-axis and the independent variable, γ, along the x-axis is depicted in Figure 1-21.

The figure reveals that the curve of τ (γ) is concave upwards. Since γ is the ratio of two quantities, it is appropriate to use a logarithmic scale to represent γ. An advantage of 10:1 for side A is identical to a superiority of 10:1 for side B (that is, an inferiority of 1:10 for side A) for the purpose of determining the duration of the engagement between the two antagonists. A logarithmic scale underscores this equality, since if we choose to indicate the initial ratio of side A to side B force along the x-axis, both the 10:1 and 1:10 ratios will be equidis-

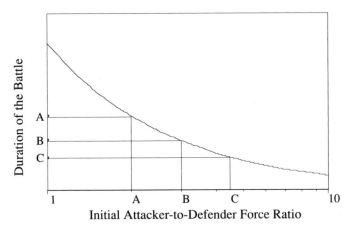

Figure 1-21   The Battle Length as a Function of the Initial Force Ratio. Note the diminishing marginal returns.

tant from the origin ($\log_{10} 10 = 1$ and $\log_{10} 0.1 = -1$, both of which are at unit distance from the origin, $\log_{10} 1 = 0$). The diminishing marginal returns property can also be better appreciated by considering the delineated regions of the graph, AB and BC. An increase in initial deployed force of AB reduces battle time by A'B'. However, if an equal percentage increase, BC, is made to the initial force level but at a higher base deployment, the incremental reduction in the duration of the conflict, B'C', is less than A'B'.

So far we have not examined how a difference in force utilization capability between the two adversaries affects battle duration. While both sides might possess the same aggregate firepower, there might be systematic differences in the dynamic ability of the two opponents to employ firepower, logistics, support and command and control systems in conflict; these differences might not be faithfully represented in the static tally of initial firepower. Factors such as troop training, morale, national public support, whether the territory being defended is home for the fighters or whether the combat force is playing surrogate for the home defense, the degree of fortifications and terrain preparations, the extent of tactical surprise enjoyed by the initiator of the attack, the mental dexterity and creativity of the chain of command in exploiting unexpected opportunities and the tactical maneuverability of the forces all feed into the equation that determines the relative combat effectiveness of the two sides. Let a represent the battle effectiveness per unit force for the aggressor and d be the corresponding measure of efficacy for the defender. The exact interpretation and formulation of a and d depend on the particular set of "laws of combat" accepted by the force planner. Duration Postulate III relates the length of the engagement, τ, to the relative effectiveness, a/d, of the two combatants:

DURATION POSTULATE III: *For a given initial force ratio, if the side inferior in force strength displays a higher combat effectiveness than the numerically superior combatant, the duration of the battle will be extended beyond the time of conflict that would prevail if the two foes were matched in fighting efficacy. On the contrary, if the numerically superior adversary is also the possessor of a higher combat effectiveness coefficient, the numerically inferior loser will be destroyed in a length of time shorter than the battle duration for the scenario of equal force utilization efficiency on both sides.*

In other words, the weaker side can hold out longer if it is more efficient in utilizing force. However if the larger opponent is also superior in fighting effectiveness, the side with lower initial force strength will suffer defeat in a shorter period of time less than in the base case of equal combat efficacy. Figure 1-22 which depicts the duration of the engagement, τ, as a function of the initial attacker-to-defender force ratio, γ, for several values of attacker-to-defender combat effectiveness, a/d, is the pictorial representation of Duration Postulate III.

The duration curve for equal force effectiveness (a/d = 1), highlighted in Figure 1-22, indicates that battle duration falls off with increasing imbalance of

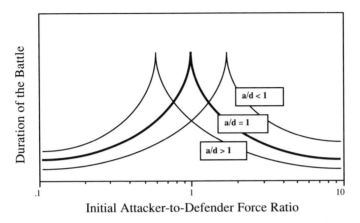

Figure 1-22   Duration of the Battle as a Function of the Initial Force Imbalance for Varying Values of Relative Combat Effectiveness.

initial deployed force irrespective of the identity of the superior side. The initial force deployment of the attacker relative to the defender increases as one proceeds from left to right along the x-axis. Thus on the right side of the x-axis, where the attacker is numerically superior, the duration curve for a/d > 1 falls below the duration curve for the base scenario of a/d = 1 while the reverse holds for the left side of the x-axis. Hence with a/d > 1, the attacker crushes the defender in a relatively short interval for $\gamma > 1$, while the attacker prolongs the battle beyond the equal effectiveness base case if the offensive onslaught is conducted with $\gamma < 1$. Finally it should be noted that the initial force ratio that results in a stalemate is shifted by changing relative force effectiveness. Thus while stalemate occurs at $\gamma = 1$ for a/d = 1, the stalemate is displaced to the left for a/d > 1, that is, the attacker continues to win even when outnumbered by the defense. Analogously, the stalemate is displaced to the right for a/d < 1 since the defender continues to win for small inferiorities in initial force as a consequence of superior defensive fighting efficacy.

The Average Attacker-to-Defender Casualty Exchange Ratio, ψ

We need to hypothesize a determining relationship for the casualty exchange ratio between the two sides for two reasons. First, we have to ensure that a given dispersed forward defense satisfies the Casualty Exchange Condition—namely, that the defense succeeds in destroying the total invading lethality at each focus of invasion using no more than the number of units allocated by the attacker to that particular focus of infiltration. This condition is essential to maintain overall parity between the forces of the two sides. The second reason for studying the casualty exchange ratio is less obvious. When a dispersed defense is confronted by a concentrated attack, the defender dispatches a series of reinforcing echelons to the initial point of contact until the attacking lethality is destroyed. To satisfy the Duration Condition for defense robustness, we must track the length of each successive engagement between the invading lethality and the defense. Duration Postulates I and II indicate that the length of an engagement is determined by the initial attacker-to-defender force ratio at the start of the engagement. However the initial strength of the attacker at the start of the second engagement is equal to the residual strength of the attacker at the end of the first. Thus to determine the initial strength of the attacker at the start of any engagement after the first, we need to know the residual strength of the attacker at the close of the previous engagement. The residual strength of the attacker after a battle depends on the average casualty exchange ratio that prevailed during the encounter. Hence we require a model of casualty exchange to determine the residual strength of the invading spearhead at the close of successive engagements. These attacking residual strength figures, in turn, determine the length of succeeding encounters.

The casualty exchange ratio measures the rate of attrition of one side relative to the other. The attacker-to-defender casualty exchange ratio is an indicator of the number of attacking combatants (or the quantum of attacking lethality or aggregated firepower) destroyed per unit decrease in the number of defenders (or defending lethality or aggregated firepower). For an individual engagement, we can calculate the average attacker-to-defender casualty exchange ratio as the ratio of total offensive attrition in the course of the conflict to the total attrition undergone by the defense. Thus if $A(0)$ and $D(0)$ represent the initial force strengths of the attacking and defending contingents and $A(\tau)$ and $D(\tau)$ are the corresponding residual force levels at the conclusion of the engagement, τ being the duration of the battle as established earlier, the average offense-to-defense exchange ratio, denoted by ψ, is given as:

$$\psi = \frac{A(0) - A(\tau)}{D(0) - D(\tau)} \tag{1-18}$$

If the defending contingent is completely annihilated in the encounter, $D(\tau) = 0$ and the formula for ψ reduces to:

$$\psi = \frac{A(0) - A(\tau)}{D(0)} \tag{1-19}$$

We advance the following three assumptions about the casualty exchange ratio.

CASUALTY EXCHANGE POSTULATE I: *The attacker-to-defender casualty exchange ratio declines with an increasing initial force strength of the attacker, assuming the initial force deployment of the defender is unchanged. Thus:*

$$\frac{\partial \psi}{\partial \gamma} < 0 \qquad (1\text{-}20)$$

CASUALTY EXCHANGE POSTULATE II: *The attacker-to-defender casualty exchange ratio shows diminishing marginal returns with an increasing initial force strength of the aggressor. Thus though the exchange ratio can be reduced by the stronger side through escalation to higher initial force levels, the reduction in the exchange ratio itself decreases with each incremental increase in the initial force deployment of the attacker. In symbolic notation:*

$$\frac{\partial^2 \psi}{\partial \gamma^2} > 0 \qquad (1\text{-}21)$$

The first casualty exchange postulate implies that the numerically superior side suffers lower average attrition through the course of the conflict than its adversary does. The critical assumption here is that the war commanders on either side are "smart" and adept at the optimal utilization of force; thus each iota of superiority enjoyed by the offense is employed effectively in lowering the attacking casualties per defender killed, producing a smaller average casualty exchange ratio for the engagement. The second casualty exchange postulate limits the benefits accruing to the superior side from the initial force imbalance; as the initial force ratio increases, the returns to the numerically superior opponent in terms of a lowered overall exchange ratio increase at a progressively slower rate. Essentially we believe in the saturation of force. If one side fields a redundancy of force on the battleground, the outermost deployed units will simply be unable to engage the limited firepower of the enemy and will contribute only peripherally to the offensive onslaught.

Figure 1-23 depicts the fundamental relationship between the casualty exchange ratio, ψ, and the initial force ratio, γ. Both the independent variable, γ, and the dependent variable, ψ, are plotted on a logarithmic scale. If the initial force ratio in the figure is conceived of as a ratio of attacking to defending force units, then the graph suggests that for high values of γ ($\gamma \gg 1$), the attacker-to-defender exchange ratio favors the offense; while for low values of γ ($\gamma \ll 1$), it is the defender who imposes stiffer relative attrition on the aggressor. All things being equal, for an initial force ratio of unity, there is no reason to expect the exchange ratio to differ from 1. This symmetry is reflected in our diagram by constraining the exchange ratio curve to pass through the point (1, 1). However all humans are not created equal and neither are the attacker and defender in battle. We are considering a class of engagements in which, courtesy of the defense locus and our assumption of perfect information capability for the defense on home ground, the defender knows in advance the exact locations along the length-M front where the attacker will possibly have to be confronted. The defender can scout the terrain around the defense locus for

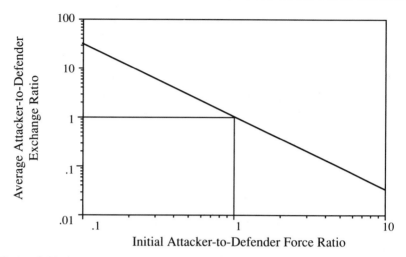

Figure 1-23   The Average Casualty Exchange Ratio as a Function of the Initial Force Ratio. The diminishing marginal returns are disguised by the log y-axis and the curve is a straight line on a log-log scale.

optimal defensive positions, amass supplies and construct fortifications. The supply depots and fortifications would probably be structured to maintain a low profile in times of peace with easy accessibility and rapid activation in times of crisis. For all these reasons, we systematically expect the defense to outperform the offense in the effectiveness of force utilization. This assumption is summarized as Casualty Exchange Postulate III.

CASUALTY EXCHANGE POSTULATE III: *The intelligent and determined defender can display in battle greater combat effectiveness per unit lethality than the invader, forcing the average attacker-to-defender casualty exchange ratio to be higher than would be predicted by the initial force ratio of the two combatants.*

Figure 1-24 which plots the attacker-to-defender casualty exchange ratio, ψ, as a function of the initial attacker-to-defender force ratio, γ, for different relative force utilization efficacies, imposes the requirements of the third casualty exchange postulate on Figure 1-23. As can be evidenced from the diagram, the casualty exchange curve for higher defensive force effectiveness, that is a/d < 1, lies above the one for equal fighting efficacy, namely a/d = 1. At any given initial force ratio, the defender, with its dominant force utilization capability, is able to exact a heavier penalty from the offense for each defensive lethality unit forgone. Thus the curve for a/d < 1 lies above the point (1, 1) (exchange ratio

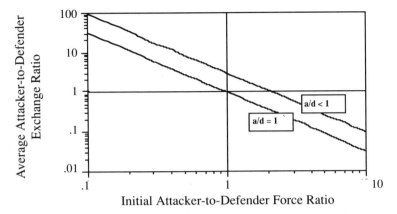

Figure 1-24   The Average Casualty Exchange Ratio as a Function of the Initial Force Ratio for Various Values of Relative Combat Effectiveness

greater than 1 for initial force ratio equal to unity), while the curve for a/d = 1 is constrained to contain the point (1, 1).

We can now relate the casualty exchange ratio that prevails in an engagement to the residual strength of the victor of that battle. Assuming complete annihilation of the loser, the residual force of the victor, $A(\tau)$, and the casualty exchange ratio, ψ, are related by the equality:

$$A (\tau) = A (0) - \psi D (0) \qquad \textbf{(1-22)}$$

Let us adopt $D(0)$ as the unit for measuring force; in effect, we are assuming that the defender dispatches one force unit to the battlefield. The symbol ρ can represent the residual force strength of the victor measured in units of $D(0)$. Then an expression for ρ can be derived by dividing both sides of Equation 1-22 by $D(0)$.

$$\rho = \frac{A (\tau)}{D (0)} = \frac{A (0)}{D (0)} - \psi \frac{D (0)}{D (0)} = \gamma - \psi \qquad \textbf{(1-23)}$$

A graph of the victor's fractional residual force strength, ρ, as a function of the initial attacker-to-defender force ratio, γ, is depicted in Figure 1-25. Figure 1-25 displays the residual force strength for the case of equal offensive and defensive force utilization capability (a/d = 1). Thus we expect ψ to decrease monotonically from unity as γ increases from 1, and Equation 1-23 tells us that ρ will increase monotonically from 0 as γ extends beyond 1. For large values of γ

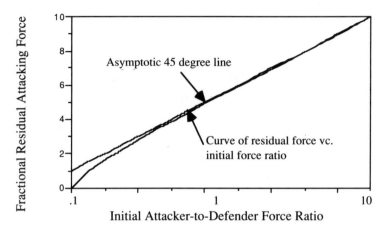

Figure 1-25   The Fractional Residual Force of the Victor as a Function of the Initial Force Ratio. The residual force curve tends asymptotically toward the 45 degree line, indicating the residual force is almost equal to the initial force of the attacker for large values of the initial force ratio.

($\gamma \gg 1$), ψ is very small and ρ approaches γ but never equals the initial force ratio as a result of our diminishing marginal returns assumption stated in Casualty Exchange Postulate II.

A Minimalist Framework for τ and ψ

In keeping with our minimalist approach to modeling combat, we have attempted to relate the duration of battle and the casualty exchange ratio to only two combat variables: the attacker-to-defender force ratio at the start of an engagement and the relative combat effectiveness, or force utilization efficacy, of the two sides. Specifically, $\tau = \tau(\gamma, a/d)$ and $\psi = \psi(\gamma, a/d)$. In addition, we have strived to expose the symmetry between the manner in which τ is related to γ and a/d as indicated by the Duration Postulates and the manner in which ψ is determined by γ and a/d as dictated by the Casualty Exchange Postulates. Both the Lanchester Square Law and Joshua Epstein's Adaptive Dynamic Model,[15] two of the most widely accepted and employed combat attrition models, easily

---

[15]Joshua M. Epstein, *The Calculus of Conventional War: Dynamic Analysis without Lanchester Theory* (Brookings, 1985). An extended version of the model is described in Joshua M. Epstein, "The 3:1 Rule, the Adaptive Dynamic Model, and the Future of Security Studies," *International Security*, vol. 13 (Spring 1989), p. 90.

satisfy our Duration and Casualty Exchange Postulates.[16] These popular formulations of the laws of attrition may thus be used to determine battle duration and the average casualty exchange ratio as a function of the initial force ratio.

The relative combat effectiveness of the two sides, a/d, is determined by factors such as the identity of the combatants (whether the battle is being fought between India and Pakistan or between Iran and Iraq or between Israel and Syria), the location of the battlefield (whether the conflict is in Central Europe along the Franco-German border or along the West Bank) and the level of defense fortification and preparation. The majority of the determining factors for a/d are independent of the solution to the generalized Defense Positioning Problem, that is, they are not affected by the decision of where to locate the defensive units. We can therefore determine a value for a/d independent of our choice of defense placement and choose the appropriate duration and casualty exchange curves before we attempt to solve the generalized Defense Positioning Problem. In other words, the relative force utilization efficacy of the two sides, a/d, is an exogenous variable in our formulation of the generalized Defense Positioning Problem while the initial attacker-to-defender force strength, γ, is an endogenous variable determined by our choice of a particular defense geometry. Hence all we require to isolate the optimal dispersed forward defense are curves of τ and ψ plotted as functions of the initial attacker-to-defender force ratio, γ. More formally, we are specifying $\tau = \tau(\gamma)$ and $\psi = \psi(\gamma)$ with the $\tau(\gamma)$ and $\psi(\gamma)$ functions satisfying the following properties:

$$\frac{\partial \tau}{\partial \gamma} < 0 \quad \frac{\partial^2 \tau}{\partial \gamma^2} > 0 \quad \frac{\partial \psi}{\partial \gamma} < 0 \quad \frac{\partial^2 \psi}{\partial \gamma^2} > 0 \qquad \textbf{(1-24)}$$

These four properties are our only assumptions about the nature of combat.[17] We related τ and ψ to the relative combat effectiveness of the two sides, a/d, to show how the influence of parameters other than the initial force ratio could be accounted for by choosing the appropriate curves for τ and ψ before embarking on the quest for the solution to the generalized Defense Positioning Problem.

---

[16]Appendix 1D proves the adherence of the Lanchester Square Law and the Adaptive Dynamic Model to our Duration and Casualty Exchange Postulates.

[17]In fact, if we are modeling the initial stages of the attempt of a highly dispersed forward defense to contain a concentrated attacking spearhead, we do not even require a complete specification of the curves for τ and ψ as functions of γ. Consider the extreme case of a N-constrained defense faced with a single concentrated invading spearhead. The invading force will be engaged at the point of initial contact by the single defending unit closest to the focus of infiltration. The successive reinforcing defensive echelons

also consist of a single force unit. Each solitary defending unit is heavily outnumbered in combat at least for the first few engagements between the offense and the defense, and this translates mathematically to a very large attacker-to-defender force ratio at the start of each engagement, that is $\gamma \gg 1$. Let us go through the war campaign step by step:

1. The first defending unit that intercepts the attacker is subjected to an initial force imbalance of $\gamma 1$ and succumbs to the invader in a period of time, $\tau 1$, as determined by the relationship between the duration of the battle, τ, on the one hand and the initial force ratio, γ, and the relative attacker-to-defender combat effectiveness, a/d, on the other. Treating a/d as fixed for the particular aggressor and defender under consideration, the battle time reduces to a function of only the initial force ratio between the two sides. Thus the first engagement culminates in an interval given by:

$$\tau 1 = \tau \ (\gamma 1)$$

The attacker's fractional residual force at the termination of the first engagement, $\rho 1$, is determined as:

$$\rho 1 = \gamma 1 - \psi \ (\gamma 1)$$

2. Suppose the second defending force unit arrives at the arena in time to prevent the unhindered advance of the invader and engages in battle the residual force, $\rho 1$, remaining with the attacker after the first defensive engagement. The duration of the second engagement, $\tau 2$, can be approximated as follows.

$$\tau 2 = \tau (\rho 1) = \tau \ [\gamma 1 - \psi \ (\gamma 1)]$$

Using a Taylor series expansion for $\tau(\gamma)$ about the point $\gamma = \gamma 1$:

$$\tau 2 \cong \tau \ (\gamma 1) - \left. \frac{\partial \tau}{\partial \gamma} \right|_{\gamma = \gamma 1} \psi \ (\gamma 1)$$

But $\tau \ (\gamma 1) = \tau 1$ and $\psi \ (\gamma 1) = \psi 1$

$$\tau 2 \cong \tau 1 - \psi 1 \ \tau' (\gamma 1)$$

The residual force of the attacker after the second engagement can be similarly estimated:

$$\rho 2 = \rho 1 - \psi \ (\rho 1)$$

But $\rho 1 = \gamma 1 - \psi \ (\gamma 1)$

Hence $\rho 2 = \gamma 1 - \psi \ (\gamma 1) - \psi \ [\gamma 1 - \psi \ (\gamma 1)]$

But $\psi \ (\gamma 1) = \psi 1$

$$\rho 2 = \gamma 1 - \psi 1 - \psi \ [\gamma 1 - \psi 1]$$

Expanding $\psi \ [\gamma 1 - \gamma 1]$ in a Taylor series about $\gamma = \gamma 1$:

$$\rho 2 \cong \gamma 1 - \psi 1 - \psi \ (\gamma 1) + \left. \frac{\partial \psi}{\partial \gamma} \right|_{\gamma = \gamma 1} \psi 1$$

For large enough values of $\gamma 1$, $\psi 1$ and $\psi'(\gamma 1)$ are both small and the partial derivative term in the above expression can be neglected. Thus:

$$\rho 2 \cong \gamma 1 - \psi 1 - \psi \ (\gamma 1)$$
$$\rho 2 \cong \gamma 1 - 2\psi 1$$

3. If the defense is robust and satisfies the Duration Condition, the tertiary protecting echelon will arrive on the battlefield before the termination of the second defensive entanglement and join the battle. If we are justified in assuming that the attacking lethality surviving the second entanglement, $\rho 2$, is significantly larger than the size of a defending force unit, the duration of the third engagement, $\tau 3$, can be approximated as before.

$$\tau 3 = \tau(\rho 2) \cong \tau \ (\gamma 1 - 2\psi 1)$$

Employing the first-order Taylor series expansion:

$$\tau 3 \cong \tau 1 - 2 \ \psi 1 \tau' \ (\gamma 1)$$

Similarly, for the residual force of the aggressor after the third battle:

$$\rho 3 = \rho 2 - \psi \ \rho 2) \cong \gamma 1 - 2\psi 1 - \psi \ (\gamma 1 - 2\psi 1)$$
$$\psi \ (\gamma 1 - 2 \ \psi 1) \cong \psi \ (\gamma 1) - \left. \frac{\partial \psi}{\partial \gamma} \right|_{\gamma = \gamma 1} 2\psi 1$$
$$\rho 3 \cong \gamma 1 - 2\psi 1 - \psi 1 + \left. \frac{\partial \psi}{\partial \gamma} \right|_{\gamma = \gamma 1} 2\psi 1$$

Once again for sufficiently large $\gamma 1$, the last term can be dropped yielding:

$$\rho 3 \cong \gamma 1 - 3\psi 1$$

Generalizing the pattern of our results, the duration of the nth conflict, τn, is determined as:

$$\tau n \cong \tau 1 - (n - 1) \psi 1 \tau' \ (\gamma 1)$$

while the attacker's lethality remaining at the close of the nth engagement, ρn, is given by:

$$\rho n \cong \gamma 1 - n \ \psi 1$$

If we are willing to accept that the invader's initial force concentration, $\gamma 1$, along the primary axis of penetration is far in excess of the strength of a defending contingent and that, at least for the initial few engagements, the attacker's residual lethality, ρi, at the termination of each encounter also dwarfs the reinforcing defensive echelons, then the prognosis of the preliminary stages of the war campaign can be described solely in terms of the duration of the first engagement, $\tau 1$, the casualty exchange ratio for the first engagement, $\psi 1$, and the rate of change of duration with respect to the initial force ratio evaluated at $\gamma = \gamma 1$, $\tau'(\gamma 1)$. The table below summarizes our conclusions.

An Algorithm for Solving the Generalized Defense Positioning Problem

Consider a defender armed with N force units who must protect a length-M front from an adversary also possessing N units. If the defender is willing to make the following assumptions:

1. The information capabilities of both sides are governed by the on-off function;
2. There is a uniform probability of attack at any point along the length-M front;
3. The defense and the offense can transport force with equal speed over defense terrain;
4. The total defending force is divided into an integral number of defense contingents of equal lethality with the integral number less than or equal to N;

Engagement number	Duration of the engagement	Residual force remaining with the attacker at completion of the engagement
0	-	$\gamma 1$
1	$\tau 1 = \tau (\gamma 1)$	$\rho 1 = \gamma 1 - \psi (\gamma 1) = \gamma 1 - \psi 1$
2	$\tau 2 \cong \tau 1 - \psi 1\ \tau'(\gamma 1)$	$\rho 2 \cong \gamma 1 - 2\ \psi 1$
3	$\tau 3 \cong \tau 1 - 2\ \psi 1\ \tau'(\gamma 1)$	$\rho 3 \cong \gamma 1 - 3\ \psi 1$
4	$\tau 4 \cong \tau 1 - 3\ \psi 1\ \tau'(\gamma 1)$	$\rho 4 \cong \gamma 1 - 4\ \psi 1$
5	$\tau 5 \cong \tau 1 - 4\ \psi 1\ \tau'(\gamma 1)$	$\rho 5 \cong \gamma 1 - 5\ \psi 1$
n	$\tau n \cong \tau 1 - (n - 1)\ \psi 1\ \tau'(\gamma 1)$	$\rho n \cong \gamma 1 - n\ \psi 1$

It should be realized when using the above general expressions for τ that since $\tau'(\gamma)$ is nonpositive for all values of γ, $- \tau'(\gamma)$ is a nonnegative quantity and hence the duration of combat increases with each successive engagement. This is to be expected since the attacker loses lethality in the course of each encounter and commences the following battle with a reduced force level while the defender always dispatches a constant contingent of one force unit to each entanglement. The increase in the length of each successive engagement, given approximately by $- \psi 1\ \tau'(\gamma 1)$, has a very intuitive interpretation. $- \tau'(\gamma 1)$ measures the rate at which the duration of the battle increases with decreasing imbalance on the battlefield. $\psi 1$ is a measure of the reduction in initial force ratio imbalance that occurs between the commencement of successive encounters. The product of $- \tau'(\gamma 1)$ and $\psi 1$ thus estimates the rise in battle time with each succeeding encounter.

We have **linearized** the problem of estimating battle durations and residual force strengths for the initial stages of an encounter between a concentrated offense pitched against a dispersed defense. For surveying the outcome of the initial defensive attempts at restraint, it is sufficient to estimate the parameters $\tau 1$, $\psi 1$ and $\tau'(\gamma 1)$ for the opening encounter. Knowledge of the complete curves for the battle duration, τ, and the casualty exchange ratio, ψ, as functions of the initial force ratio, γ, is superfluous; only a point on each curve needs to be located.

5. The defense adheres to a null-overlap methodology for implementing the dispersion of force: The front is partitioned into nonoverlapping segments, and a one-to-one mapping of responsibility is maintained between each front segment and corresponding defense contingent;

then there are N potentially optimal geometries for force positioning available to the defender. The simplest geometry would be to position all N units at $(M/\sqrt{12}, M/2)$. This positioning corresponds to an unconstrained or 1-constrained defense. A second possibility would be to divide the N units equally between two bases, one at $(M/2\sqrt{12}, M/4)$ and the other at $(M/2\sqrt{12}, 3M/4)$, leading to a 2-constrained defensive structure. A third option would involve partitioning the length-M front into three length-$(M/3)$ fronts and locating N/3 defensive units at each of three bases corresponding to three front subsections, implementing a 3-constrained defense posture. Continuing with this procedure for force dispersion, the limiting choice available to the defender is to partition the length-M front into N length-(M/N) fronts and position a single defending unit at each of the N bases corresponding to a N-constrained defense. The defender's complete spectrum of choice for force placement is tabulated in the following table for the case of N = 10 and graphically represented in Figure 1-26.

The ultimate objective of the defense is to minimize offensive infiltration and defeat the invading forces as close to the border as possible. The defender thus seeks a force positioning geometry which is robust *and* minimizes offensive infiltration. Any force positioning geometry is robust if it satisfies the Duration Condition, the Casualty Exchange Condition and the Completeness Condition defined earlier. The attacker will always be accosted by the defense at an initial point of contact along the defense locus. A force positioning geometry will succeed in restricting the attacker's infiltration to the boundary of the defense locus associated with the particular geometry only if:

1. Defensive reinforcements always arrive at each focus of penetration before the invading spearhead has annihilated the defending lethality engaging the attacker at the initial point of contact.

2. The defense can defeat the J attacking units at a focus of penetration with J or less defending units.

3. The above two conditions hold for the entire universe of attack plans.

In brief, the defense locus holds only if our three conditions for robustness hold. The defender's problem is to find which of the N defense postures satisfies these conditions for robustness and concurrently minimizes offensive infiltration.

The optimal dispersed forward defense that we seek minimizes unopposed offensive infiltration; it does not minimize the displacement of the defending units from the front. If all we desire is to place defending units as close to the

Number of front segments	Optimal force positioning geometry corresponding to each front division
1	$(M/\sqrt{12}, M/2)$
2	$(M/2\sqrt{12}, M/4)$, $(M/2\sqrt{12}, 3M/4)$
3	$(M/3\sqrt{12}, M/6)$, $(M/3\sqrt{12}, M/2)$, $(M/3\sqrt{12}, 5M/6)$
4	$(M/4\sqrt{12}, M/8)$, $(M/4\sqrt{12}, 3M/8)$, $(M/4\sqrt{12}, 5M/8)$, $(M/4\sqrt{12}, 7M/8)$
5	$(M/5\sqrt{12}, M/10)$, $(M/5\sqrt{12}, 3M/10)$, $(M/5\sqrt{12}, M/2)$, $(M/5\sqrt{12}, 7M/10)$, $(M/5\sqrt{12}, 9M/10)$
6	$(M/6\sqrt{12}, M/12)$, $(M/6\sqrt{12}, M/4)$, $(M/6\sqrt{12}, 5M/12)$, $(M/6\sqrt{12}, 7M/12)$, $(M/6\sqrt{12}, 3M/4)$, $(M/6\sqrt{12}, 11M/12)$
7	$(M/7\sqrt{12}, M/14)$, $(M/7\sqrt{12}, 3M/14)$, $(M/7\sqrt{12}, 5M/14)$, $(M/7\sqrt{12}, M/2)$, $(M/7\sqrt{12}, 9M/14)$, $(M/7\sqrt{12}, 11M/14)$, $(M/7\sqrt{12}, 13M/14)$
8	$(M/8\sqrt{12}, M/16)$, $(M/8\sqrt{12}, 3M/16)$, $(M/8\sqrt{12}, 5M/16)$, $(M/8\sqrt{12}, 7M/16)$, $(M/8\sqrt{12}, 9M/16)$, $(M/8\sqrt{12}, 11M/16)$, $(M/8\sqrt{12}, 13M/16)$, $(M/8\sqrt{12}, 15M/16)$
9	$(M/9\sqrt{12}, M/18)$, $(M/9\sqrt{12}, M/6)$, $(M/9\sqrt{12}, 5M/18)$, $(M/9\sqrt{12}, 7M/18)$, $(M/9\sqrt{12}, M/2)$, $(M/9\sqrt{12}, 11M/18)$, $(M/9\sqrt{12}, 13M/18)$, $(M/9\sqrt{12}, 5M/6)$, $(M/9\sqrt{12}, 17M/18)$
10	$(M/10\sqrt{12}, M/20)$, $(M/10\sqrt{12}, 3M/20)$, $(M/10\sqrt{12}, M/4)$, $(M/10\sqrt{12}, 7M/20)$, $(M/10\sqrt{12}, 9M/20)$, $(M/10\sqrt{12}, 11M/20)$, $(M/10\sqrt{12}, 13M/20)$, $(M/10\sqrt{12}, 3M/4)$, $(M/10\sqrt{12}, 17M/20)$, $(M/10\sqrt{12}, 19M/20)$

border as possible, then the solution is patently obvious. We should adopt a forward-deployed defense, which is a rudimentary placement of all N force units at equal distances from each other at the frontal edge of the demarcation line between the two sides. Figure 1-27 depicts a forward-deployed defense for the case of N = 10. Basing defending units as close to the front as possible does not minimize infiltration. It is a blind hope that placing men forward will somehow defeat the invader at the border.

The Completeness Condition requires that we evaluate the robustness of the defense posture for all possible plans of attack. From the point of view of the ambitious conqueror, the fundamental problem of attack is to determine the campaign plan that will maximize the likelihood of breaking through the defender's forward line of defense. In our modeling universe, both sides are assured overall parity and the aggressor can be victorious only through a strategic

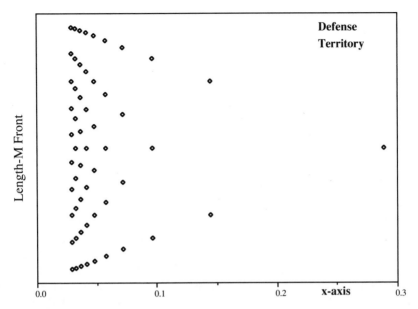

Figure 1-26 The Defensive Force Placement Choice Space for N = 10. The x-axis is calibrated in units of M. Each set of triangles at the same perpendicular distance from the front denotes a potentially optimal force positioning geometry.

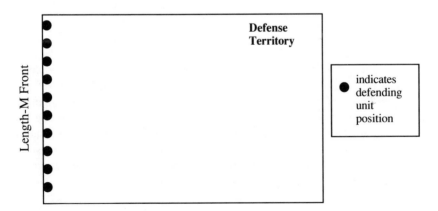

Figure 1-27 Forward Deployed Defense for N = 10

and operational breakthrough. Once a breakthrough has been accomplished, the invading forces may attack outflanked defensive bases from the rear, consolidate control over occupied territory, continue to advance into the adversary's terrain or prepare for a counterattack by defending forces. The attacker has three options in formulating a plan of attack:

1. Whether to conduct a one-period attack or spread the campaign over several time periods.
2. In each period, which foci of penetration along the length-M front to choose.
3. How many offensive force units to allocate to each point of infiltration in each time period.

It is important to comprehend what is meant by a plan of attack that is prosecuted across more than one time period. The attacking general can decide to dispatch simultaneously and in a single stroke all offensive divisions earmarked for the invasion. This scenario is covered by a single time period model in which all penetration occurs at a single instant in time. Conversely, the invading commander may determine that the optimal campaign is to hold back some forces in reserve initially and launch two, three or more consecutive waves of incursion into the defense terrain. Such a situation can only be faithfully simulated through a multiperiod model for attack. Constructing the multiperiod description requires the aggressor to first decide upon the sequence of attacks and subsequently determine the time interval between each step in the battle plan. For simplicity, we limit consideration to single time period scenarios of attack.

The problem of evaluating defense robustness is simplified by the inherent symmetry of the length-M front. For a probability distribution of attack, such as the uniform density function, that is symmetric about the midpoint, M/2, of the border, all parameters that enter into the determination of the optimal defensive force structure are also symmetric about the line y = M/2. Since all inputs to our infiltration minimization model and the theoretical structure of the model itself display bilobed symmetry, it is reasonable to expect the model output to transmit this intrinsic symmetry, and the optimal defending force positioning will also be symmetric with respect to M/2. It is hence sufficient to impose the constraint that all defensive force structures considered for optimality be symmetric about the center of the front. All the N force positioning geometries from which our defender is trying to choose satisfy this symmetry constraint. On the side of the offense, we only need consider half the total universe of possible attack plans, since any campaign allocation and its reflection about the line y = M/2, together constitute a dual and bode identical consequences for defensive force placement. Thus we need to evaluate defense robustness only for a single element of the dual pair of invasion schemata, cutting in half the number of attack plans that must be tested against the defensive force geometry.

We can use a statistical syntax to think about the various options for attack schemes available to the offense. The aggressor can choose the primary axes along which large offensive force concentrations will spearhead the attempt at infiltration and then determine the supporting force distribution around each major focus of penetration. If the invader's plan of attack be conceptualized as a distribution of force along the front, determining the primary axes of attack is the analog of setting the local maxima or modes of the force distribution function, and assigning supportive firepower around each main axis is equivalent to defining the local variance of force density in the neighborhood of each mode. As an example, a bimodal attack conducted with N force units may either be dispersed and exhibit a high standard deviation around each mode as in Figure 1-28.1 or may be fairly concentrated at the twin centers as displayed in Figure 1-28.2.

Thus defining a plan of invasion reduces to the specification of the modes and associated local variances of the offensive force density function along the front.[18] Given a particular defensive force positioning arrayed against a specific plan of attack, the procedure for determining the outcome of the offensive onslaught is as follows. The offense will breach the border at various points and the defender needs an assignment rule for transferring defending divisions from their peacetime encampments to the various points of offensive infiltration along the front. The simplest assignment mechanism is to allocate the responsibility for engaging the J infiltrating force units at a particular focus of penetration to the J defending units nearest that point of incursion. In general, the assignment rule must ensure that the initial point of contact between the invading legions and the first defensive echelon lies along the defense locus; this condition requires that along each axis of penetration the defensive base nearest the focus of infiltration must be allocated to confront the advancing lethality of the aggressor along that specific axis. For a null-overlap methodology of implementing defensive force dispersion, the task of confronting an incursionary expedition at any point along the length-M front should be attributed to the defending contingent in charge of protecting that portion of the front. Each of the J defending units assigned to engage a particular attacking contingent move quickly and directly to intercept the advancing invader. Our criterion for preventing a breakthrough requires the J defending units to pin the intruder to the initial point of contact along the defense locus and prevent any further ingress into defense terrain. In addition, when the last encounter between the invader and the defense has been concluded, all J offensive units must stand annihilated by the J defending force units; the residual lethality of the enemy must be zero along each axis of invasion at the close of the exchange with the Jth defending unit.

---

[18]For multiperiod models of attack, this definitional procedure of specifying modes and local variances may be repeated for each time period during which the envisioned masterplan is to be executed.

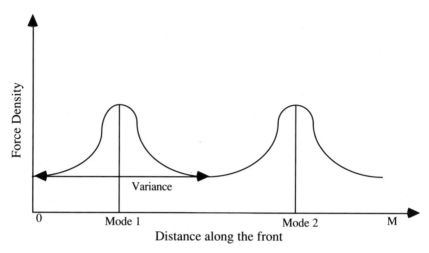

Figure 1-28.1 Bimodal Force Distribution of Attack with High Local Variance. The x-axis maps points along the length-M front. The y-axis indicates the number of invading force units assigned to each point along the front.

To conduct this dynamic campaign evaluation, we need to specify how the length of a battle between the two sides, τ, and the attacker-to-defender exchange ratio exhibited in an engagement, ψ, are determined as functions of the offense-to-defense force ratio at the outbreak of combat, γ. The τ- and ψ-curves must be of the form displayed in Figures 1-29 and 1-30, respectively, as per the Duration and Casualty Exchange Postulates. It should be noted that the average exchange ratio in an encounter with initial parity of firepower between the two sides is greater than unity. This bias in favor of the defense reflects several factors, all of which inhibit the attacker in one way or another, such as the invader's enforced mobility in unfamiliar terrain and the defender's ability to pre-position fortifications and supplies along the defense locus in anticipation of an invasion.

Once τ and ψ have been specified as functions of γ, the dynamic of determining the war outcome at each focus of penetration is straightforward. As an example of the calculations involved, consider an invading spearhead comprising 5 units which breaches the front at the point $(0, f)$. The defense assigns two units stationed at $(x1, y1)$, two units based at $(x2, y2)$ and a single unit located at $(x3, y3)$ to meet and defeat the enemy as far forward as possible. Assume the spatial geometry of the defense is such that $(x1, y1)$ is the defensive force center nearest to the point of infiltration, $(x2, y2)$ is farther removed than $(x1, y1)$ from the focus of invasion and $(x3, y3)$ is the remotest. Further, suppose that the aggressor's speed of transporting force over defense territory, v_a, is equal to the defender's velocity, v_d. Hence $v_a = v_d = v$. The attacker will achieve an infil-

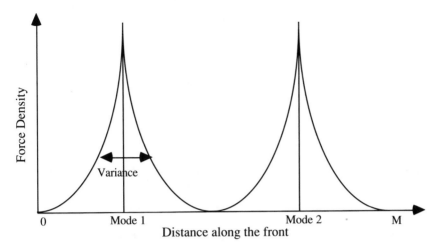

Figure 1-28.2 Bimodal Force Distribution of Attack with Small Local Variance

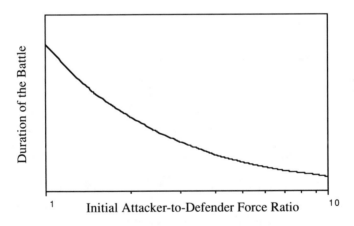

Figure 1-29 Battle Length as a Function of Initial Force Ratio

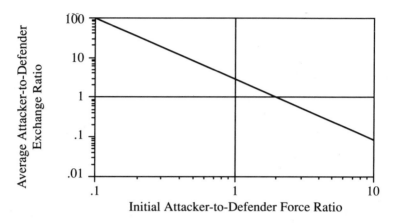

Initial Attacker-to-Defender Force Ratio

Figure 1-30   Average Casualty Exchange Ratio as a Function of Initial Force
Ratio

tration I before the initial engagement with the two defending force units mobilized from $(x1, y1)$.

$$I = \frac{x1^2 + (y1 - f)^2}{2\,x1} \tag{1-25}$$

The initial encounter between offense and defense will be conducted at the point (I, f). The attacker-to-defender force ratio at the start of this initial entanglement is 5:2 or 2.5:1. The duration of this encounter, $\tau1$, may simply be read off the curve of battle duration versus initial force ratio; analogously, the average exchange ratio prevailing in this battle, $\psi1$, is the point on the casualty exchange curve corresponding to the abscissa $\gamma1 = 2.5$. The second stage in the defense campaign plan unfolds as the second echelon of two defensive force units arrives at the site of the initial engagement, (I, f). The transit time available to the reinforcements is given by $I/v + \tau1$. If the defending units fail to materialize before the previous encounter concludes, the invader will achieve a breakthrough. Thus the defense is robust only if:

$$\frac{\sqrt{(x2 - I)^2 + (y2 - f)^2}}{v} \leq \frac{I}{v} + \tau1 \tag{1-26}$$

Assuming the second defense wave arrives as the initial engagement is drawing to a close, the initial attacker-to-defender force ratio for the second round of combat is determined as $\gamma2 = (5 - 2\psi1)/2 = 2.5 - \psi1 = \gamma1 - \psi1$. Again, this value for the initial force ratio may be inputted to the τ and ψ functions yielding the duration, $\tau2 = \tau(\gamma2)$, and the average exchange ratio, $\psi2 = \psi(\gamma2)$, of the second encounter. The next requirement the defense must satisfy is that the tertiary force echelon must arrive at (I, f) before the end of the battle between the secondary defending echelon and the attacking lethality that survived the first defensive onslaught. Thus the defense prevents the breakthrough if and only if:

$$\frac{\sqrt{(x3 - \text{I})^2 + (y3 - f)^2}}{v} \leq \frac{\text{I}}{v} + \tau1 + \tau2 \tag{1-27}$$

Finally, there must be no offensive firepower surviving at the end of the third and last battle between the attacker and the defender. The average exchange ratio, $\psi3$, prevailing in the final engagement is given by $\psi3 = \psi(5 - 2\psi1 - 2\psi2)$ and we may express the requirement of zero residual offensive lethality as:

$$5 - 2\psi1 - 2\psi2 - \psi3 \leq 0 \tag{1-28}$$

If the casualty exchange ratio in earlier encounters is significantly greater than one, the offense might be completely annihilated before the final defending echelons even arrive at the scene of combat, obviating the need to prolong the analysis of defense robustness to the ultimate stage as illustrated above. In fact, since the defense is aware of the nature of the casualty exchange curve, the redundant hindmost defending force units might be allocated to stem a different offensive attempt at conquest.

For a single period plan of attack, the procedure above may be applied to each individual focus of penetration to discover whether the defending force structure fulfills the Duration and Casualty Exchange Conditions and prevents breakthroughs. To make clear the methodology for evaluating the effectiveness of a particular defense positioning given a specific plan of attack, a numerical example is presented below.

Example: Consider a front 500 kms long separating two sides each armed with 10 units of force. The defender adopts the most forward geometry of deployment; each defending unit occupies one of the 10 locations dictated by a 10-constrained basing. Thus the defending lethality is strung out in a thin line along the front at a distance $M/10\sqrt{12} = 500/10\sqrt{12} = 14.4$ kms behind the demarcation line. The protecting units are equispaced from each other with the first unit located 25 kms along the front (in graphical terms, along the y-axis), the second unit 25 + 50 = 75 kms along the front, the third unit 75 + 50 = 125 kms, the fourth 125 + 50 = 175 kms and so on. The invader launches a single attempt at infiltration with all 10 offensive units aggregated at one extremity of the front. We may take (0, 0) as the coordinates of the focus of penetration. As diagrammed in Figure 1-31 the preliminary encounter between the solitary defending unit nearest the focus of attack and the invading spearhead will occur at the location (28.868, 0). This location is the initial point of contact.

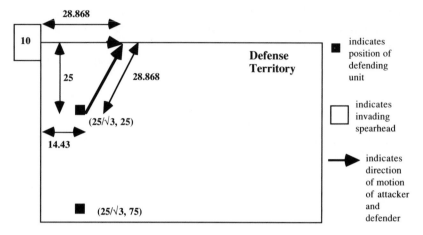

Figure 1-31   Determination of the Point of Initial Confrontation

The attacker and defender can transport force along any orientation over defense territory at a velocity of 50 kms a day. For the defensive force positioning to be robust, each succeeding unit must arrive at the initial point of contact prior to the termination of the previous engagement. Since we know the base location of each unit, the abscissa and the ordinate of the initial point of contact and the speed of transportation of the defensive force, we can calculate the time of arrival of the reinforcing echelons by dividing the separation between each unit and the initial point of contact by the defensive speed.

Unit number	Distance (kms) to the point of contact	Arrival time (days) at the scene of conflict (t = 0 corresponds to the commencement of the incursion by the offense)
1	28.868	0.577
2	76.376	1.528
3	125.831	2.517
4	175.594	3.512
5	225.462	4.509
6	275.379	5.508
7	325.320	6.506
8	375.278	7.506
9	425.245	8.505
10	475.219	9.504

For the duration and casualty curves we choose the following simplistic but analytically tractable formulations:

$$\tau = 10/\gamma \text{ days}$$

$$\psi = \gamma - (\gamma^2 - 10)^{0.5} \quad \text{for} \quad \gamma^2 \geq 10 \quad \text{and}$$

$$1/\psi = 1/\gamma - (1/\gamma^2 - 0.1)^{0.5} \quad \text{for} \quad \gamma^2 < 10$$

where γ is the attacker-to-defender force ratio at the beginning of each entanglement. These formulae for τ and ψ are in accordance with our Duration and Casualty Exchange Postulates. The attacker-to-defender force ratio at the start of the first engagement is 10 to 1. Thus the duration of the first engagement is $10/10 = 1$ day and the exchange ratio is $10 - (100 - 10)^{0.5} = 0.513$. By the close of the initial engagement, the attacking lethality is reduced to $10 - 0.513 = 9.487$ units. This is the initial attacker-to-defender force ratio at the start of the second engagement. Hence the second encounter will last for $10/9.487 = 1.054$ days and the exchange ratio that will prevail during this encounter is $9.487 - (9.487^2 - 10)^{0.5} = 0.543$. The exchange ratio for the second encounter may be used to calculate the attacking strength at the commencement of the third engagement, and the process is repeated until the attacker's residual lethality at the close of each of the 10 encounters with individual defensive units and the length of each confrontation have been determined.

Encounter number	Duration (days)	Attacking lethality at start of engagement	Attacking lethality at termination of engagement
1	1.000	10.000	9.487
2	1.054	9.487	8.944
3	1.118	8.944	8.367
4	1.195	8.367	7.746
5	1.291	7.746	7.071
6	1.414	7.071	6.325
7	1.581	6.325	5.477
8	1.826	5.477	4.472
9	2.236	4.472	3.162
10	3.163	3.162	0.000

The first unit engages the attacker within 0.577 days of the initiation of the attack. Therefore the second unit has a respite of 0.577 days + the length of the first battle = 0.577 + 1.000 = 1.577 days in which to mobilize to the initial point of contact. Analogously, the third unit receives the 1.577 days plus an additional period equal to the duration of the second entanglement between the two sides in which to arrive at the scene of the battle. The table below depicts the time by which each succeeding unit must arrive at the initial point of contact and the *actual* time required by each defending division to get there.

Unit number	Time (days) by which mobilization to the point of contact must be completed	Actual time (days) required for arrival at the point of contact
1	...	0.577
2	1.577	1.528
3	2.631	2.517
4	3.749	3.512
5	4.944	4.509
6	6.235	5.508
7	7.649	6.506
8	9.230	7.506
9	11.056	8.505
10	13.292	9.504

Each of the 9 reinforcing echelons arrives at the point of contact before the previous engagement has ended. In addition, all 10 attacking units are annihilated by the 10 defending units, and the residual lethality of the invader is zero at the termination of the tenth and final encounter between the two sides. The defense is robust in preventing a breakthrough for the specific attack plan simulated in this example and the offensive infiltration is restricted to 28.9 kms. It should be noted that for the particular scenario considered above, all defending force waves subsequent to the fifth echelon arrive sufficiently early at the scene of battle to be fully integrated with the entrenched defending forces while the previous encounter is still in progress. In a more careful analysis, this intermediate addition of reinforcing firepower during the course of each conflict should be assimilated into the calculation of the exchange ratio and the battle duration.

Finally, we chose a relatively benign plan of attack for the above analysis wherein all 10 invading units launched the invasion from a single point along the front. A far more threatening scenario is one in which the majority of the offensive firepower is concentrated along a single penetration axis while the remaining lethality pins down defensive units immediately adjacent to the main spearhead of attack. Thus reinforcing echelons have to travel much longer distances to arrive at the initial point of contact. For instance, consider an attack plan where the invading commander prosecutes a 3-pronged campaign. Attack Wave 1 consists of 3.675 units which infiltrate defense territory at the point (0, 0), Attack Wave 2 comprises 3.162 units launched into defense terrain at the point (0, 75) and Attack Wave 3 is made up of 3.162 units penetrating at the point (0, 125). All three Attack Waves advance into the defender's homeland at the same time. Our assignment rule for allocating defensive units to stem the advancing enemy columns requires us to assign the single defending unit at (14.43, 25) to Attack Wave 1, the defending unit at (14.43, 75) to Attack Wave 2 and the defending unit at (14.43, 125) to Attack Wave 3. Let us first explore the outcome of the onslaught by Attack Waves 2 and 3. Attack Wave 2 is intercepted by a single defending unit at (7.22, 75), while the advance of Attack Wave 3 is blocked by a solitary defending unit at (7.22, 125). The exchange ratio observed in each of these engagements is $3.162 - (3.162^2 - 10)^{0.5} = 3.162$, and thus the entire offensive lethality along each of these particular axes of penetration is eliminated by the defending forces. Attack Waves 2 and 3 are totally destroyed by the two defending units with peacetime bases at (14.43,75) and (14.43,125), respectively. In the process the two defending units are themselves annihilated.

Next let us consider what happens to Attack Wave 1. In the case of Attack Wave 1 the initial point of contact is 28.86 kms inward from the border along the x-axis. The offensive lethality of 3.675 units engages in combat with the defending unit dispatched from (14.43, 25). The exchange ratio manifested in this engagement is $3.675 - (3.675^2 - 10)^{0.5} = 1.803$, and the residual lethality of the invader at the conclusion of this preliminary encounter is $3.675 - 1.803 = 1.872$ units. Clearly timely reinforcements are essential if the defensive force geometry is to prevent a strategic breakthrough. The closest defensive unit not engaged in combat with Attack Waves 2 and 3 is the unit at (14.43, 175). The total period of time available to this defending echelon to arrive at the scene of battle is the sum of the time taken by Attack Wave 1 to infiltrate 28.86 kms and the duration of the first engagement. If both attacker and defender can transport forces at a speed of 50 kms a day over defense terrain, the time taken by the offense to arrive at the initial point of contact is $28.86/50 = 0.577$ days. The duration of the battle between Attack Wave 1 and the first defending regiment is $10/\gamma = 10/3.675 = 2.721$ days. The time by which the the second defense wave must arrive at the initial point of contact is $0.577 + 2.721 = 3.298$ days. The distance between the peacetime base of the reinforcing division and the battlefield location is $[(14.43 - 28.86)^2 + (175 - 0)^2]^{0.5} = 175.6$ kms and the defending regiment requires a minimum of $175.6/50 = 3.512$ days to translocate to the initial point of contact. The defending unit therefore fails to arrive in time to pin down the invader to the site of the initial battle, and the aggressor succeeds in infiltrating past the defense locus.

The 10-constrained defending force geometry is too dispersed and fails to satisfy the Duration Condition for at least one campaign of attack. It is paramount that the defensive lethality matrix maintain its robustness for the entire universe of attack plans requiring the defending commander to exhaustively test the defensive force geometry before accepting the viability of a particular K-constrained geometry.

From the example above, the methodology for testing a particular dispersed, forward-emplaced defensive force geometry against various plans of attack should be clear. The objective is to ensure that the Duration and Casualty Exchange Conditions are rigorously satisfied at each focus of penetration for every imaginable invasion campaign. The generalized Defense Positioning Problem may thus be concisely stated:

What is the most dispersed and forward positioned force geometry that the defending forces can adopt while satisfying the Duration, Casualty Exchange and Completeness Conditions and minimizing the infiltration of the invader ?

Minimizing the infiltration of the invader is the same as limiting the invader's advance to the defense locus associated with the most forward-located defense positioning permitted by the Duration, Casualty Exchange and Completeness Conditions. The defender can determine the optimal dispersed forward defense using the step-by-step algorithm outlined below.

1. Commence with the most dispersed and forward positioned defense geometry, namely the N-constrained basing.

2. For each distinct plan of attack, evaluate the robustness of the N-constrained defense. If the N-constrained defense succeeds in preventing a breakthrough for the entire universe of attack plans, the N-constrained defense is the optimal dispersed forward defense. If the N-constrained defense fails to satisfy the Duration and Casualty Exchange Conditions for any plan of attack, it must be abandoned in favor of a less dispersed defense geometry.

3. Repeat the dynamic robustness evaluation for the (N - 1)-constrained force positioning geometry. If the (N - 1)-constrained defense is robust under all plans of attack, it is the optimal forward defense. If not, the (N - 2)-constrained defense must be examined for robustness.

4. This process is continued using defense positionings characterized by progressively decreasing dispersion and increasing inward displacement from the front until a robust defense is found. The algorithm is guaranteed to produce a

solution since the 1-constrained or unconstrained defense is a robust forward defense.

Among all the force positioning geometries, the one that is the most dispersed and deploys defending units closest to the front and concurrently satisfies the robustness criterion is the optimal forward defense. This optimal geometry minimizes the unopposed infiltration achieved by the offense while maximizing defensive force dispersion and meeting and defeating the enemy as close to the front as possible. Thus the generalized Defense Positioning Problem is solved.

Outline of Part One

The Basic Assumptions
1. Simple definition of a length-M front as a contiguous border between two opposing nations.
2. Isotropy of the battlefield terrain parallel to the front.
3. Information on the force distribution of the enemy is governed by an on-off function.
4. Uniform probability distribution of attack at each point along the length-M front.
5. Total units of force possessed by the defense equal the aggregate lethality of the offense.
6. The defender must match the attacking forces unit for unit at each focus of penetration.
7. No constraints on the local concentration of force.

The Fundamental Defense Positioning Problem
Where should the defending force units be stationed to be assured of meeting and defeating the invader as far forward as possible? In other words, the defender's objective is to minimize the expected infiltration of the attacking forces.

Solutions to the Fundamental Defense Positioning Problem
For a single unit force ($N = 1$):

Relative Velocity	Optimal Defense Position
$v_a = v_d$	$(M/\sqrt{12}, M/2)$
$v_a < v_d$	Figure 1-8
$v_a > v_d$	Figure 1-9

For an arbitrary number of force units ($N \geq 1$):

Concentrate all force units at the optimal defense position determined for the N = 1 situation. Defense locus is unchanged.

Highlights and Insights

1. The optimal position for the defending forces is not along the front but at a nonzero distance behind the front. Forward defense is better than forward-deployed defense.

2. The defense locus is the set of points where the defending forces, if optimally positioned, are first able to confront the invader. The defense locus indicates the minimum inward penetration of the defender's territory inevitably achieved by the offense and is thus a measure of stability. The closer the defense locus is to the frontier, the smaller is the portion of defense terrain vulnerable to preemptive capture by the enemy and the lower is the award for a first strike by the adversary.

3. For enhancing conventional stability the absolute speed of transporting force is essentially irrelevant. Outcomes depend only on the ratio of attacking-to-defending force velocity. The defense locus is pressed outwards if each side is capable of outstripping the offense when subjected to an invasion and, in turn, is surpassed by the opponent when initiating the attack.

Relaxing the Basic Assumptions

Uniform Probability of Attack Assumption: An arbitrary probability density function of invasion.

For an arbitrary number of force units ($N \geq 1$):

Relative Velocity	Optimal Defense Position
$v_a = v_d$	(σ, μ)

σ is the standard deviation while μ is the mean of the arbitrary probability distribution of attack. In comprehending the μ part of the σ - μ Theorem, it is hardly surprising that the defender is required to position all defending lethality diametrically opposite the point along the front where the invader is expected to attempt an infiltration. What is more interesting is the σ portion of the σ - μ Theorem. σ measures the spread of the probability distribution of attack along the front. Intuitively it should be clear that the greater the variance associated with the universe of possible attacks—that is, the larger the spread of the foci of infiltration along the front—the farther removed from the line of partition the defender must be to minimize offensive incursion.

Simple definition of a length-M front: Refining the concept of a length-M front.

A nation's borders with its neighbors can be divided into discrete segments such that the nation is always cognizant of the total number of enemy force units behind each segment, the transfer of hostile forces between segments is easily discernible while intrasegment force mobility can be perfectly fluid and the terrain adjoining each segment on either side is reasonably isotropic. Each such segment constitutes a length-M front.

Any two segments separated by a natural barrier such as a river or a mountain range or an institutional or man-made obstacle should be treated as two distinct length-M fronts. It is not unduly restrictive to assume that the topography of the land bordering a particular length-M front displays isotropy parallel to the front since severe violations of terrain isotropy parallel to the border should be used to define the barrier between adjacent length-M fronts.

The goal of each country is to be able to divide the border regions it faces into several, small length-M fronts while compelling its neighbors to define a few, large length-M fronts from its own border terrain. As a consequence, the fortunate country can position its forces close to the frontier and decrease the area of its territory vulnerable to capture by an attacker, while simultaneously forcing its adversaries to locate their troops at large displacements inward from their common frontier. A country can increase the length of the length-M front by developing the capability to fluidly and unobtrusively transport force parallel to the frontier. On the other hand, a state can partition the border districts of its neighbors into smaller length-M fronts by obtaining better information on the enemy's force distribution.

On-off Information Function Assumption: The defender has better than on-off information about the force distribution of the enemy.

Better intelligence permits the defender to monitor the total enemy strength in progressively smaller regions creating the opportunity to define smaller and smaller length-M fronts. Superior reconnaissance also imbues the defender with confidence in forming its expectation of the functional nature of the probability distribution of attack.

No limits on local force concentration: The solution to the fundamental Defense Positioning Problem requires all defending units to be stationed at a single encampment. Unfortunately localized force concentrations are alluring targets for raids by deep interdiction aircraft and C^3I strikes and suffer from the fallacy of putting all the defender's eggs in one basket. A second major shortcoming of the force structure advocated by the solution to the fundamental Defense Positioning Problem is the expansive loss of terrain allowed by the defense locus. Depending on the focus of penetration, the defense locus permits the attacker to capture without opposition anywhere from $M/2\sqrt{12}$ to $2M/\sqrt{12}$ of

defense territory. For an invasion conducted over urbanized and densely populated tracts of land, the generous incursions permitted by the defense locus
could be disastrous unless M is very small.

Generalize the fundamental Defense Positioning Problem: For a defense that
seeks to disperse its total lethality among K discrete force centers, where
should the K base encampments be located in order for the defending units
meet and defeat the invader as far forward as possible? How should the aggregate defensive lethality be distributed among the K disparate force centers?

Potential Solutions to the Generalized Defense Positioning Problem

Front Segmentation   Potential "Optimal"
   Methodology   Force Structures
   With overlap   Infinite
   Null-overlap   {1-constrained,
                                      2-constrained, ...,
                                        K-constrained, ...,
                                        N-constrained}

Example: K = 2. Defense forces may be divided into two equal contingents.
One contingent could be positioned at $(M/2\sqrt{12}, M/4)$ while the second contingent could be located at $(M/2\sqrt{12}, 3M/4)$ giving rise to a 2-constrained force
geometry. Alternatively, the two contingents could be located at $(2M/3\sqrt{12},$
$M/3)$ and $(2M/3\sqrt{12}, 2M/3)$ respectively, yielding 2-force lethality matrix with
both contingents assigned to protect the middle third of the front. Clearly if a
section of the front may be assigned to more than one defense subgroup, there
is an infinite number of possible force structures available to a defender who
wishes to divide its forces between two distinct bases.

We adhere throughout to a null-overlap methodology for partitioning the
length-M front.

The Trade-off between Perfect Counterconcentration and Force Dispersion

An unconstrained or 1-constrained force deployment guarantees the defense the
ability to match the attacking forces unit for unit at each focus of penetration.
For a defender who adopts a K-constrained defense with K > 1, an encampment
of N/K units, entrusted with the safekeeping of a length-(M/K) front, must be
prepared to engage in battle with a hostile strength ranging anywhere from 0 to
N force units. The overload factor is the most unfavorable offense-to-defense
force ratio that could be impressed upon the defender in any fragment of the
length-M front as a consequence of the artificially imposed partitioning of an
otherwise contiguous length-M front into K subfronts. For a K-constrained
force geometry the maximum distance to which infiltrating forces can advance

without being challenged by the defense is $2M/K\sqrt{12}$, while the overload factor is K. Thus with the adoption of an increasingly dispersed force structure, the defense trades off its capacity for perfect counterconcentration for the option of propelling the defense locus closer to the frontier.

Meeting and Defeating the Enemy at the K-constrained Defense Locus

Associated with each K-constrained force geometry is a defense locus. If perfect counterconcentration is relinquished in favor of the forward basing of units, the objective of *meeting* and *defeating* the invader at the defense locus must be precisely defined. Meeting the aggressor at the defense locus requires restraining the advance of the invading regiments to the initial point of contact between offense and defense. Because the defending contingent that first confronts an invading spearhead may be insufficient to annihilate the attacking lethality, more than one defensive wave may be required at each focus of penetration to vanquish the foe. To pin the intruder to the initial point of contact along the defense locus, defensive reinforcements must always arrive at the scene of battle prior to the close of the previous engagement (Duration Condition).

Defeating the invader at the defense locus requires the defender to destroy the invading lethality along each axis of invasion with no more than the number of units committed by the aggressor to that particular axis (Casualty Exchange Condition).

Finally, a defense is robust only if it satisfies the Duration and Casualty Exchange Conditions for the entire universe of attack plans (Completeness Condition).

If the invading troops succeed in rupturing the defense locus, the attacker has accomplished a strategic breakthrough.

The Generalized Defense Positioning Problem

What is the most dispersed and forward-positioned force geometry that the defending forces can adopt while satisfying the Duration, Casualty Exchange and Completeness Conditions and minimizing the infiltration of the invader? If a null-overlap methodology is adopted in partitioning the length-M front, the universe from which the solution to the generalized Defense Positioning Problem must be isolated is limited to the {1-constrained, 2-constrained, ..., K-constrained, ..., N-constrained} set of geometries.

Why We Need to Model Combat

To test whether a given K-constrained force geometry satisfies the Duration and Casualty Exchange Conditions, we need a model of what determines the duration of an encounter between two sides (τ) and what determines the ratio at which casualties are exchanged by two sides in combat (ψ). We use a minimalist approach of treating τ and ψ as functions of the force ratio between the two sides at the start of the engagement (γ) and the relative effectiveness per unit force of the two combatants (a/d). We prefer a minimalist approach because it is unnecessary and futile to construct more elaborate models of the combat process in the absence of historical data to verify or reject the veracity of alternative modeling schemes. The initial force ratio between the two adversaries is used as the primary explanatory variable because it is easily measured, has a massive impact on the ultimate resolution of the encounter and is the variable sought to be manipulated by most arms control agreements.

A Minimalist Approach to Combat Modeling

The Duration of Battle (τ)

$$\frac{\partial \tau}{\partial \gamma} \quad < \quad 0$$

The duration of an engagement declines with increasing initial force strength of the superior side.

$$\frac{\partial^2 \tau}{\partial \gamma^2} \quad > \quad 0$$

If an increase by the superior side in the initial force ratio from 5 to 6 decreases the period of combat by 1 day, then a subsequent increase in the initial force ratio from 6 to 7 will lower the battle time by less than a day (Diminishing Marginal Returns).

If Side A is the victor in an encounter and a/d is greater than 1, then

$$\tau_{a/d>1} \quad < \quad \tau_{a/d=1}$$

while if a/d is less than 1, then

$$\tau_{a/d<1} \quad > \quad \tau_{a/d=1} .$$

The weaker side can hold out longer if it is more efficient in utilizing force, while the stronger side can annihilate its opponent quicker if the stronger side is also more proficient in employing force effectively.

The Casualty Exchange Ratio (ψ)

A determining relationship for the casualty exchange ratio must be hypothesized for two reasons: first, to ensure that a given dispersed forward defense satisfies the Casualty Exchange Condition; and second, to calculate the residual lethality of the invading spearhead after each encounter with a defending echelon, since the residual force at the conclusion of the jth encounter is the initial force at the commencement of the j+1th engagement.

$$\frac{\partial \psi}{\partial \gamma} < 0$$

The attacker-to-defender casualty exchange ratio declines with increasing initial force strength of the attacker, assuming the initial force deployment of the defender is unchanged.

$$\frac{\partial^2 \psi}{\partial \gamma^2} > 0$$

The attacker-to-defender casualty exchange ratio shows diminishing marginal returns with increasing initial force strength of the aggressor (Saturation of Force).

If ψ is the *attacker*-to-*defender* casualty exchange ratio and a/d is greater than 1, then

$$\psi_{a/d>1} < \psi_{a/d=1}$$

while if a/d is less than 1, then

$$\psi_{a/d<1} > \psi_{a/d=1} .$$

Because of the perfect information capability of the defense on home ground and the defender's ability to pre-fortify the defense locus, the intelligent and determined defender can display in battle greater combat effectiveness per unit lethality than the invader (a/d < 1).

Let D(0) represent the quantum of force dispatched by the defense to a particular encounter. If force lethality on either side is measured in units of D(0), then the firepower of the invader that survives the engagement is given by

$$\rho = \gamma - \psi$$

where ρ equals the attacker's residual firepower calibrated in units of D(0), γ represents the attacker-to-defender initial force ratio and ψ represents the attacker-to-defender casualty exchange ratio observed during the battle.

Exogenous and Endogenous Variables

The initial force ratio observed in individual encounters between offense and defense depends on the force geometry adopted by the defense and the particular invasion campaign plan chosen by the aggressor. Hence the determination of a robust defensive force structure requires the calculation of battle duration and casualty exchange for a range of values of the initial force ratio. On the other hand, the relative combat effectiveness, a/d, is a function of factors such as the identity of the combatants, the location of the battlefield and the level of defense preparedness. a/d is unaffected for the most part by the defender's force positioning or the invader's choice of foci of penetration. Thus a/d is an exogenous variable while the initial force ratio is an endogenous variable in the generalized Defense Positioning Problem. Given a/d, all we need to specify are $\tau = \tau(\gamma)$ and $\psi = \psi(\gamma)$ with the $\tau(\gamma)$ and the $\psi(\gamma)$ functions satisfying the following properties:

$$\frac{\partial \tau}{\partial \gamma} < 0 \quad \frac{\partial^2 \tau}{\partial \gamma^2} > 0 \quad \frac{\partial \psi}{\partial \gamma} < 0 \quad \frac{\partial^2 \psi}{\partial \gamma^2} > 0$$

These four properties are the only assumptions about the nature of combat that we require.

A Linear Approximation to Our Combat Attrition Assumptions

For modeling the initial stages of the attempt by a highly dispersed forward defense to contain a concentrated attacking spearhead, only the duration of the first engagement, $\tau(\gamma 1)$, the casualty exchange ratio that prevails during the first encounter, $\psi(\gamma 1)$, and the rate of change of duration measured as the initial force ratio observed in the first engagement, $\tau(\gamma 1)$, need be specified.

An Algorithm for Solving the Generalized Defense Positioning Problem

The Nature of the Solution Sought by the Algorithm

Under assumptions of an on-off information function, a uniform probability of attack, equal offensive and defensive velocity, a defending force divisible into N or fewer contingents of equal strength and a null-overlap methodology for partitioning the front, a N-unit defense has a choice of N potentially optimal geometries—namely, the {1-constrained, 2-constrained, 3-constrained, ..., K-constrained, ..., N-constrained} set. The defender's objective is to find a force geometry that is robust, one that satisfies the Duration, Casualty Exchange and Completeness Conditions and that minimizes the unopposed infiltration of the offense. The unconstrained or 1-constrained force geometry always satisfies the three conditions for robustness but might not necessarily be the geometry that minimizes the invader's incursion since there could exist a K-constrained geometry with K greater than one that also fulfills the robustness criteria. The solution sought by the algorithm may be stated thus: Find the most forward-positioned and dispersed of the N K-constrained force geometries accessible to a N-strong defense that satisfies the Duration, Casualty Exchange and Completeness Conditions. Note that a philosophy of basing defending units as close to the front as possible at equal distances from each other is the most forward-deployed force geometry possible but does not satisfy the three conditions for robustness and is consequently unacceptable. Satisfying the Duration, Casualty Exchange and Completeness Conditions implies that the invader has been stopped and annihilated at the *defense locus*.

Pointers on Implementing the Algorithm for Solving the Generalized Defense Positioning Problem

Schemata for modeling attack plans:

1. Single-period versus multiperiod plans of attack.

2. In each time period, an attack plan can be specified as the modes of the attacker's force distribution along the length-M front and the local variances about the modes.

3. For a probability density function of invasion that is symmetric about the midpoint of the front, reflections of attack plans about the midpoint need not be tested against each defensive force geometry evaluated for robustness. This cuts in half the attack plans to be considered in fulfilling the Completeness Condition.

Schema for choosing potentially optimal defensive force geometries:

For a probability distribution of attack that is symmetric about the midpoint of the frontier, all defensive lethality matrices considered for election to the realm of optimality must be symmetric about the front midpoint as well. All the K-constrained force geometries satisfy this requirement.

Evaluating the performance of a particular defensive force geometry subjected to a specific plan of attack:

1. The rule for assigning defending contingents to infiltrating units is as follows. Begin by assigning the defending divisions in charge of a particular front segment to the invading units that penetrate through that segment. If the allocated defending divisions are insufficient to annihilate the intrusive offensive lethality, the nearest defensive contingents not previously assigned to other invading spearheads may be dispatched to the initial point of contact.

2. Formulate duration and casualty exchange ratio functions, which depend solely on the force ratio at the start of an encounter and are in accordance with the Duration and Casualty Exchange Postulates.

3. At each focus of penetration, examine whether the Duration and Casualty Exchange Conditions hold. Assign defending contingents as per the assignment rule stated in Step 1 and determine whether defensive reinforcements arrive in time to pin the invader to the defense locus and whether all the offensive lethality at the focus is destroyed prior to or concomitant with the incapacitation of the assigned defensive regiments.

4. Repeat the procedure in Step 3 at all foci of infiltration associated with a given invasion campaign plan.

Test the defensive force structure against all conceivable, nonreplicative plans of attack as elaborated above. If the Duration and Casualty Exchange Conditions are satisfied for the entire universe of invasion campaign plans, the particular defensive force geometry under scrutiny is robust. However being robust does not imply that the force-positioning geometry is optimal; to be optimal the geometry must be both robust and the most forward positioned and dispersed of all robust lethality matrices.

Outline of the Procedure for Solving
the Generalized Defense Positioning Problem

Step	Defensive geometry. under consideration	Is the defense geometry robust?	Next step
Step 1	N-constrained	Yes No	OPTIMAL - *Exit* Go to Step 2
Step 2	(N-1)-constrained	Yes No	OPTIMAL - *Exit* Go to Step 3
Step 3	. . .	. . . . . .	. . . . . .
Step N-K+1	K-constrained	Yes No	OPTIMAL - *Exit* Go to Step N-K+2
Step N-K+2	. . .	. . . . . .	. . . . . .
Step N-1	2-constrained	Yes No	OPTIMAL - *Exit* Go to Step N
Step N	1-constrained or unconstrained	Yes	OPTIMAL - *Exit*

PART TWO

Positioning a Passive Defense

IN POSING AND SOLVING the generalized Defense Positioning Problem, we have limited ourselves to a case where the offense and defense possess equal lethality. In the real world, all armed forces are not created equal and basic demographic, economic, geographic, social and political constraints can limit the capacity of a nation to wage war. Within the framework of the generalized Defense Positioning Problem, a numerically inferior defender has no choice but to increase the casuality exchange ratio in its favor in order to compensate for inferior overall lethality, to outpace the aggressor in transporting force over defense terrain and to acquire immediate and reliable information on changes in the force geometry of the offense. Thus the first issue for a numerically inferior defender is how to achieve these objectives.

A second problem involves a country with contiguous borders with more than one nation, wherein some neighbors are friendly and others are hostile. Clearly optimal use of the country's war resources dictates that lethality be focused on borders with inimical states. However there is always the possibility that a determined foe will first conquer a congenial neighbor and subsequently launch an attack into the defender's homeland using the captured contiguous territory as a base for operations, thus converting the border between the defender and the previously friendly neighbor into the battlefield. If the time taken by the aggressor to gain control over the amicable neighbor's border areas proximate to the defense is less than the period required by the defense to mobilize and position its forces along the new front, the flanking strategy of the invader could well succeed. Logistically, it might not be feasible for the defender to assign a standing force to the border region with the friendly neighbor in peacetime. Politically, it could strain relations if the defending commander insists on maintaining a battle-ready army along an ally's border.

123

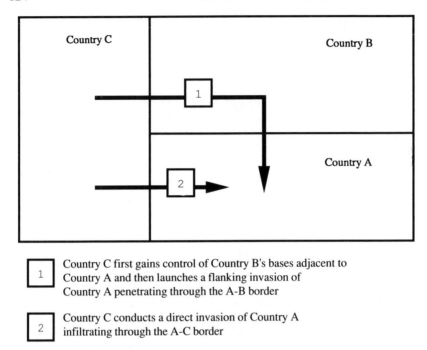

Country C first gains control of Country B's bases adjacent to Country A and then launches a flanking invasion of Country A penetrating through the A-B border

Country C conducts a direct invasion of Country A infiltrating through the A-C border

Figure 2-1   The Three-Nation Problem. Country A has amiable relations with Country B but is viewed with hostility by Country C. If A concentrates its attention and forces on the defense of the A-C border, C could catch A by surprise by first conquering Country B and subsequently launching an invasion of A through the A-B border.

The issue of multiple borders is easily visualized by considering the case of just three nations as shown in Figure 2-1.

Country A has amiable relations with Country B but fears an attack by Country C. Country C can either choose to launch a direct invasion of Country A or can first achieve a speedy conquest of Country B and prosecute its infiltration into Country A through the A-B border. If Country A cannot pre-position sufficient forces along this border, a rapid outflanking maneuver through Country B's terrain by Country C could be disastrous for Country A.

The conventional wisdom in dealing with the problems of a numerically weak defense or a defender with multiple fronts is to equip the defense with strategic counteroffensive capability. This doctrine proceeds along the lines that if a nation cannot defend its territory effectively than it must capture equal or greater tracts of the aggressor's home territory as compensation for the invader's successful conquest of defense terrain. It is therefore *imperative* that the "defender" maintain a substantial offensive war capacity to exact retaliation for a successful invasion. How the defender convinces its neighbors that the offensive capability is purely counteroffensive is a matter not addressed by the conventional wisdom. Carrying the logic of the argument one step further, the weak defender should optimally preempt the offensive onslaught and be the first to infiltrate enemy lines if there is any possibility that the enemy could defeat the defensive forces on defense terrain if allowed to mobilize fully and launch a fully prepared campaign. Basing a defense on counteroffense is a hairtrigger approach to war planning and encourages brinkmanship; it is the classic Prisoner's Dilemma, in which each player has a lot to gain by surprising the adversary but everything to lose if forced into an all-out war. Counteroffense can never replace a robust defense.

The problems of unequal forces and multiple fronts are not unique in posing obstacles for a defender attempting to implement the solution to generalized Defense Positioning Problem. Our analysis in Part One exhorted the defense to outmatch the offense in mobility and to realize favorable exchange ratios and battle durations in individual encounters. The quest for defensive systems that enhance defensive superiority on home terrain is an intrinsic part of the Defense Positioning Problem. Part Two explores defensive technologies that do not demand traditional infantry and armored divisions and associated close air support. These defense systems are singular in two respects: First, they are not manpower intensive; they make sparing use of human assistance for operation and consequently minimize casualties and the human cost of war for a demographically and numerically constrained force. Second, these technologies are inherently defensive and for the most part cannot be employed in an offensive manner. The purely defensive orientation of these systems makes it politically feasible to deploy these technologies along any border, whether that neighbor is presently hostile or friendly, and strengthens conventional force stability. We shall adopt the rubric "passive defense" to refer to these technologies—passive defense implying not inaction but limited offensive means. What distinguishes passive defense systems from other conventional forms of defense is their ability to enhance solely defensive capacity without bolstering offensive capability. As we shall see later, passive defense can be used very effectively to plug the Achilles' heels of an otherwise robust defense by slowing offensive forces to a crawl and considerably raising the casualty exchange ratio in favor of the defense.

The simplest conceptualization of a passive defense is a detect-allocate-intercept targeting system. The system consists of a detection web, an allocation routine and an interceptor load. The unsolicited entry of an alien into the space protected by the passive defense system triggers the detection mechanism. The intelligence net determines the whereabouts of as many of the intruders as permitted by the surveillance technology. All interceptors available to the system are equally allocated among the invaders and dispatched along a collision path with them. The entire detect-allocate-intercept cycle might be repeated after the interceptor pods or launchers have been reloaded.

From a theoretical perspective, it is interesting to derive an optimal design algorithm for a passive defense and compare the structure and functioning of this system with the basing modes and employment doctrine for traditional weapons. We shall advance a simple, mathematical model for a detect-allocate-intercept type of passive defense. Using the model, we will outline a set of guiding principles for the optimal design of an individual passive defense unit and then determine the most effective manner of connecting the independent passive defense modules. We will explore some of the implications of counter-attack by the invader on the passive defense system itself. Finally, we will show how passive defense can be integrated into the solution of the generalized Defense Positioning Problem to create a devastating but nonoffensive comprehensive defense system. A concise summary of all the major findings on passive defense systems advanced in Part Two is provided at the conclusion of the Part. Our conceptualization of passive defense will not only help evaluate the military efficacy of the particular passive defenses that we are proposing but also can serve as a basic axiom for the structuring of existing passive defenses such as air defense and anti-submarine warfare systems. Besides, the rising pacificity and aversion to armed conflict that has characterized the world since the end of the Second World War has significantly increased the reluctance of most Western societies to sacrifice human lives to the cause of war. Passive defense technologies with their emphasis on minimizing human loss seem likely to soon replace the existing strategic and conventional defenses that consume so many lives.

Some Real-World Examples of Passive Defense Systems

Practical, real-world examples of a passive defense could include an air defense system designed to stop close air support aircraft, escort fighters, weapon transporters, supply carriers and deep interdiction bombers that encroach upon the defender's air space. The detection web for an air defense system could range from as crude an instrument as the human lookout to light-sensitive and infrared radar and satellites. The interceptors could be anti-aircraft ground-to-air missiles dispatched by infantry units.

Another realization of a passive defense could be remote-controlled or self-regulating machine guns and anti-tank weapons located in sheltered bunkers along the border. The machine guns and anti-tank weaponry would engage all detected incursionary enemy battalions or individual tanks and infantry vehicles within shooting range of the particular defensive bunker. The allocation algorithm in this case consists of assigning rounds of machine gun fire or anti-tank guided missiles to all detected disruptions of the security network.

Such a ground defense possesses the advantage of being almost exclusively nonoffensive since the defensive force units are not mobile and and could not ordinarily be redeployed rapidly enough to conduct an intrusive maneuver into enemy territory.[1] Finally the detection system for such a passive ground defense could be a symbiotic network of electronic tripwires, remotely piloted vehicles or drones, reconnaissance aircraft and satellite observers. The detection and command mechanism for such a system must be designed to rigorous requirements of robustness to prevent the accidental triggering of the self-controlled weaponry.[2]

Other visualizations of our passive defense include anti-submarine warfare systems, in which the detection involves sonar and buoys, and anti-ballistic missile defenses, such as the existing high acceleration interceptor defense around Moscow or the area and point defenses proposed by the United States under the Strategic Defense Initiative (SDI). The continued experimentation on SDI by the United States could lead one day to the deployment of a ground or sea-based anti-ballistic missile defense, radically and fundamentally altering the risks of missile-borne nuclear attack and the future development of ballistic missile technology.

The most spectacular instance in recent history of a passive defense system in operation is offered by the Patriot system's defense of Saudi Arabia and Israel against the Scud missile launches of Saddam Hussein during Operation

---

[1]However, the loss of mobility intrinsic to the fixed, sheltered basing envisioned above might erode the survivability of the defensive weapon clusters if subjected to heavy aerial and long-range artillery bombardment. The tremendous destructive power of modern artillery shells and air bombardment might render the cost of constructing sufficiently hardened shelters prohibitive. Nevertheless there are redeeming features to such a defensive doctrine; for instance, if the force centers are sufficiently dispersed across numerous locations, the reward to the attacker for incapacitating a single bunker might be incommensurate with the firepower and effort devoted to the tasks of locating and destroying the weapon base. If the total weaponry is spread across hundreds of diminutive bunkers, the hardware housed within any single entrenchment is too small to warrant a full-scale artillery salvo or air assault. Finally the survivability of each bunker can be enhanced by adding anti-aircraft weapons such as surface-to-air missiles to its arsenal to protect against carpet bombing by the enemy air force.

[2] The robustness and dependability of the information network can be improved by instituting cross-verifications as an integral part of the identification routine and possibly placing the ultimate go-ahead signal prior to the commencement of fire in a central, manned command and control unit. Of course, designating the final authority to a manned control headquarters is not only expensive but also exposes to preemption the means of communication between outlying individual bunkers and the commander of the passive network.

Desert Storm in January and February of 1991. The rapidly launched, fast-moving Patriot intercepted the slower moving Scud and detonated its warhead in the last stage of the Scud's ballistic flight, just before impact at ground zero.

A Simple Model for a Detect-Allocate-Intercept System

Consider a passive defense system with the following features.

1. The system protects a fixed land area or volume in space and, when fully loaded, has a total of I interceptors.

2. The detection web of the system has an infinite band width; that is, there is no limitation on the total number of intruders detected. However only a fixed percentage, D, of the total incoming foreign bodies is detected by the detection network. Thus if the system is barraged by an attacking strength of A units, only DA of the attackers will be detected and targeted upon entering the system space.

3. Each interceptor has a constant single shot probability of kill, p, when targeted against the prototype attacker.

4. All I interceptors are instantaneously, or at least very rapidly, allocated among the DA detected aliens equally. Thus each attacker is subjected to an onslaught of I/DA interceptions.

Since p is the probability of destruction resulting from a single encounter with an interceptor, the likelihood of surviving a single interception is given by 1 - p. Each detected attacker is confronted with I/DA interceptors in the course of its passage through the system space. Surviving each interception is a statistically independent event; in other words, surviving one interception does not influence in any way the probability distribution of surviving the subsequent interception. Hence the probability of an individual intruder emerging unscathed from the defending system space is $(1 - p)_1(1 - p)_2(1 - p)_3 \ldots (1 - p)_{I/DA} = (1 - p)^{I/DA}$. The total number of survivors, S, who manage to evade destruction comprises those attackers who are not detected by the passive defense system's intelligence network, namely $(1 - D)A$, and the residual attackers who are detected but survive the interceptors The latter term is the product of the total number of detected attacking bodies and the probability of survival of an individual detected alien, $DA(1 - p)^{I/DA}$. Thus the total residual strength of the invading contingent is:[3]

$$S = \left(1 - D\right)A + D A \left(1 - p\right)^{\frac{I}{DA}} \qquad (2\text{-}1)$$

---

[3]The author was introduced to this equation and the underlying framework for modeling defense systems by Joshua M. Epstein, Senior Fellow at Brookings.

and the number of intruders destroyed is given by:

$$K = A - S = DA \left[1 - (1 - p)^{\frac{I}{DA}} \right] \qquad (2\text{-}2)$$

Guiding Principles for Designing a Single Passive Defense Unit

For the defense planner with a limited budget, there are three options available for improving defense efficacy:

1. Increase the number of interceptors, I.
2. Raise detection capability, D.
3. Improve single shot probability of kill, p.

Henceforth we normalize the total number of attackers to 100. Figures 2-2 and 2-3 show the number of surviving intruders as a function of the total interceptor capability of the system for various "plausible" values of D and p. While constructing Figure 2-2, the detection capability of the defensive system is held constant at 70 percent, while the kill probability is allowed to range from 0.2 to 0.8.

Figure 2-3 holds the single shot kill probability fixed at 0.5 and varies the detection capacity of the system from 0.2 to 0.8

An examination of the figures suggests that the defender can occupy three states with respect to the total number of deployed interceptors:

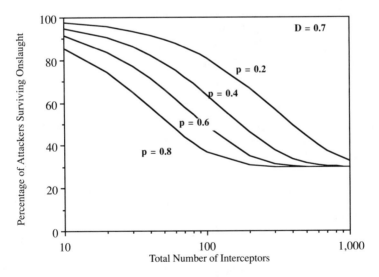

Figure 2-2 Number of Attackers Surviving as a Function of the Number of Defending Interceptors for Various Kill Probabilities

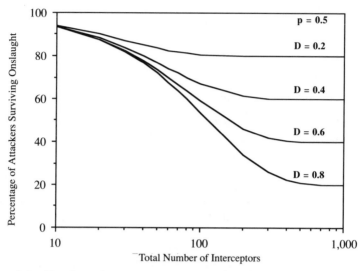

Figure 2-3   Number of Attackers Surviving as a Function of the Number of Defending Interceptors for Various Detection Capabilities

1. I << A. The number of interceptors is significantly less than the expected number of attackers. This corresponds to the region around I = 10 in our curves above.

2. I ≈ A. The number of interceptors and intruders is equal. This is the section of the x-axis surrounding I = 100.

3. I >> A. The number of interceptors is much larger than the number of attackers. This situation is reflected in the area at the extreme right of our graphs, namely I = 1000.

If the passive defense is in the first state, (I << A), the most significant improvement in effectiveness can be achieved by increasing the number of deployed interceptors. Without more interceptors, other steps are futile. For instance, improving kill probability would destroy more attackers, but the improvement would be marginal because there are not enough interceptors available to exploit the increase in kill probability. Similarly improving detection capabilities at low deployment levels is useless since even poor detection exposes more attackers to interception than there are interceptors deployed.

The scenario for an abundance of interceptors, (I >> A), is also straightforward. If each detected attacker is subjected to a barrage of interceptors, the kill probability of an individual interceptor is no longer the bottleneck variable, since despite a low one-on-one success rate, the attacker will still be incapacitated provided it encounters a large number of interceptors. Rather than increasing kill probability, the defender should improve the detection threshold of the system. As evident from Figure 2-3, for high interceptor deployment levels the efficacy of the defense system is limited by its detection capability. This is intuitively reasonable since there is a redundancy of available interceptors, and the higher the number of detected infiltrators, the more efficiently the interceptors can be allocated.

The situation for median levels of interceptor deployment, $(I \approx A)$, is slightly more involved. As expected, the defense efficiency increases for improvements in all three directions: I, p and D. However, if the defense is equipped with a poor detection network, it is inefficient to increase I since the greatest marginal benefit in terms of attackers shot down can be derived by improving detection capability. On the other hand, if the system possesses a sophisticated surveillance network, the optimal defense strategy would be to capitalize on the superior intelligence by increasing interceptor deployment. With regard to the kill probability, a diminishing marginal return limitation applies but in a weaker form. For the same percentage increase in p and I, it is generally preferable to relinquish the increase in interceptor deployment for the improvement in p, except at very high levels of kill probability such as $p \geq 0.9$. However, developing the technology to raise the kill probability is usually far more expensive and laborious than duplicating existing electronics to increase I. Thus, when confronted by a stiff budget constraint, it might still be desirable to eschew the investment in research and development needed to enhance the kill probability in favor of producing more "assembly-line" interceptors. The following table summarizes our rules for passive defense design.[4]

Current situation[†]	Test variable[‡]	Optimal decision[¶]
I << A	Is I low ?	Increase I
I >> A	Is D low ?	Increase D
I ≈ A	Is D low ?	Increase D
	Is D medium to high ?	Increase I
	Is p low to medium ?	Increase p
	Is p high ?	Increase I

[†]The current situation column locates the defense planner along the spectrum of choices for interceptor deployment.

[‡]The test variable poses the critical question that the system designer must ask herself.

[¶]The optimal decision category provides the response that will maximize defense effectiveness measured as the proportion of attackers annihilated.

---

[4]In its most general form, the problem of designing a single passive defense module to maximize the percentage of incoming intruders annihilated is a maximization problem

Connecting Passive Defense Modules: Parallel vs. Cascade

So far we have concentrated on establishing a set of rules that will maximize the efficiency of a single passive defense system. We now address the problem of how several such individual systems should be interconnected to create a comprehensive layer of defense. We shall treat each individual system as an independently functioning module. Systems theory defines two basic forms of interconnection[5] between independent systems: parallel and cascade. In parallel alignment, systems are linked so that all subsystems simultaneously access the incoming signal and process it concomitantly. The net result of the parallel processor is the sum of the outputs generated by each individual component. In contrast, for systems implemented in cascade, the input signal or trigger is processed sequentially by each individual module; the subsystems are linked end to end, and the input to the series cascade is initially fed to the foremost subsystem along the chain. The output of the first subsystem is the input to the second subsystem, whose output, in turn, constitutes the input for the third component and so on. The net result of the cascade processing is identical to the output of the last subprocessor in the hierarchy. Figures 2-4.1 and 2-4.2 are pictorial visualizations of the concept of parallel and cascade systems.

---

with a budget constraint. The designer's objective is to choose p, D and I/A so as to maximize K/A, where K is the number of attackers destroyed by the passive defense. Simultaneously, the designer is constricted by a budget constraint, $F(p,D,I/A) = Q$, which limits total spending to Q and forces the designer to trade off increases in p, D and I/A against one another. Thus designing an individual passive defense unit requires:

$$\underset{p,D,\frac{I}{A}}{\mathrm{Max}} \left[\frac{K}{A}\right]$$

with the constraint:

$$F\left(p,D,\frac{I}{A}\right) - Q = 0$$

The Lagrangian for this constrained maximization problem is:

$$\Lambda = D\left[1-(1-p)^{\frac{I}{DA}}\right] - \lambda\left[F\left(p,D,\frac{I}{A}\right) - Q\right]$$

where λ is the Lagrange multiplier. The optimal values of p, D and I/A can be determined by taking the partial derivatives of Λ with respect to p, D and I/A and equating them to zero.

---

[5]There are more complicated forms of interconnection between independent systems, such as *feedback loops,* which are not relevant to our discussion of passive defense design.

INPUT

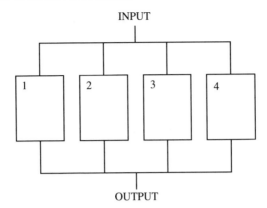

OUTPUT

Figure 2-4.1 Parallel System Interconnection. Blocks denote independently functioning modules.

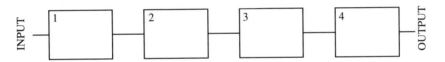

Figure 2-4.2 Cascade System Interconnection. Blocks denote independently functioning modules.

Consider our prototype passive defense system with a total of I interceptors, a detection capability D and a single shot probability of kill p. This system can be divided into two independent systems with interceptor loads I_1 and I_2 such that the sum of I_1 and I_2 equals I. We can apply our two paradigms of system interconnection to the two components of our passive defense. The two subsystems might be linked in parallel; this is identical to operating as a single defense system of interception strength $I_1 + I_2 = I$. Let S represent the attacking force strength surviving at the completion of the passage of A attackers through a parallel defense implementation. Then S is determined as in Equation 2-1.

$$S = (1 - D)A + DA(1 - p)^{\frac{I}{DA}} \qquad (2\text{-}3)$$

Alternatively, the two modules might be juxtaposed in cascade; thus the A attacking bodies will first encounter the component with I_1 interceptors. The survivors of this initial barrage, S_1, will then face the second defense module equipped with I_2 interceptors, yielding a net surviving complement of S_2. The expressions for S_1 and S_2 follow immediately from our previous discussion.

$$S_1 = (1-D)A + DA(1-p)^{\frac{I_1}{DA}} \qquad \qquad \text{(2-4)}$$

$$S_2 = (1-D)S_1 + DS_1(1-p)^{\frac{I_2}{DS_1}} \qquad \qquad \text{(2-5)}$$

$$\text{where } I_1 + I_2 = I$$

We would recommend a cascade interconnection of the systems, provided the number of attackers that escaped the cascade defense, S_2, was less than the number of attackers emerging unscathed from the parallel defense, S. Our advice to the defense planner would be reversed if S_2 exceeded S. We shall not present a general mathematical proof of the relationship between S_2 and S, but we do note the results of a graphical analysis performed in Appendix 2A.[6]

$$\text{1. } S_2 \leq S \; \forall \; p, D, I : A \text{ and } I_1 : I_2.$$

S_2 is *never* more than S. It is always preferable to interconnect passive defense systems in cascade. When compared to a parallel implementation, a cascade connection is at least equally efficient in destroying attackers and in most cases, offers a higher attrition of the offensive force.

$$\text{2. Let } S - S_2 = \Delta S. \text{ Then } \Delta S \text{ increases with increasing } I : A.$$

The benefits from a cascade configuration are greater for a larger overall interceptor to attacker ratio. Thus when a defense designer is confronted with a fixed number of attackers, the need to adopt a cascade system increases with rising deployment levels of the interception vehicle.

$$\text{3. Defense efficiency is maximized by choosing } I_1 : I_2 = 1.$$

To maximize the percentage of intruders annihilated, it is optimal to split the interceptor load equally between the two cascaded passive defense systems.

While Appendix 2A derives these relationships only for the interconnection between two passive defense subsystems, the generalization to an unspecified or indefinite number of passive defense components follows immediately. Defense effectiveness is maximized by deploying a total interceptor load of I as two equally armed defensive systems of strength I/2 in cascade. Applying the identical logic to each constituent system of strength I/2 suggests that even greater destruction will be achieved if both subsystems are themselves organized as two cascade-connected components each armed with I/4 interceptors.

---

[6]Appendix 2A uses a heuristic graphical approach to determine whether two independent passive defense modules should be connected in parallel or in cascade to maximize attacker attrition.

This 4-component chain composed of I/4-strong independent interception systems should, by the same logic, be replaced by an 8-component linkage of I/8-strong passive defense systems. The 8-component system, in turn, should be discarded in favor of a 16-tuple of I/16-strong interception units; in the limit, each interceptor would be an independent passive defense system, and the overall interceptor defense would be structured as the interconnection of I interceptors in cascade.

Each passive defense system operates in a rigid succession of three time-ordered phases: detection, allocation and interception. The invaders trespassing in the system space are detected, the total interception supply of the system is allocated among the detected infiltrators and the interceptors are dispatched on a collision course with their intended target. When we forge a cascade connection between passive defense systems, we essentially interpose detection and allocation phases between the phases of interception. After the dispatch of the interception load of the first defense system, a certain fraction of the attackers will be destroyed or incapacitated. Redetecting the residual invaders and reallocating interceptors among them before dispatching the next contingent of interceptors ensures that no interceptors are wasted on infiltrators that have already been destroyed. The more frequently the redetection-reallocation procedure is interspersed with phases of interception, the smaller is the loss of defensive resources through misallocation or superfluous assignment to previously exterminated invaders. Herein lies the strength and power of cascade defensive structures.

Cascade Interconnection and Deployment in Depth

Cascade interconnection dictates that the optimal structure for a passive defense is to decompose the detect-allocate-intercept system into the smallest possible modules and to deploy the modules in succession. When applied to ground warfare, cascade interconnection is an argument for force dispersion and deployment in depth. Using our bunker defense as an example, cascade interconnection requires the dispersion of the total lethality of the bunker force among as large a number of bunkers as is economically and technologically feasible. Connection in cascade translates into the condition that each successive bunker be confronted with the residual attacking lethality left after previous defensive actions. Cascade implementation thus spreads the bunkers as far inward from the demarcation line as possible. There is a fundamental difference between what dictates the separation of bunkers parallel to the front and what determines the displacement of bunkers orthogonal to the front. The distance between neighboring bunkers along the front is dictated purely by the range of the deployed weaponry, the maximum allowed separation between adjacent units being constrained by the requirement that their firing ranges overlap at the edges. Thus if R is the minimum of the range of the interception vehicles and

Figure 2-5.1   Parallel Realization of a Dispersed Bunker Defense. The large shaded circles represent the range of the deployed interceptors. The number at the center of each circle indicates the quantity of interceptors deployed at the point. To cover the length of the front the distance between bunkers measured parallel to the front cannot exceed twice the range of an interceptor. This minimum front coverage requirement holds for both parallel and cascade bunker defenses. In a parallel implementation, all interceptors are based as far forward as possible.

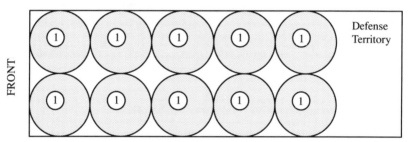

Figure 2-5.2   Cascade Realization of a Dispersed Bunker Defense. Each bunker is armed with a single interceptor. Bunkers are positioned one behind the other orthogonally inward from the front. A cascade implementation produces maximum dispersion and inward displacement of the interceptor defense.

detection net, the maximum distance between bunkers along the border can be 2R. The minimum number of bunkers required along a front of length M is M/2R. Parallel implementation of a passive bunker defense would divide all interceptors equally among the M/2R bunkers deployed along the front as shown in Figure 2-5.1.

Conversely, a cascade force structure demands the dispersal of firepower in a linear progression orthogonally inward from the front. Thus if the defense possesses a total of I interceptors, the ideal cascade implementation would disperse the I interceptors among I bunkers and locate the bunkers in strips of M/2R passive force elements parallel to the front. The total number of such parallel strips would be $I/(M/2R) = 2IR/M$. Bunkers positioned in the strip nearest to the border would initiate the attack on the invading force elements. Bunkers belonging to the second strip would be confronted by the residual attacking forces that survive the first onslaught. Similarly, bunkers in the third strip would be faced with the offensive lethality that manages to survive the bombardment of the second strip and so on. The passive bunker defense would thus be organized as a rectangle of force, with a length of $2IR/M$ bases and a width of $M/2R$ bases. A cascade implementation is depicted for the scenario where $M = 4R$ and $I = 10$ in Figure 2-5.2.

A second formidable reason for dispersing passive defense forces over a large number of bases, which is independent of the choice of a parallel or cascade passive defense implementation, is to lower the attractiveness to the aggressor of incapacitating an individual base. The smaller and more inconspicuous a base, the more difficult it is for the offense to pinpoint. The cheaper and less armed an individual passive defense module, the lower is the invader's gain from wiping it out.

In conclusion, acceptance of the optimality of cascade implementation is an argument for the maximum dispersion of passive defense lethality and its deployment in depth. It is striking how a forward-deployed defensive force geometry, namely a parallel implementation of passive defense, is inefficient in imposing the greatest attrition on the invading forces. In Part One we came to the conclusion that for a force structure consisting of conventional mobile fighting units, basing defending units as close to the front as possible does not minimize the infiltration of the aggressor into defense terrain. Once again we find that for passive defense systems, parallel implementation, or the physical forward basing of lethality, is a misguided approach to the optimal utilization of defensive force and does not maximize attacking force casualties.

Drawbacks of Cascade Interconnection

We might conclude that all passive defense systems should be structured as linear cascades of maximum chain length. However cascade defense has its drawbacks. There are hidden trade-offs in the adoption of a cascade defense that have not been explicitly explored thus far. An obvious drawback of intensive cascading is the cost of multiple detection-allocation systems. While the quantity of interception vehicles deployed is unaffected by the choice between a parallel or cascade defense implementation, the number of required detection-allocation phases increases linearly with the length of the implemented cascade. For instance, each bunker in our dispersed, remote-controlled ground defense requires its own detection-surveillance web and firing control apparatus. There is a compensating trade-off, though, in that each individual detection network for the cascade defense may be only a fraction of the huge reconnaissance net necessary to cover the entire border if all bunkers were lumped into a single

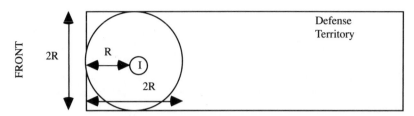

Figure 2-6   Parallel Realization of a Bunker Defense along a Front of Length 2R. All I interceptors are positioned at the center of a circle of radius R. The circle is tangential to the midpoint of the front.

parallel defense. In some cases, such as an air defense system, it might be feasible to call upon the same detection-allocation system to guide each individual surface-to-air missile allocation. However even cascade systems that surmount the obstacle of multiple detection-allocation layers are subject to a second shortcoming.

Each detection-allocation cycle requires a finite amount of processing time and adds to the lag in defense response to the invasion. The delay caused by each redetection and reallocation routine allows the invaders to penetrate further into the defender's space. This might be fatal if the strategic objective of the invader is simply to gain a limited penetration into the enemy's territory. For example, a bombing air raid not destroyed or rebuffed by the air defense before it reaches its target will render the defense a failure irrespective of how many enemy aircraft are shot down. For our dispersed bunker defense, connection in cascade translates to a deployment in depth. A cascade implementation, while it destroys more invaders and thus exacts a higher cumulative price from the offense, permits deeper infiltrations into defense territory as a result of the lower density of interceptors up front along the border between the two sides.

For a bunker defense the depth of the invader's incursion permitted by a parallel implementation is easily compared with the corresponding infiltration allowed by a cascade implementation. If R is the lesser of the range of the interception vehicles and the radius of the detection web, then a parallel implementation of a passive defense deployed along a front of length 2R would simply base all I interceptors at the center of a circle of radius R tangential to the front at its midpoint as depicted in Figure 2-6.

The quantum of offensive lethality destroyed by the parallel defense is given by:

$$K = DA \left[1 - (1 - p)^{\frac{I}{DA}} \right] \tag{2-6}$$

Thus the parallel form of passive defense succeeds in inflicting K casualties on the invading hordes while restricting the advance to 2R.

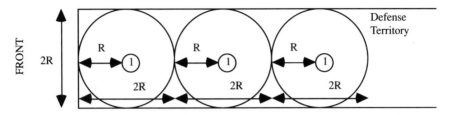

Figure 2-7 Cascade Realization of a Bunker Defense with Maximum Dispersion along a Front of Length 2R. Each circle of radius R houses a single interception vehicle at its center.

Next consider the cascade implementation of an I-interceptor passive defense deployed to protect a front of length 2R. In the extreme case of maximum force dispersion, the cascade will be organized as a linear chain of I single interceptor units with ranges that overlap at the edges. The first bunker will be located at the center of a circle of radius R tangential to the front at its midpoint. The second bunker will be based at a distance $2R + R = 3R$ from the demarcation line and halfway along the length of the frontier. The third bunker will be positioned at $4R + R = 5R$ from the front and also halfway along the front and so on. Each bunker will house exactly one interceptor. The Ith and final bunker will be deployed at a distance of $2(I - 1)R + R = (2I - 1)R$ from the front. The anterior portion of the cascade defense is sketched in Figure 2-7.

The invading lethality incapacitated by the first bunker is given by:

$$K_1 = DA\left[1 - (1-p)^{\frac{1}{DA}}\right] \tag{2-7}$$

The offensive force that survives the onslaught of the first bunker is $A - K_1$ and represents the invading force trespassing on the domain of the second bunker. The attacking force neutralized by the second bunker is given by:

$$K_2 = D\left(A - K_1\right)\left[1 - (1-p)^{\frac{1}{D\left(A - K_1\right)}}\right] \tag{2-8}$$

The third bunker is faced with $A - K_1 - K_2$ invaders. Passage of the attacking force through the region controlled by the third bunker forces K_3 losses on the invader, where K_3 is determined by the following equation.

$$K_3 = D\left(A - K_1 - K_2\right)\left[1 - (1-p)^{\frac{1}{D\left(A - K_1 - K_2\right)}}\right] \tag{2-9}$$

The general expression for the invading lethality destroyed by the ith cascade defense element follows immediately.

$$K_i = D\left(A - \sum_{j=1}^{j=i-1} K_j\right)\left[1 - (1-p)^{\overline{D\left(A - \sum_{j=1}^{j=i-1} K_j\right)}}\right] \qquad \textbf{(2-10)}$$

How far is the attacker able to penetrate into defense terrain before the attacker's cumulative attrition equals the casualties that would have been imposed by a parallel implementation? To answer this question let N be the number of layers of back-to-back cascaded defense elements that the offense manages to infiltrate before suffering cumulative attrition of K. (K is the total attacker attrition inflicted by a parallel implementation and is summarized by Equation 2-7 above.) Then N is the smallest integer that makes the following inequality true.

$$\sum_{i=1}^{i=N} K_i \geq K \qquad \textbf{(2-11)}$$

ΣK_i is the cumulative attrition of the attacking forces after passage through N layers of a cascade implementation and can be expressed in terms of the individual K_is as follows.

$$\sum_{i=1}^{i=N} K_i = \sum_{i=1}^{i=N} D\left(A - \sum_{j=1}^{j=i-1} K_j\right)\left[1 - (1-p)^{\overline{D\left(A - \sum_{j=1}^{j=i-1} K_j\right)}}\right] \qquad \textbf{(2-12)}$$

N measures how much farther the attacker, when subjected to the same attrition, is able to penetrate against a cascade implementation of passive defense when compared with a parallel implementation.

Below we examine graphically the relationship between the relative penetration of defense terrain, N, and the three fundamental parameters of passive defense, namely, I, p and D. We assume throughout that the total number of attackers is 100. As before there are three scenarios of interest with respect to I, namely, I:A = 0.1, I:A = 1 and I:A = 10. Figure 2-8 depicts the relative infiltration achieved by the invader for the case of I = 0.1A. It is assumed that the cascade defense is organized as a 10-component system of bunkers positioned end to end orthogonally inward from the front, and each bunker holds exactly 1 interception vehicle.

Figure 2-9 graphs N for the scenario of I = A. While plotting the figure, it is assumed that the cascade implementation of the passive defense is organized as a linear chain of 10 bunkers with each bunker housing 10 interceptors. The number of bunkers is limited to 10 as opposed to the most dispersed force geometry of a 100 bunkers, each armed with one interception vehicle, in order to maintain comparability between the I = 0.1A and the I = A cases.

Figure 2-10 diagrams the relative penetration, N, for the I = 10A situation. In analogy with the I = 0.1A and the I = A cases, the total number of bunkers

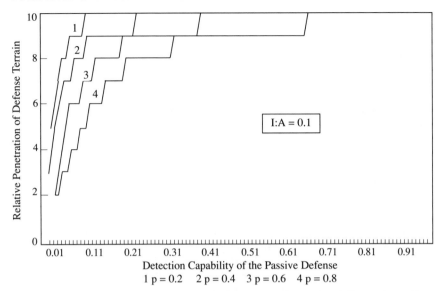

Figure 2-8 Relative Penetration of Defense Terrain by the Offense for a Cascade Implementation as Compared with a Parallel Implementation for Identical Attacker Attrition. The relative penetration is calculated as a function of D for the case of I:A=0.1 for various values of p.

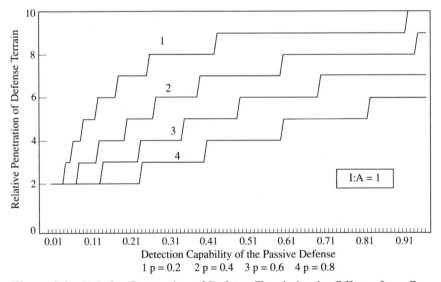

Figure 2-9 Relative Penetration of Defense Terrain by the Offense for a Cascade Implementation as Compared with a Parallel Implementation for Identical Attacker Attrition. The relative penetration is calculated a function of D for the case of I:A=1 for a range of values of p.

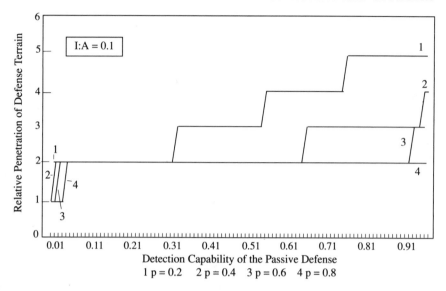

Figure 2-10 Relative Penetration of Defense Terrain by the Offense for a Cascade Implementation as Compared with a Parallel Implementation for Identical Attacker Attrition. The relative penetration is calculated as a function of D for the case of I:A=10 for various values of p.

for the cascade implementation is restricted to 10 and each bunker constitutes the base for 100 interceptors. Note the different y-axis scales for Figures 2-8, 2-9 and 2-10.

The following conclusions are immediately drawn from the graphical analysis above:

1. For the same attacker attrition, the relative penetration, N, accomplished against a cascade passive defense implementation can be significantly greater than the infiltration against a parallel implementation.

2. N decreases with increases in p and I:A. N increases with increases in D. In other words, the relative penetration of the invading legions into defense territory is lower with a high overall ratio of total interceptors and large single shot probability of kill. The relative ingress of the aggressor into the defender's homeland is greater if the passive defense possesses a sophisticated detection capability.

3. Passive defenses with the characteristics shown in the following table should be structured as relatively concentrated cascade defenses with all available interceptors distributed equally among a *few* cascaded layers.

Interceptor : Attacker ratio	Detection capability D	Probability of kill p
I << A		
I ≈ A	D high	
	D low	p low
I >> A	D high	p low

It is sensible to frontload the defensive force geometry in these cases to prevent too muck leakage of offensive lethality through the preliminary layers of the cascaded passive defense.

    4. Passive defense systems that display the following values of I, D and p are best structured as widely dispersed cascade implementations with the total interceptor contingent distributed over a *large number* of cascaded layers.

Interceptor : Attacker ratio	Detection capability D	Probability of kill p
I ≈ A	D low	p high
I >> A		p medium to high
	D low	p low

For these passive defenses a single element of the cascade is almost as effective as the entire parallel force structure in inflicting casualties on the invader. Thus defenses with the above characteristics might be dispersed over a large number of bases without fear of permitting excessive offensive lethality to make deep inroads into defense territory.

    What depth of penetration by the offense is acceptable to the defender clearly depends on the defender's aversion to the loss of home terrain and to the defender's desire to inflict attrition on the invader. A more cascaded deployment of the passive defense elements leads to greater cumulative attrition of the attacker; however, it also permits a larger segment of the invading legions to penetrate deep into defense terrain. The trade-off between the benefits of cascading and the costs of accepting deep incursions can be summarized by comparing the *attrition profiles* of the aggressor for various degrees of cascading. The attrition profile measures surviving attacking lethality as a function of distance penetrated by the offense into the defender's homeland. Figure 2-11 depicts the prototypical attrition profiles for a parallel and a cascade defense.

    It is evident from the figure that offensive penetration beyond the break-even infiltration is better dealt with by a cascade defense because of the cascade's ability to inflict higher cumulative attrition on the invading forces. On the contrary, if the invader's master plan is simply to capture and occupy defense territory within the confines of the break-even penetration, a parallel defense would be more effective. What degree of cascading is appropriate for a

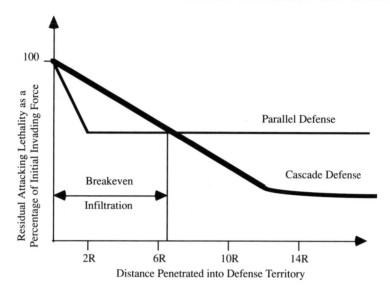

Figure 2-11   Attrition Profile of the Attacker versus a Parallel and a Cascade Passive Defense. The y-axis measures the surviving attacking lethality as a percentage of the invading force that initiates the onslaught. The breakeven infiltration is the distance at which the attrition imposed by the cascade defense equals the attrition exacted by the parallel defense. Beyond the breakeven infiltration, a cascade implementation outperforms a parallel defense.

particular defender is therefore a function of which attrition profile the defending commander wishes to impose on an advancing aggressor.

The third somewhat unrealistic assumption that is intrinsic to our development of passive defense is that we have not allowed for the possibility of counterattack by the invaders. The passive defense system has no monopoly on the capability to destroy enemy forces. The intelligence and command and control apparatus that implements the detection and allocation algorithms of the passive defense can be castrated by the offense either prior to or concurrent with an incursionary attempt. The launch mechanisms and interception vehicles can themselves be incapacitated in a counterattack. In part, it is because of this implicit acceptance of the invulnerability of the passive defense elements that we have arrived at an optimal force structure for passive defense involving maximum dispersion of the individual firepower units. This dispersed defense philosophy is radically opposed to the usually promulgated conventional force doctrine, such as the Lanchester Square Law, of relying on local force concentration. The ideal structure for our passive defense spreads interceptors out in a gigantic cascade and requires that a single defending vehicle be launched at the invaders at any one time. We assume that each individual bunker is a relatively inconspicuous, hardened and mechanically reinforced structure, which requires considerable effort and expense on the part of the invader to locate and incapacitate. Further, the benefit to the aggressor of incapacitating a single bunker is miniscule because the interceptor contingent housed by any one bunker is very small and the total interceptor force is dispersed over a large multitude of bunkers. With this visualization of a passive defense, the consequences of counterattack are negligible. In sharp contrast to this one-by-one engagement philosophy, if the combat between passive defense elements and the invading spearhead exhibits even traces of Lanchester Square type and certain other Lanchester types of force-on-force attrition, we would advocate a joint, concerted onslaught simultaneously conducted by all defensive force elements. In a Lanchester Square universe a defensive strategy of dispatching a single interceptor to each individual encounter with the invader would be foolhardy as the numerically inferior defending concentrations would be cheaply exterminated by the superior offense. Thus, while it is reasonable to ignore the consequences of counterattrition on some of the passive defense systems we have conceptualized, one must keep in mind that there could be a limit on total dispersion if counterattack were significant and obeyed certain Lanchester type formulations.

The Implications of Counterattack for Distributed Defense

To explore the consequences of counterattack on passive defense systems let us introduce a distributed defense system in which the defense is highly susceptible to a counterattack by the invading legions. The real-world analog of our modified passive defense with counterattrition could be a defense composed of small, rapidly mobilized, highly mobile, fighting squads armed with light weaponry, which would race to the scene of invasion and delay the advancing enemy columns until defending armored divisions arrived. The fighting squads could be manned by trained reserves who are native to the border regions and who would be ideally positioned to engage an intruder immediately and could relay their early reconnaissance to the defending central command. From a macro perspective the defender is scattered along the entire length of the front in small discrete units. Each unit has a limited range of mobility as a consequence of its lightly armored, improvised means of ground transport and is vulnerable to attack by the enemy. Such a defense is passive and nonoffensive since the dispersed, lightly armored scouting units can hardly be expected to lead a diehard invasion of a neighbor's well-defended homeland. At the same time our border patrol defense is by its very nature distributed all over the region adjoining the front in small, local concentrations; the defending warriors are inhabitants of the border districts who have the misfortune of waking up one morning to find a full-fledged incursionary expedition in their backyard. Finally, the border civilians who bravely engage the inimical invader are not blessed with minimal counterattrition. Quite likely these defending soldiers will be wiped out long before the fully mobilized infantry and armored divisions and close air support of the defense arrive to contain the advancing columns. In brief, our border patrol is a distributed passive defense with significant problems of counterattack.

The next question to be addressed is what is an appropriate model for the interaction in battle between each fighting squad and the invading lethality. Let us assume very generally that the instantaneous rate of decay of each side's lethality in combat is a fixed function of the instantaneous firepowers of the two sides. The relationship between the rate of change of lethality at any point in time and the instantaneous firepowers of the two sides at that time is fixed in the sense that it retains the same functional form for the entire duration of the battle. Then letting $R(t)$ and $B(t)$ represent the engaged lethalities of the two sides in combat at time t, and r and b represent the combat effectiveness, or force utilization coefficients per unit, of the two sides respectively, the attrition of the combatants is described by the following rules.

$$\left.\begin{array}{l} \dfrac{dR}{dt} = -b\,B^{\lambda_1}\,R^{\lambda_2} \\[2mm] \dfrac{dB}{dt} = -r\,R^{\lambda_3}\,B^{\lambda_4} \end{array}\right\} \qquad \text{(2-13)}$$

This is the general Lanchester family of equations where λ_1, λ_2, λ_3 and λ_4 are constants. Different values of the λs correspond to different Lanchester models of combat. The incremental losses on either side are in proportion to the instantaneous aggregated firepower of each adversary raised to the appropriate power of λ. We are assuming that the interaction between the dispersed passive defense units and the attacking concentration of lethality can be described by a generalized Lanchester formulation not because of any conviction on our part that the actual conflict will display Lanchester behavior. Rather, the Lanchester family of equations is an elegant and mathematically tractable expression of the attrition process in battle and is of great convenience to us in understanding the effect of counterattack on distributed defense. Besides, we have adopted the most general form of the Lanchester differential equations, and all we are really claiming is that the attrition of each side in battle is influenced by the engaged lethalities of the two contestants.

The state equation for the general Lanchester family is easily derived.

$$\frac{dR}{dB} = \frac{b}{r}\,B^{\lambda_1-\lambda_4}\,R^{\lambda_2-\lambda_3} \qquad \text{(2-14)}$$

where dR/dB is the instantaneous casualty exchange ratio. Separating variables and integrating yields:

$$r \int_{R(0)}^{R(t)} R^{\lambda_3-\lambda_2}\,dR = b \int_{B(0)}^{B(t)} B^{\lambda_1-\lambda_4}\,dB \qquad \text{(2-15)}$$

Performing the indicated integration gives the most general form of the Lanchester state equation:

$$\frac{r}{\lambda_3 - \lambda_2 + 1}\left[R(t)^{\lambda_3 - \lambda_2 + 1} - R(0)^{\lambda_3 - \lambda_2 + 1}\right]$$

$$= \frac{b}{\lambda_1 - \lambda_4 + 1}\left[B(t)^{\lambda_1 - \lambda_4 + 1} - B(0)^{\lambda_1 - \lambda_4 + 1}\right] \tag{2-16}$$

with the requirement that $\lambda_3 - \lambda_2 + 1$ not equal zero and $\lambda_1 - \lambda_4 + 1$ not equal zero.

Let B(0) represent the aggregate defensive lethality of the border patrol defense at the commencement of hostilities. B(0) is divided among K fighting squads each of strength B(0)/K. Consider a class of encounters where the border patrol defense, B, is eventually defeated. If all itinerant squads were to launch a unified, simultaneous onslaught on the invading concentration of force, then the residual offensive lethality after the culmination of the battle is determined by setting $B(t) = B(\tau) = 0$ in Equation 2-16 above.

$$\frac{r}{\lambda_3 - \lambda_2 + 1} R(\tau)^{\lambda_3 - \lambda_2 + 1} = \frac{r}{\lambda_3 - \lambda_2 + 1} R(0)^{\lambda_3 - \lambda_2 + 1} - \frac{b}{\lambda_1 - \lambda_4 + 1} B(0)^{\lambda_1 - \lambda_4 + 1} \tag{2-17}$$

On the other hand if the offense is engaged by each fighting squad of lethality B(0)/K in strict succession, then the fighting force of the invader surviving the first defending echelon, $R(\tau 1)$, is given by:

$$\frac{r}{\lambda_3 - \lambda_2 + 1} R(\tau 1)^{\lambda_3 - \lambda_2 + 1} = \frac{r}{\lambda_3 - \lambda_2 + 1} R(0)^{\lambda_3 - \lambda_2 + 1}$$

$$- \frac{b}{\lambda_1 - \lambda_4 + 1}\left[\frac{B(0)}{K}\right]^{\lambda_1 - \lambda_4 + 1} \tag{2-18}$$

Analogously, the residual attacking strength after the second encounter with a border patrol squad, $R(\tau 2)$, is determined as:

$$\frac{r}{\lambda_3 - \lambda_2 + 1} R(\tau 2)^{\lambda_3 - \lambda_2 + 1} = \frac{r}{\lambda_3 - \lambda_2 + 1} R(\tau 1)^{\lambda_3 - \lambda_2 + 1}$$

$$- \frac{b}{\lambda_1 - \lambda_4 + 1}\left[\frac{B(0)}{K}\right]^{\lambda_1 - \lambda_4 + 1} \tag{2-19}$$

Substituting the expression for $R(\tau 1)$ from Equation 2-18 into the formula for $R(\tau 2)$ in Equation 2-19 results in:

$$\frac{r}{\lambda_3 - \lambda_2 + 1} R(\tau 2)^{\lambda_3 - \lambda_2 + 1} = \frac{r}{\lambda_3 - \lambda_2 + 1} R(0)^{\lambda_3 - \lambda_2 + 1}$$

$$- 2\frac{b}{\lambda_1 - \lambda_4 + 1}\left[\frac{B(0)}{K}\right]^{\lambda_1 - \lambda_4 + 1} \tag{2-20}$$

We may generalize immediately to the expression for the residual offensive lethality at the conclusion of the Kth and final encounter, $R(\tau K)$.

$$\frac{r}{\lambda_3 - \lambda_2 + 1} R(\tau K)^{\lambda_3 - \lambda_2 + 1} = \frac{r}{\lambda_3 - \lambda_2 + 1} R(0)^{\lambda_3 - \lambda_2 + 1}$$

$$- K \frac{b}{\lambda_1 - \lambda_4 + 1} \left[\frac{B(0)}{K} \right]^{\lambda_1 - \lambda_4 + 1}$$

$$\frac{r}{\lambda_3 - \lambda_2 + 1} R(\tau K)^{\lambda_3 - \lambda_2 + 1} = \frac{r}{\lambda_3 - \lambda_2 + 1} R(0)^{\lambda_3 - \lambda_2 + 1}$$

$$- K^{\lambda_4 - \lambda_1} \frac{b}{\lambda_1 - \lambda_4 + 1} B(0)^{\lambda_1 - \lambda_4 + 1} \qquad (2\text{-}21)$$

Under what circumstances will a dispersed defense produce greater cumulative attrition of the invading forces than a concentrated defense? This is exactly the question we posed at the beginning of Part Two which led us to choose a cascade defense over a parallel defense. Our advocacy of a cascade defense, however, did not take into account the possibility of counterattrition of the passive defense elements. The war framework based on the general Lanchester family of equations that has been advanced above explicitly accounts for counterattack by the offense and allows us to revisit the question of which defensive force geometry is most effective in imposing attrition on the aggressor in the context of counterattack.

For the multiple battles engaged in by a dispersed border patrol to be more effective than a concerted onslaught by a single defensive force concentration it must be true that $R(\tau K) < R(\tau)$. Recall that $R(\tau K)$ is the offensive lethality surviving the Kth and final encounter with a dispersed border patrol defense and is given by Equation 2-21. $R(\tau)$ is the attacker's residual fighting strength at the culmination of the single engagement with an aggregated defending force and is denoted by Equation 2-17. There are four distinct cases of interest in investigating the implications of the condition $R(\tau K) < R(\tau)$ for defensive force geometry:

(1) $\lambda_3 - \lambda_2 + 1 > 0$ and $\lambda_1 - \lambda_4 + 1 > 0$
(2) $\lambda_3 - \lambda_2 + 1 > 0$ and $\lambda_1 - \lambda_4 + 1 < 0$
(3) $\lambda_3 - \lambda_2 + 1 < 0$ and $\lambda_1 - \lambda_4 + 1 > 0$
(4) $\lambda_3 - \lambda_2 + 1 < 0$ and $\lambda_1 - \lambda_4 + 1 < 0$

For illustrative purposes we work through the first case, $\lambda_3 - \lambda_2 + 1 > 0$ and $\lambda_1 - \lambda_4 + 1 > 0$, below. The requirement $R(\tau K) < R(\tau)$ translates mathematically to:

$$\frac{r}{\lambda_3 - \lambda_2 + 1} R(\tau K)^{\lambda_3 - \lambda_2 + 1} < \frac{r}{\lambda_3 - \lambda_2 + 1} R(\tau)^{\lambda_3 - \lambda_2 + 1} \qquad (2\text{-}22)$$

Using Equations 2-17 and 2-21:

$$\frac{r}{\lambda_3 - \lambda_2 + 1} R(0)^{\lambda_3 - \lambda_2 + 1} - K^{\lambda_4 - \lambda_1} \frac{b}{\lambda_1 - \lambda_4 + 1} B(0)^{\lambda_1 - \lambda_4 + 1}$$

$$< \frac{r}{\lambda_3 - \lambda_2 + 1} R(0)^{\lambda_3 - \lambda_2 + 1} - \frac{b}{\lambda_1 - \lambda_4 + 1} B(0)^{\lambda_1 - \lambda_4 + 1} \qquad (2\text{-}23)$$

Eliminating common terms on either side of the inequality yields:

$$K^{\lambda_4 - \lambda_1} > 1 \qquad (2\text{-}24)$$

Taking the natural logarithm of both sides:

$$(\lambda_4 - \lambda_1) \ln(K) > 0 \qquad (2\text{-}25)$$

For a dispersed defense K must be greater than 1, implying ln (K) > 0. Dividing both sides of Equation 2-25 by ln (K) gives the condition under which a dispersed defense outperforms its concentrated counterpart.

$$\lambda_4 - \lambda_1 > 0 \qquad (2\text{-}26)$$

It can easily be shown that the identical condition for dispersed defense optimality is obtained in each of the other three cases for $\lambda_3 - \lambda_2 + 1$ and $\lambda_1 - \lambda_4 + 1$. Note that the condition for distributed defense optimality is independent of the initial force strengths of the offense and the defense, the number of discrete units into which total defensive lethality is divided, the force utilization efficacy of either combatant and the manner in which offensive force lethality enters the equations of battle. The effectiveness of defensive dispersion depends only on the manner in which the war dynamic is influenced by defensive lethality; more specifically, it depends solely on the relationship between the way in which defensive firepower causes attacker attrition and the way in which defensive force concentration causes defending losses. We may summarize our findings through the following theorem.

LANCHESTER THEOREM OF UNLIMITED DISPERSION FOR A PASSIVE DEFENSE UNDER COUNTERATTACK: *If battle between combatants is governed by the general Lanchester family of equations, namely:*

$$\frac{dR}{dt} = -b B^{\lambda_1} R^{\lambda_2}$$

$$\frac{dB}{dt} = -r R^{\lambda_3} B^{\lambda_4}$$

and if $\lambda_4 > \lambda_1$, then the cumulative attrition of the invader, R, is maximized by dispersing the defensive lethality, B, into as large a number of independent units as possible and requiring each individual unit to engage the attacker in battle separately from the other defending units.

The rate of attrition of B is related to the instantaneous engaged lethality of B through λ_4. Similarly the rate of attrition of R is related to the instantaneous engaged lethality of B through λ_1. If $\lambda_4 > \lambda_1$, all other things being equal, a larger initial value of B causes faster attrition of the defense than of the offense. Consequently dispersing the defense is in relative terms more beneficial in alleviating defensive attrition than it is less potent in imposing casualties on the offense. Hence we can observe the bias towards distributed defense evinced by Lanchester warfare with the characteristic $\lambda_4 > \lambda_1$.

The instantaneous casualty exchange ratio for the general Lanchester family of equations is given as:

$$\frac{dR}{dB} = \frac{b}{r} \frac{R^{\lambda_2 - \lambda_3}}{B^{\lambda_4 - \lambda_1}} \tag{2-27}$$

If $\lambda_4 > \lambda_1$ then the casualty exchange ratio at any point in time is a decreasing function of the engaged lethality of B at that point in time. The condition $\lambda_4 > \lambda_1$ for distributed defense optimality thus translates generally to the requirement that the attacker-to-defender casualty exchange ratio decrease with increasing defensive deployment. This result is independent of whether the engagement between the two foes is determined by the general Lanchester family of equations and is encapsulated below.

GENERAL THEOREM OF UNLIMITED DISPERSION FOR A PASSIVE DEFENSE UNDER COUNTERATTACK: *If the attacker-to-defender casualty exchange ratio between two combatants decreases with increasing engaged defensive lethality, then the cumulative attrition of the aggressor is maximized by dividing the aggregate defensive lethality into as large a number of discrete units as possible and requiring each individual unit to engage the attacker in battle separately from the other defending units.*

Choosing between a concentrated and a distributed force geometry for a defender subject to counterattack is actually an assessment of the nature of the casualty exchange function likely to prevail in battle. If the ratio of attacker-to-defender casualties increases with increasing defensive deployment, a concentrated defense will maximize attacking attrition; on the contrary, if the casualty exchange ratio displays a decreasing relationship with increasing concentration of engaged defensive lethality, the optimal defending force structure is one of maximum dispersion. The ideal defensive force geometry is independent of all other battle parameters such as the attacker's initial force strength.

Is it at all possible for the defender to disperse forces in a universe where the casualty exchange ratio increases with increasing defensive force deployment? The defense can afford to distribute its forces even if $\lambda_4 < \lambda_1$ provided the defense has superior overall effective lethality. Overall effective lethality is simply total firepower including the force utilization coefficient as it enters the state equation. Thus the overall effective lethality of side B for the general Lanchester family of equations is

$$\frac{b}{\lambda_1 - \lambda_4 + 1} B(0)^{\lambda_1 - \lambda_4 + 1}$$

and the analogous overall effective lethality of side R is given by

$$\frac{r}{\lambda_3 - \lambda_2 + 1} R(0)^{\lambda_3 - \lambda_2 + 1}$$

A preliminary constraint imposed in situations where $\lambda_4 < \lambda_1$ is that only the side with a higher overall effective lethality enjoys the luxury of force dispersion; that is, while no side can improve its battle performance in terms of maximizing enemy attrition by force dispersion, the combatant with higher overall effective lethality can disperse its forces to a limited extent while still ensuring a stalemate. If the assailant with superiority in effective firepower chooses not to distribute its forces and commits all firepower simultaneously to the battlefield, it would have nonzero forces remaining after destroying all the other side's lethality. To the extent that the assailant chooses to disperse its forces, it relinquishes its ability to retain residual military strength after defeating the enemy. Unlike the $\lambda_4 > \lambda_1$ scenario, the superior side in the $\lambda_4 < \lambda_1$ case does not gain anything by force distribution. In fact, it loses what it can afford to, namely, its surviving lethality after the last encounter with the foe. Therefore the maximum dispersion that the stronger fighter can afford to engage in is exactly equal to that force distribution that results in a stalemate.

Since the defender with its knowledge of defense terrain can reinforce and fortify in peacetime the points along the front where an invader might have to be confronted, we may award the defender a superiority in overall effective lethality. In the language of algebra:

$$\frac{b}{\lambda_1 - \lambda_4 + 1} B(0)^{\lambda_1 - \lambda_4 + 1} = M \frac{r}{\lambda_3 - \lambda_2 + 1} R(0)^{\lambda_3 - \lambda_2 + 1} \tag{2-28}$$

with M > 1. M is the relative superiority in overall effective lethality of the defender. Let the defense be dispersed across K identical units that engage the attacker independently in a linear progression. Each defensive echelon is B(0)/K strong. The expression for the residual attacking lethality that survives the Kth and ultimate encounter between the offense and the defense is given by Equation 2-21 derived earlier and is repeated below.

$$\frac{r}{\lambda_3 - \lambda_2 + 1} R(\tau K)^{\lambda_3 - \lambda_2 + 1} = \frac{r}{\lambda_3 - \lambda_2 + 1} R(0)^{\lambda_3 - \lambda_2 + 1}$$
$$- K^{\lambda_4 - \lambda_1} \frac{b}{\lambda_1 - \lambda_4 + 1} B(0)^{\lambda_1 - \lambda_4 + 1} \tag{2-29}$$

If the war results in a stalemate, the residual attacking lethality at the culmination of the final engagement between the two enemies, $R(\tau K)$, is zero, implying:

$$K^{\lambda_4 - \lambda_1} \frac{b}{\lambda_1 - \lambda_4 + 1} B(0)^{\lambda_1 - \lambda_4 + 1} = \frac{r}{\lambda_3 - \lambda_2 + 1} R(0)^{\lambda_3 - \lambda_2 + 1} \tag{2-30}$$

From Equation 2-28 we introduce the relative superiority in overall effective lethality of the defender:

$$K^{\lambda_4 - \lambda_1} \frac{b}{\lambda_1 - \lambda_4 + 1} B(0)^{\lambda_1 - \lambda_4 + 1} = \frac{1}{M} \frac{b}{\lambda_1 - \lambda_4 + 1} B(0)^{\lambda_1 - \lambda_4 + 1} \tag{2-31}$$

Eliminating expressions common to both sides of Equation 2-31 we have:

$$K = M^{\frac{1}{\lambda_1 - \lambda_4}} \tag{2-32}$$

Let $\lambda_1 - \lambda_4 = \Delta\lambda$ where $\Delta\lambda > 0$. Then:

$$K = M^{\frac{1}{\Delta\lambda}} \tag{2-33}$$

K is the number of equal-sized discrete units into which the defense might divide its total lethality. M is the relative superiority of the defense in overall effective firepower. $\Delta\lambda$ is the exponent to which defensive lethality is raised in the expression for the casualty exchange ratio between the two sides. Higher values of $\Delta\lambda$ cause the attacker-to-defender casualty exchange ratio to increase sharply with rising levels of engaged defensive lethality. K increases with increasing M and decreases with increasing $\Delta\lambda$. Thus the number of distinct units into which the defense might disperse while still ensuring a stalemate increases with increasing defensive superiority in overall effective lethality. Conversely, allowed defensive dispersion is lower if the casualty exchange ratio between the two sides in battle is a rapidly growing function of defensive force deployment.

The three variants of the Lanchester family of equations most widely used for modeling warfare are the Square Law, the Linear Law and the Ambush Law. Let us see what defensive force dispersion is permissible under each of these combat modeling regimes.

Lanchester law	λ_1	λ_2	λ_3	λ_4	$\lambda_1 - \lambda_4$	Maximum permitted defensive dispersion
Square	1	0	1	0	1	$K = M^{1/1} = M$
Linear	1	1	1	1	0	$K = $ Infinity
Ambush	1	1	1	0	1	$K = M^{1/1} = M$

The Square and Ambush variants of the Lanchester family of equations impose an upper limit on the distribution of defensive lethality. Only the side with superior overall effective lethality may engage in the luxury of force dispersal. The number of independent discrete units into which the superior side may divide its forces is equal to $bB(0)^2/rR(0)^2$ in the case of the Square Law and $bB(0)^2/2rR(0)$ in the case of the Ambush Law, assuming side B is the stronger adversary. For the Linear Law $\Delta\lambda$ equals zero and the dispersion of side B has no direct effect on the outcome of the battle. The defender can disperse to whatever degree it desires without any detrimental or beneficial consequences for its performance in war. More generally, for any combat model in which the ratio of attacker-to-defender casualties does not depend on the magnitude of lethality deployed by the defender, the outcome of the conflict is indifferent to the degree of defensive force dispersion. Below we summarize our conclusions regarding the upper limit on force dispersal prescribed by certain formulations of counterattack on passive defenses.

LANCHESTER THEOREM OF FINITE DISPERSION FOR A PASSIVE DEFENSE UNDER COUNTERATTACK: *If battle between combatants is governed by the general Lanchester family of equations elaborated earlier and if $\lambda_4 < \lambda_1$, then the defense can afford to distribute its forces only if the defense possesses a higher overall effective lethality. The maximum number of independent equal strength units, K, into which the total force of the dispersed side might be divided while ensuring a stalemate is given by:*

$$K = M^{\frac{1}{\Delta\lambda}}$$

where M is the relative superiority in overall effective lethality of the stronger opponent and $\Delta\lambda = \lambda_1 - \lambda_4$.

Generalizing beyond the Lanchester family of equations:

GENERAL THEOREM OF FINITE DISPERSION FOR A PASSIVE DEFENSE UNDER COUNTERATTACK: *If the attacker-to-defender casualty exchange ratio observed in battle between two combatants increases with increasing engaged defensive lethality then only a defense with superior overall effective lethality may engage in the luxury of force dispersal. In addition, there is an upper bound on the number of independent discrete units into which the superior side may divide its firepower. This threshold on force dispersion relaxes with increas-*

ing defensive force superiority and tightens with a casualty exchange ratio that grows sharply with rising defensive force deployment.

Finally for the case of a casualty exchange ratio that does not depend on the level of defensive force deployment:

INDIFFERENCE THEOREM OF DISPERSION FOR A PASSIVE DEFENSE UNDER COUNTERATTACK: *If the attacker-to-defender casualty exchange ratio observed in battle between two combatants does not depend on the magnitude of engaged defensive lethality then the outcome of the conflict is not affected by the degree of defensive force dispersal. The defender can distribute his forces into any number of independent discrete units with no positive or negative influence on the final result of the war. In the case of the general Lanchester family of equations the outcome of the conflict is indifferent to the extent of defensive force dispersal if $\lambda_4 = \lambda_1$.*

The implications of counterattack for structuring passive defenses thus depend on the nature of the attacker-to-defender casualty exchange ratio. If concentrating defending forces increases defensive vulnerability and reduces the number of attacking casualties for each defending warrior forgone, our recommendation is to disperse the defender's military strength into as large a number of units as is practically feasible. In diametric opposition, if the conflux of defending firepower causes the aggressor to lose more men for each point of defensive lethality, there is an absolute bound on the number of independent force units into which the defending forces might be distributed while guaranteeing a stalemate. Expressing a view on the desirability of force dispersion is in fact a statement on the nature of the casualty exchange ratio between the two sides. For passive defenses where counterattack is a significant problem one cannot address the question of force diffusion without probing the dynamics of casualty exchange likely to be observed in combat.

Using Passive Bunker Defense Systems to Create a Robust Defense

At the commencement of Part Two we stated that the quest for defensive systems that enable the defense to outmatch the offense in mobility over defense terrain and to realize favorable exchange ratios in combat is an integral part of the Defense Positioning Problem. Passive defense technologies such as a dispersed bunker defense possess several properties that make them extremely desirable as complements to, or even substitutes for, more conventional armored and infantry divisions:

1. Passive defenses such as an unmanned, remote-controlled bunker defense with hardened, stationary bunkers, each housing limited weaponry, distributed over a large region are intrinsically nonoffensive and inherently defensive. They cannot be used to lead an invasion of the neighbor's home territory.

2. Passive technologies can reduce the invader's speed of locomotion to a crawl and dissipate the forward momentum of the attacking force concentration. They constitute a wedge between the aggressor's velocity, v_a, and the defender's mobility, v_d, and give the defender more time for mobilization. The differential between v_a and v_d is key to enhancing conventional stability. Both sides can employ passive defenses to curb an attacker's speed on defense territory without impairing defense mobility. At the same time, each side suffers identical disadvantages in terms of reduced velocity when it plays the role of aggressor.

3. Passive defenses can take a big bite out of the aggressor's lethality. They can impose heavy attrition on the advancing invader facilitating the task of conventional military forces.

4. Passive technologies can be structured to minimize human involvement. In this aspect, perhaps their biggest virtue, they can keep the loss of human life as low as possible.

5. The feedback from deployed passive defense systems can serve as conveniently available and highly reliable intelligence on the progress of the invading columns through the defender's home territory. Information on the exact coordinates and evolving trajectory of the enemy's forces can be used to surmise the intents of the foe and to orchestrate an effective deployment of defending divisions in response to the invasion.

6. A passive defense on the outskirts of the border between two sides can be transformed into an effective political signalling tool. Each combatant can forcefully assert that any violation of its outlying passive defense would signify an act of war and could lead to full-scale retaliation through air raids on the trespasser's territory. Any incursion into a region protected by a passive defense would be highly visible due to the weaponry it would trigger. Use of this signal as a tripwire by the defending side to accelerate mobilization and hostilities if necessary would provide legitimacy to the martial preparations of the defender in the eyes of the international community, establish a clear picture of the order in which events escalate and imbue the defender's efforts to mobilize with decisiveness and urgency.[7]

Some of the ways in which passive defenses can be used to augment the optimal K-constrained force positioning geometries described in Part One are as follows.

1. Consider a defender who is outpaced and outnumbered by its enemies in any sector of the length-M front. The rapid speed with which the invader can transport force over defense terrain compels the defender to position the units assigned to that particular segment of the border at a substantial inward dis-

---

[7]In addition, most cease-fires and peace treaties between nations would clearly make for easier drafting if each side had a passive defense that could be used as a tripwire.

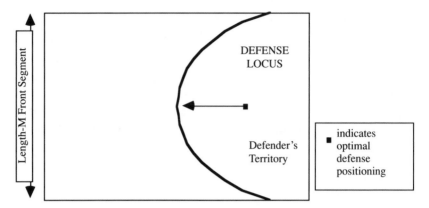

Figure 2-12   The Attackers Superiority in Transporting Force Allows the Attacker to Seize Large Portions of Defense Territory without Encountering Any Opposition from the Defending Units.

placement from the frontier. The defense locus permits vast unopposed infiltrations by the offense as depicted in Figure 2-12.

The defending commander can deploy a passive defense system in the portion of defense territory along the frontier between the two sides. The passive defense will have the effect of slowing down the attacking force concentration and reducing the disparity between v_a and v_d, propelling the defense locus forward and reducing drastically the defense terrain exposed to uncontested conquest by the offense. As shown in Figure 2-13 the passive defense elements should be based only in the region between the length-M front and the new or post-bunker defense locus. Locating bunkers beyond the new defense locus can impede defensive mobility if the passive defense does not differentiate between friendly and hostile aliens. The new defense locus and optimal location for the defending divisions is determined by the solution to the Defense Positioning Problem outlined in Part One, adjusting for the reduction in the attacker-to-defender velocity ratio, v_a/v_d. Another benefit of the passive defense is to impose heavy attrition on the advancing legions of the invader, countering the imbalance between the numerically superior offense and weaker conventional defense. Thus when the armored and infantry divisions of the two sides engage in combat along the defense locus the defender will enjoy a more favorable initial force ratio on the battlefield.

How should the areal density of the passive defense elements in the region between the front and the defense locus be determined? One obvious methodology is to disperse the total interceptor population uniformly over the entire deployment area. Thus if A is the total deployment area and R is the lesser of the range of the detection network and the range of an interception vehicle, then the number of individual interceptor basings would be given by $A/\pi R^2$. If U is the

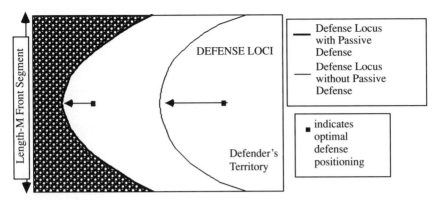

Figure 2-13 Improvement in the Defense Locus with Passive Defense. The passive defense is deployed in the shaded area between the front and the new defense locus. The passive defense decreases the attacker's velocity and causes the defense locus to be displaced forward reducing unopposed infiltration.

total interceptor population, the number of interceptors housed in each bunker would be $U/(A/\pi R^2) = \pi UR^2/A$. This methodology of deploying the passive defense accomplishes reasonable cascading and slows the attacker down uniformly for incursions at any point along the length-M front. The invader's velocity is independent of the focus of penetration since the bunker density is identical at each point along the demarcation line. Thus the speed of the invading columns is uniformly depressed. However this technique for distributing passive defense lethality has a shortcoming—the quantum of offensive firepower that survives the passage through the passive defense differs from point to point along the defense locus. At locations along the defense locus that are closer to the border, a higher proportion of offensive lethality arrives unscathed at the defense locus. At positions at either extremity of the length-M front segment, the invading spearhead has to navigate far more layers of the defensive cascade and is severely attrited by the time it appears at the defense locus.

A second methodology for deploying the passive defense is to position the same number of cascade layers between each point along the length-M front and the defense locus. Consequently, the deployed bunkers are more compressed in the region adjoining the central portion of the front and are spaced relatively further apart in the endzones. If one proceeds inward from any point along the demarcation line one encounters exactly the same number of cascade layers of the passive defense system before arriving at the defense locus. Each layer of the cascade defense is armed with an identical number of interception vehicles. This passive defense geometry ensures that the number of intruders who survive the interceptors and make it to the defense locus is the same at each point along the defense locus. On the other hand, it is no longer true that

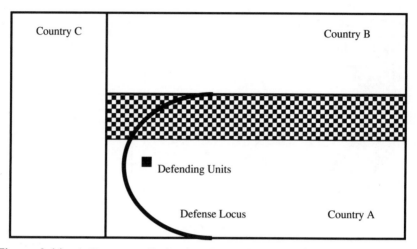

Figure 2-14   A Prototype Defensive Force Geometry for the Three Nation Problem. Country A deploys a passive defense, indicated by the shaded area, along the border with Country B and focuses its conventional lethality along the border with Country C.

the attacker's velocity is the same for an incursion launched at any focus of penetration along the frontier. The invader will be slowed to a crawl in the central region of the length-M front because of the high density of bunkers in this area. However, the aggressor will make relatively rapid progress in prosecuting an attack at either extremity of the front as a consequence of the lower density of passive defense elements in those regions. Note that the dependence of v_a on the point of infiltration requires a slight modification to the solution to the Defense Positioning Problem. We have to choose the optimal defensive encampment, (x, y), so as to minimize the expected value of offensive infiltration, I, which has the functional form: $I(f, x, y, v_a(f), v_d)$.

In constructing the passive defense between the length-M front and the new defense locus the hardened bunker defense can be used to slow down and decimate the ground forces of the enemy while an anti-aircraft defense composed of a battery of surface-to-air missile launchers, for example, can be used to impede and wear down the airpower of the adversary.

2. Passive defenses can be used to address the problem of multiple fronts faced by a country with more than one nation along its borders. The defender's nightmare is that an inimical neighbor will seize control of a friendly neighbor's territory and launch an invasion of the defense terrain through the border between the previously amicable neighbor and the defending state. If it is logistically and politically impossible for the defense to maintain a standing, battle-ready army along the front between two friendly nations in peacetime, a compromise solution is to deploy an extensive passive defense in the region

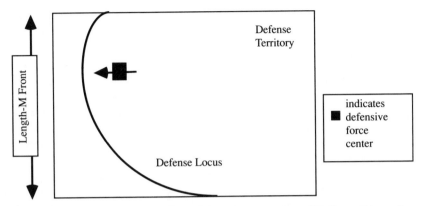

Figure 2-15 Optimal Unconstrained Force Geometry and Defense Locus for a Probability Density Function of Attack with Most of the Mass of the Function Concentrated in the Upper Third Region of the Length-M Front.

adjoining the frontier with the allied country. The inherently nonoffensive posture of a bunker-type passive defense can allay any fears of aggression invoked in the neighbor. At the same time, the blockade imposed by the passive defense in the path of an advancing aggressor can provide the defense with the respite needed to transfer lethality from the border with its hostile neighbor to the new front should a flanking action be attempted by the enemy. Figure 2-14 depicts a prototype defensive force geometry for the three-nation problem considered at the beginning of Part Two.

Thus in peacetime Country A should deploy a passive defense along the border with Country B and focus all its conventional lethality and attention on the frontier with Country C. If Country C conquers Country B and attempts a flanking invasion of Country A through the A-B border, the passive defense will slow down the invading force concentration and impose heavy casualties on Country C's columns while Country A reassigns divisions from the A-C front to the new battlefield.[8]

---

[8]Our championship of a passive defense should not be confused with the disastrous concept of the Maginot Line promulgated by the French in the Second World War and other similar "impregnable" fortified defenses. The Maginot Line was not dispersed, remote controlled or light on the use of manpower. In fact, defending the Maginot Line occupied the majority of French forces, leaving a sprinkling of lethality to safeguard other regions of the French frontier. Finally the principle of deployment in depth was alien to the French. The French were based so far forward that the Germans were able to simply "walk" through admittedly hilly terrain and outflank the divisions protecting the rear of the Maginot Line. The lesson to be learnt is that drawing a line on a map and emplacing conventional defensive units in close proximity to the front do not constitute a passive

3. Often the defense does not expect a uniform probability of attack at each point along the length-M front and has an indication of which regions of the border are most vulnerable to an incursive attempt by the enemy. The invader's decision of where to attack is influenced by a number of factors such as topography, the locations of targets of high strategic value and the likelihood of encountering large defensive force concentrations in the immediate vicinity of the focus of infiltration. Appendix 1A, which solves the generalized Defense Positioning Problem for a nonuniform probability density of attack, leads us to expect that for nonuniform distributions the optimal positioning of the defensive units can be significantly displaced from the usual 1-constrained basing opposite to the center of the length-M front. For instance Figure 2-15 graphs an optimal force geometry and associated defense locus for a probability density of attack favoring the upper one-third segment of the length-M front. Consequently the defender is persuaded that there is a very high probability of attack along the upper third of the front and a very small chance that the border will be breached elsewhere.

However if the attacker does choose a point along the lower two-thirds of the front as the main axis of penetration, the defender will have forgone an immense portion of defense terrain while offering no opposition because of the large inward sweep of the defense locus in the lower two-thirds of the border. Reinforcing this area with passive defense systems can create a significant velocity differential between offense and defense should a campaign be launched through this part of the frontier and can inflict heavy attrition on the aggressor. The deployment of the passive defense arrests the inward sweep of the defense locus in the lower half of the defense terrain and also gives the defender more time to transport forces from the upper portion of defense territory. Figure 2-16 depicts the dramatic improvement in defensive capability engendered by the combination of a passive defense with a conventionally structured solution to the Defense Positioning Problem when faced with a nonuniform probability of attack.

In Figure 2-16 the lightly shaded area between the front and the new defense locus along the upper one-third of the border is outfitted with a low-density bunker defense. The heavily shaded area along the lower two-thirds of the demarcation line is home to a high-density passive defense. The low-density passive defense causes the defense locus to be displaced slightly outward towards the border while the high-density passive defense slows down the attacking legions significantly, enabling the defending units to intercept the invader materially closer to the frontier. As is evident from the Figure, selective deployment

---

defense. A passive defense is a truly nonmanpower-intensive, dispersed, remote-controlled defense system with its own detection and surveillance web, which functions independently of the conventional armored might of the defender and complements the role of armored and infantry divisions rather than using up all their resources.

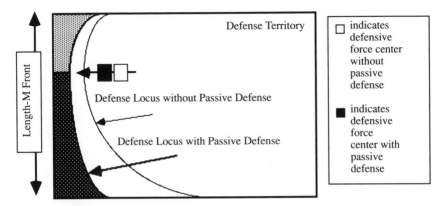

Figure 2-16 Improvement in Defense Response to a Nonuniform Probability Distribution of Attack. The lightly shaded area indicates a low density passive defense deployment while the heavy shaded region is the home of a high density passive defense.

of a passive defense smooths the uneven and asymmetrical defense locus that is the outcome of implementing the solution to the Defense Positioning Problem with an uneven probability of attack.

Thus for nonuniform probability distributions of attack, passive defenses can be used to "cheaply" plug the gaps in the defensive force geometry, that is, where the attacker is considered least likely to invade. This maintains balance in the overall defensive response to an incursive attempt and hedges the defender against the occurrence of improbable attack sequences or gross miscalculations in the determination of the expected probability of attack at each point along the front.

Outline of Part Two

What Are Passive Defense Systems?
Passive defenses are defensive systems that exhibit two salient features:

1. They make sparing use of human assistance for operation, thus minimizing the human cost of war.

2. They are inherently defensive.

By passive defense is implied not inaction but rather limited flexibility to be deployed in an offensive mode. The simplest conceptualization of a passive defense is a detect-allocate-intercept targeting system, which detects alien entities that intrude into the space protected by the system, allocates available interception vehicles among the detected aliens and dispatches the interceptors on a collision path with the foreign bodies. The whole detect-allocate-intercept cycle is repeated after the interceptor pods or launchers have been reloaded.

Real-World Examples of Passive Defense

System	Alien to be Targeted	Detection Web	Interception Vehicle
Air-defense	Aircraft, cruise missiles	Radar, satellite	Surface-to-air (SAM) missiles
Bunker defense	Battalions, individual tanks and armored fighting vehicles	Electronic trip-wires, drones, airborne reconnaissance	Machine guns, anti-tank weaponry
Anti-submarine defense	Submarines	Sonar, buoys	Depth charges, anti-submarine warfare (ASW) missiles
Strategic Defense Initiative	Ballistic missiles	Satellite, airborne reconnaissance	X-ray laser, high-speed interceptors

The Utility of Passive Defense Systems

The solution to the generalized Defense Positioning Problem exhorts the defense to outmatch the offense in mobility over defense terrain and to realize favorable exchange ratios and battle durations in individual encounters. Passive defenses enable the defender to achieve these objectives and are essential for the defense of numerically inferior nations or countries with multiple fronts. Conventional wisdom would require a defender not confident of repulsing an invasion by an unfriendly neighbor to equip itself with strategic counteroffensive capability and launch a preemptive first strike if necessary to deter incursive forays by the enemy. Deploying passive defenses can obviate the need to indulge in the games of brinksmanship that inevitably accompany a conventional balance where either or both sides lack a robust defense capable of defeating the offense on the defender's home ground.

A Simple Model for a Detect-Allocate-Intercept Unit

A = The total number of intruding aliens.

I = The number of defensive interceptors available for launch when all interceptor pods are fully loaded.

D = The percentage of total incoming foreign bodies detected by the intelligence net.

p = The single shot kill probability of an interceptor when targeted against the prototypical attacker.

The residual strength of the invader that survives the passage through the passive defense unit is given by:

$$S = (1 - D) A + D A (1 - p)^{\frac{I}{DA}}$$

while the number of intruders destroyed by the detect-allocate-intercept module is:

$$K = A - S = DA \left[1 - (1 - p)^{\frac{I}{DA}} \right]$$

Designing the Optimal Passive Defense System

We approach the design of the optimal detect-allocate-intercept system in two steps. First, we establish a set of design principles that will maximize the efficiency of a single passive defense unit. Second, we address the problem of how such individual units should be interconnected to create a comprehensive layer of defense.

Trade-offs in the Design of a Single Passive Defense Unit

A defense planner seeking to maximize the percentage of incoming intruders annihilated by a passive defense unit can increase the number of interception vehicles, I, raise detection capability, D, or improve single shot probability of kill, p. Cost constraints imposed by a limited budget can prevent the force planner from increasing all three. If I is very much smaller than the expected number of invading bodies, A, then it is preferable to increase I and leave D and p unchanged. If I is very much greater than A, defense efficiency is maximized by raising D. If I is comparable to A, D and p should be increased until they are relatively close to unity before adding interceptors to the installed interceptor base.

Interconnecting Individual Passive Defense Modules

Systems theory defines two basic forms of interconnection between independent systems: parallel and cascade. In parallel alignment, all component subsystems simultaneously access and process the incoming signal, and the net result of the parallel processor is the sum of the outputs generated by each individual component. In cascade interconnection, component subsystems are linked end to end; the input to the series cascade is fed first to the foremost component along the chain, whose output forms the input to the second component and so on, with the net result of the cascade processor being identical to the output of the final component along the chain.

A passive defense system with I interceptors may be split into two component subsystems armed with I_1 and $I_2 = I - I_1$ interceptors respectively. Connecting the components in parallel is equivalent to detecting the incoming intruders, allocating all I interceptors among the detected aliens and dispatching the total interceptor load against the enemy barrage in a single shot. Linking the passive defense subsystems in cascade requires a first stage of identifying incident foreign bodies, allocating I_1 interception vehicles among the detected trespassers and dispatching I_1 interceptors on a collision path; coupled with this is a second stage of redetecting the location and trajectory of the intruders that survive the first stage of the cascade, allocating the I_2 interceptors among the redetected aliens and dispatching I_2 interceptors. By interposing detection and allocation phases between two phases of interception, the cascade interconnection ensures that no interceptors are wasted in pursuit of infiltrators that have already been annihilated by earlier stages of the cascade. A cascade interconnection with $I_1 = I_2$ maximizes the percentage attrition of the offensive force encroaching upon the space protected by the passive defense. Parallel or single-layer passive defenses are nonoptimal and wasteful in their use of interception vehicles. In the limit, each individual interception vehicle should form an independent passive defense subsystem, and the overall interceptor defense should be structured as the interconnection of I interceptors hitched together in cascade.

When applied to ground warfare, cascade implementation is an argument for the maximum dispersion of passive defense lethality and its deployment in depth. For instance, a cascade interconnection of a bunker defense distributes the total lethality of the bunker force among as large a number of bunkers as is economically and technologically feasible and spreads bunkers in a straight line stretching as far inward from the frontier as possible. Dispersing passive defense forces over a large number of bases also lowers the attractiveness to the aggressor of incapacitating an individual base and makes it harder for the offense to pinpoint the base.

In Part One we came to the conclusion that for a force structure consisting of conventional mobile fighting units, basing defending units as close to the front as possible does not minimize the infiltration of the aggressor into defense terrain. Once again we find that a forward-deployed defensive force geometry, namely a parallel implementation of passive defense, is not optimal. A parallel geometry does not impose the greatest attrition on the invading forces.

The Drawbacks of Cascade Interconnection

1. Cascade interconnection interposes detection and allocation phases between interception routines. The number of detection-allocation elements increases

linearly with the length of the cascade, thus increasing the procurement and maintenance cost of the passive defense system.

2. Each detection-allocation cycle requires a finite amount of processing time, adding to the lag in defense response to the invasion and allowing the intruders to penetrate further into the defender's space. Because of its lower up-front interceptor density, a cascade implementation, while imposing greater cumulative attrition on the offense, permits invading force concentrations to accomplish greater inroads into defense territory when compared with a parallel system design. A parallel defense inflicts its entire damage on the incoming aliens in a single dose and then allows the survivors to continue along their path unhampered. Conversely, a cascade linkage gradually attrites the invading lethality as the intruder progresses through the defender's home territory. At break-even infiltration, the attrition exacted by a cascade defense equals the attrition imposed by a parallel interconnection of the same interception vehicles. If penetration up to break-even infiltration allows the attacker to capture strategically significant tracts of the defender's home territory, the passive defense is best structured as a relatively concentrated cascade defense with all available interceptors distributed equally among a few cascaded layers. On the other hand, if penetration up to the break-even distance can be endured by the defense, the passive interception system is optimally structured as a widely dispersed cascade with the total interceptor contingent distributed over a large number of cascaded layers. The break-even infiltration increases with increasing D and decreases with increasing p and increasing I:A.

3. Some forms of passive defense are susceptible to counterattack by the offense. If the equations of combat between the passive defense elements and the invading force possess a Lanchester Square-type quality, it might be inadvisable for the defense to disperse lethality across a large number of cascaded layers. The diminutive force complement of a single layer of the cascade would be cheaply eliminated by the preponderant might of the offense.

The Impact of Counterattack on a Distributed Defense

To study the effects of counterattack on a distributed defense, we replace the hardened remote-controlled bunker structure considered earlier with a defense composed of small, lightly armed fighting squads manned by trained reserves residing along the border. Such a defense is dispersed by its very nature since the soldiers are inhabitants of frontier districts. At the same time a border patrol defense is inherently nonoffensive as the dispersed, lightly armored scouting units cannot be expected to lead an invasion into enemy territory. Finally, these border civilians will most likely be wiped out by an armored invader and thus face significant problems of counterattack.

Like its cascaded counterpart does a dispersed border patrol defense with each unit fighting independently impose greater cumulative attrition on invading force concentrations when compared with a single, concerted onslaught by all scouting units acting in unison? The response depends on the nature of the equation governing combat between the passive defense elements and the infiltrating spearhead.

Case I

If the attacker-to-defender casualty exchange ratio decreases with increasing engaged defensive lethality, then the aggressor's attrition is maximized by dividing the defense into as large a number of independent discrete units as possible. If battle between the combatants is governed by the general Lanchester family of equations, namely:

$$\frac{dR}{dt} = -b B^{\lambda_1} R^{\lambda_2}$$

$$\frac{dB}{dt} = -r R^{\lambda_3} B^{\lambda_4}$$

the condition for unlimited defensive dispersion translates to $\lambda_4 > \lambda_1$. Distributing defensive lethality is optimal in situations where dispersing the defense is in relative terms more beneficial in alleviating defensive attrition than it is less potent in imposing casualties on the offense.

Case II

If the attacker-to-defender casualty exchange ratio increases with rising engaged defensive lethality, the defense can afford the luxury of force dispersal only if the defense has superior overall effective lethality. To the extent that the defender chooses to disperse its forces, it relinquishes its ability to retain residual military strength after the last encounter with the attacker. In addition, there is an upper bound on the number of independent fighting units into which the superior side may divide its firepower. For the Lanchester family, the maximum number of independent equal strength units, K, is given by:

$$K = M^{\frac{1}{\Delta \lambda}}$$

where M is the relative superiority in overall effective lethality of the stronger opponent, and $\Delta \lambda = \lambda_1 - \lambda_4$. In general, K increases with increasing defensive force superiority and decreases with a casualty exchange ratio that grows *sharply* with rising defensive force deployment.

Case III

If the attacker-to-defender casualty exchange ratio does not depend on the magnitude of engaged defensive lethality, the defender can distribute its forces into any number of independent discrete units with no positive or negative influence on the final result of the war. In the Lanchester universe, Case III corresponds to $\lambda_4 = \lambda_1$.

For passive defenses where counterattack is significant, cascade-type force diffusion cannot be advocated without probing the dynamics of casualty exchange likely to be observed in combat between the passive defense elements and the penetrating spearhead.

Why Passive Defenses Are the Force Structure of the Future

Passive defenses are extremely desirable as complements or even substitutes for more conventional armored and infantry divisions for the following reasons.

1. Passive defenses such as an unmanned, remote-controlled bunker defense with hardened, stationary bunkers each housing limited weaponry distributed over a large region are intrinsically nonoffensive and inherently defensive. They cannot be used to lead an invasion of the neighbor's home territory.

2. The biggest virtue of passive defenses is that they can be structured to be nonresource intensive in exactly that resource, namely human lives, that is the most scarce and valuable to the defender.

3. Passive defenses can curb the attacker's speed of transporting force on defense terrain without impairing defense mobility, constituting a wedge between the aggressor's velocity, v_a, and the defender's speed, v_d. By displacing the defense locus towards the front, the differential between v_a and v_d is key to enhancing conventional stability.

4. Passive defenses can take a big bite out of the aggressor's lethality by imposing heavy attrition on the advancing invader.

5. The feedback from deployed passive defense systems contains accurate and reliable intelligence on the progress of the invading columns through the defender's border districts.

6. A passive defense on the outskirts of the border between two sides can be used as an effective political signalling tool. Each combatant can forcefully assert that any violation of its outlying passive defense would signify an act of war and lead to full-scale retaliation. Any incursion into a region protected by a passive defense would be highly visible and would provide legitimacy to the martial preparations of the defender in the eyes of the international community.

Combining Passive Bunker Defenses with K-constrained Defense Geometries

A defender who is *outpaced* and *outnumbered* by its enemies in any sector of the length-M front should deploy a passive defense system in the portion of defense territory along the frontier between the two sides. The passive defense has the effect of slowing down the attacking force concentration, reducing the disparity between v_a and v_d and propelling the defense locus forward. The passive defense elements should be based only in the region between the length-M front and the new, or post bunker, defense locus. Locating bunkers beyond the new defense locus can impede defensive mobility if the passive defense does not differentiate between friendly and hostile aliens. The new defense locus and optimal force geometry is determined by solving the Defense Positioning Problem, adjusting for the reduction in the attacker-to-defender velocity ratio, v_a/v_d. Another benefit of the passive defense is to impose heavy attrition on the invading legions, thus countering the imbalance between the numerically superior offense and the weak conventional defense. When the infantry and armored divisions of the two sides engage in combat along the defense locus, the defender will enjoy more favorable initial force ratios on the battlefield resulting in higher attacker-to-defender casualties and longer battle durations than in the absence of a passive defense.

Determining the Areal Density for a Passive Defense System

There are two choices for the areal density of the passive defense elements in the region between the front and the defense locus.

1. The total interceptor population can be uniformly dispersed over the entire deployment area between the length-M front and the new defense locus. This methodology depresses the speed of the invading columns uniformly since the bunker density is identical at each point along the frontier. However, the percentage of offensive firepower that survives the passage through the passive defense differs from point to point along the defense locus since there are fewer cascade layers in the regions where the defense locus is closer to the front and many more interceptor layers in the areas where the defense locus is distant from the front.

2. A second option is to position the same number of cascade layers between each point along the length-M front and the defense locus. Consequently, the density of deployed bunkers is much greater in regions where the defense locus is close to the front while the bunkers are spaced relatively further apart in areas where the defense locus is distant from the border. Since all intruders must navigate the same number of interceptor layers to get to the defense locus, the proportion of offensive lethality that survives the passage through the passive defense is identical at each point along the defense locus and is independent of the focus of infiltration. However, the velocity of the aggressor's forces will be higher in regions of low bunker density and lower in areas of high bunker density. Since the bunker density is not uniform along the front, the attacker's velocity, v_a, will be a function of the point along the border chosen as a focus of penetration.

A second benefit from the combination of passive defense systems with K-constrained force geometries is in solving the quandary of a country with multiple fronts. The country has contiguous borders with more than one nation, with some neighbors friendly and others hostile. The defender's nightmare is that an inimical neighbor will seize control of the territory of a friendly adjacent nation and launch an invasion through the border between the previously amicable neighbor and the defending state. It might be logistically and politically impossible for the defense to maintain a standing, battle-ready army along the front between two friendly nations in peacetime. A compromise solution is to deploy an extensive passive defense in the region adjoining the frontier with the allied country. While the inherently nonoffensive posture of a bunker-type defense can allay any fears of aggression invoked in the friendly neighbor, the blockade posed by the passive defense in the path of an advancing aggressor can provide the defense with the respite needed to transfer lethality from the border with hostile neighbors to the new front should a flanking action be attempted by an enemy.

A third opportunity for combining passive defense systems with K-constrained lethality matrices is in situations where the defender expects a nonuniform probability distribution of attack. As shown in Appendix 1A, for skewed probability distributions of attack the optimal positioning of defensive force units can be significantly displaced from the usual 1-constrained basing opposite the center of the length-M front. For instance, if the defender is convinced that there is a very high probability of an incursionary attempt by the enemy in the upper third of the length-M front, then the unconstrained solution to the generalized Defense Positioning Problem will require all defending lethality to aggregate at a location opposite the upper one-third of the frontier. The adoption of this optimal force geometry by the defense exposes a very large portion of defense territory—that adjoining the lower two-thirds of the length-M front—to uncontested conquest by the offense. Reinforcing this area with passive defense systems arrests the inward sweep of the defense locus in the lower two-thirds of defense terrain and slows down the attacking forces should a campaign be launched through the lower part of the border, providing the defense with more time to transport forces from the misguided peacetime base. Thus for nonuniform probability density functions of attack, passive defenses can be used to "cheaply" plug the gaps in the defensive force geometry, points that the attacker is considered least likely to designate as major foci of penetration. The defender is hedged against the occurrence of improbable attack sequences or gross miscalculations in the determination of the expected probability density function of attack.

PART THREE

What Optimal Defense Geometries Mean for Low Force Levels and Arms Control

WE UNDERSTAND WHAT IS AN OPTIMAL FORCE GEOMETRY for the defense and what it depends on. Ideally the defender would like to position all its forces at a single base. The exact location of this base would depend on the defender's expectations of the probability distribution of attack along the front and the relative speed with which the offense and defense can transport forces over defense terrain. If the two sides are evenly matched in mobility across defense territory, all the defending forces should be located at a distance along the length-M front equal to the mean of the probability density function of attack and at a distance behind the border equal to the standard deviation of the probability density function. The adoption of this optimal force geometry with no limitations on local force concentration guarantees the defense the ability to minimize unopposed offensive penetration while matching the invader unit for unit at each focus of infiltration.

Notwithstanding the benefits of an unconstrained force structure, the defender might be unwilling or incapable of basing all its lethality at a single location, which could be significantly distant from the front. The desire to disperse defensive lethality and deploy units as far forward as possible to reduce uncontested offensive incursion compels the defending commander to trade off perfect counterconcentration for forward deployment. The optimal force geometry for a defense is hence the most dispersed and forward deployed of the K-constrained lethality matrices that satisfy the Duration, Casualty Exchange and Completeness Conditions. The defender can reinforce its K-constrained conventional defense by deploying a passive defense system along the border with its enemy. The passive defense slows down invading columns and inflicts heavy attrition on the advancing foe. The defense can employ a hardened bunker-type system to compensate for numerically inferior or slow-moving forces or along frontiers with friendly neighbors as a safeguard. The inherently nonoffensive and therefore stabilizing nature of passive defenses and their sparing use of human involvement make these systems essential components of the force structure of the future.

The end of the Cold War and the demise of the Warsaw Pact have removed many of the political and ideological obstacles to reducing forces to minimal levels. It is now conceivable for both military superpowers and their allies in Eastern and Western Europe, as well as in North and South Korea, to make deep reductions theaterwide—lowering force densities to the bare minimum needed for a coherent and robust defense. Any restrictions on force reductions stem from militarily and strategically advocated thresholds, not from political ill will or misunderstanding. It is for the generals to decide how far-reaching and deep they want mutual force cuts to be and what kind of inspection and monitoring regime they require in the aftermath of the weapon cuts.

Similar issues of global disarmament arise amid regional power balances: the Middle East, the China-India-Pakistan-Soviet Union axis and South Africa. In the Middle East, for instance, the crucial question after the vanquishing of Iraq becomes ensuring sustainable peace in a region plagued by tension, unrest and bloodshed. It would be immensely beneficial for the Middle East as a whole if all parties agreed to disarm themselves to the minimum level essential for an effective and deterrent defensive capability. How deep can mutual cuts go without irreparably damaging defensive capability and upsetting conventional stability? To answer this question it is imperative to examine the dynamics of defense at low force densities. What determines the minimum viable density of conventional forces? Note that deep cuts in deployed armaments can occur either through mutual agreement in the form of an arms control treaty or through amputation as happened to the German forces after World War I or the Iraqi army after Operation Desert Storm.

Our understanding of the optimal geometry for defensive forces and its determinants must be applied to answer three critical questions:

1. How do deep force cuts, such as a fifty percent reduction in deployed lethality, affect the optimal geometry of defensive forces? What changes in defensive force structure and operating philosophy must inevitably follow as a direct consequence of deep cuts? How do these changes in force structure enhance or imperil defensive capability and robustness?

2. Is there a minimum force-to-space density below which the defense cannot prevent an invader from accomplishing strategic breakthroughs and routing all defending units?

3. How should cooperative arms control agreements that implement deep cuts be structured to maximize stability and make unprovoked aggression prohibitively expensive and futile?

Deep Conventional Force Reductions and Forward Defense

A question of great importance, on which views diverge widely, is the advocacy of deep conventional force reductions and the viability of defense at low force densities. While large decreases in conventional forces are highly desirable because of the economic resources they liberate for civilian use, it is sometimes believed that theaterwide reductions as deep as a fifty percent are impossible because of their detrimental consequences for mutual stability and defense robustness or because of the extensive restructuring of conventional forces they involve. It is therefore a matter of primary significance that our conclusions regarding optimal defensive force posture and passive defense technologies are carefully applied to the problem of deep conventional force reductions.

Part of the loss in defensive firepower caused by deep force cuts can be compensated through the deployment of passive defense systems such as the distributed detect-allocate-intercept bunker defense described in Part Two. There are strong grounds for encouraging the proliferation of passive defense systems as replacements for or supplements to standing infantry and armored divisions. Passive defenses, based solely on the defender's territory and limited in their mobility and counteroffensive capability, are inherently nonoffensive and therefore stabilizing. At the same time, they can impose heavy attrition on the advancing invader, in addition to reducing to a crawl the forward momentum of the attacking force concentration.

Despite the contribution of passive defense to a post-reduction environment, the major burden of the reduction in lethality must be borne by the massive, traditional infantry and armored divisions of both sides. We have proven that the optimal force positioning for a defender, who is confronted with an attacker possessing *parity* in overall military might and who wants to match that attacker unit for unit at each focus of penetration, is to base all defending units at a single point behind the front. The exact location of this point depends on the defender's expectations of the probability distribution of attack and the relative attacker-to-defender velocity of transporting force. In deriving this result the defender is assumed to possess limited or no information on the deployment of enemy forces. This optimal defensive posture is based exclusively on an assumption of equivalence between the total force strengths of the two sides; nowhere is there any constraint or expectation levied on the actual numbers of units or quanta of lethality available to either side. A decrease in total lethality, for whatever reason and magnitude, if matched one on one by the opponent, does not affect either the optimal defensive force positioning or the defender's dynamic wartime allocation and combat stratagems. A N-strong defender should station all its forces at a single fixed location irrespective of the value of N. We may crystallize our basic result for conventional arms cuts as Deep Force Reductions Postulate I.

DEEP FORCE REDUCTIONS POSTULATE I: *In a world where all parties are equipped with comparable firepower and are able and willing to adopt the optimal unconstrained defensive posture, there is no militarily or strategically justifiable limit on the levels to which nation-states may reduce their deployed forces by mutual agreement as long as overall parity in lethality is maintained.*

For defense configurations that are compelled to suboptimize because of a minimum dispersion constraint or for reasons of reducing unopposed offensive incursion, problems might arise with substantial force decreases. Posit an arms control agreement that decrees a fifty percent reduction in deployed units on both sides. Thus each side must reduce forces from N units to N/2 units. While the solution to the fundamental Defense Positioning Problem, which does not allow any constraint on the local concentration of forces, does not depend on the absolute number of units possessed by either side, the solution to the generalized Defense Positioning Problem is a function of the absolute level of lethality. For a defender who adopts a null-overlap methodology for implementing the dispersion of force, the possibilities for defense positioning before reductions range from the 1-constrained geometry to the N-constrained formation. After the fifty percent cuts are implemented, the possible defense basings are halved and are limited to the set {1-constrained, 2-constrained, ..., N/2-constrained}. In general, the number of robust solutions to the Defense Positioning Problem, with an upper bound on local concentration, decreases as the number of defending units falls. Correspondingly, the defender's choices for dispersed forward defenses shrink with deep force cuts.

What this constraint on defense choices implies for the restructuring of the defender's conventional forces depends on the nature of the force geometry before reductions and the extent of the mandated cuts. If the defensive force posture prior to reductions is not too heavily dispersed or forward-based and the force cuts required are moderate, the defending militia can retain, under arms control, the earlier force geometry by applying the overall reduction ratio uniformly to each position in the pre-reduction defensive lethality matrix. For example, consider a defender armed with 8 units before cuts are announced. The units are based in a 4-constrained geometry, with 2 units each at the locations $(M/4\sqrt{12}, M/8)$, $(M/4\sqrt{12}, 3M/8)$, $(M/4\sqrt{12}, 5M/8)$ and $(M/4\sqrt{12}, 7M/8)$. Now if the defense accepts a fifty percent decrease in overall force levels, 1 unit may be dismantled from each of the 4 defensive force centers. Thus the defense will have satisfied the arms control treaty, and, at the same time, the defensive force geometry will be untouched by the reductions as the remaining units will still be positioned in a 4-constrained basing. We are assured that the defensive force basing obtained by applying the overall reduction percentage uniformly to each point of deployment is robust and is a solution to the N/2 generalized Defense Positioning Problem, since the attacker has also undergone the same proportionate reduction in offensive lethality, leaving any ratio of attacker-to-defender lethality, such as the force ratio at the start of an engagement, unchanged.

However, if the force reductions mandated by the arms control legislation are too deep or if the defender has opted for an extremely dispersed and forward-based force geometry, the defense might have no choice but to abandon its earlier basing for a less dispersed and more inwardly displaced positioning. Returning to our hypothetical 8-unit defender whose forces are initially configured as a 4-constrained defense, an arms control agreement that decrees a seventy-five percent reduction in deployed force units would lower defensive lethality to 2 units. If we require that each point of deployment in the defensive force geometry be occupied by *at least one whole unit*, it is clear that 2 units cannot be configured in a 4-constrained geometry.[1] The maximum degree of dispersion that can be attained with 2 units is a 2-constrained geometry and thus the defender has no choice but to restructure forces, once the reductions take effect.

The complementary scenario, which also compels the defender to reposition units, is where the defense has a highly dispersed initial basing. For example, if the 8-unit defender had deployed forces in an 8-constrained geometry prior to the arms control treaty, then even a twenty-five or fifty percent decrease in overall force strength will impose substantial restructuring on the defense. A twenty-five percent cut leaves the defender with 6 units while a fifty percent cut leaves only 4 units. The farthest forward that 6 units can be deployed is a 6-constrained basing. The analogous limit on dispersion for 4 units is a 4-constrained geometry. The inward displacement from the front of the defending units when aligned in a 4-constrained configuration is twice that dictated by an 8-constrained scenario. Thus the diminution in force levels mandated by the arms control accord impels the defender with an initially forward posture to accept a force restructuring that compresses forces inward from the front. We may formalize these intuitions as Deep Force Reductions Postulate II.

DEEP FORCE REDUCTIONS POSTULATE II: *In a world where defenders impose a minimum dispersion constraint on forward defenses, deep force cuts may affect the dispersed defensive force geometry in one of two ways. If the defensive force positioning prior to reductions is not too highly dispersed and the reduction in forces required by the arms control treaty not too extreme, the defense may simply apply the reduction ratio uniformly to each point of deployment in the defensive force geometry, leaving the basic lethality matrix*

---

[1]We deny the possibility of independently functioning fractional units. There is definitely a minimum unit size such as a regiment or a brigade beyond which conventional weapons cannot function effectively. Thus while a site in the defensive lethality matrix may be occupied by 1.5 defending units, it cannot be protected by stationing 0.5 defending units at the location.

unchanged. However, if the defense posture before reductions is highly dis-
persed and extremely forward based or the level of force cuts is very deep,
the arms control treaty will involve substantial restructuring and relocation
of defensive firepower. In general, the restructured defensive lethality matrix
is constrained to be less far forward than its pre-reduction predecessor.

We can proceed further in the determination of the restructured defensive
force structure; all that the defense planner must do is recompute the perfect forward defense structure using the step-by-step algorithm for solving the generalized Defense Positioning Problem outlined in Part One with the reduced force
levels as inputs. Thus while the defender had a choice of N force geometries pri-
or to the force cuts, the universe of K-constrained basings available to the defender will be lowered two-fold to N/2 for a fifty percent cut in overall lethality.
Correspondingly, the invader's potential range of attack plans will also shrink as
the total offensive firepower declines from N to N/2. Using the algorithm for
solving the generalized Defense Positioning Problem, we can test the entire set
of invasion campaign plans against each of the N/2 defensive force geometries
to reveal the ideal dispersed forward defense. As before the optimal forward defense is the one that is the most dispersed and forward emplaced while satisfying
the Duration, Casualty Exchange and Completeness Conditions. Again it must
be realized that since the most forward line of defense has been forcibly transformed from a N-constrained configuration to a (N/2)-constrained structure, the
defense locus might be forced to recede inward from the border, exposing the
defender to the peril of deeper offensive intrusions.

So far we have focused exclusively on the increased inward displacement of
the defense line with decreasing force levels. However, concomitant with the
displacement of forces from the front is the important and as yet unanalyzed
phenomenon of the thinning out of forces parallel to the front. While the average separation between adjacent defending units in a N-constrained scenario is
M/N, the intervening distance between successive units doubles to 2M/N for a
(N/2)-constrained basing. The consequences of this vertical diminution in
force-to-space density parallel to the front become clear when the actual battle-
by-battle progression of the war is taken into consideration. We shall hence pur-
sue in greater detail the reformations and modifications in the actual war dynamic that accompany substantial cuts in deployed force levels.

For concreteness, we will consider a relatively simple, extremely forward defensive regime, namely one where a 10-strong defender bases its lethality units
in a 10-constrained line of defense prior to force reductions. An arms control
treaty depresses force levels by half, and the defending commander who wishes
to retain an extreme forward posture opts to restructure the 5 remaining units in
a 5-constrained positioning. For the identical attack plan, the response of the
pre- and post-reduction defensive force structures can be vastly divergent and in-

congruous. Imagine an attacker's masterplan in which all the invading lethality is concentrated at a single focus of penetration at one extremity of the length-M front, say the origin (0, 0). We may now observe the evolution of the battle dynamic in both the pre-reduction and post-reduction scenarios.

Description of parameter	Value before force reductions	Value after fifty percent reductions
Defensive force posture	10-constrained	5-constrained
Distance of defending units from the front	$M/10\sqrt{12}$	$M/5\sqrt{12}$
Shortest distance between neighboring defending units	$M/10$	$M/5$
Strength of invading force concentration	10 units	5 units
Unopposed penetration accomplished by the attacker	$M/5\sqrt{12}$	$2M/5\sqrt{12}$
Initial point of contact where first battle is fought	$(M/5\sqrt{12}, 0)$	$(2M/5\sqrt{12}, 0)$
Attacker-to-defender force ratio at the start of the first engagement	10 to 1	5 to 1

We expect the duration of the preliminary encounter between the cumulative offensive lethality and the solitary defending unit closest to the focus of infiltration to be greater for the post-reduction $\gamma = 5$ case than for the pre-reduction $\gamma = 10$ case, with its larger attacker-to-defender force imbalance. However as a consequence of the vertical dilution of firepower in the 5-constrained positioning, the first reinforcing echelon is twice as far removed from the scene of hostilities as it was in the 10-constrained scenario. Before the implementation of the weapons reduction the second defense wave had to traverse a distance of $M\sqrt{7}/10\sqrt{3}$ to arrive at the battlefield while its counterpart in the post–arms control world mobilizes across a distance of $M\sqrt{7}/5\sqrt{3}$. In the pre-reduction world the total time available to the second defending echelon to arrive at the initial point of contact is the sum of the time taken by the invading columns to penetrate a distance $M/5\sqrt{12}$ into defense terrain and the duration of the preliminary battle between the invading spearhead and the first defense wave. Therefore in the 10-constrained scenario if the second defending unit arrives just as the opening encounter between the two adversaries is drawing to a close, it must be true that $M/v5\sqrt{12} + \tau1 = M\sqrt{7}/v10\sqrt{3}$, where v is the speed of force transportation over defense terrain and $\tau1$ is the duration of the first engagement between offense and defense. The corresponding condition for defense robustness in the 5-constrained universe is $2M/v5\sqrt{12} + \tau1' = M\sqrt{7}/v5\sqrt{3}$. From the form of the two equations it is apparent that $\tau1'$ must equal $2\tau1$ if the defense is to satisfy the Duration Condition and prevent the aggressor from gaining a strategic breakthrough.[2] Thus if the 10-constrained defense was robust in its capability to contain breakthroughs for the specific attack plan being elaborated, similar robustness will be shown by the 5-constrained placement if and only if the length of the preliminary engagement in the post-reduction universe is twice that in the pre-reduction case. Corresponding relationships hold also for the succeeding engagements between the offense and the defense in the pre- and post-reduction environments. All encounters in the world of lower vertical force-to-space density must be twice as time intensive as they were under circumstances of greater force abundance; this criterion is a prerequisite for the fulfillment of the Duration Condition by the defense. We may generalize this relationship between weapon cuts and the duration of individual engagements.

THEOREM I: *For a defender that deploys a fully dispersed and forward emplaced defense both before and after arms reductions, assuming the defender's velocity of transporting firepower is unchanged, an arms cut of k percent is justified only if the duration of all conflicts is augmented by 1/1-k after the reductions are in place.*[3]

This theorem is actually a comment on the relation between battle duration and the initial attacker-to-defender force ratio. A reduction in force levels uniformly applied to both sides lowers the maximum imbalance the aggressor can hope to achieve at the commencement of any single encounter with the defense. Thus a reduction in deployed forces translates to a decrease in the initial force ratio, γ. If the length of an individual engagement is to increase in proportion to the decrease in γ, the battle duration curve must be relatively steep. If the τ-curve is flat instead, there will be little or no increase in battle length with decreasing initial force ratio. Figures 3-1.1 and 3-1.2 illustrate graphically the distinction between steep and flat duration functions.

From the perspective of deep force reductions, the battle duration curve must be sufficiently steep so that the increase in the length of an individual con-

---

[2]If the velocity of defensive forces in the post-reduction world was greater than the defense speed of transporting firepower in the pre-reduction scenario, $\tau 1'$ need not be as large as $2\tau 1$ to prevent an offensive breakthrough. The defense can compensate somewhat for the increased distance between ground units that results from the adoption of a forward defense under a ceiling on total armaments by investing heavily in aerial firepower and airlift capacity, both of which dramatically increase the speed with which defending lethality arrives at the battle scene.

[3]A k percent cut reduces the defender's forces from N to N(1 - k). Hence the separation between adjacent units increases from M/N to M/N(1 - k). All distances in the post-reduction environment scale accordingly and are increased by a factor of 1/(1 - k). Therefore the duration of successive conflicts must increase by 1/1 - k to satisfy the Duration Condition.

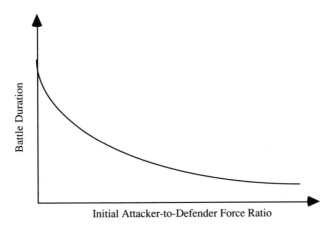

Figure 3-1.1   A Steep-sloped Battle Duration Curve. The battle duration function is in concordance with our Duration Postulates.

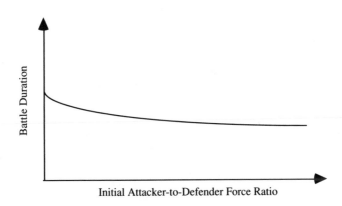

Figure 3-1.2   A Flat Battle Duration Curve. The battle duration function is in concordance with our Duration Postulates.

frontation with a decreasing initial force ratio compensates for the larger average distance that reinforcing defensive units must travel in a post-reduction world. If the τ-curve is relatively flat, the time period occupied by each engagement in a force-depleted situation will be unchanged from its pre-reduction value, but the defender's reinforcing echelons will be compelled to travel over far greater tracts of territory; thus, the aggressor might accomplish a breakthrough.

Let us quantify how steep the battle duration curve should be to accommodate force reductions. Consider the case of a defender whose N units are positioned as a U-constrained geometry before arms control cuts of k percent. The imposed force reduction will entail substantial restructuring of the defensive lethality matrix provided that $N(1 - k) < U$. Note that if $N(1 - k)$ were greater than or equal to U we could simply apply the k percent cut to each of the U positions in the pre-reduction force distribution, leaving the U-constrained force geometry undisturbed by the arms cuts. On the contrary, if $N(1 - k)$ is less than U, the defensive force positioning closest to the pre-reduction force geometry will be one in which defensive firepower is arranged in a $N(1 - k)$-constrained lethality matrix with each point in the matrix occupied by a single defending unit.

As before let us compare the response of the pre- and post-reduction geometries to an offensive onslaught with all invading lethality concentrated at the focus of penetration (0,0). In a world with force abundance the time constraint that must be satisfied by the second defending echelon is $2M/vU\sqrt{12} + \tau(U) \geq M\sqrt{7}/vU\sqrt{3}$ (Inequality 1). The force ratio at the commencement of the preliminary encounter between the invading spearhead and the defense contingent mobilized from $(M/U\sqrt{12}, M/2U)$ is $N:N/U = U$; thus the duration of the opening encounter is $\tau(U)$. Examining the response of the post-reduction $N(1 - k)$-constrained force geometry to the invasion leads to the following mathematical translation of the requirement that the second defending unit arrive at the initial point of contact prior to the end of initial engagement between the two sides: $2M/vN(1 - k)\sqrt{12} + \tau[N(1 - k)] \geq M\sqrt{7}/vN(1 - k)\sqrt{3}$ (Inequality 2). The duration of the first encounter between offense and defense is $\tau[N(1 - k)]$ because the force ratio at the initiation of combat is $N(1 - k):1 = N(1 - k)$. Since the U-constrained defense in the pre-reduction world is a robust force geometry it must be true that $2M/vU\sqrt{12} + \tau(U) \geq M\sqrt{7}/vU\sqrt{3}$. Multiplying both sides of this inequality by $U/N(1 - k)$ yields $2M/vN(1 - k)\sqrt{12} + U\tau(U)/N(1 - k) \geq M\sqrt{7}/vN(1 - k)\sqrt{3}$ (Inequality 3). Comparing Inequality 3 to the expression for the Duration Condition in a world with diminished vertical force-to-space density, Inequality 2, exposes a simple relationship between battle durations in the pre- and post-reduction environments: $\tau[N(1 - k)] \geq U\tau(U)/N(1 - k)$. In more technical terminology given that Inequality 3 is true, Inequality 2 holds if and only if $\tau[N(1 - k)] \geq U\tau(U)/N(1 - k)$. Separating variables reveals the basic condition on the nature of the functional relationship between battle duration and the initial force ratio essential for force dispersion under depleted force densities:

$$N(1 - k)\,\tau[N(1 - k)] \geq U\,\tau(U) \quad \forall \quad N(1 - k) < U \qquad \text{(3-1)}$$

Since $N(1 - k)$ is less than U we may replace $N(1 - k)$ with the initial force ratio, γ, and U with $\gamma + \delta$, where δ represents an incremental positive change in γ. Inequality 3-1 is thus transformed to:

$$\gamma\,\tau(\gamma) \geq (\gamma + \delta)\,\tau(\gamma + \delta) \qquad \delta > 0 \qquad \text{(3-2)}$$

Rearranging terms in Inequality 3-2 produces:

$$\frac{\tau(\gamma + \delta) - \tau(\gamma)}{\delta} \leq - \frac{\tau(\gamma + \delta)}{\gamma} \tag{3-3}$$

In the limit as δ tends to zero the left side of Inequality 3-3 becomes the slope of the battle duration curve, $\partial\tau/\partial\gamma$, while the right side approaches $- \tau(\gamma)/\gamma$. Substituting these limiting values into Inequality 3-3 gives:

$$\frac{\partial\tau}{\partial\gamma} \leq - \frac{\tau(\gamma)}{\gamma}$$

$$\frac{\dfrac{\partial\tau}{\tau}}{\dfrac{\partial\gamma}{\gamma}} \leq -1 \tag{3-4}$$

The expression $\partial\tau/\tau \, / \, \partial\gamma/\gamma$ is the initial force ratio elasticity of the battle duration function. The initial force ratio elasticity measures the percentage change in battle duration for a unit percentage change in the initial force ratio between the two sides. Thus if an increase of 1 percent in the force ratio at the beginning of an engagement causes the length of time required by the superior side to defeat the weaker side to decrease by 0.75 percent, the elasticity of the battle duration curve at the abscissa corresponding to the initial force ratio that prevailed in the encounter is -0.75. Similarly if a decrease of 0.5 percent in the initial force ratio produces an increase of 1.3 percent in battle duration, the initial force elasticity at that point is -2.6. As a consequence of Duration Postulate I, both the slope and the elasticity of the battle duration function are negative. Inequality 3-4 requires the initial force ratio elasticity of the battle duration curve to be less than -1, which is the same as requiring the absolute value of the elasticity to be greater than unity. We may thus draw the following conclusion on the ability of a defender to deploy a dispersed defensive force geometry under deep force reductions.

THEOREM II: *For force cuts that require a substantial restructuring of the pre-reduction defensive lethality matrix, the defender will be able to adopt a dispersed and forward emplaced force geometry in the post-reduction universe if the absolute value of the initial force ratio elasticity of the battle duration curve is not less than unity. In other words, the percentage increase in battle length that accompanies a reduction in the initial force ratio must be equal to or greater than the percentage decrease in the initial force ratio that caused the rise in battle duration.*

The elasticity constraint on defensive force dispersal under deep cuts is a sufficient condition but not a necessary one. If the battle duration curve is elastic, the defender is assured of finding robust forward geometries in the force-depleted scenario; however, there might be dispersed defensive force distributions available to the defending commander even if the battle duration function is inelastic to changes in the initial force ratio.[4] Graphically, the constraint on the initial force ratio elasticity of the battle duration function can be interpreted as requiring a slope of less than -1 at each point of the battle duration curve when plotted on a log-log scale.[5]

The ability to deliver reinforcements in time is only one precondition for defense robustness; a second crucial requirement that must be fulfilled by the defensive force structure is that the total lethality of the invader at each focus of penetration must be reduced to zero at the end of all encounters between the offense and the defense. If the invader dispatches J offensive units along a particular axis of invasion, all J attacking units must be annihilated by J or less defending units (the Casualty Exchange Condition). Along any axis of infiltration there will, in general, be series of encounters between the offensive force concentration and the successive defending echelons. The Casualty Exchange Con-

---

[4]Recall that the elasticity condition was derived by comparing the response of the *first and second* defending echelons in the pre- and post-reduction worlds to an invasion by a concentrated attacking spearhead. The initial force ratio evidenced in encounters subsequent to the premier engagement depends on the casualty exchange ratio that prevails in the initial encounter. Force cuts result in lower initial attacker-to-defender force ratios and correspondingly higher offense-to-defense casualty exchange ratios when compared with the pre-reduction universe. Higher casualty exchange ratios in earlier encounters, in turn, give rise to even lower initial force ratios in subsequent engagements. As a result while the constraints imposed by the diminution of vertical force-to-space density on the absolute duration of encounters after the preliminary battle are no less stringent than the performance required of the first defense wave to confront the aggressor, the burden on battle duration to increase sharply with decreasing initial force ratio is reduced because of the additional fall in the initial force ratio itself due to higher casualty exchanges in previous encounters. In deriving the elasticity condition we have implicitly assumed that the battle duration function must show similar percentage increases for unit percentage reductions in the initial force ratio for the entire sequence of engagements between offense and defense in the post-reduction world. We have not accounted for any of the benefit in lower initial force imbalances in the later stage of the war accruing to the defense as a consequence of the improvement in casualty exchange ratios in a world with reduced armaments. The elasticity constraint, while assuredly sufficient, might thus be stricter than necessary to allow force dispersion in lethality-deficient scenarios.

[5]From Inequality 3-4:

$$\frac{\frac{\partial \tau}{\tau}}{\frac{\partial \gamma}{\gamma}} \leq -1 \quad \Rightarrow \quad \frac{\partial(\ln \tau)}{\partial(\ln \gamma)} \leq -1$$

$\frac{\partial(\ln \tau)}{\partial(\ln \gamma)}$ is the slope of the resulting curve when the logarithm of battle duration is plotted as a function of the logarithm of the initial force ratio.

dition will be satisfied provided the weighted arithmetic mean of the average attacker-to-defender casualty exchange ratios prevailing in each of these engagements is not less than unity. Each exchange ratio is weighted by the number of defensive units involved in the particular encounter in which the exchange ratio is observed.[6] The maximum initial force imbalance that can occur in an individual encounter is depressed by the adoption of identical force cuts

---

[6]Let A be the number of offensive units dispatched by the attacker along a particular axis of invasion. Assume there are K encounters between the offense and the defense before the attacking lethality is annihilated. If D_1, D_2, D_3, ..., D_k, ..., D_{K-1}, D_K are the strengths of the defending units that engage the invader in each of the K encounters, then the Casualty Exchange Condition requires:

$$\sum_{k=1}^{K} D_k \leq A$$

$$\frac{A}{\sum_{k=1}^{K} D_k} \geq 1 \tag{1}$$

Let ψ_1, ψ_2, ψ_3, ..., ψ_k, ..., ψ_{K-1}, ψ_K be the average attacker-to-defender casualty exchange ratios that prevail in each of the K encounters. Then if the attacker is to be prevented from accomplishing a strategic breakthrough it must be true that:

$$A - \sum_{k=1}^{K} \psi_k D_k \leq 0 \tag{2}$$

Let $\hat{\psi}$ represent the weighted arithmetic mean of the K casualty exchange ratios. Thus:

$$\hat{\psi} = \frac{\sum_k \psi_k D_k}{\sum_k D_k} \tag{3}$$

and

$$\sum_k \psi_k D_k = \hat{\psi} \sum_k D_k$$

Substituting this expression for $\sum_k \psi_k D_k$ in equation 2 above yields:

$$A - \hat{\psi} \sum_k D_k \leq 0$$

$$A \leq \hat{\psi} \sum_k D_k$$

$$\frac{A}{\sum_k D_k} \leq \hat{\psi} \tag{4}$$

Combining equations 1 and 4 gives:

$$1 \leq \frac{A}{\sum_k D_k} \leq \hat{\psi} \tag{5}$$

implying that the weighted arithmetic mean of the casualty exchange ratios must not be less than unity.

by the two antagonists,[7] and the casualty exchange ratio increases with decreasing γ. Thus the average casualty exchange observed in a force-depleted environment cannot be lower than the corresponding average for the pre-reduction situation. Hence if the mean casualty exchange before deep force cuts is sufficient to annihilate the invading spearhead, the nature of the ψ-curve ensures that the defender will be able to destroy the offensive lethality in the post-reduction phase too. Let us investigate in greater detail the effect of deep force reductions on the fulfillment of the Casualty Exchange Condition.

The defending commander's problem is to determine whether a given defensive force geometry can satisfy the Casualty Exchange Condition for a particular invasion campaign. The specific plan of attack determines the total lethality of the adversary at each focus of penetration. The force posture adopted by the defense and the overall invasion blueprint of the attacker determine the number of defending echelons and the firepower allocated to each echelon. If defending echelon 1 consists of D_1 units, defending echelon 2 is armed with D_2 units and so on, we may represent the sequence of defending waves assigned to a focus of penetration as D_1, D_2, D_3, ..., D_k, ..., D_K. If J is the attacking lethality at the focus of invasion, then the defender's problem is to determine whether the K defending echelons can annihilate the J invading units.

For simplicity assume that the K defending echelons are equal in lethality. Let us use this quantum of firepower as the unit for measuring force, implying $D_1 = D_2 = D_3 = ... = D_k = ... = D_K = 1$. Thus there are K defending echelons each armed with a single unit of firepower. On the attacker's side, there are A invading regiments each equal to the lethality of a single defending echelon.[8] Because of the overall parity of force between the two sides the total defensive lethality assigned to confront the aggressor along any axis of invasion, K, must equal the total offensive firepower, A, launched into defense territory along that particular axis.

To gain an intuitive appreciation of how the nature of the casualty exchange curve affects the fulfillment of the Casualty Exchange Condition, it helps to adopt a graphical approach. The casualty exchange curve, ψ, as a function of the initial force ratio, γ, is of the form depicted in Figure 3-2.

---

[7]To see why this is true, consider a defender and an attacker armed with ten units each before reductions. The maximum imbalance that can occur between the two sides is a ten unit attack on a single defending unit. Thus $\gamma_{max} = 10$ in the pre-reduction world. If both sides agree to fifty percent cuts, the total strength of each antagonist will be reduced to five units. The highest value the initial force ratio can assume in the post-reduction universe is limited to five.

[8]$A = J / D_k$ with J and D_k calibrated using the same unit for measuring force.

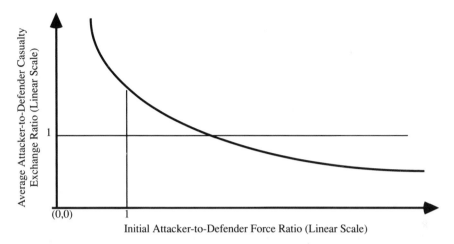

Figure 3-2   The General Form of the Casualty Exchange Curve as a Function of the Initial Force Ratio between the Two Sides. Note the linear x- and y-axes scales. For an initial force ratio equal to one, the casualty exchange ratio is assumed to be greater than unity.

Because of the assumed superiority of the defense on home terrain, the casualty exchange ratio is greater than unity (in favor of the defense) for an initial force ratio of 1. What initial force ratio of offense-to-defense will lead to the complete annihilation of the offense at the culmination of the encounter? This question is readily answered by the following construction. Plot a 45° line through the origin, (0,0), of the graph depicting the ψ-curve as a function of γ. The 45° line will connect points whose x and y coordinates are equal. Thus the 45° line is the locus of points for which $\psi = \gamma$. From the point where the 45° line intersects the ψ-curve, drop a perpendicular to the x-axis as shown in Figure 3-3.

The foot of the perpendicular is the value of γ for which the attacking forces are completely attrited by unit defending lethality. Note that the foot of the perpendicular is constrained to lie beyond 1 on the γ-axis since $\psi > 1$ for $\gamma = 1$. Let us denote the value of the initial force ratio determined by this graphical construction as $\gamma 1$. Thus, $\gamma 1$ is the maximum amount of attacking lethality that can be eliminated by a solitary defending unit. We shall refer to $\gamma 1$ as the first pole of the casualty exchange function. $\gamma 1$ is that initial force ratio for which the casualty exchange ratio equals the initial force ratio itself.[9]

The logical next step in the process of evaluating defense robustness is to ask what is the total attacking lethality that can be annihilated by two succes-

---

[9]Mathematically, the first pole is the solution to the equation $\psi (\gamma 1) = \gamma 1$.

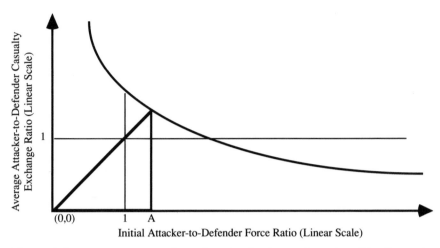

Figure 3-3   The First Pole of the Casualty Exchange Function. The first pole is denoted by point A and lies beyond one along the x-axis.

sive defending echelons each armed with a single unit of firepower. To answer this query, draw a 45° line through the point ($\gamma1$, 0) parallel to the 45° line constructed through the origin as graphed in Figure 3-4. Drop a perpendicular to the γ-axis from the point where the second 45° line intersects the ψ-curve. The foot of the perpendicular, ($\gamma2$, 0), represents the second pole of the casualty exchange function.[10]

Here, $\gamma2$ is the maximum offensive lethality that can be destroyed by two consecutive defense waves each equipped with a solitary quantum of firepower. The casualties inflicted by the first defending echelon on the attacking force concentration are given by $\psi(\gamma2)$. The residual attacking lethality at the termination of the initial encounter is $\gamma2 - \psi(\gamma2)$. But from Figure 3-4 it is apparent that $\psi(\gamma2)$ is equal to $\gamma2 - \gamma1$ since $\psi(\gamma2)$ lies on the 45° line through the point ($\gamma1$, 0). Therefore the residual attacking lethality at the close of the first engagement, which is also the initial force ratio at the commencement of the second round of combat, is given by $\gamma2 - \psi(\gamma2) = \gamma2 - (\gamma2 - \gamma1) = \gamma1$. The initial force imbalance at the start of the second engagement, $\gamma1$, is the first pole of the casualty exchange function and is the amount of offensive lethality that can be annihilated in battle by a single unit of defending firepower. Hence the entire invading force of $\gamma2$ units can be destroyed by the independent onslaughts of two defending echelons each armed with a single unit of lethality.

---

[10]In algebraic terms, the second pole of the casualty exchange function is the solution to the equation $\psi(\gamma2) = \gamma2 - \gamma1$.

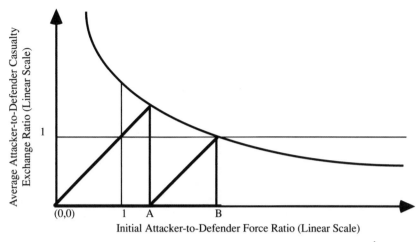

Figure 3-4   The Second Pole of the Casualty Exchange Function. The second pole is denoted by point B and lies beyond the first pole denoted by point A.

Extending the process of determining the poles of the casualty exchange function, we may ask what is the maximum amount of attacking lethality that can be annihilated by three successive defense waves each consisting of a single fighting unit. The solution to this problem is discerned by constructing a 45° line through the point ($\gamma 2$, 0) parallel to the 45° lines through the origin and the point ($\gamma 1$, 0). From the point where the 45° line intersects the ψ-curve drop a perpendicular to the x-axis as shown in Figure 3-5. The foot of the perpendicular denoted by ($\gamma 3$, 0) represents the third pole of the casualty exchange function.[11]

Thus if the defensive force geometry is dispersed into three discrete locations each the home of a single unit of firepower, the maximum offensive lethality that can be destroyed by the three defense waves arriving at the scene of battle in succession is $\gamma 3$. For the Casualty Exchange Condition to be satisfied $\gamma 3$ must be greater than or equal to 3, that is, the point corresponding to $\gamma 3$ on the γ-axis must lie on or beyond 3 on that axis. Deriving the poles of the casualty exchange function is fundamentally the same as determining the response of a defense divided into K echelons each armed with unit lethality. The defense waves attack the A invading columns one after the other in linear progression. The total number of defense echelons available to stem the offensive intrusion determines which pole is relevant to the determination of defense ro-

---

[11]The third pole of the casualty exchange function is the root of the equation ψ ($\gamma 3$) = $\gamma 3 - \gamma 2$.

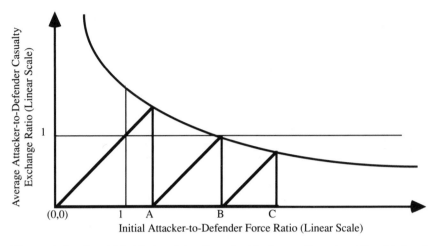

Figure 3-5   The Third Pole of the Casualty Exchange Function. The third pole is denoted by point C on the x-axis and lies beyond the first two poles denoted by points A and B respectively.

bustness. The first pole indicates the maximum amount of enemy lethality that can be destroyed by a single defensive unit, the second pole measures the maximum attacking lethality that can be annihilated by two defensive units and the Kth pole indicates the maximum offensive firepower that can be destroyed by K defensive onslaughts each conducted with a single quantum of lethality. If the Kth pole lies on or beyond A on the initial force ratio axis, the defensive force structure satisfies the Casualty Exchange Condition. More generally, it must be true that the N-constrained defensive force posture adopted by a defender fulfills the casualty exchange requirement if and only if the Nth pole of the casualty exchange function lies on or beyond N on the γ-axis.[12] Note that this is true by the definition of the Casualty Exchange Condition, which requires the defense to annihilate the J attacking units along any axis of penetration with J or less defending units. We may summarize this result as Theorem III.

THEOREM III: *From the perspective of satisfying the Casualty Exchange Condition, the defender can adopt a N-constrained force geometry if and only if the Nth pole of the casualty exchange function governing combat between the two sides is greater than or equal to N.*

---

[12]The Nth pole of the casualty exchange function is determined by solving the equation $\psi(\gamma N) = \gamma N - \gamma N\text{-}1$ where $\gamma N\text{-}1$ is itself given by the equation $\psi(\gamma N\text{-}1) = \gamma N\text{-}1 - \gamma N\text{-}2$ and so on.

Theorem III is a sufficient but not a necessary test for the satisfaction the Casualty Exchange Condition under a fully dispersed defense. Theorem III is sufficient because in terms of satisfying the Casualty Exchange Condition the worst scenario facing the N-constrained defense is a concerted incursion by N invading divisions at a single point along the length-M front. The Casualty Exchange Condition will certainly hold for this worst-case scenario if the Nth pole is not less than N. However, Theorem III might be too stringent a constraint on defensive force dispersal because it was implicitly assumed in deriving the theorem that defensive reinforcements arrive at the scene of battle and engage the foe only as the previous encounter with the invader is winding down. Depending on the distance between adjacent defensive camps and the speed of transporting the defending divisions, it is possible that reinforcing echelons would arrive at the initial point of contact prior to the termination of the previous engagement, biasing the casualty exchange ratio in favor of the defense and imposing greater attrition in the first few encounters than was assumed in the analysis leading up to Theorem III. As a result the initial force imbalance facing subsequent defending echelons is less than that predicted by Theorem III, moving the war toward the origin on a graph of the casualty exchange ratio versus the initial force ratio.[13] Therefore, in general, while a casualty exchange function that satisfies

---

[13]Let us demonstrate with an example how the early arrival and integration into the defending army of a reinforcing echelon benefits the defense. Consider a scenario where a defender with 10 force units deployed in a 10-constrained formation is attacked by a 10-strong incursionary spearhead. In our first simulation of defensive response the primary and secondary defensive echelons arrive at the initial point of contact in strict succession so that the first defense wave is completely annihilated before the second wave enjoins the invader in combat. The residual lethality of the offense at the completion of the first two defensive onslaughts is:

$$\rho A = 10 - \psi[10 - \psi(10)] - \psi(10) \tag{1}$$

$\psi(10)$ is the loss of attacking lethality in the first engagement, $10 - \psi(10)$ is the initial force ratio at the start of the second encounter and $\psi[10 - \psi(10)]$ is the reduction in invasive firepower in the second battle.

In our second simulation the second defensive echelon is in place on the battlefield halfway through the initial engagement between the invading spearhead and the primary defending unit. Hence after half the lethality of the first defense wave is destroyed, there is a jump in defensive firepower to 1.5 units as the remnants of the first defense wave are reinforced by the second defending echelon. The residual lethality of the invader at the close of the joint encounter with the first two defensive units may be approximated as:

$$\rho B = 10 - \frac{3}{2} \psi \left[\frac{10 - \frac{\psi(10)}{2}}{\frac{3}{2}} \right] - \frac{\psi(10)}{2} \tag{2}$$

Theorem III is sufficient to permit the deployment of a N-constrained defense, it might not be necessary that the Nth pole of the casualty exchange curve lie on or beyond N for the adoption of a N-constrained geometry by the defense.

Theorem III is actually a specific instance of the requirement for fulfillment of the Casualty Exchange Condition expressed earlier—namely, that the weighted arithmetic mean of the casualty exchange ratios observed in the N en-

---

$\psi(10)/2$ is the diminution in attacking firepower in the encounter with the defending unit nearest to the focus of penetration. Halfway through this preliminary engagement the primary defending unit is joined by a second division lowering the initial force ratio for the ensuing combat to $[10 - \psi(10)/2]/1.5$ and imposing attrition equal to $1.5\psi\{[10 - \psi(10)/2]/1.5\}$ on the intrusive legions.

Under all pertinent circumstances residual invading lethality under Simulation B will be less than that under Simulation A. From equations 1 and 2 above, ρB will be less than ρA provided:

$$\frac{3}{2}\psi\left[\frac{10-\dfrac{\psi(10)}{2}}{\dfrac{3}{2}}\right] + \frac{\psi(10)}{2} \quad > \quad \psi[10-\psi(10)] + \psi(10)$$

$$\psi\left[\frac{10-\dfrac{\psi(10)}{2}}{\dfrac{3}{2}}\right] + \frac{1}{2}\psi\left[\frac{10-\dfrac{\psi(10)}{2}}{\dfrac{3}{2}}\right] \quad > \quad \psi[10-\psi(10)] + \frac{1}{2}\psi(10) \tag{3}$$

Since $\partial\psi/\partial\gamma$ is less than 0 for all values of γ in accordance with Casualty Exchange Postulate 1, inequality 3 above will hold if:

$$\frac{10-\dfrac{\psi(10)}{2}}{\dfrac{3}{2}} < 10 - \psi(10) \quad \text{and} \quad \frac{10-\dfrac{\psi(10)}{2}}{\dfrac{3}{2}} < 10$$

$$\psi(10) < 5 \quad \text{and} \quad \psi(10) > -10$$

$$-10 < \psi(10) < 5 \tag{4}$$

$\psi(10)$ will always be greater than 0, satisfying the requirement that $\psi(10)$ be greater than -10. Now if $\psi(10)$ is greater than 1, it is patent that the defense can structure its lethality in a 10-constrained geometry without violating the Casualty Exchange Condition. The only situation of interest is one where $\psi(10)$ is greater than 0 but less than 1, which immediately satisfies inequality 4, proving that invading forces suffer greater attrition if reinforcing defensive echelons arrive at the initial point of contact and join the battle while the engagement with the preceding defense wave is still in progress. In Simulation B elaborated above it is possible that the third defense wave could arrive at the scene of battle prior to the end of the encounter with the joint first and second defending

counters between the offense and the defense be greater than or equal to one.[14] If the Nth pole of the casualty exchange function lies on or beyond N, the defender is assured of destroying N or more offensive units with N defensive units dispatched individually to the initial point of contact. Under what circumstances will the Nth pole of the casualty exchange function lie on or beyond N on the initial force ratio axis? To investigate this matter further consider a casu-

---

echelons further improving the initial force imbalance in favor of the defense. The "early" or "intraencounter" availability of reinforcements can dramatically influence the casualty exchange ratio in support of the defense resulting in far greater attrition of offensive forces than would otherwise be the case.

[14]The weighted arithmetic mean of the casualty exchange ratios observed in the N encounters is given by:

$$\hat{\psi} = \frac{\psi(\gamma 1) + \psi(\gamma 2) + \psi(\gamma 3) + ... + \psi(\gamma N)}{N}$$

Each individual weight is equal to 1 because the defending commander dispatches a single unit of lethality to each encounter with the invader. The satisfaction of the Casualty Exchange Condition requires that $\hat{\psi}$ be greater than or equal to 1 implying:

$$\psi(\gamma 1) + \psi(\gamma 2) + \psi(\gamma 3) + ... + \psi(\gamma N) \geq N \qquad (1)$$

If $\gamma 1$, $\gamma 2$, $\gamma 3$, ..., γN represent poles of the casualty exchange function it must be true that:

$$\psi(\gamma 1) = \gamma 1$$
$$\psi(\gamma 2) = \gamma 2 - \gamma 1$$
$$\psi(\gamma 3) = \gamma 3 - \gamma 2$$
$$...$$
$$\psi(\gamma N - 1) = \gamma N - 1 - \gamma N - 2$$
$$\psi(\gamma N) = \gamma N - \gamma N - 1$$

Summing both the right and the left sides of the above expressions for the N poles of the casualty exchange function yields:

$$\psi(\gamma 1) + \psi(\gamma 2) + \psi(\gamma 3) + ... + \psi(\gamma N) = \gamma N \qquad (2)$$

The Nth pole, γN, of the casualty exchange function is therefore equal to N times the weighted arithmetic average of the casualty exchange ratios observed in each individual engagement between offense and defense. Comparing expression 2 with expression 1 leads to the conclusion:

$$\gamma N \geq N \qquad (3)$$

Requiring $\hat{\psi}$ to be greater than or equal to unity is hence identical to constraining the Nth pole to lie on or beyond N on the initial force ratio axis.

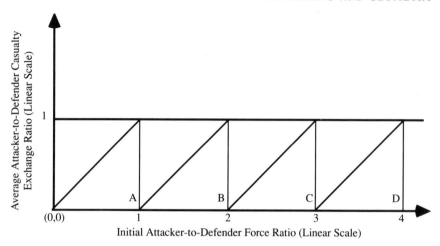

Figure 3-6   The Degree of Defensive Force Dispersion Permitted by a Casualty Exchange Function that Equals Unity for all Values of the Initial Force Ratio. A, B, C and D denote the first four poles of the casualty exchange function. The first pole coincides with the initial force ratio one, the second pole with two, the third pole with three and so on. The defender can adopt the most dispersed force geometry without violating the casualty exchange condition.

alty exchange function that is equal to unity for all values of the initial force ratio. The Nth pole of this casualty exchange function will always be coincident with N as depicted in Figure 3-6, and the defender is free to adopt the most distributed and forward-emplaced force geometry without violating the Casualty Exchange Condition.

We have claimed that for an engagement with equivalence in the initial force strengths of the two combatants, the defender will enjoy an advantage in the average casualty exchange in battle. It is therefore implied that our casualty exchange curve commences at a point above unity on the ψ-axis. Now if the ψ-curve is relatively flat, the casualty exchange ratio will not fall significantly below 1 even for large disparities in initial firepower and the Nth pole will continue to fall beyond N for large values of N as depicted in Figure 3-7.

Thus in Figure 3-7 the defender is free to adopt a 5-constrained force geometry since the fifth pole lies beyond five on the initial force ratio axis. For a flat casualty exchange function the defender can rest assured that even for a large degree of force dispersion, the total offensive lethality will be exterminated by the end of the last encounter between the offense and the defense.

However we must approach with an air of healthy skepticism the proposition that the casualty exchange curve is a benign, mildly downward-sloping function of the initial force ratio. It is quite possible that the casualty exchange

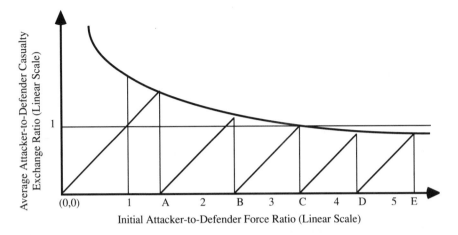

Figure 3-7 The Degree of Defensive Force Dispersion Permitted by a Casualty Exchange Function that is Greater Than Unity for an Initial Force Ratio of One and Declines Gradually as the Initial Force Ratio Increases. The poles A, B, C, D and E lie beyond 1, 2, 3, 4 and 5 permitting the defense to adopt at least a 5-constrained force geometry.

curve slopes steeply downward, crosses the line of exchange equality for an early value of the initial force ratio and descends significantly below unity for excessive initial force imbalances as graphed in Figure 3-8.

The defender confronted with a casualty exchange function of the form depicted in Figure 3-8 can at best adopt a 3-constrained force posture since the third pole is the last pole to succeed or coincide with its corresponding initial force ratio. If the defender insists on implementing a highly dispersed defense, the ensuing series of encounters between the attacking force concentration and the succession of solitary defending units might display such one-sided initial force ratios that the entire war might be restricted to a region of the downward-sloping ψ-curve well below the line of parity in casualty exchange. An extremely forward line of defense might distribute forces so thinly over the defense terrain that the extreme disparities in firepower between the attacker and the defender at the onset of each engagement coupled with a steeply declining casualty exchange curve could render the defense ineffective and incapable of satisfying the Casualty Exchange Condition. It would appear that a relatively flat casualty exchange curve, which allows higher-order poles to lie beyond their corresponding initial force ratios, is a prerequisite for the extensive dispersion and forward basing of defensive force units.

We may summarize our analysis of the consequences of the diminution in vertical force-to-space density parallel to the front with decreasing force levels as Deep Force Reductions Postulate III.

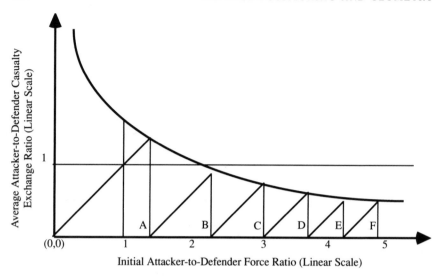

Figure 3-8   The Degree of Defensive Force Dispersion Permitted by a Casualty Exchange Function that is Greater Than Unity for an Initial Force Ratio of One and Declines Steeply as the Initial Force Ratio Increases. The poles A and B lie beyond 1 and 2 on the initial force ratio axis. The pole C is coincident with 3, while pole D lies before 4. The defense is therefore constricted to a 3-constrained force geometry by the Casualty Exchange Condition.

DEEP FORCE REDUCTIONS POSTULATE III: *Defenders who are committed to the extreme forward emplacement of defensive firepower are faced with a thinning out of lethality along the most forward line of defense as deep force reductions are implemented. Assuming the forward defensive posture adopted in the pre-reduction world was robust, the restructured forward defense in the force-depleted situation will also be robust provided the nature of the duration function is such that the duration of each individual encounter between the attacker and the defender increases sharply with decreasing force disparity between the two sides at the start of the encounter. In particular, the defender will be able to adopt a dispersed and forward force geometry in the post-reduction universe if the absolute value of the initial force ratio elasticity of the battle duration curve is not less than unity. In other words, the percentage increase in battle length accompanying a reduction in the initial force ratio must be equal to or greater than the percentage decrease in the initial force ratio that caused the rise in battle duration. From the perspective of casualty exchange, the newly constituted forward defense will be at least as efficient as its ante-reduction precursor in annihilating the total offensive lethality along each axis of invasion.*

The Muddle over Force-to-space Ratios

The literature and discussion on conventional force planning and arms control often makes use of the term force-to-space ratio or force-to-space density.[15] While it is difficult to find a clear, unequivocal definition of the phrase "force-to-space," the conventional wisdom on this topic is that there are restrictions on the length of front that can be defended by a unit of force.[16] For example, Jack Snyder and Barry Posen advance the view that "roughly one ADE (Armored Division Equivalent) is required to hold every twenty-five kilometers of front."[17] John J. Mearsheimer has formulated his constraint on force-to-space in terms of brigades. He has popularized the view that "a brigade can hold a front approximately seven to fifteen kilometers long."[18] It is claimed by the proponents of force-to-space that the defense must deploy a minimum force-to-space density along the entire length of the front if breakthroughs are to be prevented. The lower threshold on force-to-space density is a necessary prerequisite for robust defense and is independent of the nature and number of hostile forces. This philosophy of defense was chiefly applied to the Central Front between NATO and the Warsaw Pact in Europe, leading to the conclusion that NATO required a certain minimum of defending lethality to maintain the necessary force-to-space ratios along the inter-German and West German-Czechoslovak borders. Thus according to the proponents of force-to-space, NATO could not have tolerated a reduction of its overall strength that would have undermined the threshold force-to-space density.[19] In effect, NATO's force requirements were supposed to be independent of the Warsaw Pact's deployed forces.

---

[15]See the writings of Barry Posen, Jack Snyder, John J. Mearsheimer, Robert D. Blackwill, Jeffrey Record, and David B. Rivkin, Jr.

[16]In Appendix 3A we argue that the term force-to-space should be replaced with the term firepower-to-space in the lexicon of defense studies. Once combat commences it is not the number of physical divisions present on the killing field that affects the evolution of the battle; rather it is the actual firepower-to-space ratio achieved by all units firing within their ranges that is the crucial determinant of the course of the conflict.

[17]Jack Snyder, "Limiting Offensive Conventional Forces," *International Security*, vol. 12 (Spring 1988), p. 66, and Barry R. Posen, "Measuring the European Conventional Balance," in Steven E. Miller, ed., *Conventional Forces and American Defense Policy* (Princeton University Press, 1986), p. 106.

[18]John J. Mearsheimer, *Conventional Deterrence* (Cornell University Press, 1983), p. 181.

[19]This point is repeatedly stressed in the literature on conventional force reductions. Jeffrey Record and David B. Rivkin Jr. state: "NATO has to maintain a certain force-to-

The imposition of a minimum force-to-space requirement had disastrous consequences for deep arms reductions in Europe. The Central Front is roughly 750 kilometers long. If NATO absolutely had to deploy an ADE for every 25 kilometers of the front, then NATO required a minimum of 30 standing divisions along the border between the two sides. In peacetime NATO had 15 ADEs deployed along the front and could position an additional 10 ADEs at the demarcation line within five days of the start of mobilization.[20] Therefore, even assuming successful and timely mobilization of all its resources, NATO could barely satisfy the one ADE per 25 kilometers dictate of the force-to-space adherents. It was therefore inadvisable for NATO to accept any weapon cuts whatsoever, even if they were more than symmetrically matched by the Soviet Union and its allies.[21] Seen in this light, the dogmatic application of force-to-space ratios was one of the major stumbling blocks to achieving deep conventional force reductions in Cold War Europe.[22]

---

space ratio along the inter-German border; it cannot afford major reduction in its forward-deployed forces." From "Defending Post-INF Europe," *Foreign Affairs*, vol. 66 (1988), pp. 753-54. This view is endorsed by Robert D. Blackwill: "Anything more than token U.S. troop withdrawals would upset the post-war political balance within Western Europe... [and] weaken required NATO force-to-space ratios on the Central Front." In "Conceptual Problems of Conventional Arms Control," *International Security*, vol. 12 (Spring 1988), p. 36. Or in the words of John J. Mearsheimer: "In fact, it would be a major mistake for NATO to agree to any reductions in its force size, not only because of force-to-space ratio considerations, but also because there is no reason to think that a somewhat smaller Pact force would be any less dangerous than the present one." From "Strategy, Numbers and the European Balance," *International Security*, vol. 12 (Spring 1988), p. 185.

[20]These figures for NATO's peacetime force deployment and mobilization potential are from Appendix C of Joshua M. Epstein's book, *Conventional Force Reductions: A Dynamic Assessment* (Brookings, 1990).

[21]The use of force-to-space constraints in the construction of its theater battle model for the Central Front led the RAND Corporation to advocate that arms reductions between NATO and the Warsaw Pact would be stabilizing only if the Warsaw Pact was willing to match the western alliance at levels of asymmetry as high as 7 to 1 in cuts.

[22]In the words of Jonathan Dean, long a proponent of conventional arms control in Europe: "This 'force-to-space' issue is a major reason why NATO governments view the pending [conventional arms control talks] as a trap rather than as an opportunity, and why they are determined to hold NATO reductions to a minimum. NATO appears to be locked by its own strategy into continuing the East-West confrontation." From "Can NATO Unite to Reduce Forces in Europe," *Arms Control Today*, vol. 18 (October 1988), p. 15.

With reference to the situation in Central Europe, the dissolution of the War-saw Pact and the subsequent unification of the two Germanys has meant the United States and its allies must withdraw from the front between Eastern and Western Europe, regardless of force-to-space ratios along the frontier. Yet, in its strictest form the doctrine of force-to-space espouses that NATO's threshold force-to-space density is unaltered by any changes in the size, composition or potency of the Soviet forces. Thus as long as there is *any* threat of an attack by the Russians, Ukrainians, Belorussians or Kazakhs, NATO should retain its full force complement in the European arena. In reality, the force-to-space school of thought has not insisted that NATO maintain Cold War levels of military force, recognizing the drastic changes in absolute and relative lethalities that have oc-curred since the dissolution of the Warsaw Pact. Nevertheless, the force-to-space theory is still applicable to a more general world setting: Is there a mini-mum density of defensive force deployment parallel to the front below which the defense is incapable of organizing an effective and robust rebuttal to the in-vader's onslaught?

Let us apply our conclusions on forward defense optimization to the force-to-space argument. Does it make any sense to insist that a unit of force such as an ADE or a brigade is essential to defend a given length of front? We have shown earlier that to defend a sector of the front of length M, the defense must allocate the same number of units to that sector as there are offensive units on the enemy's side of that region of the border. All the defending units must be located at a single position behind the front. Under the assumptions of equal of-fensive and defensive velocity on defense terrain and a uniform probability of attack at each point along the front, this position is given by $(M/\sqrt{12}, M/2)$. If the defender adopts this optimal 1-constrained force posture, it is assured of minimizing offensive infiltration and of maintaining a perfect counterconcen-tration capability. Where does the requirement of a minimum force-to-space density emerge from this analysis?

The problem with requiring a minimum density of force along the front is that no account is taken of the inward positioning of defending units from the front. Depending on its distance from the border, the same unit can defend a front 25 kilometers long, 50 kilometers long, or 1,000 kilometers long. If the front is length M, the unit is optimally positioned to defend the front if it is situ-ated at $(M/\sqrt{12}, M/2)$; M can take any value in this expression. As the length of the front defended by the unit increases, so does the inward displacement of the unit from that border, though the unit still succeeds in meeting and defeating its offensive counterpart as close to the front as possible. What does occur with in-creasing front length is that the defense locus is swept inward from the border and the invader is able to accomplish deeper infiltrations in terms of absolute mileage. The attacker is guaranteed a minimum unopposed infiltration of $M/2\sqrt{12}$ even if the invasion is launched directly opposite the defender's peace-time base. As M increases, so does the aggressor's penetration, and presumably so does the reward for launching an attack. It cannot be denied that it is fool-hardy for the defense to permit the invader to penetrate deep into defense terri-tory without encountering any opposition. Thus, if we are going to place a spe-cific numerical boundary or threshold on a parameter, it should be on the infiltration of the attacker orthogonal to the front. We should be trying to struc-ture defensive forces to minimize offensive infiltration, and this aim requires us to solve the Defense Positioning Problem. It might be true that for a specific front between two specific opponents, the optimal force geometry for the de-fense as determined by solving the Defense Positioning Problem involves plac-ing one ADE along every 25 kilometer stretch of the front. However there still remains the question of how far behind the front the unit should be located; a question to which the force-to-space rule offers no solution. It is rather unlikely that for the various potential war zones around the world the solution to the De-fense Positioning Problem will always require one ADE for every 25 kilome-ters of front. Without solving the Defense Positioning Problem for a specific arena of confrontation, it is impossible to determine the optimal geometry of the defending forces.

The force-to-space approach tends to neglect several important variables: the defender's expectations of the probability distribution of attack, the relative ve-locities of the two sides, the defender's information gathering capabilities and the strategic objectives of the defense. Let us consider these shortcomings sepa-rately. If an attacker can launch an invasion at only one point along the front because of the topography of the border region, all the defender's forces should be focused at that point. This fact will be reflected while solving the Defense Positioning Problem in a probability distribution of attack with a probability of one at the indicated point and a probability of zero at all other positions along the frontier. There is no such mechanism for adjusting the force-to-space rule for different probability distributions of attack. The solution to the Defense Po-sitioning Problem explicitly takes into account the intelligence capabilities and velocities of the two adversaries. The force-to-space doctrine, by contrast, does not incorporate any such factors into its calculations. One of the prime objec-tives of arms control has been to improve intelligence capabilities of potential adversaries in a nonintrusive manner. Because the law of force-to-space has no way of accounting for improvements is information exchange, the force-to-space advocates saw little benefit in implementing confidence-building mea-sures and information exchanges in Central Europe. Lastly, the force-to-space approach does not make explicit its assumptions about the strategic goals of the defender in the one ADE per 25 kilometers rule. Is the defender trying to mini-mize offensive infiltration, to minimize defensive casualties, to minimize the product of offensive infiltration and defensive casualties, to maximize offensive casualties or to maximize the ratio of offensive casualties to offensive infiltra-tion? As a practical matter it is impossible from the force-to-space rule to infer exactly what is being minimized or maximized by the defense.

Finally, stationing defending units in accordance with a law of force-to-space density is a static procedure; it says nothing about the robustness of the defensive force structure or its ability to fulfill the Duration, Casualty Exchange and Completeness Conditions. Implementation of the force-to-space law leads to dispersed and forward-positioned defensive force geometries, the effectiveness of which varies greatly with the attacker's choice of an invasion blueprint. Thus while ADEs stationed 25 kilometers apart might curb a broad-based, multi-pronged attack, the same defense might be an utter disaster when confronted by a concentrated, one- or two-pronged onslaught. It is very dangerous to not subject any rule for defensive force positioning to a sensitivity analysis. Nowhere do the force-to-space adherents address the vulnerability of their proposed defensive force structure to different invasion plans or justify the ability of their defensive force geometry to defend against the large majority of such plans.

In summary, postulating a minimum force-to-space density has the effect of making a country's armament level proportional to the length of its frontiers with adjoining states and independent of the quantity of firepower possessed by its neighbors. While the importance of knowing the length and nature of a country's frontiers with its neighbors cannot be denied, it is a bit skewed to base a nation's aggregate force level only on front length, oblivious of all other factors. Territory comes with two dimensions and the dimension orthogonal to the front simply cannot be overlooked.

We may now examine in greater detail two of the most common claims about real world defensive force structures and the prospects for arms control that have been advanced on the basis of force-to-space arguments.

CLAIM I: *The defender is already below the threshold force-to-space density for a robust defense and immediate augmentation of the defender's weapon stockpiles is warranted; or, alternatively, the defense should adopt an operational doctrine based on counteroffense, deep attack and early nuclear use.*

Discussion: If the defender's current defensive force distribution is incapable of preventing a strategic and operational breakthrough and if the defender possesses overall parity in aggregate firepower when compared with the would-be invader, one of the following must hold true.

1. The defender's force structure is nonoptimal. It is not based on any premise of minimizing offensive infiltration and loss of territory.[23] As examples

---

[23] Let us be clear that a real-world force configuration is not nonoptimal simply because it does not match any element of our {1-constrained, 2-constrained, ..., K-constrained, ..., N-constrained} set of geometries. We derived these geometries under a constraint of null-overlap and insisted that responsibility for any segment of the front be assigned to exactly one defense base. The defender's force positioning may be nonoptimal because it might not be a solution to the most general formulation of the Defense Positioning Problem, which permits overlap among defense contingents and front segments.

of nonoptimal force postures, the defender's force distribution might be too heavily frontloaded with a dangerously low reserve-to-forward deployed ratio, it might be located at nonoptimal base encampments or it may be too thinly dispersed given the steepness of the casualty exchange curve confronting the defense. In fact, the defending commander, by virtue of historical and institutional inertia, may simply be pursuing a philosophy of forward-deployed defense and hoping that the placement of a sufficiently high force concentration as far forward along the front as possible will somehow contain and vanquish an invading spearhead. In all likelihood, it is this faith in the philosophy of forward-deployed defense that leads to the insistence on maintaining large force-to-space densities near to the front. Clearly if the defender's present geometry is nonoptimal, the defender must determine the ideal force posture by solving the generalized Defense Positioning Problem and not authorize expensive renovations in deployed arsenals or adopt an operational doctrine based on counteroffense or early vertical escalation.

2. While the defender has adopted an optimal force geometry as determined by solving the generalized Defense Positioning Problem, the command hierarchy of the defense is incapable of executing its functions in a real war situation. The inability to perform effectively under the pressure of a crisis may be the result of a lack of communication between defense bases, an extremely lethargic and leisurely mobilization of reinforcements, incompetence in the transfer of units parallel to the front, haphazard monitoring of enemy maneuvers once the foe has crossed into home territory or the nonformulation of a dynamic wartime resource-allocation algorithm. It would seem that the direct approach of rectifying the lacunae in the defender's capabilities is preferable to postulating a force-to-space constraint.

> CLAIM II: *The defender cannot endure even moderate decreases in deployed force levels even if it is more than symmetrically matched by a comparably armed attacker because the defender's force structure will fall below a threshold force-to-space density beyond which coherent and effective defense is impossible.*

Discussion: The belief in a threshold force-to-space density is advanced as an absolute dictum that emerges spontaneously from an analysis of conventional war in the twentieth century and is completely unaffected by the force levels of an opponent. Under an assumption of overall parity between offensive and defensive forces, we have managed to minimize the invader's infiltration into the defender's territory, and no magical force-to-space threshold has emerged from our analysis. If it is indeed true that the defense cannot allow force cuts without endangering its capacity to impede breakthroughs and if the present defensive force distribution is an optimal forward defense, then the following must hold.

1. The defender is constrained to seek maximum dispersion and forward emplacement of its defending force units.

2. The battle duration curve is not steep enough to allow reductions to low levels of lethality. Consequently, the thinning out of forces along the front, which is the inevitable accompaniment of a reduction in defending firepower, cannot be compensated for by an increase in the length of individual engagements between the concentrated attacker and the dispersed defending units.

Even if the above Draconian pronouncements are valid representations of the prevailing situation, they do not instantaneously rule out the possibility of accomplishing deep force reductions based on innovative arms control proposals. The flatness of the battle duration function can be artificially amended by human connivance. The defender can deploy passive defense systems to slow down the advancing columns and provide the reinforcing defensive echelons additional time to arrive at the scene of combat. The attrition imposed on the invading lethality by the deployed passive defense systems lowers the initial force ratio in the first encounters between the survivors of the passive defense and the defensive echelons nearest to the foci of penetration, further increasing battle duration. In addition, the reduced initial force imbalance raises the casualty exchange ratio in favor of the defense. The other key issue that must be addressed if substantial force reductions are to be realized is the demand for the dispersal and forward deployment of defensive troops. The major obstacle to permitting the inward recession of defending units from the demarcation line with decreasing force levels is the significant strategic value of even minor losses of territory in the highly urbanized, densely populated and industrially advanced regions adjacent to most battle frontiers in today's world. We will outline in the next section a few suggestions for arms control that may be successful in overcoming the problem of receding defense loci.

Returning to the proliferation of the force-to-space concept, the term force-to-space is simply a misleading and undefined proxy for other parameters of the war dynamic such as the slope of the battle duration and casualty exchange curves, which have no connection with the density of force deployments. Perhaps it is up to the force-to-space enthusiasts to specify what quantity they are optimizing under which set of suppositions to produce this threshold.

Arms Control Regimes that Facilitate Deep Cuts

Weapon reductions compel the defense to abandon its pre-reduction force geometry and accept a less forward and less dispersed lethality matrix if either the defense posture before reductions is *highly* dispersed and *extremely* forward or the level of force cuts is very deep or both. For a defender with N force units prior to a k percent cut, the most forward geometry achievable after the cut is a N(1 - k)-constrained basing. If the defender had deployed a U-constrained force geometry before the arms control treaty and if U is greater than N(1 - k), the defense must experience an inward displacement of the defense locus even if it employs the most dispersed and forward-positioned force geometry in the post-reduction world. Besides, the inelasticity of the battle duration curve may make it impossible for the defense to position forces in a N(1 - k)-constrained formation, forcing an even less forward force geometry on the defense. Any inward displacement of the defense locus is destabilizing and invites each side to preempt by raising the reward for first strike since the attacker is able to capture larger tracts of territory unchallenged. A second concern is the decrease in force dispersal that accompanies the switch from a more forward to a less forward force geometry and the consequent increased vulnerability of the defensive forces to deep strikes and decapitation. These hindrances in the path of substantial arms reductions can snuff out any hope of a new world of lower across-the-board force densities.

If two sides want to overcome these barriers and reduce force levels substantially while maintaining a stable military balance, how should they structure an arms control regime to achieve their aims? Are there ways to convert a spirit of cooperation into agreements that permit low force levels? A few suggestions for structuring disarmament protocols, which go a long way towards overcoming the obstacles in the path of deep force reductions, are described below.

Horizontal Lines of Arms Control

Offering both sides the opportunity to define shorter length-M fronts from the entirety of a two-nation border permits the positioning of defending units closer to the demarcation line. If the adversary can fluidly transfer force along the entire border without alerting the defender to the force displacement, then the defender is compelled to treat the full length of the border as a single length-M front. The only path open to a defender, confronted with an excessively long front, who wishes to disperse forces and base units forward is to adopt a suboptimal constrained defense and trade off counterconcentration capability for dispersion and forward position. Such a suboptimal defense is risky and testing its robustness is difficult and based on assumptions about the nature of combat. However if the long border can somehow be partitioned into several smaller length-M fronts, the defense can adopt an optimal unconstrained geometry in each front segment. For instance, consider a length-M front along which there is a uniform probability of attack. The optimal posture for the defense is to base all units at $(M/\sqrt{12}, M/2)$. However if the front could be split into two length-$(M/2)$ fronts, the defending units can be located at two separate bases each at a distance $M/2\sqrt{12}$ from the demarcation line. Figure 3-9 depicts the forward displacement of the defense locus if a length-M front could be treated as two length-$(M/2)$ fronts.

It may be recalled that a length-M front is defined by the ability of the defender to predict accurately at all times the total number of units deployed by the enemy behind that front, although the defender may be utterly ignorant of the actual geographical distribution of the hostile units along the particular segment.

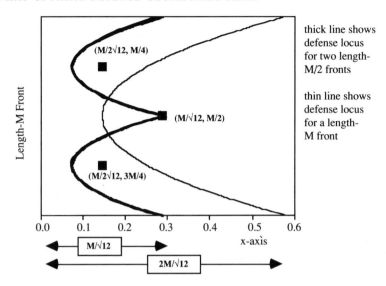

Figure 3-9 Forward Displacement of the Defense Locus if a Length-M Front Can Be Treated as Two Length-M/2 Fronts. The x-axis is calibrated in units of M.

Thus the two sides can construct by mutual consent horizontal lines of arms control as graphed in Figure 3-10 such that each side is always aware of the opponent's total lethality in each region bounded by adjacent arms control lines.

Force mobility is perfectly fluid within a segment bounded by the horizontal lines while the transfer of force across segments must be easily detectable.[24] Thus if one side's troops must be mobilized across segments for field exercises or other domestic purposes, the troop transfer must be announced well in advance and must be verifiable by the other side. The defense can then allocate the same number of units to a front segment as that deployed by the enemy. Within a region bounded by the horizontal lines, the defender can adopt a perfect forward defense with all units in that sector concentrated at the optimal location dictated by the 1-constrained, or unconstrained, solution to the Defense Positioning Problem.

The separation between the horizontal lines of arms control should be based

---

[24]Suppose horizontal lines of arms control are constructed at distances of M/5, 2M/5, 3M/5 and 4M/5 along the length-M front. Thus the horizontal arms control line at M/5 proceeds orthogonally inward on either side of the border at a distance of M/5 from the beginning of the boundary between the two nations. The arms control treaty guarantees Side A an information function, $r_A(x, y)$, of the form:

on the maximum infiltration either side is willing to suffer. As an illustration, the spacing between horizontal arms control lines for a front along which there is a uniform probability of attack may be determined as follows. If ΔM is the separation between adjacent horizontal lines, then the maximum unopposed infiltration that can be accomplished by the offense is $2\Delta M/\sqrt{12}$. To restrict this maximum infiltration to, say, 30 kms, we equate the maximum possible incursion, $2\Delta M/\sqrt{12}$, to 30 to determine the value of ΔM: $\Delta M = 30\sqrt{12}/2 = 15\sqrt{12} = 52$ kms. Thus the horizontal lines should be spaced 52 kilometers apart.

Defining shorter length-M fronts by constructing horizontal lines of arms control has two major advantages.

1. It permits each side to deploy units close to the border while at the same time maintaining the optimal unconstrained force geometry within the confines of each individual segment bounded by the horizontal arms control lines. By making lethality transfers between segments highly conspicuous, the horizontal arms control lines provide both opponents with perfect counterconcentration capability. On the other hand, the opportunity for unchallenged conquests of large portions of defense terrain is drastically reduced by keeping the separation between adjacent horizontal lines small.

2. It allows both sides the luxury of misjudging the expected probability distribution of attack along the front without any disastrous consequences. Since ΔM is small in absolute terms, the defense can grossly miscalculate the expected probability density function of invasion and still find its peacetime base only a few kilometers away from the optimal position dictated by the true probability distribution. In general the defense should not make the blunder of locating its base very close to the frontier unless it is extremely confident that the offensive attempt at penetration will occur at or close to the section of the front op-

---

$r_A(0, y) = 1 \ \forall \ y \in [0, M]$
$r_A(x, M/5) = 1 \ \forall \ x \in [0, \infty)$
$r_A(x, 2M/5) = 1 \ \forall \ x \in [0, \infty)$
$r_A(x, 3M/5) = 1 \ \forall \ x \in [0, \infty)$
$r_A(x, 4M/5) = 1 \ \forall \ x \in [0, \infty)$
$r_A(x, y) = 1 \ \forall \ x < 0$
$r_A(x, y) = 0$ for all other values of x and y

Similarly Side B enjoys an information function, $r_B(x, y)$, of the form:

$r_B(0, y) = 1 \ \forall \ y \in [0, M]$
$r_B(x, M/5) = 1 \ \forall \ x \in [0, -\infty)$
$r_B(x, 2M/5) = 1 \ \forall \ x \in [0, -\infty)$
$r_B(x, 3M/5) = 1 \ \forall \ x \in [0, -\infty)$
$r_B(x, 4M/5) = 1 \ \forall \ x \in [0, -\infty)$
$r_B(x, y) = 1 \ \forall \ x > 0$
$r_B(x, y) = 0$ for all other values of x and y

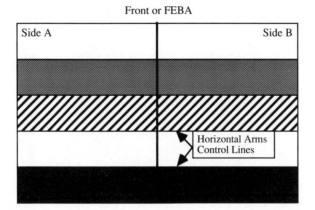

Figure 3-10   Horizontal Lines of Arms Control. The border is divided into length-M segments by the arms control lines. Any two segments with identical shading must contain the same number of deployed units for stability.

posite the base. If the defensive force base is reasonably distant from the border, the small distance between successive horizontal arms control lines guarantees that the exact probability density function of attack does not really matter; for most practical purposes the force units assigned to the defense of a particular segment can base themselves at $(\Delta M/\sqrt{12}, \Delta M/2)$ and be confident of coming very close to minimizing the expected infiltration of the offense.

Vertical Lines of Arms Control

The vertical analogue of horizontal arms control lines is to specify zones parallel to the length-M front and limit the total lethality that can be fielded in each zone. Each zone is bounded by two vertical lines of arms control running parallel to the front. Interzonal force transfers across vertical arms control lines require prior notification and are easily discernible; at the same time, each side has complete freedom in the intrazonal deployment of its forces.[25] As shown in

---

[25]Suppose two countries agree to impose vertical lines of arms control at distances of x_1, x_2, x_3 and x_4 proceeding outward from the length-M front. Thus the first pair of vertical arms control lines is located at a distance of x_1 to the right and a distance of x_1 to the left of the length-M front. Each line extends from $y = 0$ to $y = M$ parallel to the entire length of the border. Similarly the second pair is positioned at $x = x_2$ and $x = -x_2$ on either side of the frontier. The peace accord enhances the intelligence capabilities of Side A from an on-off information function to one of the form:

$$r_A(0, y) = 1 \ \forall \ y \in [0, M]$$
$$r_A(x_1, y) = 1 \ \forall \ y \in [0, M]$$

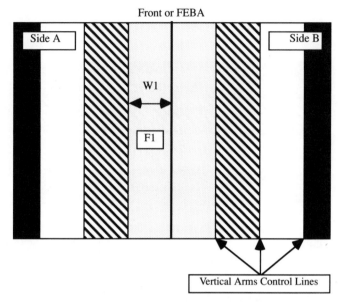

Figure 3-11 Vertical Lines of Arms Control. The territory on each side of the front is divided into vertical zones by the arms control lines. Any two zones with identical shading have the same ceiling on the number of force units that may be deployed within the zones.

Figure 3-11 the corresponding zones on either side of the length-M front are subject to identical ceilings on the total force permitted within them.

Under vertical lines of arms control the side choosing to launch an invasion into enemy territory has two options. The first strategy is a standing start attack in which only the units stationed in the zone closest to the front infiltrate defense territory in the first wave of the invasion. This attack plan provides the aggressor with the advantage of strategic surprise since the defense has no advance warning of the impending invasion. However since only the units allowed in the zone nearest the frontier can be launched into the defender's territory in the first attack wave, the maximum possible imbalance between offensive and defensive forces at the start of the first battle is lowered from N-

---

$$r_A(x_2, y) = 1 \; \forall \; y \in [0, M]$$
$$r_A(x_3, y) = 1 \; \forall \; y \in [0, M]$$
$$r_A(x_4, y) = 1 \; \forall \; y \in [0, M]$$
$$r_A(x, y) = 1 \; \forall \; x < 0$$
$$r_A(x, y) = 0 \text{ for all other values of x and y}$$

Analogously the information function for Side B has the property:

to-1 to F_1-to-1, where F_1 is the force ceiling on the zone nearest to the front. For a standing start attack vertical lines of arms control can dramatically reduce attacker-to-defender force imbalances, aiding the defense in fulfilling the Casualty Exchange and Duration Conditions.

The second option open to the attacker is to transport forces from zones farther back from the front to locations closer to the border before initiating the incursion into defense terrain. While the defense may no longer enjoy advantagous attacker-to-defender force ratios, the defending commander is provided with advance warning of at least W_1/v_{aa}—where W_1 is the width of the zone closest to the front and v_{aa} is the attacker's speed of transporting force across this zone—to prepare for an onslaught by the additional offensive units from Zones 2 and beyond. An unexpected crossing of a vertical arms control line sends an early alarm to the defense of the potentially aggressive intentions of its neighbor and of the possibility that the initial offensive onslaught may be conducted with more than F_1 units.[26]

The objective of a vertical grid of arms control lines is to compel both sides to disperse firepower inward from the front and thus adopt a defensive posture. How should the lethality cap on and the width of each zone parallel to the front be determined? These parameters should be chosen to allow each side to deploy optimal defensive force geometries. If the most general formulation of the Defense Positioning Problem, which permits overlap in the assignment of front segments to defending bases, is solved, there will usually emerge a large number of defense geometries that satisfy the Duration, Casualty Exchange and Completeness Conditions. Among these force geometries each side should

---

$r_B(0, y) = 1 \ \forall \ y \in [0, M]$
$r_B(-x_1, y) = 1 \ \forall \ y \in [0, M]$
$r_B(-x_2, y) = 1 \ \forall \ y \in [0, M]$
$r_B(-x_3, y) = 1 \ \forall \ y \in [0, M]$
$r_B(-x_4, y) = 1 \ \forall \ y \in [0, M]$
$r_B(x, y) = 1 \ \forall \ x > 0$
$r_B(x, y) = 0$ for all other values of x and y

[26]In general let W_1, W_2, W_3, ..., W_j, ..., W_J represent the widths of the J vertical arms control zones parallel to the front agreed upon by two sides and let F_1, F_2, F_3, ..., F_j, ..., F_J be their corresponding force ceilings. Let v_{aa} be the velocity of the attacker's forces on their home turf. If the invader wishes to increase the initial force imbalance in its favor by employing more than the F_1 units allowed in the vertical zone closest to the front to initiate its attack, the attacker must transport force units from Zones 2, 3, ..., j, ..., J to Zone 1 prior to the commencement of the offense campaign. However this interzonal transfer of lethality provides the defender with advance warning that the incursive at-

choose the solution that keeps unopposed offensive incursion to a minimum. The width of the vertical zones and the force ceilings associated with each zone should be determined to allow each side to deploy that force geometry that yields the least territory to the invader. The agreement to abide by vertical lines of arms control leaves each side with *no choice* but to deploy the optimal defensive force geometry as determined by the most general form of the Defense Positioning Problem. To summarize, the spacing of the vertical grid and the ceilings on force levels should be chosen to permit the fielding of the optimal defensive force geometry. Once each side has agreed to adhere to the vertical lines of arms control, both nations are automatically compelled to position troops in close, or at least approximate, concordance with the optimal defensive force structure.

Demilitarized Zones

The creation of demilitarized zones parallel to the front on either side of a two-country border enables both sides to move bases nearer the length-M front.

---

tempt might involve more than F_1 units. If the invader decides to dispatch the total allowed lethality in the first two zones, namely $F_1 + F_2$, into defense territory it provides the defending commander advance warning of W_1/v_{aa} since the F_2 force units must be transported across Zone 1. If the aggressor seeks to conduct its attempt at conquest employing $F_1 + F_2 + F_3$ units, it is compelled by the vertical arms control regime to warn its adversary of its designs a time period $[W_1 + W_2]/v_{aa}$ prior to the penetration of the front. The schedule below indicates the minimum advance warning before infiltration available to the defending commander for increasing values of the maximum attacker-to-defender initial force imbalance achievable by the offense.

Scenario number	Maximum possible offense-to-defense initial force imbalance	Advance warning time available to the defense
1	$F_1 : 1$	0
2	$F_1 + F_2 : 1$	W_1/v_{aa}
3	$F_1 + F_2 + F_3 : 1$	$[W_1 + W_2]/v_{aa}$
4	$F_1 + F_2 + F_3 + F_4 : 1$	$[W_1 + W_2 + W_3]/v_{aa}$
...		
j	$F_1 + F_2 + F_3 + ... + F_j : 1$	$[W_1 + W_2 + ... + W_{j-1}]/v_{aa}$
...		
J	$F_1 + F_2 + F_3 + ... + F_J : 1$	$[W_1 + W_2 + ... + W_{J-1}]/v_{aa}$

In Scenario J, the invader launches all its lethality into defense terrain in a single stroke. This situation is identical to an incursive attempt by all N offensive units. As a result of the vertical lines of arms control, the defense receives an advance notice of $[W_1 + W_2 + ... + W_{J-1}]/v_{aa}$ that all its neighbor's N force units could be headed for an invasion of the defense homeland.

The demilitarized zone can be visualized as a region immediately adjacent to the front where neither side can position armored, mechanized or infantry divisions and with a very low ceiling on total deployed lethality. Further the information capabilities of each side no longer fall off at the front; each nation has perfect intelligence on the whereabouts of enemy battalions within the demilitarized zone of its neighbor. The on-off information function switches off only past the demilitarized zone of the adversary.[27] Thus the instant the opponent's forces cross the vertical tripwire posed by the edge of its own demilitarized zone, the defender is alerted and can monitor the progress and trajectory of the enemy units as they traverse their own demilitarized zone. Because the attacking units are fully visible to the defender once in their own demilitarized zone, they must proceed as quickly as possible towards their targets inside defense territory. In response the defender may dispatch forces into the adversary's demilitarized zone to contain the advancing spearhead. A demilitarized zone of width W propels the defense locus forward by a distance W and allows the defense to move all defensive encampments a distance W towards the front. Figure 3-12 depicts how the defense locus is pulled forward by the demilitarized zone, thereby tremendously reducing the depth of uncontested offensive penetration into defense territory.

An increase of ΔW in the width of the demilitarized zones on either side of the length-M front allows each side to move forces a distance ΔW closer to the front. For comparison purposes note that reducing the distance between horizontal lines of arms control by ΔM allows units on either side to move closer to the border by a distance of approximately $\Delta M/\sqrt{12} = 0.29\Delta M$ only. However there is a limit on how far back the demilitarized zones can be extended from the frontier. One way to compare the relative merits of horizontal arms control lines and demilitarized zones is to examine which of the two schemes permits greater forward positioning of the defense. Let us investigate how far forward an unconstrained defense can base itself if facilitated by a demilitarized zone. To truly contrast the effectiveness of horizontal lines with demilitarized zones one must assume that the defense deploys the unconstrained solution to the generalized Defense Positioning Problem in the demilitarized zone scenario,

---

[27]Suppose the demilitarized zones extend for a distance W on each side of the length-M front. Then the information function of Side A, $r_A(x)$, is given by:

$$r_A(x) = 1 \ \forall \ x \leq W$$
$$r_A(x) = 0 \ \forall \ x > W$$

Similarly Side B's information function takes the form:

$$r_B(x) = 1 \ \forall \ x \geq -W$$
$$r_B(x) = 0 \ \forall \ x < -W$$

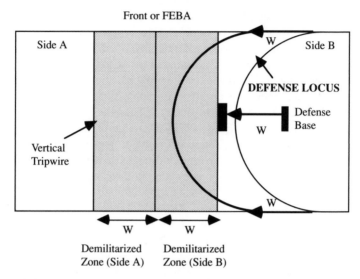

Figure 3-12 Demilitarized Zones. Shaded region indicates demilitarized zones. Arrows depict forward displacement of Side B's defense locus and defense base as a consequence of Side A's demilitarized zone. The thick curve is Side B's new defense locus after the vertical tripwire is put in place.

since the force geometries protecting each segment of the length-M front in the horizontal arms control lines scenario are also unconstrained and guarantee the defense a perfect counterconcentration capability. Suppose two neighbors, A and B, agree to create demilitarized zones of width W on either side of their common front. Side B adopts an unconstrained force geometry and bases all its units at a single base. The demilitarized zone on Side B's territory cannot extend beyond the location of Side B's force center. Since Side B's information function extends into A's demilitarized zone and since B is free to dispatch units into A's demilitarized region to repulse any of A's troops that infiltrate the outer edge of A's demilitarized zone, B's force units should position themselves at a distance of $M/\sqrt{12}$ from the remote boundary of A's demilitarized zone. In other words B's optimal unconstrained force geometry is to locate all units at $(M/\sqrt{12} - W, M/2)$ to account for the forward displacement of distance W experienced by the defense locus. But Side B's demilitarized zone cannot contain any force units and hence can extend only as far as the edge of the defensive lethality base implying $M/\sqrt{12} - W_{MAX} = W_{MAX}$. Hence $W_{MAX} = M/2\sqrt{12}$. W_{MAX} is the maximum permissible width of a demilitarized zone. Thus the closest an unconstrained defense can approach the front through the construction of demilitarized zones is $M/2\sqrt{12}$. The same proximity to the front can be gained by the construction of a single horizontal arms control line at $M/2$. Furthermore, if

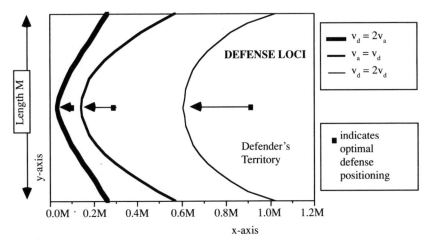

Figure 3-13   Defense Locii for $v_d = 2v_a$, $v_a = v_d$ and $v_a = 2v_d$. The x-axis is calibrated in terms of the length of the front.

the two combatants are willing to partition the length-M front into more than two horizontal zones, each side can achieve still greater dispersion and forward positioning of forces while maintaining the ability to match the invader unit for unit at each focus of penetration.

Velocity Differentials

The introduction of a velocity differential in favor of the defense is another technique for rationalizing the forward placement of forces. If v_d represents the average velocity of the defender on home terrain and v_a denotes the average velocity of the attacking forces travelling over defense terrain, then the objective is to maximize the differential between v_d and v_a. Figure 3-13 shows how both the optimal force location and the defense locus are pushed forward when the defense can transport force over its home terrain faster than the offense can.

Thus the arms control accord should seek by mutual consent to structure forces, equipment and terrain in a manner that ensures units unequivocal superiority in locomotion over home territory. Each side must be capable of outstripping the attacking forces when subjected to an invasion and, in turn, must be surpassed by the opponent when initiating the attack. Functionally, the goal of v_d greater than v_a might be accomplished by the deployment along the border of a network of barriers and minefields or even of a remote-controlled, hardened-bunker passive defense system equipped with immobile machine guns, anti-tank missile launchers and artillery batteries as envisioned in Part Two. Passive defense technologies such as these can be deployed in the region between the frontier and the defense locus to slow the would-be conqueror, allowing defending divisions more time to travel from their peacetime bases to the point of interception with the incursionary columns along the defense locus. Short-range close air support aircraft can also be used to engage enemy airpower in aerial combat and to bombard and carpet-bomb the advancing ground forces, further hindering the invader in its progress over unfamiliar terrain.

Passive Defenses and Mobility Constraints

Passive defenses such as an unmanned, remote-controlled bunker defense with hardened, stationary bunkers each housing limited weaponry, such as machine guns, anti-tank missiles, anti-aircraft guns and anti-missile missiles, should be distributed over the region adjoining the front. The passive defense network can use drones or Remotely Piloted Vehicles (RPVs) for reconnaissance and intelligence on the whereabouts of the enemy. The single biggest virtue of passive defenses is that they can be constructed such that few human lives are at risk. Since they do not demand much manpower, passive defenses can afford to be quite large and can run the entire length of the border to prevent the adversary from outflanking the stationary elements of the passive defense system.

Passive defenses are intrinsically nonoffensive. It is hardly a serious threat to a neighbor that the deployer of a passive defense will uproot its buried, hardened bunkers or vandalize the firepower within its bunkers to *secretly* launch an invasion into the neighbor's territory. The neighbor would receive ample advance warning of any intentions to use the passive defense system for purposes of aggression. Because of their nonoffensive nature, passive defenses can be deployed in the region adjoining the frontier with an allied country in order to guard against surprises—either the unexpected predatory designs of that neighbor or the possibility of an enemy seizing the territory of the friendly neighbor and then using the captured border districts as a base from which to attack the defender.

As mentioned earlier, a bunker-type defense can reduce the invader's speed over defense terrain, dissipate the forward momentum of the attacking force concentration and take a big bite out of the aggressor's lethality. The painful progress of the enemy through the defender's bunker network leaves accurate and conveniently available traces of the coordinates and evolving trajectory of the hostile forces. Arms control agreements must force the transfer of lethality from conventional basing modes to modes with limited mobility and minimal offensive potential. One method may be to mandate mobility constraints on each side's residual lethality after outright k percent cuts. An example of such a regime is elaborated in the following table.

Percentage of each side's residual lethality subject to the mobility constraint	Maximum range over which the lethality unit can be transported (in kms)
10	5
10	15
15	25
15	50
50	No limit

Such a regime automatically compels both sides to structure a significant portion of their allowed firepower in passive defense-like configurations. Thus if Side A has $N(1 - k)$ lethality units after mandated arms reductions, one-tenth of the $N(1 - k)$ units must be structured so that their maximum mobility is less than 5 kilometers. Note that the mobility constraints on the permitted physical displacement of firing platforms must also include restrictions on the range of their projectiles to truly limit the offensive potential of the passive defense. If the launch platforms are fixed within a circle of radius 5 kilometers but the missiles discharged by the platforms can accurately target locations 500 kilometers away, the ability of the platforms to strike targets deep within the neighbor's homeland has not been vitiated by the mobility constraint.

Traditionally military commanders have been extremely reluctant to limit the mobility of their forces. Immobility has been considered synonymous with weakness and vulnerability. And elsewhere we have demonstrated the advantages that flow from maintaining agility and fluidity in transporting forces both orthogonal to and parallel to the frontier. However it should be emphatically clear that in our discussion of mobility constraints we are advocating that only a small but significant minority of the total forces of *both* sides be structured as a dispersed passive defense with limited mobility. Further, such a nonthreatening basing should be forced upon both sides only as part of a comprehensive arms control agreement, the paramount objective of which is to first and foremost reduce the aggregate war-waging capacity of both sides by a third or a half. A massive truncation of the current force levels fielded by all nations would reduce the perceived threat of a concentrated offensive attack, considerably increasing the viability and attractiveness of a distributed and inert passive defense system. Besides, if the passive defense is light on the utilization of manpower, shifting lethality into passive defense-type deployment modes will, over the long run, free up significant human resources for employment in activities of far greater benefit to society, such as basic and applied scientific and

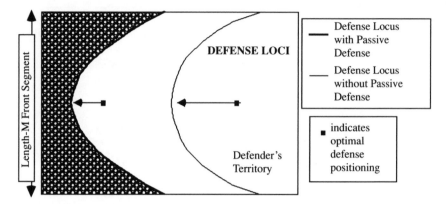

Figure 3-14 Implementation of an Arms Control Treaty with Mobility Constraints. The mobility constrained units are configured as a passive defense deployed in the shaded area between each segment of the front and the new defense locus associated with that segment. The passive defense decreases the attacker's velocity and causes the defense locus to de displaced forward reducing unopposed offensive infiltration.

medical research. Finally, if all parties to an accord willingly agree to base roughly the same proportion of their total permitted lethality as a bunker-type or other passive defense system, no side has any advantage relative to its neighbors in its flexibility to relocate divisions.

A bunker-style passive defense can be integrated with the optimal K-constrained geometry adopted by the defense as shown in Figure 3-14. The mobility-constrained lethality units of the defender can be positioned as a passive defense in the region between each segment of the length-M front and the new, or postbunker, defense locus associated with that segment. The defending units assigned to the K peacetime bases of the K-constrained force geometry are not inhibited in their mobility by the passive defense since the passive defense elements extend inward only to the edge of the defense locus. Thus the passive defense truly succeeds in impeding offensive velocity over defense terrain while leaving the defense speed of transporting force unchanged. A final, nontrivial application of a passive defense is as a political tripwire. A passive defense on the outskirts of the border between two sides can be transformed into a diplomatic signalling device wherein each combatant can assert that any violation of its outlying passive defense would constitute an act of war and lead to full-scale retaliation, say through air raids on the trespasser's territory. Any incursion into a region protected by a passive defense system would be highly visible to the international community, establishing a clear sequence of the order in which events escalate and justifying the defender's determination to mobilize fully. If both countries facing each other across a common border deploy passive defenses, it might be possible to treat any mobile expedition possessing firepower greater than a specified limit that crosses into its own passive defense territory as indicative of hostile intentions and meriting a full-scale response from its neighbor if not immediately withdrawn and explained. As discussed earlier, pushing the vertical tripwire forward into the enemy's territory allows the defender to position its forces closer to the length-M front and lowers the unopposed conquest of defense terrain that the would-be invader across the border can hope to accomplish. Thus passive defenses can serve as effective and efficient *early* tripwires while denying either side any strategic benefit of surprise in launching an invasion.

Nuclear Decoupling

One source of pressure for the dispersal of defending lethality is generated by the possibility of nuclear bombardment of local force concentrations. The need to distribute forces leads to the relinquishment of optimal force geometries, which tend to concentrate defensive forces at a few locations as opposed to more dispersed and forward positions. These latter positions relinquish the defender's perfect counterconcentration capability in exchange for force dispersal and might be unable to fulfill the Casualty Exchange and Duration Conditions. Often the need to distribute forces becomes the driving force in the defender's force structuring algorithm, leading to the adoption of thinly distributed force structures completely incapable of containing offensive attempts at a breakthrough. The nuclear threat against local concentration can be alleviated by adopting policies of no first-use of nuclear weapons by both sides, by decoupling the nuclear command and control structure and the capacity to employ nuclear warheads from conventional force authority and, if both sides are amenable, by eliminating tactical nuclear weapons from the theater of war. Nuclear decoupling in itself will not cure the vulnerability problem of local force concentrations but is a big step towards allowing the defender to optimize its force geometry.

Relaxing the Information Functions

On a more idealistic note, if both combatants are willing to accept completely defensive postures and give up the ideology of counteroffense, it might be feasible to ban deep interdiction aircraft and fighters and long-range precision-guided munitions from the theater of war. If the defensive force structure is truly robust, the defense only needs information on the offensive intentions of the attacker; there is really no imperative for retaining the capability to engage hostile forces on enemy territory.[28] The defender can utilize the information on offensive deployment to optimize its force distribution and patiently await the arrival of the first invading unit. If the means for executing a deep attack can be eliminated, each side may permit its opponent to deploy information-collecting webs within its territory in order to relax the steepness of the information functions confronting the nations and extend them beyond the front into hostile terrain. The extended knowledge of mutual force deployments that comes with the relaxed information functions can enhance the optimization of defensive force positioning for both sides. However, this knowledge can only be exchanged if each nation is guaranteed that the knowledge will not be used to destroy its armed forces on home ground in a preemptive attack. Only then is conventional stability enhanced. In this idyllic scenario, even if one side does decide to launch an invasion, the only means for gaining control over the opponent's territory is to dispatch attacking units into defense terrain, a war situation for which the forewarned defense will hopefully be optimized, racing to fortified and prepared points of conflict along the defense locus. Of course, in an optimistic vein, if both sides possess optimal defensive force structures, the futility of attempting a conquest and the extreme unlikelihood of success will in themselves obviate any desire for armed interaction.

Conclusion

While some of the seven schemes for structuring arms control agreements illustrated above are mutually exclusive, most of the schemes complement each other very well to create an atmosphere conducive to achieving deep weapons cuts. As an example, two sides could agree to create horizontal lines of arms control

---

[28]Needless to say, there will always be strong arguments, such as the need for power projection, for retaining *some* offensive capability to engage enemy forces on their home territory. Invasions are often launched not for the purpose of gaining territory but to liberate the peoples of the invaded lands from an unpopular or repressive regime. Given the tremendous range of strategic and political missions that are often fulfilled by military means, it is impossible to convince nations to disavow all weapons of aggression. However tremendous improvement from the status quo in the stability of conventional force balances and deep cuts might be accomplished if the driving philosophy behind the structuring and positioning of forces was *predominantly* defensive among the *majority* of nations. The cornerstone of defense doctrine should be developing an ability to defeat enemy units as they penetrate into defense terrain, not capturing equivalent portions of enemy territory, conducting preemptive strikes or encouraging vertical escalation. Nevertheless, a handful of bricks in the defender's force structure might permit the means for counteroffense and power projection. It is not really necessary that all countries forgo all means for engaging hostile forces on enemy territory to accomplish very deep force cuts.

spaced 50 kilometers apart. Within each horizontal zone, the two sides could create demilitarized regions extending for a distance of 6 kilometers on either side of the border. Further, 25 percent of each side's total lethality could be constrained in its mobility and could be structured as a passive defense in each horizontal zone. The two treaty signatories could limit deep interdiction aircraft and long-range missiles and grant the opponent inspection rights and air rights for a specified number of drones up to a distance of 100 kilometers inward from the front. Such a combination of concrete concessions and confidence-building measures might allow both sides to become comfortable with a 50 percent cut in overall force levels. An arms control treaty could also take a slightly different approach. Both sides could create a demilitarized zone 25 kilometers wide on either side of a common front of 200 kilometers. The territory beyond the demilitarized zones could be divided by vertical arms control lines with a cap on the total lethality that may be deployed in a particular vertical zone. In addition both sides could agree to eliminate tactical and intermediate-range nuclear weapons from the war zone and to impose a mobility constraint on a fifth of their total firepower.

The precise nature of the weapons reduction regime most suitable for a specific region will obviously depend on factors such as the topography of the physical terrain, the kinds of weapons possessed by the opposing entities, the risk tolerance of the involved nations, the economic, human and psychological costs of negotiating, implementing, monitoring and enforcing the chosen arms control treaty and the aversion to allowing the dictates of the arms control agreement to disrupt the normal way of life of each country's citizens. The power of the approaches to arms control described above lies in the fact that when employed in conjunction with one another their ability to encourage very deep reductions and foster low force-to-space densities is multiplicative rather than additive. It remains to be seen whether the political will, vision and daring exists to do away with the vast stockpiles of the instruments of war that have been amassed by all nations. The ultimate challenge is whether we have the courage to rely on a philosophy of robust defense on our own territory as our *primary* deterrent against attack instead of yielding to the temptation of counteroffense and counteraggression.

Outline of Part Three

The Impact of Deep Arms Reductions on Optimal Force Geometries

How do deep force cuts, such as a 50 percent reduction in fielded lethality, change the optimal force geometry of the defense? Part of the loss in defensive firepower caused by deep force cuts can be compensated through the deployment of hardened bunker-type passive defenses, which are limited in their mobility and counteroffensive capability and are inherently nonoffensive and

therefore stabilizing. Nevertheless, the major burden of the reduction in lethality must be borne by the traditional infantry and armored divisions of both sides.
Consider a N-strong defender confronted by an opponent also armed with N
force units. The defending units are positioned in a U-constrained geometry pri-
or to an arms control treaty that reduces the aggregate lethality of both sides by
k percent. The restrictions on defensive force positioning imposed by the arms
control regime depend on how forward and dispersed is the pre-reduction U-
constrained lethality matrix and on how deep are the mandated force cuts:

Pre-reduction Force Geometry	Post-reduction Optimal Defensive Force Positioning Options
Unconstrained with all N units at a single base	Unconstrained with all N(1 - k) units at the same base. The unconstrained defensive force geometry was derived based on parity in overall might between the two opponents and does not depend on absolute force levels. Whether each side has N or N(1 - k) units is irrelevant.
U-constrained with N(1 - k) >= U	No change in defensive force geometry necessary. Apply the k percent reductions uniformly to each base in the defensive lethality matrix.
U-constrained with N(1 - k) < U	The defender is limited to the universe {1-constrained, 2-constrained, ..., N(1 - k)-constrained} with N(1 - k) less than U. To determine determine which of the N(1 - k) geometries is is optimal the defender must resolve the generalized Defense Positioning Problem with N(1 - k) units as the input. Since the most dispersed geometry available to the defense is limited to N(1 - k)-constrained, the defense is compelled to adopt a less forward positioned force geometry, permitting the invader to achieve greater unchallenged incursions into defense territory. Besides, even the deployment of a N(1 - k)-constrained geometry might not be feasible because of the diminution in the defender's vertical force-to-space density parallel to the front.

In a world where all parties are equipped with comparable firepower and are
able and willing to adopt the optimal unconstrained defensive force posture,

there is no militarily justifiable lower limit on the levels to which nation-states may reduce their deployed forces by mutual agreement as long as parity in overall lethality is maintained. However, if the defense posture before reductions is highly dispersed and based far forward or the level of force cuts is very deep, an arms control treaty could compel the relocation of defensive firepower in a far less forward lethality matrix than its pre-reduction predecessor.

In general, the defense planner can determine the optimal post-reduction force geometry by recomputing the most forward positioned and least permissive of the robust defensive force structures identified by using the step-by-step algorithm for solving the generalized Defense Positioning Problem outlined in Part One with the reduced force levels as inputs.

Satisfying the Duration and Casualty
Exchange Conditions under Deep Force Cuts

The Duration Condition

Concomitant with the increased inward displacement of defending units from the frontier caused by deep force cuts is the thinning out of forces along the direction of the front. For instance, while the average separation between adjacent defending units in a N-constrained scenario is M/N, the intervening distance between successive units doubles to 2M/N for a N/2-constrained basing. As a consequence of this vertical diminution in force-to-space density parallel to the front, reinforcing defensive echelons are forced to travel greater distances in the post-reduction environment to arrive at the initial point of contact with an invading spearhead. If the reinforcing echelons are to satisfy the Duration Condition and arrive at the interception location prior to the termination of the prior engagement, battle durations in the force-depleted world must increase to accommodate the longer distances traversed by the secondary and tertiary defending waves.

The increase in battle duration required to justify weapon cuts for a defender who deploys a fully dispersed and forward-positioned defense both before and after arms reductions is easily calculated. If the defender possesses N_1 units located as a N_1-constrained basing prior to a cut of $(N_1 - N_2)/N_1$ percent and the defender positions its N_2 units after the reductions in a N_2-constrained force geometry, the post-reduction geometry will satisfy the Duration Condition only if the length of all battles is augmented by the factor N_1/N_2 once the arms cut is in place.

A reduction in force levels uniformly applied to both sides lowers the maximum imbalance the aggressor can hope to achieve at the commencement of any single encounter with the defending units. Thus a reduction in deployed forces translates to a decrease in the initial force ratio, γ. If the duration of an individual engagement is to increase in proportion to the shrinkage in γ, the battle duration curve must be relatively steep. If the τ-curve is flat instead, there will be little or no increase in battle length with decreasing initial force ratio, making it very difficult for reinforcing echelons to travel the greater distances between units in a force-depleted situation and arrive in time to prevent the offense from accomplishing a breakthrough.

How steep should the curve of battle duration relative to the initial attacker-to-defender force ratio be to permit force dispersion and forward emplacement under circumstances of low force-to-space density? A *sufficient but not necessary* condition on steepness is that the absolute value of the initial force ratio elasticity of the battle duration curve be not less than unity. Mathematically:

$$\frac{\dfrac{\partial \tau}{\tau}}{\dfrac{\partial \gamma}{\gamma}} \leq -1$$

In other words, the percentage increase in battle length that accompanies a reduction in the initial force ratio must be equal to or greater than the percentage decrease in the initial force ratio that caused the rise in battle duration. Battle duration must be an *elastic* function of the initial force ratio.

The Casualty Exchange Condition

Along any axis of infiltration there will, in general, be a series of encounters between the offensive force concentration and successive defending echelons. The Casualty Exchange Condition will be satisfied provided the weighted arithmetic mean of the average attacker-to-defender casualty exchange ratios prevailing in each of these engagements is not less than unity. Each exchange ratio is weighted by the number of defensive units involved in the particular encounter in which the exchange ratio is observed.

A sufficient condition for a K-constrained defense to satisfy the Casualty Exchange Condition is that the Kth pole of the casualty exchange function lie on or beyond K on the initial force ratio axis. The first pole of the casualty exchange function is the maximum amount of attacking lethality that can be eliminated by a solitary defending unit. The second pole of the casualty exchange function is the maximum offensive lethality that can be destroyed by two consecutive defense waves each equipped with a single unit of firepower. The second defense wave arrives at the initial point of contact and engages the enemy immediately after the annihilation of the first defense wave; there is no overlap between the two defending echelons. Analogously, the third pole of the casualty exchange function is the maximum offensive firepower that can be incapacitated by three defense waves arriving in strict succession at the battlefield. Given a graph of the casualty exchange function for a particular pair of opponents, the poles of the casualty exchange function can be very easily constructed by a simple graphical approach of drawing 45° lines and dropping perpendiculars to the x-axis. An estimate of the degree of dispersion allowed by the casualty exchange function is immediately available by observing which is the last pole to coincide with or succeed its corresponding initial force ratio. The requirement that the Kth pole must be greater than or equal to K for a K-constrained defense to satisfy the Casualty Exchange Condition is a simple rule of thumb which can be used to estimate the number of bases into which defensive forces may be divided by visual inspection of the casualty exchange curve. A relatively flat casualty exchange curve allows higher-order poles to lie beyond their corresponding initial force ratios, permitting extensive dispersion and forward basing of defensive force units, while a steeply downward-sloping casualty exchange function may severely limit defensive dispersion. The Kth pole rule is a special instance of the requirement that the weighted arithmetic mean of the casualty exchange ratio be greater than or equal to unity.

How do deep force cuts affect the satisfaction of the Casualty Exchange Condition by a defensive force geometry? Equal force reductions on both sides reduce initial attacker-to-defender force ratios since the maximum imbalance is lowered from N-to-1 to N(1 - k)-to-1. Lower initial force ratios mean higher casualty exchange ratios because of the downward-sloping nature of the casualty exchange function. Hence a weighted arithmetic mean of casualty exchange ratios in the post-reduction universe will be at least as large as its antecedent in the pre-reduction world. If the defensive force geometry prior to weapon cuts displayed casualty exchange ratios whose weighted arithmetic mean was not less than unity, the decrease in initial force ratios that accompanies an across-the-board lethality cut ensures that weighted arithmetic mean casualty exchange ratios in the post-reduction world will also be greater than or equal to unity. The newly constituted defense will therefore be at least as efficient as its ante-reduction precursor in annihilating the total offensive lethality along each axis of invasion.

The capability of the defense to prevent offensive breakthroughs and protect its homeland without invading the enemy's territory is strengthened by steep battle duration curves and flat casualty exchange functions. Steep battle duration curves allow deep force cuts while flat casualty exchange functions permit highly dispersed and forward-positioned defensive force geometries.

The Muddle over Force-to-space Ratios

Many prominent thinkers in the field of conventional force planning have expressed the view that there are restrictions on the length of front that can be defended by a unit of force. For example, one belief is that roughly one ADE (Armored Division Equivalent) is required to hold every 25 kilometers of front. According to the force-to-space proponents, the defense must deploy this minimum force-to-space density along the entire length of the front to prevent offensive breakthroughs. In its strictest form, the doctrine of force-to-space espouses that the requirement on the defense to maintain a threshold force-to-space density is not altered by any changes in the size, composition or potency of the enemy forces. The force-to-space argument was primarily used prior to the collapse of the Warsaw Pact to justify NATO's inability to make any cuts in deployed lethality in Central Europe.

There are several fatal flaws in the logic behind the philosophy of force-to-space:

1. It was proved in Part One that under the assumptions of a uniform probability distribution of attack and equal offensive and defensive velocities of transporting force on defense terrain, a defense geometry that bases all units at $(M/\sqrt{12}, M/2)$ minimizes unopposed offensive infiltration and possesses perfect counterconcentration capability. For the 1-constrained force geometry there are no restrictions of any kind on how large M can be. Depending upon its removal from the border, the same unit can *optimally* defend a front 25 kilometers long, 50 kilometers long or 1,000 kilometers long. However as the length of the front defended by the unit increases, so does the inward displacement of the unit from the partitioning border. As M increases, the defense locus is pushed inward, permitting the opponent to seize larger tracts of defense terrain unchallenged and increasing the enemy's reward for a first strike. Thus it might be prudent to prescribe a specific numerical threshold on the invader's infiltration *orthogonal* to the front, but without solving the Defense Positioning Problem there is no way to come up with a minimum force-to-space density *parallel* to the front.

2. In requiring a minimum density of force along the front no account is taken of the probability distribution of attack. The density of defensive forces at a location along the front must represent the defender's expectations of the likelihood of attack at that point and cannot be independent of the probability of penetration.

3. The force-to-space approach does not recognize or incorporate any differences in the intelligence, reconnaissance and surveillance capabilities of the two sides in determining the one ADE per 25 kilometers rule.

4. There is no mechanism for adjusting the force-to-space rule for the different relative speeds at which the offense and defense can mobilize and transport force units.

5. It is impossible from the statement of the force-to-space rule to infer the strategic goals of the defense. Is the defender minimizing offensive infiltration, maximizing offensive casualties, maximizing the ratio of offensive casualties to offensive penetration or maximizing the ratio of offensive casualties to defensive casualties? It is not clear in what sense the force-to-space rule is optimal.

6. Stationing units in accordance with the law of force-to-space is a static procedure. No dynamic analysis is conducted to demonstrate that at least under a simulated invasion, the one ADE per 25 kilometers defense does indeed succeed in preventing offensive breakthroughs for the universe of possible attack plans. There is no analogue of the Duration, Casualty Exchange and Complete-

ness Conditions, and no sensitivity analysis of defensive response to different infiltration scenarios is deemed necessary by the force-to-space adherents.

7. Postulating a minimum force-to-space density has the effect of making a country's armament level proportional to the length of its frontiers with adjoining states and independent of the quantity of lethality possessed by its neighbors. The correct method of determining optimal force geometries is to solve the generalized Defense Positioning Problem. Reducing the science of structuring defensive forces to a universally applicable one ADE per 25 kilometers rule is misleading and could be extremely dangerous. *Territory comes with two dimensions and the dimension orthogonal to the front cannot be ignored.*

Arms Control Regimes That Facilitate Deep Cuts

Weapon reductions compel the defense to abandon its pre-reduction force geometry and accept a less forward and less dispersed lethality matrix if either the defense posture before reductions is *highly* dispersed and *extremely* forward based or the level of mandated force cuts is *very deep* or both. The backward displacement of the defense locus that accompanies the adoption of a less forward force geometry is destabilizing and raises the reward for first strike. A second concern is the concomitant decrease in defensive force dispersal and the consequent increased vulnerability of defensive force concentrations to decapitation. These obstacles in the path of deep force reductions can be overcome by structuring disarmament protocols in an innovative fashion, keeping in mind what we have learned about the optimal force geometry for the defense and its determinants. A few arms control regimes that facilitate deep cuts are described below.

Horizontal Lines of Arms Control

If the adversary can fluidly transfer force along the entire front without alerting the defender to the force displacement, then the defender is compelled to treat the full length of the border between the two states as a single length-M front. The only path open to a defender, confronted with an excessively long front, who wishes to disperse forces and base units forward is to adopt a suboptimal constrained defense and trade off counterconcentration capability against dispersion and forward emplacement. Such a suboptimal defense is risky and testing its robustness is difficult and based on assumptions about the nature of combat. However if the long border tract can somehow be partitioned into several, smaller length-M fronts, the defense can adopt an optimal unconstrained geometry in each front segment. Such a border partitioning can be accomplished if both sides agree to construct horizontal lines of arms control such that each side is always aware of the opponent's *total* lethality in each region bounded by adjacent horizontal arms control lines. Each side can easily and reliably detect any force transfers across horizontal segments by its neighbor and can match the force transfer so as to always allocate a corresponding number of units to the front segment. Within a region bounded by the horizontal lines, the defender is free to base all units assigned to that sector at the 1-constrained location, because of the relatively small length of the front segment. The separation between the horizontal lines of arms control should be based on the maximum infiltration either side is willing to suffer. For a front with a uniform probability of attack, the distance between the horizontal lines should be $\sqrt{3}I_{MAX}$, where I_{MAX} is the maximum unopposed infiltration either side is willing to tolerate.

Horizontal arms control lines enable both sides to deploy units close to the border without any sacrifice in the capability to counterconcentrate perfectly. A horizontal arms control regime also allows both sides the luxury of misjudging the expected probability distribution of attack of the enemy along the front without any disastrous consequences. Since the front segment defined by the horizontal arms control lines is small in absolute terms, the defense can grossly miscalculate the expected probability density function of invasion and still find its peacetime base only a few kilometers away from the optimal positioning indicated by the true probability distribution of infiltration.

Vertical Lines of Arms Control

The vertical analogue of horizontal arms control lines is to specify zones *parallel* to the length-M front and limit the total lethality that can be fielded in each zone. Interzonal force transfers across vertical arms control lines are easily discernible. The corresponding zones on either side of the length-M front are subject to identical ceilings on the total force permitted within the zones. Under a vertical arms control regime, if the attacker wishes to preserve the advantage of strategic surprise in launching its invasion, it is compelled to initiate the onslaught using only the units allowed in the zone nearest the frontier. Therefore the maximum imbalance that can possibly be experienced by the defense in confronting the first attack wave is lowered from N-to-1 to F_1-to-1, where F_1 is the force ceiling on the zone nearest the front. Alternatively, if the attacker wishes to transport forces from zones removed from the front to locations close to the border before initiating the incursion into defense terrain, the defending commander is provided with advance warning of at least W_1/v_{aa}—where W_1 is the width of the zone closest to the front and v_{aa} is the attacker's speed of transporting force across this zone—to prepare for an onslaught by the additional offensive units from Zones 2 and beyond. As the attacker attempts to achieve higher and higher values of the initial attacker-to-defender force imbalance, the defense is automatically provided with earlier and earlier notification of the impending invasion. The vertical arms control regime thus compels the side with aggressive intentions to sacrifice the element of strategic surprise on the altar of more favorable force imbalances.

The lethality cap on and the width of each zone parallel to the front should be determined so as to allow both sides to deploy a force geometry that solves the most general formulation of the Defense Positioning Problem, with overlap permitted in the assignment of front segments to defending bases. In other words, the primary objective of a vertical grid of arms control lines is to compel both sides to disperse firepower inward from the front and adopt a defensive posture. Since the placement of and force limitations on the vertical zones delineated by the vertical arms control lines correspond to an optimal defensive force geometry, obeying the vertical arms control regime automatically lets each side end up with an optimal or close-to-optimal defensive lethality matrix.

Demilitarized Zones

Demilitarized zones can be visualized as regions immediately adjacent to the frontier where neither side can position armored, mechanized or infantry divisions and with a very restrictive limit on total deployed lethality. Further the intelligence capabilities of each side no longer fall off at the front but extend into the demilitarized zone of its neighbor, switching off only past the demilitarized zone. Thus the instant the opponent's heavy firepower crosses the vertical tripwire posed by the edge of the demilitarized zone on the side of the length-M front away from the defense, the defender is alerted and can dispatch forces into the adversary's demilitarized zone to contain the advancing spearhead. A demilitarized zone of width W on either side of a length-M front propels the defense locus forward by a distance W and allows the defense to displace all defensive encampments a distance W towards the front, thereby reducing considerably the expanse of the defender's heartland open to uncontested conquest by the foe.

Comparison between Horizontal Arms Control Lines and Demilitarized Zones

An increase of ΔW in the width of the demilitarized zones on either side of the length-M front allows each side to move forces a distance ΔW closer to the front. In contrast, reducing the distance between horizontal arms control lines by ΔM allows force units on either side to approach closer to the border by a distance of approximately $\Delta M/\sqrt{12} = 0.29\Delta M$ only. However, there are two drawbacks associated with the concept of demilitarized zones. First, there is a limit on how far back the demilitarized zones can be extended from the frontier. For a length-M front with a uniform probability of attack at each point along the front the closest an unconstrained defense can approach the front through the construction of demilitarized zones is $M/2\sqrt{12}$. For a border with an arbitrary probability density function of infiltration, an unconstrained defense would normally be positioned at a perpendicular distance of σ from the length-M front, where σ is the standard deviation of the probability distribution of attack. An agreement to create demilitarized zones would at most displace the defensive lethality base forward to a separation of $\sigma/2$ from the border. The identical proximity to the frontier can be gained by the construction of a single horizontal arms control line at M/2. Second, the trade-off between force dispersion and perfect counterconcentration is not eliminated by the adoption of demilitarized zones. Note that to truly contrast the effectiveness of horizontal lines with demilitarized zones one must assume that the defense deploys the unconstrained solution to the generalized Defense Positioning Problem in the demilitarized zone scenario, since the force geometries protecting each segment of the length-M front in the horizontal arms control lines scenario are also unconstrained. However, while total defending lethality is divided among the various segments defined by the horizontal lines, the entire defending force in the demilitarized zone scenario must be based at a single location to provide the same kind of perfect counterconcentration ability available with horizontal lines. In conclusion, if the two combatants are willing to partition the length-M front into more than two horizontal zones, each side can achieve greater dispersion and forward emplacement of forces through horizontal arms control lines as opposed to demilitarized zones.

Velocity Differentials

The introduction of a velocity differential in favor of the defense makes room for the forward emplacement of forces. Arms control accords should seek by mutual consent to structure forces, equipment and terrain in a manner that ensures force units unequivocal superiority in locomotion over home territory. Each side must be capable of outstripping the attacking forces when subjected to an invasion and, in turn, must be surpassed by the opponent when initiating the attack. Increasing the differential between v_d and v_a propels both the optimal defensive force location and the defense locus forward. Functionally, the goal of v_d greater than v_a might be accomplished by deploying along the border a network of barriers and minefields or a remote-controlled, hardened-bunker passive defense system and policing the air with short-range close air support aircraft.

Mobility Constraints and Passive Defenses

Arms control agreements must force the transfer of lethality from conventional basing modes to modes with limited mobility and minimal offensive potential. One method may be to mandate mobility constraints on each side's residual lethality after outright k percent cuts. An example of mobility constraints would be as follows. If Side A has $N(1 - k)$ lethality units after the arms reductions mandated by a treaty, mobility constraints would require one-tenth of the $N(1 - k)$ units to be structured so that their maximum mobility is less than 5 kilometers. Another tenth must remain within a radius of 15 kilometers. Further, another 15 percent cannot leave a 25 kilometer radius while another 15 percent have a mobility limitation of 50 kilometers. For the remaining 50 percent of Side A's lethality there are no constraints on mobility. Thus in this illustration some form of mobility constraint would be applied to one-half of Side A's total lethality. Note that the mobility constraints on the permitted physical displacement of firing platforms must also include restrictions on the range of the projectiles launched by the firing platforms to truly limit the offensive potential of the mobility-constrained units.

One very effective manner in which to structure mobility-constrained lethality is to deploy it as a passive defense in the region adjacent to the front. The passive defense system could take the form of an unmanned, remote-controlled bunker defense with hardened, stationary bunkers each housing limited weaponry, such as machine guns, anti-tank missiles, anti-aircraft guns and anti-missile missiles, distributed over the region adjoining the front. The passive defense web could use drones or Remotely Piloted Vehicles (RPVs) for reconnaissance and intelligence on the whereabouts of the enemy. Since the passive defense would not demand much manpower for operation, it can afford to be quite large and can run the entire length of the border to prevent the adversary from outflanking the stationary elements of the passive defense system.

Traditionally, military commanders have been extremely reluctant to limit in any way the mobility of their forces. Immobility has been considered synonymous with weakness and vulnerability. Elsewhere we have demonstrated the advantages that flow to the defense when it maintains agility and fluidity in transporting forces both orthogonal to and parallel to the frontier. However it should be emphatically clear that in our discussion of mobility constraints we are advocating that only a small but significant minority of the total forces of **both** sides be structured as a dispersed passive defense with limited mobility. Further such a nonthreatening basing should be forced upon both sides only as part of a comprehensive arms control agreement whose paramount objective is to first and foremost reduce the aggregate war-waging capacity of both sides by a third or a half. Besides, if all parties to an accord willingly agree to base roughly the same proportion of their total permitted lethality as a bunker-type or other passive defense system, no side has any advantage relative to its neighbors in its flexibility to relocate divisions.

A passive defense can be integrated with the defender's optimal K-constrained force geometry by positioning the passive defense elements in the region between each segment of the length-M front and the post-bunker defense locus associated with that segment. Passive defenses are intrinsically nonoffensive, making it politically feasible to deploy them in the region adjoining the frontier with an allied country just in case the seemingly friendly neighbor turns out to have predatory designs. A bunker-type defense can reduce the invader's speed over defense terrain to a crawl and dissipate the forward momentum of the attacking force concentration, placing a big wedge between the offensive and defensive force velocities, in addition to taking a big bite out of the aggressor's lethality. Finally, a passive defense on the outskirts of the border between two sides can be transformed into an effective diplomatic signalling device wherein each combatant can assert that any violation of its outlying passive defense would constitute an act of war and lead to full-scale retaliation.

Nuclear Decoupling

One source of pressure for the dispersal of defending lethality is generated by the possibility of nuclear bombardment of local force concentrations. The need to distribute forces leads to the relinquishment of optimal force geometries, which tend to concentrate defensive forces at a few locations in exchange for risky, suboptimal substitutes. The nuclear threat against local concentration can be alleviated by adopting policies of no first-use of nuclear weapons, by decoupling the nuclear command and control structure and the capacity to employ nuclear warheads from conventional force authority and, if both sides are amenable, by eliminating tactical nuclear weapons from the theater of war.

Relaxing the Information Functions

If the means for executing a deep attack can be eliminated, each side may permit its opponent to deploy information collating networks within its territory in order to relax the steepness of the information functions confronting the nations and extend them beyond the front into hostile terrain. The extended knowledge of force deployments and mutual intentions that comes with the relaxed information functions can enhance the optimization of defensive force positioning for both sides. However, this knowledge can only be exchanged if each nation is guaranteed that the knowledge will not be used to destroy its armed forces on their own home territory in a preemptive attack. One way to guard against misuse of the information gained through relaxed information functions is to ban deep interdiction aircraft and fighters and long-range precision-guided munitions from the theater of war. Ideally, if the defensive force structure is truly robust, the defense only needs information on the offensive intentions of the attacker; there is really no imperative for retaining the capability to engage hostile forces on enemy territory. Further, if each side can convince the other of the optimality and robustness of its defense and the extreme unlikelihood of success in attempting a conquest, there should be little desire on either side to go to war against its neighbor.

The Defense Positioning Problem and a Nonuniform Probability of Attack

In deciding where to attack along a length-M front, no would-be invader can afford to belittle the significance of surveying the physical layout of the territory to be conquered. Warfare today is dominated by mass motorized units, and the ease with which various regions of the intervening terrain between the two combatants facilitate rapid, large-scale, mechanized and armored vehicle maneuvers is a variable of primary importance in choosing the locations along the front most suited to motorized incursion. In addition to terrain layout, the decision of where to attack is also influenced by factors such as the proximity of the axis of penetration to targets of high strategic value and the likelihood of encountering large defensive force concentrations in the immediate vicinity of the focus of infiltration. Ceteris paribus, the aggressor will always seek to attack those regions of the front that are closest to sites the invader most wishes to occupy, that are less likely to hold defensive forces lying in wait to ambush the unsuspecting foe and that will provide the offense with greater natural cover from the defender's firepower once the no man's land between the two nations has been breached.

Consequently, we expect an attacker if confronted by a length-M front to have some preferences about choosing various points along the front for its onslaught. The defender would doubtless formulate its own expectations of where the offensive penetrations would most likely occur. In terms of probability theory, the defender can attribute a certain probability of assault to each point along the length-M front, giving rise to a probability density function of attack. In the real world, it might not always be true that the invader is equally likely to launch an attack at any point along the front and hence we relax our earlier assumption of a uniform probability of attack along the length-M front. Let P represent the arbitrary probability density function that the defender expects the invader to follow. Then P(f) is the probability that the defender associates with the event that point f along the length-M front will be chosen by the attacker for a penetration. We shall make the simplifying assumptions that each side possesses a single unit of force and that the offensive and defensive velocities over defense terrain are equal. Thus if (x, y) represents the optimal defensive force encampment and f is the point along the length-M front subjected to an offensive penetration, then the unopposed infiltration, I, achieved by the invader is given below (also see Equation 1-6 in Part One).

$$I(x,y;f) = \frac{x^2 + (y - f)^2}{2x} \tag{1A-1}$$

The expected value of the adversary's infiltration into the defender's territory is determined as:

$$\bar{I}(x,y) = \int_0^M I(x,y;f)\, P(f)\, df \tag{1A-2}$$

Substituting for I (x, y; f) from Equation 1A-1:

$$\bar{I} = \int_0^M \frac{x^2 + (y - f)^2}{2x} P(f)\, df \tag{1A-3}$$

To determine the optimal defensive emplacement, x and y are chosen to minimize the expected infiltration.

$$\min_{(x,y)} \left[\int_0^M \frac{x^2 + (y - f)^2}{2x} P(f)\, df \right] \tag{1A-4}$$

$$\frac{\partial}{\partial x}\left[\int_0^M \frac{x^2 + (y - f)^2}{2x} P(f)\, df \right] = 0$$

$$\text{and} \quad \frac{\partial}{\partial y}\left[\int_0^M \frac{x^2 + (y - f)^2}{2x} P(f)\, df \right] = 0 \tag{1A-5}$$

Invoking the Leibniz Rule for interchanging the order of partial differentiation and integration yields:

$$\int_0^M \frac{\partial}{\partial x}\left[\frac{x^2 + (y - f)^2}{2x} \right] P(f)\, df = 0$$

$$\text{and} \quad \int_0^M \frac{\partial}{\partial y}\left[\frac{x^2 + (y - f)^2}{2x} \right] P(f)\, df = 0 \tag{1A-6}$$

Performing the differentiations:

$$\int_0^M \left[1 - \frac{(y - f)^2}{x^2} \right] P(f)\, df = 0$$

$$\text{and} \quad \int_0^M \left[\frac{y - f}{x} \right] P(f)\, df = 0 \tag{1A-7}$$

The integral for y is resolved first.

$$y \int_0^M P\,(f)\,df \ = \ \int_0^M f\,P\,(f)\,df \qquad\qquad \text{(1A-8)}$$

But P(f) is a probability density function that extends from f = 0 to f = M and the following must hold.

$$\int_0^M P\,(f)\,df = 1 \qquad\qquad \text{(1A-9)}$$

This yields:

$$y = \int_0^M f\,P\,(f)\,df \qquad\qquad \text{(1A-10)}$$

$$y = \mu\,(f) \qquad\qquad \text{(1A-11)}$$

where μ (f) denotes the expected or mean value of f and is the point along the length-M front where the aggressor is expected to launch an invasion. Thus the defender should station its forces at a distance along the length-M front equal to the expected value of the probability density function of attack.

Replacing y with μ (f) in the integrand for x gives:

$$\int_0^M \left[1 - \frac{[\mu\,(f) - f]^2}{x^2} \right] P\,(f)\,df = 0 \qquad\qquad \text{(1A-12)}$$

$$\frac{1}{x^2} \int_0^M [\mu\,(f) - f]^2\,P\,(f)\,df \ = \ \int_0^M P\,(f)\,df \qquad\qquad \text{(1A-13)}$$

However, Equation 1A-9 indicates that the right side of the equality is unity, yielding:

$$x^2 \ = \ \int_0^M P\,(f)\,[\mu\,(f) - f]^2\,df \ = \ \text{Var}\,(f) \qquad\qquad \text{(1A-14)}$$

where Var(f) denotes the variance of f and is a measure of the dispersion of the attacker's probability density function about its mean value. It has therefore been proved that:

$$x = \sigma\,(f) \qquad\qquad \text{(1A-15)}$$

where $\sigma(f)^2 = \text{Var}(f)$ and $\sigma(f)$ is the standard deviation of the probability density function of attack.

Thus the defender must base its unit at a distance behind the length-M front equal to the standard deviation, or spread, of the probability density function of attack about its mean. The optimal defense emplacement is wholly and exactly determined by the first two moments, namely, the mean and the standard deviation, of the probability distribution of attack. We generalize our conclusion to the scenario in which each side is armed with N force units as the σ - μ Theorem.

σ - μ THEOREM: *The defense commander can minimize expected offensive infiltration into defense territory and simultaneously match the invader unit for unit at each focus of penetration if all the defending units are concentrated at a distance μ along the length-M front and at a distance σ inward from the border. μ is the mean and σ is the standard deviation of the probability density function of attack the defense expects the would-be conqueror to follow. In terms of our coordinate system established earlier, the optimal point of placement for the defense is given by (σ, μ). In deriving this result it is assumed that the aggressor and the defender possess equal velocities of transporting force over defense territory.*

In comprehending the μ part of the σ - μ Theorem, it is hardly surprising that the defender is required to position all defending lethality diametrically opposite the point along the front where the invader is expected to attempt an infiltration. What is more interesting is the σ portion of the σ - μ Theorem. σ measures the spread of the probability distribution of attack along the front. However when applied to the determination of the optimal defense posture, σ is transformed to a depth perpendicular to the front. Thus a measure of dimension along the front is translated into a dimension orthogonal to the front. Intuitively it should be clear that the greater the variance associated with the universe of possible attacks, that is the larger the spread of the foci of infiltration along the front, the farther removed from the line of partition the defender must be to minimize offensive incursion.

Earlier we advanced the idea of using the defense locus as a proxy for the guaranteed reward accruing to the aggressor for launching the preliminary attack. Our justification for treating the defense locus as a prize for preemption is contained in the ability of the defense locus to measure how far the invader can advance *unchallenged* into the defender's territory for any choice of penetration strategy. The farther the defender's peacetime encampment is removed from the demarcation line, the more permissive is the incursion permitted by the defense locus. However, it has been shown that the inward displacement of the defensive base is equal to the standard deviation of the adversary's probability density function of attack. Thus if the award for a first strike is to be minimized and stability enhanced, the two sides should try to reduce the dispersion or spread of the points along the front that can possibly be transformed into foci of infiltration.

We work through a few examples to clarify the relationship between optimal defense placement and different probability density functions of attack.

$$P\ (f) = \frac{1}{M} \qquad f \in [\,0, M\,]$$

Example 1

This is the uniform probability density function of attack considered earlier.

$$\mu\ (f) = \int_0^M \frac{f}{M}\ df = \frac{f^2}{2M}\bigg|_0^M = \frac{M^2}{2M} = \frac{M}{2}$$

$$Var\ (f) = \int_0^M \left(f - \frac{M}{2}\right)^2 \frac{1}{M}\ df = \frac{1}{3M}\left(f - \frac{M}{2}\right)^3\bigg|_0^M = \frac{2M^3}{2\,4M} = \frac{M^2}{12}$$

Thus for a uniform probability of attack, $(x, y) = [\sqrt{Var(f)}, \mu(f)] = (M/\sqrt{12}, M/2)$, which soundly confirms our direct derivation performed earlier.

Example 2

$$P\ (0) = \frac{1}{2}$$

$$P\ (M\ ) = \frac{1}{2}$$

$P\ (f) = 0\ \forall\ f\ between\ 0\ and\ M$

P(f) as depicted in Figure 1A-1 is a discrete probability density function restricting the possible locations along the front accessible to attack to two, one at each end of the front. It is equally probable that either of the two points will be the focus of infiltration.

The physical realization of such a probability distribution could be a front where the only easily navigated means of ingress, such as flat plains or paved roads, into the defender's territory are at either extremity of the front. In general, discrete probability density functions are ideal for modeling fronts that are extremely hilly or interspersed with bodies of water; thus while the enemy can reallocate forces at leisure behind the cover of the intervening mountainous tract or river without providing any warning to the distant defender, the actual paths along which the adversary can gain entry into the defender's territory are limited and far apart. It is sufficient for the purposes of our model to assign nonzero probabilities of attack to only these potential foci of infiltration and to restrict to zero the probability of penetration in all sections

Figure 1A-1   Example 2: The 2-focus Probability Density Function

between them, thus giving rise to a discrete probability distribution of attack. For the probability density function described above:

$$\mu \ (f) = \left(\frac{1}{2}\right)0 + \left(\frac{1}{2}\right)M \ = \frac{M}{2}$$

$$\text{Var} \ (f) = \left(\frac{1}{2}\right)\left(\frac{M}{2} - 0\right)^2 + \left(\frac{1}{2}\right)\left(\frac{M}{2} - M\right)^2 = \frac{M^2}{4}$$

Hence the optimal defense position for this 2-horned probability distribution is (M/2, M/2). The defensive base is farther removed from the front for this case than is the base for a uniform probability of attack. This is a consequence of the larger variance associated with the 2-focus probability density function when compared with the uniform likelihood of attack distribution ($M^2/4$ as opposed to $M^2/12$). Thus, though in one scenario there are only two points along the front where an attack is envisioned while the other permits the possibility of an attack at every location along the border, it is the former situation that offers the greater prize for preemption and poses a greater threat to mutual stability.

The probability distributions described in Examples 1 and 2 possess a significance above and beyond that addressed in our earlier discussion. Consider the problem of a defense commander charged with the protection of a relatively flat and uniform border district adjoining a length-M front. The demarcation line between the two neighbors is permeable at most locations, and the population density and industrial base of the defender are also smoothly spread over the total defense terrain. The defending regime has little information on which to base its determination of the probability distribution of attack. In such circumstances, the risk-neutral defense planner will assume a uniform probability density of attack since each point along the front is equally accessible and attractive to the aggressor for initiating an attempt at infiltration. The acceptance of a uniform likelihood of incursion minimizes the total tract of defense territory between the length-M front and the defense locus that can be conquered by the invader without encountering any opposition from the defender's forces. This region between the defense locus and the length-M front can be viewed as the summation of all possible infiltrations into defense terrain. Thus the adoption of a uniform probability density function of attack is the *minisum* (*mini*mizing the *sum* of all infiltrations) approach to optimal defense placement.

Conversely, a defending commander who is highly risk averse will seek to minimize the maximum depth of penetration into defense territory that can be accomplished by the aggressor. Such a commander will opt for the 2-focus probability density of attack, since this is the distribution with the highest variance of attack. The maximal spread of the 2-horned discrete probability distribution compels the defender to locate the defensive base at the largest inward distance from the border and consequently minimizes the maximum distance infiltrated by the antagonist. For instance, the maximum incursion permitted by the uniform probability density function is $2M/\sqrt{12} = 0.577M$ while the greatest incursion allowed by the 2-focus distribution is $M/2 = 0.5M$. Thus adherence to the 2-horned discrete probability density function of attack is the *minimax* (*mini*mizing the *max*imum infiltration) approach to the optimization of defensive force positioning.

What if the defense suspects that the attacker might be able to locate the defender's peacetime base prior to the commencement of hostilities? The attacker does not need to pinpoint the x-coordinate or the displacement of the defensive force encampment from the length-M front. All the invader needs to discern is the y-coordinate, or the position along the front, of the defense base. The aggressor can then conduct an infiltration at f = 0 if y is greater than M/2 or at f = M if y is less than M/2. If the enemy is aware of the defensive force geometry, the defender has no choice but to position its unit midway along the length-M front to ensure that the vertical displacement of the defending legions from the focus of penetration is not greater than M/2. Once the defender has chosen y = M/2 as the home for the defensive division, the attacker will be indifferent between the choice of f = 0 and f = M as foci of infiltration. Thus there will be an equal probability of attack at either extremity of the length-M front and a zero probability of incursion at all points in between. In effect, the defender will be confronted by the 2-horned discrete probability distribution of attack described in Example 2 above. The defender should therefore position its unit at a distance of M/2 from the border. Hence if the defender suspects that a potential invader is capable of acquiring accurate intelligence on the location of the defensive homebase, the defender should adopt the point (M/2, M/2) as the optimal force geometry. Stated differently, if the offense has no constraints on its ability to "see" into defense territory while the defense is constricted in its intelligence by an on-off information function, the defender should determine the optimal lethality matrix for positioning defensive forces based on a 2-focus probability density function of attack. This approach is optimal since it minimizes the maximum unopposed infiltration into defense territory accomplished by the invader; in a situation where the aggressor has perfect knowledge of defensive force positioning, the defender can rest assured that the attacker will choose an invasion campaign that guarantees the offense the greatest uncontested penetration into the defender's homeland.

Example 3

$$P(f) = \frac{4}{M^2}f \;\;\forall\;\; f \text{ between } 0 \text{ and } \frac{M}{2}$$

$$P(f) = \frac{4}{M} - \frac{4}{M^2}f \;\;\forall\;\; f \text{ between } \frac{M}{2} \text{ and } M$$

This probability density function of attack is graphed in Figure 1A-2.

$$\mu(f) = \int_0^{\frac{M}{2}} f\left[\frac{4}{M^2}f\right]df + \int_{\frac{M}{2}}^M f\left[\frac{4}{M} - \frac{4}{M^2}f\right]df = \frac{M}{2}$$

$$Var(f) = \int_0^{\frac{M}{2}}\left(f - \frac{M}{2}\right)^2\left[\frac{4}{M^2}f\right]df + \int_{\frac{M}{2}}^M\left(f - \frac{M}{2}\right)^2\left[\frac{4}{M} - \frac{4}{M^2}f\right]df = \frac{M^2}{24}$$

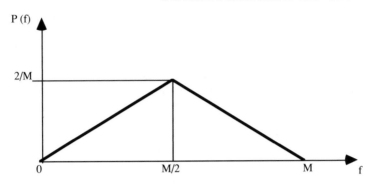

Figure 1A-2   Example 3: The Triangular Probability Density Function

The spread of the triangular probability density function is small with the majority of the "mass" condensed around the mid-point. Thus x is reduced to $M/\sqrt{24}$ while the even symmetry of the probability distribution sets y equal to $M/2$ as before.

So far we have assumed that the defender is willing to base all its forces at a single location. If the defense seeks to disperse force along the front, the optimal defense positioning can be determined by optimizing independently the probability density functions of attack for each sector or subdivision of the front. In each sector the integral of the probability density function of attack over the length of the sector must equal unity; that is, each defensive force commander expects an onslaught somewhere along the fragment of the border assigned to him or her. Any sector where an attempt at infiltration is not expected does not require a defensive base. Mathematically, the overall probability density function of attack for the entire length-M front is sliced into portions corresponding to the division of the length-M front into fragments and the probability distribution for each front segment is normalized to unity before invoking the infiltration minimization routine. The normalization in any given sector should be performed by multiplying the integral of the portion of the overall probability density that is associated with the sector by an appropriate constant. In other words, we require multiplicative normalization to preserve the identity of the mean and variance of the probability subdistribution. The normalized subdensity function in each segment of the length-M front can be used to determine the coordinates of the optimal defense encampment corresponding to that section of the border. The number of defending units assigned to a particular segment is equal to the area of the overall probability density function enclosed within that section multiplied by the total force strength of the defense. Thus the defending lethality is distributed among the front segments in propor-

tion to the area of the overall probability distribution contained within the segment.[1]
This suboptimization procedure is illustrated in Examples 4 and 5 below.

---

[1]Let P(f) be the probability density function of attack along a length-M front that is partitioned by the defender into N equal segments each of length M/N. The kth segment extends from $f = (k-1)$ M/N to $f = k$ M/N. If both the offense and the defense are in possession of J units of firepower, the number of defensive units assigned to the kth sector of the length-M front, U_k, is given as:

$$U_k = J \frac{\int_{\frac{(k-1)M}{N}}^{\frac{kM}{N}} P(f) df}{\sum_{k=1}^{k=N} \int_{\frac{(k-1)M}{N}}^{\frac{kM}{N}} P(f) df} \qquad (1)$$

$$U_k = J \frac{\int_{\frac{(k-1)M}{N}}^{\frac{kM}{N}} P(f) df}{\int_{0}^{\frac{M}{N}} P(f) df + \int_{\frac{M}{N}}^{\frac{2M}{N}} P(f) df + \int_{\frac{2M}{N}}^{\frac{3M}{N}} P(f) df + \ldots + \int_{\frac{(N-1)M}{N}}^{M} P(f) df} \qquad (2)$$

$$U_k = J \frac{\int_{\frac{(k-1)M}{N}}^{\frac{kM}{N}} P(f) df}{\int_{0}^{M} P(f) df} \qquad (3)$$

But $\int_{0}^{M} P(f) df = 1$

Hence $\quad U_k = J \int_{\frac{(k-1)M}{N}}^{\frac{kM}{N}} P(f) df \qquad (4)$

Note that $\quad \sum_{k=1}^{N} U_k = J \sum_{k=1}^{N} \int_{\frac{(k-1)M}{N}}^{\frac{kM}{N}} P(f) df = J \int_{0}^{M} P(f) df = J$

Example 4

Returning to the probability density function considered in Example 2, we impose
the additional constraint that the defensive units must be divided equally between
two separate concentrations. The region of the front from $f = 0$ to $f = M/2$ can be
considered as one sector, while the area from $f = M/2$ to $f = M$ constitutes a second
independent sector. Hence for our 2-pronged probability distribution of attack, there
is a normalized probability of one in the upper sector that an onslaught will be executed at $f = 0$. Thus $N/2$ of the defending force strength will base their camp at $(0, 0)$.
In the lower sector, there is also a normalized probability of one that the attack will
be initiated at $f = M$, leading the remaining $N/2$ defensive force units to base themselves at $(0, M)$. This 2-center defense will satisfy the Duration Condition provided
the defender can transport $N/2$ units of force from one extremity of the front to the
other in the time required by an offensive force of N to annihilate a defense contingent half its magnitude in lethality.

The sum of all the force allotments to individual sectors of the length-M front equals the total
lethality available to the defender.

To determine where the U_k defending forces allocated to the kth subdivision of the front must
be positioned, we must normalize to unity the portion of the overall probability distribution of attack that falls within sector k. The normalized subdensity function, $P_k(f)$, is obtained from the
overall probability density function, $P(f)$, by multiplying $P(f)$ with a constant α_k determined as follows.

$$\alpha_k = \frac{1}{\int_{\frac{(k-1)M}{N}}^{\frac{kM}{N}} P(f) df} \tag{5}$$

The normalization constant, α_k, differs from segment to segment of the border. The normalized
probability subdistribution, $P_k(f)$, may therefore be represented as:

$$P_k(f) = \alpha_k P(f) \tag{6}$$

The optimal defensive base in the region adjoining the kth segment of the front, (σ_k, μ_k), is determined as the standard deviation and mean of the normalized probability subdensity function of attack, $P_k(f)$.

$$\mu_k = \alpha_k \int_{\frac{(k-1)M}{N}}^{\frac{kM}{N}} f P(f) df \tag{7}$$

$$\sigma_k = \sqrt{\alpha_k \int_{\frac{(k-1)M}{N}}^{\frac{kM}{N}} (f - \mu_k)^2 P(f) df} \tag{8}$$

Example 5

As a final instance of distributed defense optimization, we impose a 2-center restriction on the probability density function elaborated in Example 3. In the upper sector of the front, the probability distribution, $P_1(f)$, is given by:

$$P_1(f) = \frac{8}{M^2} f \qquad f \in \left[0, \frac{M}{2}\right]$$

while in the lower sector the following probability density function, $P_2(f)$, prevails.

$$P_2(f) = \frac{8}{M} - \frac{8}{M^2} f \qquad f \in \left[\frac{M}{2}, M\right]$$

As a consequence of the symmetry of the overall probability density function, the probability distribution areas enclosed within each of the two sectors are equal and thus each segment is assigned N/2 defending units. The two moments of interest for $P_1(f)$ are:

$$\mu(f) = \int_0^{\frac{M}{2}} f^2 \frac{8}{M^2} df = \frac{8}{M^2} \frac{f^3}{3}\Big|_0^{\frac{M}{2}} = \frac{8}{M^2} \frac{M^3}{24} = \frac{M}{3}$$

$$\text{Var}(f) = \int_0^{\frac{M}{2}} \left(f - \frac{M}{3}\right)^2 \frac{8}{M^2} f df = \frac{M^2}{72}$$

The upper defensive force units should therefore be based at $(M/\sqrt{72}, M/3)$. The probability distribution for the lower sector is anti-symmetric to the probability distribution for the upper segment and hence the lower defensive encampment must be stationed at $(M/\sqrt{72}, 2M/3)$. Figure 1A-3 shows the different defensive force structures derived in Examples 1 through 5.

As a practical matter it might be exceedingly difficult for the defender to pin down the exact probability distribution of attack from which the invasion plans of the aggressor are likely to be derived. While the defender's expectations of the probability distribution of assault must approximate the true probability density of attack, there might exist a range of plausible attacker probability distributions. Uncertainty in the determination of the probability density function of attack translates into uncertainty in the mean and standard deviation of the probability density of penetration along the front. The y coordinate of the optimal defensive force position corresponds to the mean while the x coordinate equals the standard deviation of the probability density of invasion. Thus if the mean of the probability density function of attack is uncertain, the y coordinate must be chosen to equal the expected value of the mean. In determining the ordinate of the defender's peacetime base, it is important to be as accurate as possible in isolating the true mean of the probability density function of attack. However, when choosing x, accuracy in determining the variance of the probability distribution of infiltration is not essential. The abscissa of the defender's optimal force positioning should be picked conservatively, erring towards a larger displacement inward from the border within the bounds of uncertainty on x. In the extreme case it is almost never prudent for a defender to position

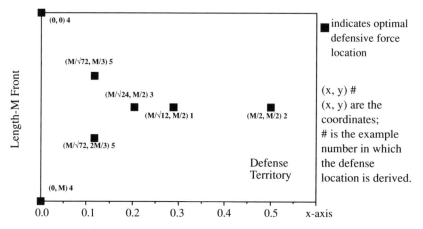

Figure 1A-3 Optimal Defensive Force Deployment for Examples 1 to 5. The x-axis is calibrated in terms of M.

all its forces at a point on the length-M front, (x = 0), unless the defender is *absolutely* certain the invasion will be launched at that point. Choosing x conservatively ensures the defense against errors in the determination of the probability density function of attack and provides the defense with breathing space to counter unexpected invasion campaigns without fear of being easily outflanked by the attacker. To summarize, while the choice of y demands accuracy, the choice of x should be dictated by level-headed conservatism. In other words, while the force planner should set y equal to the expected mean of the probability density function of attack, x might be chosen to be a bit greater than the analytically determined standard deviation.[2]

The defender's displacement inward from the frontier thus depends on two factors:

1. The absolute length of the length-M front. The larger the value of M in miles or kilometers, the greater the inward removal of the defending force base in absolute terms from the demarcation line separating the two sides.

2. The variance of the probability density function of attack from which the defender expects the aggressor to derive its campaign plan of invasion. As per the σ-μ Theorem, the defender's forces must be based at a distance equal to the standard deviation of the probability distribution of penetration inward from the front.

To minimize the defender's home ground exposed to uncontested infiltration and occupation by the enemy, the defense must be based as close to the frontier as possible. The defender's vulnerability may be reduced and stability enhanced by defining shorter length-M fronts. Shorter length-M fronts reduce the absolute displacement of the defensive peacetime base from the border; after all the farthest back the defensive forces can be from the demarcation line is M/2. Second, shorter fronts imply smaller standard deviations of the probability distribution of attack since the standard deviation is ultimately

---

[2]Of course, the maximum value of x is M/2 since the maximum standard deviation of a probability distribution of attack defined over a closed interval [0, M] is M/2.

expressed in units of M. Third and not so patently obvious, shorter fronts penalize the defender to a far smaller extent for errors in the determination of the true probability density function of attack. The defender has the leeway to make significant mistakes forming its expectation of the attacker's likelihood of assault at each point along the length-M front without disastrous consequences in terms of territory lost. How shorter length-M fronts can be created by mutual consent between the two sides is the subject of arms control and is treated in Part Three.

Calculating the Optimal Defense Position for Unequal Offensive and Defensive Velocities

In this appendix we derive the optimal position for a defender whose velocity over home ground, v_d, differs from the attacker's velocity over defense terrain, v_a. The defense is armed with one unit and is confronted by an invading force of equal strength. There is a uniform probability of attack at each point along the length-M front. Thus $P(f) = 1/M$ for all $f \in [0, M]$. The attacking unit attempts infiltration at the point $(0, f)$ and the defending unit is based at (x, y). I is the attacker's unopposed infiltration accomplished by the invader before encountering the defending unit.

The $v_a < v_d$ case

In Part One we derived the following expression relating x, y, I, f, v_a and v_d.

$$\frac{I}{v_a} = \frac{\sqrt{(x - I)^2 + (y - f)^2}}{v_d} \tag{1B-1}$$

Squaring both sides of the above equation:

$$\frac{v_d^2 \, I^2}{v_a^2} = (x - I)^2 + (y - f)^2 \tag{1B-2}$$

We rearrange the quadratic equation in I, taking into account that $v_d > v_a$ and solve for I.

$$I^2 \left(\frac{v_d^2}{v_a^2} - 1 \right) + 2xI - x^2 - (y - f)^2 = 0 \tag{1B-3}$$

$$I = \frac{-x \pm \sqrt{x^2 + \left(\frac{v_d^2}{v_a^2} - 1 \right)\left(x^2 + [y - f]^2 \right)}}{\left(\frac{v_d^2}{v_a^2} - 1 \right)} \tag{1B-4}$$

243

The sign ambiguity is resolved by choosing the positive sign since the attacker's infiltration cannot be negative. Thus I is given by:

$$I = \frac{-x + \sqrt{x^2 + \left(\frac{v_d^2}{v_a^2} - 1\right)\left(x^2 + [y - f]^2\right)}}{\left(\frac{v_d^2}{v_a^2} - 1\right)} \tag{1B-5}$$

The optimal placement of the defensive force unit can be determined by imposing the condition:

$$\int_0^M \left[\frac{\partial}{\partial x} I(x, y; f)\right] df = 0$$

$$\text{and} \quad \int_0^M \left[\frac{\partial}{\partial y} I(x, y; f)\right] df = 0 \tag{1B-6}$$

THEOREM I: *For the $v_d > v_a$ scenario, the defensive force unit must be stationed halfway along the length-M front and at a distance x behind the demarcation line, where x is determined implicitly by the following transcendental equation:*

$$\frac{x \, v_d}{\sqrt{v_d^2 - v_a^2}} \ln\left[\frac{\sqrt{\frac{x^2 v_d^2}{v_d^2 - v_a^2} + \frac{M^2}{4}} + \frac{M}{2}}{\sqrt{\frac{x^2 v_d^2}{v_d^2 - v_a^2} + \frac{M^2}{4}} - \frac{M}{2}}\right] = \frac{M \, v_a}{v_d} \tag{1B-7}$$

Equivalently, in terms of our rectangular c-ordinate system established earlier, the defensive unit must base itself at the point (x, M/2) to minimize the attacker's unopposed infiltration.

Equation 1B-5 allows us to compute the partial derivatives of I with respect to x and y.

$$\frac{\partial I}{\partial x} = \frac{-1 + \frac{\frac{x v_d^2}{v_a^2}}{\sqrt{x^2 + \left(\frac{v_d^2}{v_a^2} - 1\right)\left(x^2 + [y - f]^2\right)}}}{\left(\frac{v_d^2}{v_a^2} - 1\right)}$$

$$\text{and} \quad \frac{\partial I}{\partial y} = \frac{v_a}{v_d} \frac{(y - f)}{\sqrt{x^2 + [y - f]^2}}$$

The partial derivative with respect to y is easily integrated:

$$\int_0^M \frac{v_a}{v_d} \frac{(y-f)}{\sqrt{x^2 + [y-f]^2}}\, df = 0$$

Let $[y-f]^2 = u$

Then $-2[y-f]\,df = du$

$$-\int_{y^2}^{(y-M)^2} \frac{du}{\sqrt{x^2+u}} = 0$$

$$\sqrt{x^2+u}\; \Big|_{u=y^2}^{u=(y-M)^2} = 0$$

$$x^2 + (y-M)^2 = x^2 + y^2$$

Thus $y = \dfrac{M}{2}$

We now integrate the expression for $\partial I/\partial x$ with respect to f:

$$\int_0^M -1 + \frac{\dfrac{x v_d^2}{v_a^2}}{\sqrt{x^2 \dfrac{v_d^2}{v_a^2} + \left(\dfrac{v_d^2}{v_a^2} - 1\right)(y-f)^2}}\, df = 0$$

$$\frac{x v_d^2}{v_a^2} \int_0^M \frac{df}{\sqrt{x^2 \dfrac{v_d^2}{v_a^2} + \left(\dfrac{v_d^2}{v_a^2} - 1\right)(y-f)^2}} = M$$

Let $\sqrt{\dfrac{v_d^2}{v_a^2} - 1}\,(y-f) = u$

Then $-\sqrt{\dfrac{v_d^2}{v_a^2} - 1}\, df = du$

$$\frac{x v_d^2}{v_a^2} \int_{\sqrt{\frac{v_d^2}{v_a^2} - 1}\, y}^{\sqrt{\frac{v_d^2}{v_a^2} - 1}(y-M)} \frac{-du}{\sqrt{\dfrac{v_d^2}{v_a^2} - 1}\,\sqrt{x^2 \dfrac{v_d^2}{v_a^2} + u^2}} = M$$

$$\frac{x\,v_d^2}{\sqrt{\dfrac{v_d^2}{v_a^2}-1}\;v_a^2}\int_{\sqrt{\frac{v_d^2}{v_a^2}-1}\,(y-M)}^{\sqrt{\frac{v_d^2}{v_a^2}-1}\,y}\frac{du}{\sqrt{x^2\dfrac{v_d^2}{v_a^2}+u^2}}\;=\;M$$

$$\frac{x\,v_d^2}{\sqrt{\dfrac{v_d^2}{v_a^2}-1}\;v_a^2}\left[\ln\left|u+\sqrt{x^2\dfrac{v_d^2}{v_a^2}+u^2}\right|\right]_{u=\sqrt{\frac{v_d^2}{v_a^2}-1}\,(y-M)}^{u=\sqrt{\frac{v_d^2}{v_a^2}-1}\,y}\;=\;M$$

$$\frac{x}{\sqrt{\dfrac{v_d^2}{v_a^2}-1}}\,\frac{v_d^2}{v_a^2}\ln\left[\frac{\sqrt{\dfrac{v_d^2}{v_a^2}-1}\;y+\sqrt{x^2\dfrac{v_d^2}{v_a^2}+\left(\dfrac{v_d^2}{v_a^2}-1\right)y^2}}{\sqrt{\dfrac{v_d^2}{v_a^2}-1}\,(y-M)+\sqrt{x^2\dfrac{v_d^2}{v_a^2}+\left(\dfrac{v_d^2}{v_a^2}-1\right)(y-M)^2}}\right]\;=\;M$$

Replacing y with M/2 yields:

$$\frac{x}{\sqrt{\dfrac{v_d^2}{v_a^2}-1}}\,\frac{v_d^2}{v_a^2}\ln\left[\frac{\sqrt{x^2\dfrac{v_d^2}{v_a^2}+\left(\dfrac{v_d^2}{v_a^2}-1\right)\dfrac{M^2}{4}}+\sqrt{\dfrac{v_d^2}{v_a^2}-1}\,\dfrac{M}{2}}{\sqrt{x^2\dfrac{v_d^2}{v_a^2}+\left(\dfrac{v_d^2}{v_a^2}-1\right)\dfrac{M^2}{4}}-\sqrt{\dfrac{v_d^2}{v_a^2}-1}\,\dfrac{M}{2}}\right]\;=\;M$$

$$\frac{x}{\sqrt{\dfrac{v_d^2}{v_a^2}-1}}\,\frac{v_d^2}{v_a^2}\ln\left[\frac{\sqrt{x^2\dfrac{v_d^2}{v_a^2}\dfrac{1}{\left(\dfrac{v_d^2}{v_a^2}-1\right)}+\dfrac{M^2}{4}}+\dfrac{M}{2}}{\sqrt{x^2\dfrac{v_d^2}{v_a^2}\dfrac{1}{\left(\dfrac{v_d^2}{v_a^2}-1\right)}+\dfrac{M^2}{4}}-\dfrac{M}{2}}\right]\;=\;M$$

Thus
$$\frac{x\,v_d}{\sqrt{v_d^2-v_a^2}}\ln\left[\frac{\sqrt{\dfrac{x^2\,v_d^2}{v_d^2-v_a^2}+\dfrac{M^2}{4}}+\dfrac{M}{2}}{\sqrt{\dfrac{x^2\,v_d^2}{v_d^2-v_a^2}+\dfrac{M^2}{4}}-\dfrac{M}{2}}\right]\;=\;\frac{M\,v_a}{v_d}$$

(1B-7)

Equation 1B-7 is a transcendental equation and cannot be solved explicitly for x. To explore the nature of the solution set to the equation, let $v_d/v_a = \lambda$, the defense-to-offense velocity ratio. For $v_d > v_a$, we must have $\lambda > 1$. The defining equation for x, Equation 1B-7, is transformed to:

$$\frac{x\lambda}{\sqrt{\lambda^2 - 1}} \ln \left[\frac{\sqrt{\frac{x^2\lambda^2}{\lambda^2 - 1} + \frac{M^2}{4}} + \frac{M}{2}}{\sqrt{\frac{x^2\lambda^2}{\lambda^2 - 1} + \frac{M^2}{4}} - \frac{M}{2}} \right] = \frac{M}{\lambda} \qquad \text{(1B-8)}$$

The above equation defines x, the distance of the defensive force unit from the front, as an implicit function of λ and M. Since we are primarily interested in understanding the relationship between the optimal defensive force location and the relative velocities of the attacking and defending forces, M can be normalized to 1 and Equation 1B-8 can be solved for x with λ as a parameter using numerical techniques of successive iteration. The solution to the equation is depicted graphically in Figure 1B-1. The independent variable along the x-axis is the defender-to-attacker velocity ratio, λ. The dependent variable along the y-axis is the location of the defending force unit behind the front. The positioning of the defending forces is expressed as a fraction of the defensive force location for the case of equal offense and defense speeds. In effect, it is assumed in constructing the graph that the defending unit would be stationed at unit distance inward from the border if the attacker and the defender were evenly matched in the speed of transporting force over defense terrain.

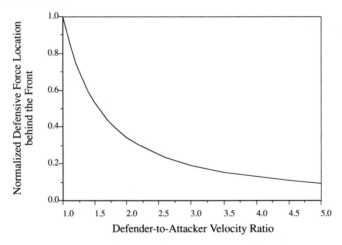

Figure 1B-1 Defense Velocity Greater than the Attack Velocity. Defensive location behind the front expressed as a fraction of the placement for the equal velocity case.

As defensive force agility begins to eclipse the speed of the invading forces, the defending force unit can be located closer and closer to the front. However there are diminishing marginal returns associated with increasing defense speed; each incremental advance in relative speed corresponds to a progressively smaller movement towards the demarcation line.

The $v_a > v_d$ case:

For the $v_a > v_d$ case, the unopposed infiltration of the attacker, I, can be expressed as:

$$I = \frac{x \pm \sqrt{x^2 - \left(1 - \frac{v_d^2}{v_a^2}\right)\left(x^2 + [y - f]^2\right)}}{\left(1 - \frac{v_d^2}{v_a^2}\right)} \tag{1B-9}$$

To resolve the sign ambiguity, consider the situation where the invader launches its onslaught diametrically opposite the defending force base. Algebraically, this translates to f = y. Let t be the time that elapses before first contact is made between the adversarial force units. Then $I = tv_a$ and $x - I = tv_d$. Eliminating the variable t between the two equations for x and I and solving for the infiltration, I, yields:

$$I = \frac{x}{1 + \frac{v_d}{v_a}} \tag{1B-10}$$

The identical result for the invading force incursion can be obtained by setting f = y and choosing the negative sign in the expression for I elaborated in Equation 1B-9. This leads us to believe:

$$I = \frac{x - \sqrt{x^2 - \left(1 - \frac{v_d^2}{v_a^2}\right)\left(x^2 + [y - f]^2\right)}}{\left(1 - \frac{v_d^2}{v_a^2}\right)} \tag{1B-11}$$

THEOREM II: *For the $v_d < v_a$ scenario, the defensive force unit must be stationed at (x, M/2) where x is determined implicitly by the following transcendental equation:*

$$\frac{1}{\sqrt{1 - \frac{v_d^2}{v_a^2}}} 2 x \frac{v_d^2}{v_a^2} \sin^{-1}\left[\sqrt{\frac{v_a^2}{v_d^2} - 1} \frac{M}{2x}\right] = M \tag{1B-12}$$

Since the process of deriving the optimal defense placement from I (f, x, y, v_d, v_a) has already been delineated above, we commence directly with the task of extricating x and y. Our quest begins with y:

$$\frac{\partial I}{\partial y} = \frac{(y - f)}{\sqrt{x^2 - \left(1 - \frac{v_d^2}{v_a^2}\right)\left(x^2 + [y - f]^2\right)}}$$

$$\int_0^M \left[\frac{\partial I}{\partial y}\right] df = 0$$

$$\int_0^M \frac{(y - f)}{\sqrt{x^2 - \left(1 - \frac{v_d^2}{v_a^2}\right)\left(x^2 + [y - f]^2\right)}} df = 0$$

Let $(y - f)^2 = u$

Then $-2(y - f)df = du$

$$\int_{y^2}^{(y - M)^2} \frac{du}{\sqrt{x^2 - \left(1 - \frac{v_d^2}{v_a^2}\right)(x^2 + u)}} = 0$$

$$\sqrt{x^2 \frac{v_d^2}{v_a^2} + u} \Bigg|_{u = y^2}^{u = (y - M)^2} = 0$$

$$x^2 \frac{v_d^2}{v_a^2} + (y - M)^2 = x^2 \frac{v_d^2}{v_a^2} + y^2$$

Thus $y = \frac{M}{2}$

We now solve for x:

$$\frac{\partial I}{\partial x} = \frac{1 - \dfrac{x \dfrac{v_d^2}{v_a^2}}{\sqrt{x^2 \dfrac{v_d^2}{v_a^2} - \left(1 - \dfrac{v_d^2}{v_a^2}\right)(y - f)^2}}}{\left(1 - \dfrac{v_d^2}{v_a^2}\right)}$$

$$\int_0^M \left[\frac{\partial I}{\partial x}\right] df = 0$$

$$x \frac{v_d^2}{v_a^2} \int_0^M \frac{df}{\sqrt{x^2 \frac{v_d^2}{v_a^2} - \left(1 - \frac{v_d^2}{v_a^2}\right)(y - f)^2}} = M$$

$$\frac{1}{\sqrt{1 - \frac{v_d^2}{v_a^2}}} \times \frac{v_d^2}{v_a^2} \int_0^M \frac{df}{\sqrt{\frac{x^2 v_d^2}{v_a^2 - v_d^2} - (y - f)^2}} = M$$

Let $(y - f) = u$

$$\frac{1}{\sqrt{1 - \frac{v_d^2}{v_a^2}}} \times \frac{v_d^2}{v_a^2} \int_{y - M}^y \frac{du}{\sqrt{\frac{x^2 v_d^2}{v_a^2 - v_d^2} - u^2}} = M$$

$$\frac{1}{\sqrt{1 - \frac{v_d^2}{v_a^2}}} \times \frac{v_d^2}{v_a^2} \left[\sin^{-1}\left(\frac{u}{\frac{x v_d}{\sqrt{v_a^2 - v_d^2}}} \right) \right]_{u = y - M}^{u = y} = M$$

Introduce $y = \frac{M}{2}$

Thus $$\frac{1}{\sqrt{1 - \frac{v_d^2}{v_a^2}}} 2 x \frac{v_d^2}{v_a^2} \sin^{-1}\left[\sqrt{\frac{v_a^2}{v_d^2} - 1} \frac{M}{2x} \right] = M$$ **(1B-12)**

x is again enmeshed in a transcendental equation and methods of successive iteration must be used to find a solution. We represent the ratio of the attacker-to-defender velocities by Ω, that is $\Omega = v_a / v_d$. $v_a > v_d$ implies $\Omega > 1$. Equation 1B-12, the defining equality for x, gets transformed to:

$$\sin^{-1}\left[\sqrt{\Omega^2 - 1} \frac{M}{2x} \right] = \Omega \sqrt{\Omega^2 - 1} \frac{M}{2x}$$ **(1B-13)**

Normalizing M to 1, x can be determined as a function of Ω employing numerical iterative techniques of solving transcendental equations. A graph depicting the relationship between x and Ω is presented in Figure 1B-2. Along the x-axis is the ratio of attacker mobility to defense speed. The y-axis indicates the optimal peacetime displacement of the defense unit behind the front. The ordinate is graduated in units of the distance behind the front of the defensive forces for the scenario of equal offense and defense velocities. Thus a 1 on the y-axis corresponds to a location behind the border equal to the optimal defense displacement for $v_a = v_d$, a 2 on the y-axis corresponds to twice the optimal distance for the equal velocity case, and so on.

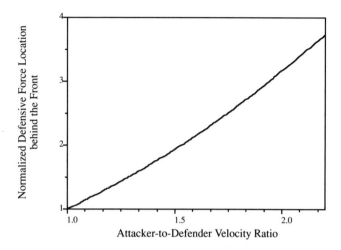

Figure 1B-2   Attack Velocity Greater than Defense Velocity. Defensive location behind the front expressed as a multiple of the placement for the equal velocity case.

It is evident from Figure 1B-2 that as the attacker's speed of transporting force exceeds that of the defender's the defender is compelled to position forces further and further inward from the demarcation line. For an attacking force velocity more than twice the average defense speed, the removal of the defensive force unit behind the front escalates sharply.

A Statistical Analysis of Twentieth-Century Warfare

The following statistical analysis is based on the US Army Concepts Analysis Agency Database, which contains data on 600 individual engagements since the turn of the century. The analysis here is restricted to 185 battles conducted during and after World War II for which relatively complete data are available. This limited subset is more representative of modern modes of warfare and is therefore more useful to today's force planners, defense analysts and arms controllers. Some of the key results arrived at from the statistical analysis are summarized toward the end of the appendix.

Caveats Regarding the Data[1]

1. Most battle parameters have extremely skewed frequency distributions. While most of the mass of the distribution is concentrated at small values of the parameter, there is a long tail that stretches towards the right to extremely high values. As an example, consider the advance rate of the attacker or the withdrawal rate of the defender in kms/day. For 80 percent of the battles the advance rate lies between 0 and 8 kms/day; for the remaining 20 percent, however, the advance rate stretches out in a tail that extends up to 50 kms/day. The extreme asymmetry of the distribution makes the arithmetic mean an inappropriate measure of location or centrality. For parameters that are ratios of two variables, the geometric mean is preferable, while the median should be used as an estimate of the center of the distribution for all other parameters. Using the geometric mean as the measure of centrality for parameters that are ratios of two variables is identical to assuming that the underlying distribution of the parameter is log normal.

2. There is no statistically consistent procedure for selecting subsets of data on which to base calculations. In other words, removing outliers or grouping the data by theater, battle terrain (such as rolling or flat), defense preparation (such as hasty or prepared), at-

---

[1]These caveats are also discussed in Robert McQuie, *Historical Characteristics of Warfare for Gaming [Benchmarks]* (Bethesda: Concepts Analysis Agency, 1988).

tacking force maneuver (such as frontal attack or double envelopment), weather conditions (such as hot or cold), and so on is unlikely to improve the quality of the conclusions. Moreover, such case-by-case analysis can be misleading since the differences between values of a parameter calculated for each subset of the data are not statistically
significant. This is because the variations in parameter values for each subset of the data
are extremely large. Thus one might find the median attacker-to-defender casualty exchange ratio to be 1.3 for battles conducted on a flat plain and 1.6 for battles conducted
on rugged land. However the difference between the two exchange ratios is not statistically significant. We cannot conclude that, on average, battles fought on rugged terrain
lead to higher attacker-to-defender casualty exchange ratios than battles fought on a flat
plain. This is because the casualty exchange ratio for flat-land battles might range from
0.2 to 8.0 and the same might hold for the spread of ratios for battles on rugged territory.
The large variance in the exchange ratio for each subset of the data makes differences
between medians calculated for each subset insignificant.

   3. The third important feature of the data is its extreme variability, as illustrated by
the following table.[2]

Battle parameter description	Extreme	Year observed	Attacking nation: Defending nation	Battle parameter value
Force ratio men	High	1967	Egypt: Israel	17: 1
(attacker: defender)	Low	1945	Japan: USA	.3: 1
Force ratio artillery	High	1945	USA: Japan	50: 1
(attacker: defender)	Low	1948	Israel: Syria	.11: 1
Mortar density dfdr	High	1943	Britain: Germany	132
(weapons/km)	Low	1973	Egypt: Israel	0.19
Artillery density attkr	High	1944	USA: Japan	444
(weapons/km)	Low	1948	Israel: Jordan	0.2
Casualty rate attkr	High	1945	USA: Japan	96%
(men % per day)	Low	1944	Britain: Germany	0.13%
Advance rate attkr	High	1967	Israel: Egypt	45
(km per day)	Low	1945	USA: Japan	0.1
attkr = attacker	dfdr = defender			

The large variability of the data sheds doubt on the hypothesis that there is one optimal
value of any parameter that should be employed when modeling war. Historically, extremely high or low values of parameters have been observed in war, and thus it is safer

---

[2]The table is from McQuie, *Historical Characteristics*, p. 13.

to conduct sensitivity analyses of any war model for a wide range of input parameter values than to rely on a historically computed, static aggregate value of the parameter.

Statistical Results

Ψ: *Average Attacker-to-Defender Casualty Exchange Ratio*

Ψ is the ratio of the total attacking casualties in battle divided by the total defending casualties during the course of the engagement.

Median Ψ: 0.946

Geometric Mean Ψ: 0.887

Standard Deviation for Geometric Mean: 3.485

The 68 percent confidence interval for the casualty exchange ratio is (0.887/3.485 = 0.255, 0.887*3.485 = 3.093), and the 95 percent confidence interval is (0.255/3.485 = 0.0731, 3.093*3.485 = 10.78).

Figures 1C-1 and 1C-2 below depict the frequency distribution of the exchange ratio. Ψ is grouped into frequency intervals of width 0.25, and the center of each frequency class is plotted along the x-axis. The y-axis indicates the number of battles that fall within each frequency class. Figure 1C-1 employs a linear scale for displaying the casualty exchange ratio along the x-axis. The frequency distribution in the figure is highly skewed with the dominant majority of battles falling between 0 and 2 on the x-axis and a long tapering tail extending out to 13. The skewness of the distribution makes it unrealistic to invoke the usual assumption of normality in analyzing the exchange ratio. The inability to treat the underlying distribution as a normal density function is severely constraining and invalidates most conventional techniques of analysis such as the use of the mean and variance as the sole descriptors of the distribution. In general, a skewed distribution will possess significant third- and higher-order moments which must also be computed when describing the characteristics of the population. The inapplicability of normality also nullifies the use of linear regression analysis, a useful statistical tool for examining the empirical validity of conflicting models through a systematic study of correlation among the various model parameters. Thus we seek a transformation of the exchange ratio that will map the skewed distribution into a normal or an almost normal density function. It is no coincidence that the casualty exchange ratio is the ratio of two variables and our inclination is to replace Ψ with its logarithm, log Ψ.

The log transformation is accomplished in Figure 1C-2 by displaying the exchange ratio on a logarithmic scale. The log frequency distribution appears to be reasonably normal implying that the original distribution is log normal. We can retain unmodified our familiar tool kit for statistical analysis as long as the logarithm of the exchange ratio rather than the exchange ratio itself is the variable under scrutiny.[3]

---

[3] For instance, it is meaningless to compute the arithmetic mean of the exchange ratio. Suppose we calculate the arithmetic mean of Ψ and the standard deviation for the arithmetic mean.

Arithmetic Mean Ψ: 1.748

Standard Deviation for Arithmetic Mean: 2.219

The 68 percent confidence interval for Ψ is (1.748 - 2.219, 1.748 + 2.219) = (- 0.470, 3.967); but this is absurd since the exchange ratio cannot be negative. The single best measure of centrality for the casualty exchange ratio is the exponential of the arithmetic mean of the logarithm of the exchange ratio, which can be directly computed as the geometric mean of the exchange ratio itself.

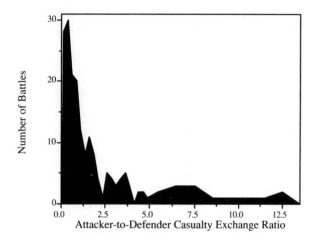

Figure 1C-1   Frequency Distribution for the Casualty Exchange Ratio. Linear x-axis scale.

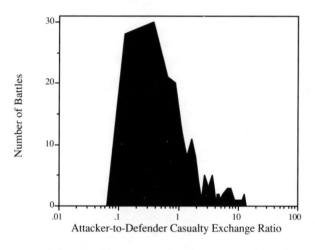

Figure 1C-2   Frequency Distribution for the Casualty Exchange Ratio. Logarithmic x-axis scale.

Γ: Initial Attacker-to-Defender Force Ratio

Γ is the ratio of attackers to defenders at the outbreak of hostilities.
Geometric Mean Γ: 1.735
Standard Deviation for Geometric Mean: 1.909
Thus we can say with 68 percent confidence that the initial attacker-to-defender force ratio must lie in the interval (0.909, 3.313) and with 95 percent confidence in the interval

(0.476, 6.325). The geometric mean Γ of 1.735 is for the entire universe of 185 battles, not all of which resulted in victory for the attacker. For the 55 battles that were attacker victories, the geometric mean Γ is 1.738, the standard deviation for the geometric mean is 1.844 and the 68 percent confidence interval is (0.942, 3.204). It is sometimes believed that the aggressor must provide an initial force superiority of 3:1 in those sectors where a breakthrough is desired.[4] However the mean initial force ratio for victorious attackers has historically been a measly 1.74, casting some doubt on the empirical validity and applicability of this 3-to-1 rule.

Figures 1C-3 and 1C-4 display the frequency and log frequency distributions of the initial force ratio, as Figures 1C-1 and 1C-2 did for the exchange ratio. Again it is noteworthy that taking the logarithm of Γ transforms the original highly skewed distribution into a density function with a fair degree of normality, thus opening the path for the usual statistical analysis.

τ: Duration of the Conflict

τ is the length of time for which the two sides engage in battle. The values calculated for τ are very susceptible to the manner in which the length of a battle is defined. The US Army Concepts Analysis Agency Database segregates data by individual encounters resulting in a rather short duration for the average conflict.

Median τ: 2.00 days
Arithmetic Mean τ: 3.99 days

α: Attacker's Average Daily Percentage Attrition

$\alpha = 100 \, [A(0) - A(\tau)] \, / \, \tau \, A(0)$, where $A(0)$ is the attacker's initial force strength, $A(\tau)$ is the attacker's terminal residual strength and τ is the duration of the engagement.

Median α: 1.06 %
Arithmetic Mean α: 1.66 %

β: Defender's Average Daily Percentage Attrition

$\beta = 100 \, [D(0) - D(\tau)] \, / \, \tau \, D(0)$, where $D(0)$ and $D(\tau)$ are the defender's initial and terminal force strengths respectively.

Median β: 2.09 %
Arithmetic Mean β: 3.68 %

---

[4]John J. Mearsheimer, "Why the Soviets Can't Win Quickly in Central Europe," *International Security*, vol. 7 (Summer 1982), pp. 16-17. The 3-to-1 rule was also frequently cited in the press reports covering Operation Desert Shield, the U.S. dispatch of forces to Saudi Arabia in response to the Iraqi invasion of Kuwait on August 2, 1990. The 3-to-1 rule was used in press reports to explain why the United States and its allies needed substantial reinforcements to their initial 250,000-strong "defensive" deployment if they desired to launch an offensive campaign to dislodge the 480,000 Iraqi soldiers camped in Kuwait and southern Iraq. In addition, Iraqi sources were cited as opining that the U.S.-led international coalition was unlikely to engage in offensive operations against the Iraqi forces because they lacked the 3-to-1 force superiority necessary for a successful attack.

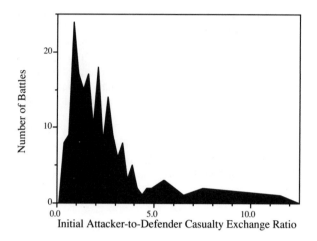

Figure 1C-3 Frequency Distribution for the Initial Force Ratio. Linear x-axis scale.

Ψ as a Function of the Attacking and Defending Force Nationality

The average attacker-to-defender casualty exchange ratio can be calculated for attacking and defending forces of different nationalities. The results are presented in the following table. As elaborated earlier, differences in Ψ across data subsets are generally statistically weak.[5]

Attacker	Defender	Number of battles	Geometric mean exchange ratio
Britain	Germany	21	2.357
Germany	Britain	10	1.231
Egypt	Israel	6	2.649
Syria	Israel	8	1.618
Israel	Egypt/Iraq/Jor/Syr	46	0.377
USSR	Germany	22	1.484
Germany	USSR	6	0.173
Germany	US	9	2.046
US	Germany	49	0.923
US	North Korea	3	0.0517

[5]Intuitively a result is statistically weak if little or no confidence can be expressed in its predictive power. Referring to the table, it is not possible to predict with any reasonable confidence what value of the geometric mean exchange ratio should be expected in a future confrontation between Britain and Germany or between Egypt and Israel. In other words, if a British force with a composition substantially similar to a World War II British army were to attack a World War II–type Ger-

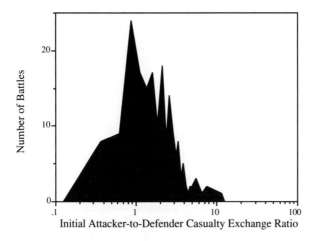

Initial Attacker-to-Defender Casualty Exchange Ratio

Figure 1C-4   Frequency Distribution for the Initial Force Ratio. Logarithmic x-axis scale.

Battle Outcomes and Withdrawal

The withdrawal of the defender is often considered a proxy for the result of the battle. Thus the attacker strives to make the defender give up ground in the hope of winning the encounter; correspondingly the defender attempts to adhere to its position in a determined effort not to permit the invader to advance. To test this relationship between battle outcome and a defender's withdrawal, the data were grouped into three subgroups depending upon the outcome of the battle as documented in the database.

1. Attacker victory (OUTCOME = 0)
2. Stalemate (OUTCOME = 1)
3. Defender victory (OUTCOME = 2)

The arithmetic average and median front displacements were as follows for each subgroup:

Outcome	Number of battles	Median withdrawal	Arithmetic mean withdrawal
Attacker victory	55	8.00 km	33.44 km
Stalemate	101	2.50 km	10.78 km
Defender victory	9	0 km	1.00 km

Thus there appears to be a meaningful relationship between front displacement and battle outcome. Attacker victories result in significantly larger withdrawals as compared with stalemate or defensive victories. It must be realized that the relationship is not perfect since the battle plains over which the battles are conducted are not homogeneous.

man contingent in a series of encounters, the geometric mean exchange ratio calculated from this new data set could be very different from the 2.357 value derived from the historical data.

The loss of 10 or 20 kilometers in a battle on the Russian front in World War II may not result in a defensive loss while a battle on the outskirts of Berlin might be lost if even one kilometer were yielded.

Testing the Lanchester Square Law of Combat

The Lanchester Square Law imposes the following state equation on the fighting strengths of the two combatants, A and D:[6]

$$a\left[A(0)^2 - A(\tau)^2\right] = d\left[D(0)^2 - D(\tau)^2\right]$$

where τ is the duration of the engagement and a and d are the combat effectiveness coefficients of the two sides in conflict. For a particular attacker and defender we would expect a/d to be fairly constant since a/d represents the relative force utilization capability of the antagonists and should be largely determined by the identity of the offense and the defense. The following table tabulates the geometric mean, the standard deviation of the geometric mean and the range of historically observed values for the Lanchester Square combat efficacy of select attackers relative to select defenders.

Attacker	Defender	Number of battles	Geometric mean for a/d	Standard deviation for a/d	Range for a/d
Britain	Germany	21	0.224	3.107	(0.0295, 1.432)
Germany	Britain	10	0.521	1.827	(0.178, 1.093)
Egypt	Israel	6	0.101	1.391	(0.0543, 0.145)
Israel	Egypt	24	3.252	3.189	(0.222, 27.313)
Germany	US	9	0.292	3.132	(0.0466, 1.938)
US	Germany	49	0.491	2.542	(0.0575, 2.641)
Germany	USSR	6	6.107	3.375	(0.808, 21.744)
USSR	Germany	22	0.233	3.725	(0.039, 3.59)
Israel	Syria	13	3.103	2.176	(1.02, 11.563)
Syria	Israel	8	0.179	3.27	(0.0558, 3.226)

For any given attacker-defender pair, the relative combat effectiveness observed in war is spread over a tremendous range. The large variance in values intrinsic to a/d is underscored by the huge standard deviation that accompanies each calculation of the geometric mean. It is highly improbable that a/d is a constant for encounters between a specific offense and defense, thus providing no affirmation of the validity of the Lanchester Square Law of Combat. In fact, in its purest form, the Lanchester Square Law makes no

---

[6]The corresponding state equation for the Lanchester Linear Law is:

       a' [A(0) – A(τ)] = d' [D(0) – D(τ)]

where a' and d' are the Lanchester Linear combat effectiveness coefficients of the two sides in battle.

distinction between attack and defense; a/d for Germany attacking Britain should be the reciprocal of a/d for Britain attacking Germany. This reciprocity of relative effectiveness is not shown by any of the 5 attacker-defender pairs above.[7]

The single most powerful test of the Lanchester Square Law or any other combat attrition model is to consider an individual engagement and compare the historically observed attrition of either side over the course of combat with the force drawdown curve predicted by the model. This analysis falls under the domain of time-series analysis since the data needed for the analysis are a sequence of numbers in time. The process of time-series analysis can be extended to and replicated for several individual encounters. This extension to a set of battles is called cross-sectional analysis. Thus a complete and general examination of a combat attrition model requires data on residual forces and front displacement for each day of combat to facilitate a time-series analysis. The daily breakdown of information on battle parameters must be available for numerous individual engagements to permit the subsequent cross-sectional survey. The Concepts Analysis Agency Database is restricted in its scope to data collection solely at the commencement and termination of each incident of conflict and thus it is possible to calculate daily statistics only through the method of averaging the overall aggregate attrition and front displacement over the duration of the battle. In this sense, the data base conveys virtually no information about the nature or process of force interaction as it evolves on the battlefield on a day-by-day basis, and consequently it is rather ambitious to attempt to prove or disprove any combat attrition model by performing statistical tests on the data base. It must be recognized that our rejection of the Lanchester Square Law is founded on a purely cross-sectional analysis and the weakness of our negative conclusion should not be underestimated.

Results of Regression Analysis

Multivariable linear regression analysis can be used to study the relationship between the various battle parameters—the casualty exchange ratio, the initial force ratio and the duration of the conflict. The notation adopted for the regression analysis is summarized in the following table.

---

[7]The relative combat effectiveness for the Lanchester Linear Law, a'/d', is the reciprocal of the average attacker-to-defender casualty exchange ratio. We have described earlier in some detail the large variance associated with any measure of the casualty exchange ratio. Analogous to the Lanchester Square Law, the Lanchester Linear relative combat efficacy varies greatly across a series of battles between the same attacker and defender. The only method of testing the validity of the Lanchester Linear Law in a cross-sectional analysis of historical data on warfare is to test whether the relative combat effectiveness of a specific attacker-defender pair is reasonably constant across a series of encounters. The constancy of the Lanchester Linear ratio of combat efficacy is not borne out by the data. History is equally hostile to both the Lanchester Linear and Square Laws.

Real variables	
CEXR	Average attacker-to-defender casualty exchange ratio
LCEXR	Natural logarithm of the average attacker-to-defender casualty exchange ratio
IFR	Initial attacker-to-defender force ratio
LIFR	Natural logarithm of the initial attacker-to-defender force ratio
DUR	Duration of the battle in days
AVGATTLOSS	Attacker's average daily percentage attrition
AVGDEFLOSS	Defender's average daily percentage attrition
WDWL	Total defender withdrawal in the encounter (km)
	Negative for an attacker repulse or a defensive counterattack
WDWLPERDAY	Defender's average withdrawal per day (km/day)

Dummy variables		
SURPRISE	-1	for the offense surprising the defense
	0	for no surprise on either side
	1	for the defense surprising the offense
OUTCOME	0	Attacker victory
	1	Stalemate
	2	Defender victory

The following set of dummy variables captures the identity of the attacker-defender pair for each engagement. Each dummy is referenced to the base case of a US onslaught on Germany, US/GER, and takes on the values 0 and 1. As an example, when the dummy variable BRIT/GER equals 1, the particular battle is a British attack on German forces. The default scenario of a US attack on Germany is triggered when all the dummy variables are zero. In our regression analysis, the attacker/defender dummies occur as explanatory variables only, that is they always appear on the x or right hand side of the regression equation. The coefficient of a particular dummy, such as BRIT/GER, indicates the change in the variable being explained or the y variable that would occur if all other parameters remaining the same, the attacker-defender pair were switched from US-Germany to Britain-Germany. In other words, the change in the y variable is always measured relative to the US/GER base scenario.

BRIT/GER	Britain attacking Germany
EGY/IS	Egypt attacking Israel
GER/BRIT	Germany attacking Britain
GER/FR	Germany attacking France
GER/US	Germany attacking the US
GER/USSR	Germany attacking the USSR
IS/EGY	Israel attacking Egypt
IS/IRQ	Israel attacking Iraq
IS/JOR	Israel attacking Jordan
IS/SYR	Israel attacking Syria
JAP/USSR	Japan attacking the USSR
JOR/IS	Jordan attacking Israel
SYR/IS	Syria attacking Israel
US/NK	US attacking North Korea
USSR/GER	USSR attacking Germany
USSR/JAP	USSR attacking Japan

The foremost issue to be addressed through the regression analysis is to determine how the outcome of war is governed by the various inputs that feed into the battle dynamic. There are two statistically viable manifestations of battle outcome: the average attacker-to-defender casualty exchange ratio and the total withdrawal of the defender. Each is analyzed in turn. In the first part of the regression analysis, we treat the attacker-to-defender casualty exchange ratio as a proxy for the outcome of battle for statistical purposes and attempt to discover what factors determine the observed values of the casualty exchange ratio. Regressions V, VI and VII replace the casualty exchange ratio with the withdrawal of the defender in kilometers as a proxy for battle outcome and conduct an inductive regression analysis analogous to the one performed on the casualty exchange ratio in Regressions I through IV. Regression VIII examines the relationship between battle duration and the initial force ratio. Regressions IX and X study the correlation between the average daily percentage attrition of the attacker and the defender on the one hand and the average daily withdrawal of the defense on the other.

Several dozen regressions were performed in compiling this analysis. The 10 regressions selected for examination and presented below are not the only ones that are worthy of dissection. The Concepts Analysis Agency Database has records for numerous other variables such as terrain features, defense preparation, tactical maneuvering of attacking forces, weapon density, front length and weather that are completely excluded from our analysis. These variables can be incorporated into the analysis in various ways. As an example all attrition and initial force calculations used in this study are based on the numbers of attacking and defending personnel. An alternative strategy would be to measure attrition and force parameters in terms of the number of tanks on the two sides. In no way is it implied that the following analysis is definitive or sufficient; interested readers are implored to undertake their own studies of the data base based on their perceptions and expectations of the relationships enduring between parameters in war.

Of fundamental significance in military doctrine is the admonition to strive for a local numerical superiority of forces at every focus of conflict with the enemy. Implicit in this philosophy is the belief that the greater the amount by which the initial imbalance favors one side, the more devastating is the defeat of its enemy. This "strength in numbers" hypothesis can be tested by regressing the logarithm of the casualty exchange ratio against the logarithm of the initial force ratio.

Regression I					
No. of observations 185		*Degrees of freedom* 183		*R-squared* 0.1312	
LCEXR	=	-0.5052	1.1708	CONSTANT	INSIG
		0.6996	0.1331	LIFR	SIG

The interpretation of our regression is fairly straightforward. The y variable (or independent variable) under analysis is indicated to the left of the equal sign while the explanatory x variables are listed in the third column to its right. The first number in each row is the regression coefficient of the particular x variable. The next number is the standard error associated with the coefficient. The last column shows whether the regression coefficient is significant or insignificant in explaining the observed variance of the ordinate. Significance is calculated by comparison with a 2-sided t-statistic at the 95 percent confidence level. The x variable CONSTANT is the y-axis intercept of the regression line or hyperplane. Hence the above regression should be read as:

LCEXR = -0.5052 + 0.6996*LIFR

or employing our earlier notation:

ln Ψ = -0.5052 + 0.6996*ln Γ

Raising the base of natural logarithms, e, to each side:

$\Psi = 0.6034*(\Gamma)^{0.6996} \approx 0.6*(\Gamma)^{0.7}$

For each defender killed, the aggressor suffers a higher number of casualties the greater the attacker's initial force superiority. This is hardly an encouraging conclusion for believers in the superiority of numbers. One complication might be that historically commanders have been inept in the utilization of excess manpower; they might fail to commit more than a certain quantity of forces to the battlefield holding the excess firepower in reserve behind the Forward Line of Own Troops (FLOT) or distribute the extra divisions along the periphery of the Forward Edge of Battle Area (FEBA) where shoddy intelligence and command and control might render the additional forces ineffective in engaging the antagonist while exposing them to enemy artillery and close air support bombardment. One possibility for tackling this issue is to restrict the regression to battles involving an attacker whose military capability is highly respected and discern whether our super-intelligent aggressor is more effective than its contemporary counterparts in the utilization of force. Fortunately Israel's attacks on Egypt, Iraq, Jordan and Syria seem to fall within this category of military acumen, and Regression II repeats the analysis of our earlier regression for this limited subset.

Regression II						
No. of observations	46	Degrees of freedom		44	R-squared	0.0137
LCEXR	=	-0.9655	1.0907		CONSTANT	INSIG
		-0.2536	0.3243		LIFR	INSIG

The equation relating Ψ and Γ for Israeli onslaughts is:

$\Psi = 0.3808*(\Gamma)^{-0.2536} \approx 0.4*(\Gamma)^{-0.25}$

The negative sign in the exponent indicates that the casualty exchange ratio falls with increasing initial strength of the attacker, restoring our confidence at least in Israeli military capability if not also in the concept of superiority of numbers. However the results are statistically insignificant because of the small sample size. Of the 185 battles available for Regression I, only 46 were initiated by Israel and the sharp reduction in data points lowers the R-squared statistic.

To understand further what determines the casualty exchange ratio, in Regression III we regress LCEXR against front displacement, the identity of the attacker-defender pair, LIFR, surprise and the battle outcome.

Regression III				
No. of observations 160		*Degrees of freedom* 143	*R-squared* 0.5207	
LCEXR	= -0.1234	0.8705	CONSTANT	INSIG
	-0.00448	0.00121	WDWL	SIG
	1.00907	0.232	BRIT/GER	SIG
	1.0959	0.4046	EGY/IS	SIG
	0.1282	0.3226	GER/BRIT	INSIG
	1.0014	0.3726	GER/US	SIG
	-1.199	0.4151	GER/USSR	SIG
	-0.8264	0.2901	IS/EGY	SIG
	0.1153	0.3846	IS/JOR	INSIG
	-0.7278	0.3418	IS/SYR	SIG
	1.5439	0.8877	JOR/IS	INSIG
	1.1459	0.4368	SYR/IS	SIG
	-2.9952	0.6361	US/NK	SIG
	0.9361	0.2568	USSR/GER	SIG
	0.04238	0.1501	LIFR	INSIG
	0.3718	0.2095	SURPRISE	INSIG
	0.08161	0.1394	OUTCOME	INSIG

The R-squared of 0.52 in Regression III indicates that 52 percent of the total variation in the exchange ratio can be explained by a handful of variables. This in itself is an impressive result when one considers the plethora of variables that are unaccounted for in our simple regression such as type of terrain, defense condition and tactical maneuvering of the attacking contingent. In a cross-sectional analysis the exchange ratio is negatively correlated with defense withdrawal; battles that involve defensive retreats display a lower number of attackers killed per defender killed. The relinquishment of territory by the defender has historically rewarded the aggressor with a lower exchange ratio. It is puzzling that tactical surprise achieved by either side at the commencement of hostilities plays no role in defining the exchange ratio; the coefficient for surprise is insignificant in the regression equation. The initial force ratio is also insignificant in explaining the attrition relationship prevailing on the battlefield. We are led to suspect that the majority of the explanatory power of our model for the exchange ratio is contained in the identity of the offense and defense. We confirm this conclusion through Regression IV, which regresses LCEXR solely against the attacker-defender dummies.

Regression IV				
No. of observations	185	Degrees of freedom	168	R-squared 0.4772

LCEXR	=	-0.1077	0.9478	CONSTANT	INSIG
		0.965	0.2472	BRIT/GER	SIG
		1.082	0.41	EGY/IS	SIG
		0.3155	0.3289	GER/BRIT	INSIG
		-1.7249	0.9574	GER/FR	INSIG
		0.8235	0.3437	GER/US	SIG
		-1.6494	0.41	GER/USSR	SIG
		-1.0332	0.2362	IS/EGY	SIG
		-0.5854	0.9575	IS/IRQ	INSIG
		-0.01807	0.3614	IS/JOR	INSIG
		-1.1098	0.2957	IS/SYR	SIG
		-0.5684	0.9575	JAP/USSR	INSIG
		1.6118	0.9575	JOR/IS	INSIG
		0.5894	0.3614	SYR/IS	INSIG
		-2.8537	0.5637	US/NK	SIG
		0.5027	0.2432	USSR/GER	SIG
		1.8921	0.6838	USSR/JAP	SIG

The 0.48 R-squared in Regression IV establishes the overwhelming importance of the identity of the aggressor and defender in governing the relative attrition on the battlefield. Hidden in this identity label are parameters such as systematic national discrepancies in troop training, morale, command dexterity, group cohesiveness and tenacity, weapon quality and employment, force organization, command, control, communication and intelligence structures and chauvinistic fervor, all of which are peculiarities of a state's military, political and social infrastructure and enter our regression equation through the attacker-defender dummy variables. In interpreting these regression equations, it must be realized that all changes are measured relative to the base case of a U.S. onslaught on Germany. For example, in Regression IV the 0.965 coefficient of BRIT/GER denotes that the natural logarithm of the exchange ratio would increase by 0.965 if Britain replaced the United States as the instigator of the attack on Germany. With reference to predictive power, the predominant dependence of the casualty exchange ratio on the identity of the combatants is disappointing. It is impossible to venture an extrapolation for the exchange ratio in a conflict between two nations who have not previously engaged each other in battle. More specifically, the regression equation offered no *a priori* estimate for the exchange ratio likely to prevail in a contemporary war situation such as the U.S. onslaught on Iraq in January 1991 since there had been no previous encounters between these two forces.

The casualty exchange ratio is only one proxy for the outcome of war. As mentioned earlier, an equally valid measure of the result of an individual engagement is the displacement of the front between the two warring entities. We begin by regressing withdrawal against the logarithm of the initial force ratio. Our expectation is that the defender's withdrawal should mount with increasing initial superiority of the attacker.

Regression V					
No. of observations	*174*	*Degrees of freedom*	*172*	*R-squared*	*0.000127*
WDWL	=	23.853	65.464	CONSTANT	INSIG
		-1.1344	7.6596	LIFR	INSIG

The 0.00 R-squared statistic of Regression V lays to rest any hopes of correlation between the initial force ratio and the withdrawal of the defender. Whatever determines the defender's abandonment of ground, it definitely is not the initial superiority of the aggressor. Undeterred by our initial lack of success in explaining front movement, we regress WDWL against the entire universe of variables in the hope of maximizing the R-squared.

Regression VI					
No. of observations	*171*	*Degrees of freedom*	*154*	*R-squared*	*0.3498*
WDWL	=	11.4965	55.7502	CONSTANT	INSIG
		-18.2259	4.8465	LCEXR	SIG
		15.2652	15.5981	BRIT/GER	INSIG
		20.8399	25.4972	EGY/IS	INSIG
		-0.9768	19.7179	GER/BRIT	INSIG
		12.2628	21.2869	GER/US	INSIG
		42.688	26.786	GER/USSR	INSIG
		-9.8571	18.1438	IS/EGY	INSIG
		1.0872	24.3978	IS/JOR	INSIG
		-24.545	20.036	IS/SYR	INSIG
		16.2947	57.2326	JOR/IS	INSIG
		18.6004	27.1748	SYR/IS	INSIG
		-58.2081	36.7082	US/NK	INSIG
		109.1754	14.5955	USSR/GER	SIG
		26.6319	41.2834	USSR/JAP	INSIG
		-8.5046	8.6149	LIFR	INSIG
		2.0267	13.2359	SURPRISE	INSIG

The parameter OUTCOME in Regression VI is excluded from the regression since the defender's withdrawal is in almost one-to-one correspondence with the consequence of the battle as expressed in the variable OUTCOME, and it is ineffectual to regress one proxy for the result against another. The 0.35 R-squared indicates that we have overcome over a third of the resistance in explaining withdrawal. However the majority of the regression coefficients in Regression VI are insignificantly different from zero. As pointed out above, withdrawal is negatively correlated with the exchange ratio. Historically, battles characterized by large cessions of territory by the defense are associated with lower attacker-to-defender exchange ratios.

It is conceivable that like its predecessor, the exchange ratio, withdrawal is also substantially determined by the nationality of the offense and defense engaged in combat. Regression VII confirms this conjecture.

Regression VII				
No. of observations 174		*Degrees of freedom 157*	*R-squared 0.2862*	
WDWL	=	6.6122	57.8933	CONSTANT	INSIG
		-1.3265	15.0997	BRIT/GER	INSIG
		-3.9456	25.0401	EGY/IS	INSIG
		-3.7122	20.0889	GER/BRIT	INSIG
		3.3878	58.481	GER/FR	INSIG
		-0.9456	20.9953	GER/US	INSIG
		80.8878	25.0401	GER/USSR	SIG
		17.7211	15.9563	IS/EGY	INSIG
		-1.6122	58.481	IS/IRQ	INSIG
		3.3878	25.0401	IS/JOR	INSIG
		2.8044	18.6468	IS/SYR	INSIG
		-5.6122	58.481	JAP/USSR	INSIG
		-6.6122	58.481	JOR/IS	INSIG
		-3.4456	25.0401	SYR/IS	INSIG
		1.3878	34.4327	US/NK	INSIG
		98.4787	14.8576	USSR/GER	SIG
		-6.1122	41.7638	USSR/JAP	INSIG

Despite the R-squared of 0.29, in Regression VII, the glaring lack of statistical significance on the right side of the regression equation undermines the suitability of withdrawal as a proxy for battle outcome. From a narrow statistical viewpoint, the exchange ratio outweighs kilometers withdrawn as a quantization of the unfolding of events on the battlefield.

So far we have not sought to relate the duration of the conflict to the initial force imbalance prevailing on the battlefield. Regression VIII rectifies this omission.

Regression VIII				
No. of observations 185		*Degrees of freedom 183*	*R-squared 0.000054*	
DUR	=	4.0375	6.849	CONSTANT	INSIG
		-0.07779	0.7787	LIFR	INSIG

If the length of the battle is a function of the initial force ratio, there is little historical evidence to substantiate this claim. However it must be noted that the Concepts Analysis Agency Database offers no explanation of how the battle time variable, DUR, was derived; in almost all the engagements under evaluation, fighting was hardly a round-the-clock affair and only a limited portion of each day was devoted to actual hostilities and exchange of fire. The compilers of the Concepts Analysis Agency Database appear to have measured duration as the total number of days involving any form of interaction between the sides rather than the actual combat hours, leaving the problem of what determines battle duration unresolved.[8]

Finally, Regressions IX and X probe the correlation between average daily withdrawal by the defender and average daily attacker and defender percentage attrition.

Regression IX				
No. of observations 174		*Degrees of freedom* 172	*R-squared* 0.009129	
AVGATTLOSS	=	0.01794	0.01833	CONSTANT	INSIG
		-0.000227	0.00018	WDWLPERDAY	INSIG

Regression X				
No. of observations 174		*Degrees of freedom* 172	*R-squared* 0.1673	
AVGDEFLOSS	=	0.0238	0.0416	CONSTANT	INSIG
		0.002406	0.000409	WDWLPERDAY	SIG

Front displacement per day displays no connection with the attacker's percentage loss of forces each day. Conversely, there is a strong positive correlation between withdrawal and defensive percentage attrition on a day-to-day basis. Battles with large AVGDEFLOSS values also depict large daily relinquishments of territory by the defense. We are not claiming that the defense exhibits higher percentage attrition on days during which the defensive forces execute large withdrawals. Unfortunately we lack *actual* day-by-day data to substantiate or refute any such conclusion. All we can assert in a cross-sectional analysis is that battles with large *average* defensive force withdrawal per day are generally associated with a higher *average* percentage attrition of defensive lethality per day.

Main Conclusions from Historical Data

Summarized below are the major findings of our statistical analysis of twentieth century warfare as embodied in the Concepts Analysis Agency data:

1. There is no empirical justification for the belief that possessing a greater local preponderance of force allows the numerically superior side to impose higher relative attrition on the quantitatively inferior opponent. One reason for the refutation of the "strength in numbers" hypothesis might be that historically commanders have been inept in the utilization of excess manpower.

2. Israeli *attacks* on Syria, Jordan, Egypt and Iraq do display decreasing attacker-to-defender casualty exchange ratios with increasing Israeli initial force superiority. However the regression coefficients are statistically insignificant.

---

[8]The relationship between battle duration and the logarithm of the initial force ratio may be nonlinear in which case no correlation between the two variables would be identified by the linear regression analysis under consideration. The same point applies in general to all the regressions performed here—the regressions seek to identify linear relationships among variables and perfect nonlinear relationships among parameters would evade detection by the regression analysis.

3. In a cross-sectional analysis the exchange ratio is negatively correlated with defense withdrawal; battles that involve defensive retreats display a lower number of attackers killed per defender killed. The relinquishment of territory by the defender has historically rewarded the aggressor with a lower exchange ratio.

4. The casualty exchange ratio predominantly depends on the identity of the attacker-defender pair. As a consequence, it is impossible to venture an extrapolation for the exchange ratio that would prevail in a conflict between two nations who have not recently engaged each other in battle.

5. Battles with large *average* defensive force withdrawal per day are generally associated with a higher *average* percentage attrition of defensive lethality per day. However in the absence of recorded day-by-day attrition and front displacement data, there is no test that can be performed to determine whether it is higher daily percentage attrition that causes large withdrawals by the defense or whether defenders in retreat are more prone to higher casualty rates. In other words, while we can isolate correlation, we can draw no conclusions regarding causation.

6. Neither the Lanchester Square Law nor the Lanchester Linear Law is validated by a cross-sectional analysis of historical data on warfare. A rigorous test of a combat attrition model requires data on residual forces and front displacement for each day of combat to facilitate a time-series analysis. Such a daily breakdown of information is not provided by the Concepts Analysis Agency Database. Hence we emphasize the weakness of our rejection of the Lanchester Laws.

7. For the 185 most recent battles in the Concept Analysis Agency Database the geometric mean attacker-to-defender casualty exchange ratio is 0.89. The attacker-to-defender casualty exchange ratio lies between 0.26 and 3.09 68 percent of the time.

8. The geometric mean initial force ratio for the entire universe of 185 battles is 1.74. The initial force ratio can be expected to lie between 0.91 and 3.31 for 68 percent of all encounters. If the analysis is restricted to the 55 battles that culminated in attacker victories, the geometric mean initial force ratio employed by the attacker is unchanged from the 1.74 value derived for the entire universe. It is sometimes believed that the aggressor must provide an initial force superiority of 3-to-1 in those sectors where a breakthrough is desired. However the mean initial force ratio for victorious attackers has historically been a measly 1.74, casting some doubt on the empirical validity and applicability of this 3-to-1 rule.

9. The historically observed median values for various battle parameters calculated in this brief statistical analysis can be used to make very rough order-of-magnitude forecasts for critical variables in future conflicts. As a first example, the average daily percentage attrition of the attacker when engaged in combat has a median value of 1 percent while the average daily percentage attrition of the defender has a median of 2 percent. These attrition figures could have been used to estimate the number of casualties the U.S.-led military coalition dispatched to Saudi Arabia in response to the Iraqi invasion of Kuwait could have expected to experience in a full-scale war against Iraq. The United States and its allies had 500,000 soldiers stationed in the Persian Gulf. If the war with Iraq had consisted of 10 encounters each involving 2 days of actual fighting and 10 percent of the total U.S. force complement, a lower end estimate of total U.S. casualties could be 10% x 500,000 x 1% x 2 x 10 = 10,000, while an upper end estimate could be 10% x 500,000 x 2% x 2 x 10 = 20,000. A second example is using the empirically observed attacker-to-defender casualty exchange ratio in battles involving an Israeli

onslaught on Egyptian, Iraqi, Jordanian and Syrian forces to estimate the casualty exchange ratio likely to prevail in a future war between Israel and its Arab neighbors in the Persian Gulf. The median casualty exchange ratio observed in 46 Israeli attacks is 0.38. A starting point for an analysis of Israel's military superiority vis-à-vis its neighbors could be the assumption that Israel can incapacitate 10 enemy soldiers for every 4 Israeli attackers put out of action.

In conclusion, we must reemphasize the incompleteness of the analysis in this appendix; the preceding discussion is only the starting point for a more detailed and comprehensive statistical examination of the Concepts Analysis Agency Database. We have engineered a first cut at some of the most poignant and germane issues in the conduct and nature of war. There remains an abundance of pertinent queries that need to be addressed by any statistical survey of armed conflict in the recent past. The driving impulse throughout the discussion has been to establish a methodology and a language for subsequent examination and inspire the quest for the collection of data that is plenary and complete.

Verifying the Duration and Casualty Exchange Postulates for the Lanchester and Epstein Models

In this appendix we apply our framework for battle duration and casualty exchange to two commonly accepted formulations of the laws of combat. The Lanchester Square Law is the classic maxim of attrition modeling and has lent credence to the use of differential equations in conceptualizing conflict. Our second illustrative application will be to Joshua Epstein's Adaptive Dynamic Equations for combat and withdrawal. We shall demonstrate that both of these popular combat modeling philosophies obey our Duration and Casualty Exchange Postulates. We also include a numerical example employing historical data on battles conducted during and after the Second World War, illustrating how the Lanchester Square Law can be applied to the combat component of the solution to the generalized Defense Positioning Problem.

The Lanchester Square Law of Attrition

Let $R(t)$ and $B(t)$ represent the aggregated firepower or lethality of the two sides in conflict. Let r and b be the combat effectiveness, or force utilization, coefficients of the two antagonists respectively. Then Lanchester Square combat would display the following behavior.

$$\frac{dR}{dt} = -bB$$
$$\frac{dB}{dt} = -rR$$

(1D-1)

The attrition of each side is driven by the force concentration and efficacy of the adversary. The state equation for the Lanchester Square Law is easily derived.

$$\frac{dR}{dB} = \frac{bB}{rR}$$

$$r \int_{R(0)}^{R(t)} R\,dR = b \int_{B(0)}^{B(t)} B\,dB$$

273

where R(0) and B(0) constitute the initial lethalities of the two sides. Performing the indicated integration yields:

$$r\left[R\ (0\ )^2 - R\ (t)^2\right] = b\left[B\ (0\ )^2 - B\ (t)^2\right]$$ **(1D-2)**

For a stalemate R(t) and B(t) must simultaneously approach zero for the same value of t. Thus a stalemate is assured if:

$$rR\ (0\ )^2 = bB\ (0\ )^2$$ **(1D-3)**

We shall assume throughout this discussion that R is the victor of the engagement. This implies:

$$rR\ (0\ )^2 > bB\ (0\ )^2$$ **(1D-4)**

If the annihilation of B is completed in a time period τ, the state equation suggests:

$$rR\ (0\ )^2 - rR\ (\tau)^2 = bB\ (0\ )^2$$

The expression for the residual offensive strength, R(τ), follows immediately.

$$R\ (\tau) = \sqrt{R\ (0\ )^2 - \frac{b}{r}B\ (0\ )^2}$$ **(1D-5)**

The quantity under the square-root sign is positive according to our supposition of R superiority, namely $rR(0)^2 > bB(0)^2$. The fractional residual force, ρ, remaining with R, measured in units of B(0), is determined as:

$$\rho = \frac{R\ (\tau)}{B\ (0\ )} = \sqrt{\frac{R\ (0\ )^2}{B\ (0\ )^2} - \frac{b}{r}}$$ **(1D-6)**

But R(0)/B(0) = γ, the initial attacker-to-defender force ratio. Thus:

$$\rho = \sqrt{\gamma^2 - \frac{b}{r}}$$ **(1D-7)**

and the average casualty exchange ratio for the encounter, ψ, is given by:

$$\psi = \gamma - \rho = \gamma - \sqrt{\gamma^2 - \frac{b}{r}}$$ **(1D-8)**

Let k represent the ratio of R-to-B combat efficiency, implying:

$$k = \frac{r}{b}$$

$$\text{and} \quad \psi = \gamma - \sqrt{\gamma^2 - \frac{1}{k}}$$ **(1D-9)**

ψ will satisfy our Casualty Exchange Postulates provided that

$$1.\ \frac{\partial\psi}{\partial\gamma} < 0 \qquad\qquad 2.\ \frac{\partial^2\psi}{\partial\gamma^2} > 0 \qquad\qquad 3.\ \frac{\partial\psi}{\partial k} < 0$$

Each of the above holds true for the Lanchester Square Law:

$$\frac{\partial \psi}{\partial \gamma} = 1 - \frac{\gamma}{\sqrt{\gamma^2 - \frac{1}{k}}} < 0$$

$$\frac{\partial^2 \psi}{\partial \gamma^2} = \frac{\frac{1}{k}}{\left(\gamma^2 - \frac{1}{k}\right)^{\frac{3}{2}}} > 0$$

$$\frac{\partial \psi}{\partial k} = - \frac{1}{2k^2 \sqrt{\gamma^2 - \frac{1}{k}}} < 0$$

Extracting the duration of the Lanchester Square battle requires the solution of the pair of equations in 1D-1. The solution which is easily verified by substitution into the original system of differential equations is presented below.

$$R(t) = \frac{1}{2}\left[R(0) - \sqrt{\frac{b}{r}} B(0)\right]e^{\sqrt{br}\,t} + \frac{1}{2}\left[R(0) + \sqrt{\frac{b}{r}} B(0)\right]e^{-\sqrt{br}\,t} \qquad \textbf{(1D-10)}$$

$$B(t) = \frac{1}{2}\left[B(0) - \sqrt{\frac{r}{b}} R(0)\right]e^{\sqrt{br}\,t} + \frac{1}{2}\left[B(0) + \sqrt{\frac{r}{b}} R(0)\right]e^{-\sqrt{br}\,t}$$

If the battle results in a stalemate, then $R(0) = \sqrt{b/r}\, B(0)$ and both $R(t)$ and $B(t)$ tend asymptotically to zero as t increases without bound, indicating that the duration of the encounter is infinite. In actuality, no commander can be expected to prosecute the conflict with no hope of victory and with manpower levels that have been attrited to a fraction of initial force strength. Once it is apparent to both combatants that the engagement is destined to result in a stalemate the fighting will stop. We will assume the battle ends when lethality on either side has fallen to 10 percent of its initial value. We can determine the duration of the stalemate battle, τ_s, by setting $B(t) = 0.1B(0)$ at time $t = \tau_s$ in Equation 1D-10. Since the encounter is a stalemate $R(t)$ is also equal to $0.1R(0)$ at $t = \tau_s$.

$$B(\tau_s) = 0.1B(0) = B(0)e^{-\sqrt{br}\,\tau_s} \qquad \textbf{(1D-11)}$$

$$\tau_s = \frac{1}{\sqrt{br}} \ln(10)$$

For an engagement where R is the eventual victor the battle length is the time required to exterminate B. In symbolic terms $B(t) = 0$ at $t = \tau$. From Equation 1D-10:

$$\left[B(0) - \sqrt{\frac{r}{b}} R(0)\right]e^{\sqrt{br}\,\tau} + \left[B(0) + \sqrt{\frac{r}{b}} R(0)\right]e^{-\sqrt{br}\,\tau} = 0$$

$$\text{Thus}\quad e^{2\sqrt{br}\,\tau} = \left[\frac{\sqrt{\frac{r}{b}} R(0) + B(0)}{\sqrt{\frac{r}{b}} R(0) - B(0)}\right] \qquad \textbf{(1D-12)}$$

$$\text{and}\quad \tau = \frac{1}{2\sqrt{br}} \ln\left[\frac{\sqrt{r}\, R(0) + \sqrt{b}\, B(0)}{\sqrt{r}\, R(0) - \sqrt{b}\, B(0)}\right]$$

Replacing $R(0)/B(0)$ with γ and r/b with k yields:

$$\textbf{(1D-13)}$$

$$\tau = \frac{1}{2\sqrt{br}} \ln\left[\frac{\sqrt{k}\,\gamma + 1}{\sqrt{k}\,\gamma - 1}\right]$$

Satisfying our Duration Postulates requires:

$$1. \frac{\partial \tau}{\partial \gamma} < 0 \qquad\qquad 2. \frac{\partial^2 \tau}{\partial \gamma^2} > 0$$

$$3. \frac{\partial \tau}{\partial k} < 0, \frac{\partial \tau_s}{\partial k} < 0$$

The first two postulates are directly verified by performing the indicated differentiations.

$$\frac{\partial \tau}{\partial \gamma} = - \frac{\sqrt{k}}{\sqrt{br}\,(k\gamma^2 - 1)} < 0$$

$$\frac{\partial^2 \tau}{\partial \gamma^2} = \frac{2k^{\frac{3}{2}}\gamma}{\sqrt{br}\,(k\gamma^2 - 1)^2} > 0$$

Proving the applicability of the third duration postulate is facilitated by holding the combat effectiveness of the opponent that is eventually defeated, b, constant and assuming that any increases in relative effectiveness, k, arise through improvements in r. This supposition permits us to replace $\sqrt{br}$ in the denominator of the expression for τ enunciated in Equation 1D-13 with $b\sqrt{k}$, and we may now take the partial derivative of τ with respect to k:

$$\tau = \frac{1}{2b\sqrt{k}} \ln\left[\frac{\sqrt{k}\,\gamma + 1}{\sqrt{k}\,\gamma - 1} \right]$$

$$\frac{\partial \tau}{\partial k} = - \frac{\gamma}{2bk\,(k\gamma^2 - 1)} - \frac{1}{4bk^{\frac{3}{2}}} \ln\left[\frac{\sqrt{k}\,\gamma + 1}{\sqrt{k}\,\gamma - 1} \right] < 0$$

Similarly for the duration of the stalemate encounter, τ_s:

$$\tau_s = \frac{1}{b\sqrt{k}} \ln(10)$$

$$\frac{\partial \tau_s}{\partial k} = - \frac{\ln(10)}{2bk\sqrt{k}} < 0$$

Figures 1D-1 and 1D-2 display the casualty exchange ratio and the duration of the battle as functions of the initial force ratio for Lanchester Square combat. The diagrams plot ψ and τ for several values of relative effectiveness, k.

Let us work through a numerical example to illustrate how the Lanchester Square Law equations can be used to calculate the duration of individual encounters, τ, between the offense and the defense and the residual force of the attacker at the termination of each engagement, $R(\tau)$. We shall model the response of a 10-constrained 10-unit defense confronted with a concentrated invading spearhead of 10 units focused at one extremity of the length-M front. The estimation of τ and $R(\tau)$ necessitates the assignment of values to the combat effectiveness coefficients of the two sides, b and r. While there are no prototypical values of b and r that emerge from a statistical analysis of data on contemporary battles or that are generally accepted in the realm of combat modeling, we can calculate very approximately what the mean values of b and r have been for battles fought during and after the Second World War. We shall assume our attacker and defender utilize force as effectively as the average offense and defense in contemporary warfare. We begin by calculating the statistical mean of the historically observed values for b and r.

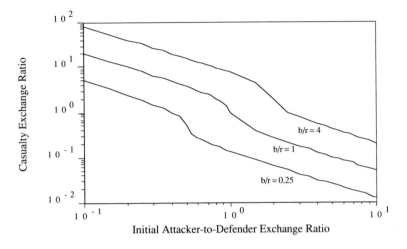

Figure 1D-1   Lanchester Square Casualty Exchange Ratio

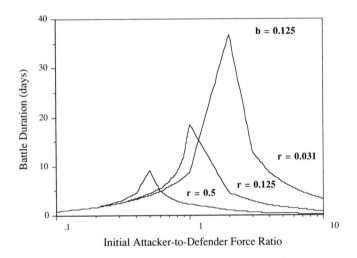

Figure 1D-2   Lanchester Square Battle Duration

Example: The Concepts Analysis Agency of the U.S. Army has compiled a data base on battles conducted in the twentieth century. For the 185 battles in the data base that occurred during or after World War II, we can estimate very roughly the defender's force utilization efficacy, b_i, for each individual engagement i using the formula:

$$b_i = \frac{A_i(0) - A_i(\tau)}{\tau_i \left[\dfrac{D_i(0) + D_i(\tau)}{2} \right]}$$

where $A_i(0)$ and $D_i(0)$ are the initial personnel strengths of the attacker and the defender, τ_i is the length of the particular encounter in days and $A_i(\tau)$ and $D_i(\tau)$ are the residual offensive and defensive strengths at the conclusion of the engagement. Since b is a ratio, the geometric mean, $\hat{b}$, is an appropriate estimator of centrality for the distribution of b.

$$\hat{b} = \left(\prod_{i=1}^{185} b_i \right)^{\frac{1}{185}}$$

The identical procedure can be used for determining a historical average for r. A gross approximation of r_i for each individual battle is:

$$r_i = \frac{D_i(0) - D_i(\tau)}{\tau_i \left[\dfrac{A_i(0) + A_i(\tau)}{2} \right]}$$

and the geometric mean, $\hat{r}$, is given as:

$$\hat{r} = \left(\prod_{i=1}^{185} r_i \right)^{\frac{1}{185}}$$

Performing the indicated computations on the engagements in the Concepts Analysis Agency Database, we arrive at the following historical averages for defense and offense effectiveness.

$\hat{b} = 0.0126$ attackers killed per defender per day[1]

$\hat{r} = 0.020039$ defenders killed per attacker per day

In other words, for every hundred defending personnel the prototypical attacker lost 1.26 men each day of active combat while the typical defender lost 2.00 men per day of battle for every hundred attacking personnel.

Let us use these historically determined values of b and r to model a conflict between a defender and an attacker each armed with 10 units of force. The defender opts for a fully forward, 10-constrained force structure while the attacker concentrates all 10 offensive units at a single focus of penetration. Each defending force unit individually engages the invading force concentration as the unit arrives at the scene of the battle. Therefore B(0) = 1 for each individual engagement between the two sides. The aggressor will have no respite between encounters with the defensive echelons if the defense fulfills the Duration Condition. We can use our formulae for the Lanchester Square Law to calculate the duration of each encounter and the residual force of the attacker at the conclusion of each engagement. For the first entanglement with the protecting forces, the attacker's initial force strength is 10. For each succeeding battle, the invader's initial manpower is exactly equal to the residual strength

---

[1]We have chosen to calculate the combat effectiveness coefficients in terms of personnel. The Concepts Analysis Agency Database also contains data on tank attrition, and thus another valid measure of combat effectiveness that could be calculated is the ratio of attacking tanks destroyed per defending tank per day.

remaining at the termination of the previous encounter. The defender always dispatches one unit to each engagement. All that remains to be determined is combat efficacy on either side. Hypothesizing a R and a B force whose combat effectiveness is the statistical average of the attacking and defending armies of the twentieth century, we assign to our invader the geometric mean combat efficiency, $\hat{r}$, and to our defender the corresponding mean combat efficiency, $\hat{b}$. We are now in a position to use Equations 1D-5 and 1D-12 to compile the following table.

Encounter	$R(0)$	$R(\tau)$	τ in days
1	10	9.9685	5.0008
2	9.9202	9.9369	5.0166
3	9.8397	9.9052	5.0326
4	9.7585	9.8734	5.0488
5	9.6767	9.8416	5.0651
6	9.5942	9.8096	5.0816
7	9.5109	9.7775	5.0983
8	9.4269	9.7452	5.1151
9	9.3422	9.7129	5.1321
10	9.2567	9.6805	5.1492

The first column in the table indexes the sequence of successive encounters between the offensive force concentration and the solitary defending units. The second column tabulates the attacker's strength that is brought to bear on the battlefield at the start of each engagement. The third column displays the residual force strength remaining with the aggressor at the end of the particular entanglement. The fourth column is the duration of each Lanchesterian battle in days.

It should be a matter of some consternation to the defender that even if the Duration Condition were fulfilled, the invader has a residual lethality of 9.1704 units available for conquering the defender's home terrain after the last defending unit has been annihilated. This violation of parity is a consequence of the application of the Lanchester Square Law. The Square Law is a panegyric to the virtues of concentration of force; it rewards the quantitatively superior opponent in proportion to the square of its numerical advantage. Consequently, if two sides each with 10 units engage in battle with all units simultaneously, the outcome is a stalemate, assuming identical combat efficacies for the two antagonists. However if the 10 force units of one side function in unison while the other side dispatches only fragments of its force strength to each individual conflict, the local superiority enjoyed by the first side will be rewarded by the Lanchester Square Law and after the last battle has ended, the more concentrated opponent will have a residual force left standing on the battlefield. Besides, in this particular example $\hat{r}$ exceeds $\hat{b}$ by 59 percent, contributing significantly to the inexpensive demise of the side with lower combat efficacy.

The Adaptive Dynamic Model

We now turn to an examination of Epstein's Adaptive Dynamic Model of combat.[2] Epstein's model is implemented as a system of discrete difference equations with step size governed by the time unit used to measure the length of the conflict. Intrinsic to Epstein's conceptualization is the attacker-to-defender exchange ratio per time period, ρ. ρ specifies in each time period the quantum of attacking lethality destroyed per unit of defender lethality exterminated. We adopt the form $\rho = \sqrt{D/A}$ to simulate the benefit of lower relative casualties accruing to the numerically superior force. Epstein's extended model itself does not impose any specific formulation or behavior on the exchange ratio and is a generalization and extension of the Lanchester Square Law and the Lanchester theory of attrition modeling through differential equations. By our choice of values for ρ we are inducing the model output to obey our Casualty Exchange Postulates. To discover how the battle duration and the average attacker-to-defender casualty exchange ratio as determined by the Adaptive Dynamic Model are related to the initial attacker-to-defender force ratio, we "run" the Epstein model with the following inputs.

The unit time period for the simulation is a day.

$$\left.\begin{array}{l} \rho[n] = \dfrac{D[n]^{\lambda_d[n]}}{A[n]^{\lambda_a[n]}} \\[2ex] \lambda_d[n] = \lambda_a[n] = 0.5 \; \forall \; n \end{array}\right\} \quad \text{Exchange Ratio in time period } n.$$

$\alpha_g[0] = 0.05$ Attacker's initial ground prosecution rate.
Unit: Percentage attacker attrition per time period.

$\alpha_{AT} = 0.05$ Attacker's threshold attrition.
Unit: Percentage attacker attrition per time period.

$\alpha_{DT} = 1.00$ Defender's threshold attrition.
Defender does not withdraw under any circumstances.

ACAS = 0   Attacker's close air support.

DCAS = 0   Defender's close air support.
Airpower is zero; only ground units are involved.

We now vary the initial attacker-to-defender force ratio, $\gamma = A[0]/D[0]$, and determine the duration of the engagement, τ, and the average casualty exchange ratio, ψ, for each choice of γ. ψ differs from the Epsteinian exchange ratio, ρ; ψ is the total number of attackers killed in an encounter divided by the total number of defenders incapacitated while ρ is the daily relative attrition. Thus if the battle lasts for a total of N days with $\Delta A[1], \Delta A[2], ..., \Delta A[n], ..., \Delta A[N]$ the attacker's casualties on successive days and $\Delta D[1], \Delta D[2], ..., \Delta D[n], ..., \Delta D[N]$ the corresponding lethrality losses of the defender on successive days, then

$$\rho[1] = \frac{\Delta A[1]}{\Delta D[1]} \quad \rho[2] = \frac{\Delta A[2]}{\Delta D[2]} \quad ... \quad \rho[n] = \frac{\Delta A[n]}{\Delta D[n]} \quad ... \quad \rho[N] = \frac{\Delta A[N]}{\Delta D[N]}$$

---

[2]Joshua M. Epstein, *The Calculus of Conventional War: Dynamic Analysis without Lanchester Theory* (Brookings, 1985). An extended version of the model is described in Epstein, "The 3:1 Rule, the Adaptive Dynamic Model, and the Future of Security Studies," *International Security*, vol. 13 (Spring 1989), p. 90.

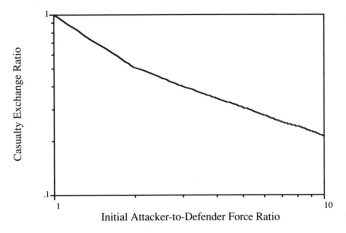

Figure 1D-3   Adaptive Dynamic Model Casualty Exchange Ratio

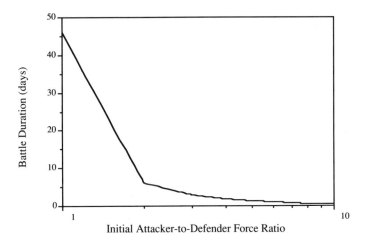

Figure 1D-4   Adaptive Dynamic Model Battle Duration

while

$$\psi = \frac{\Delta A[1] + \Delta A[2] + ... + \Delta A[n] + ... + \Delta A[N]}{\Delta D[1] + \Delta D[2] + ... + \Delta D[n] + ... + \Delta D[N]}$$

and there is no simple formula relating ψ and the $\rho[n]$.

Figures 1D-3 and 1D-4 graph the average casualty exchange ratio and the battle duration as functions of the initial force ratio as determined by the Adaptive Dynamic

Model. It is evident from the shape and slope of the curves that Epstein's model is in concordance with our Duration and Casualty Exchange Postulates.

In conclusion it has been demonstrated that the Duration and Casualty Exchange Postulates hold for both the Lanchester Square Law and the Adaptive Dynamic Model. Both these commonly accepted formulations of the laws of attrition may thus be used to determine battle duration and the average casualty exchange ratio as a function of the initial force ratio, and the τ and ψ curves thus generated may be used to simulate the response of a dispersed defense to various plans of attack.

A Graphical Demonstration of the Superiority of Cascade Interconnection

THEOREM: *It is always desirable to interconnect passive defense systems in cascade as opposed to a parallel implementation. Cascade interconnections annihilate a higher proportion of the incoming attackers when compared with linking the modules side by side in parallel.*

Demonstration: We shall "demonstrate" the truth of the theorem for the case of *two* independent defense modules. Using the notation established in Part Two, there are four dimensions of choice available to the system designer:

1. The total interceptor-to-attacker ratio, I:A. This can range from low (I:A = 1:10) through medium (I:A = 1:1) to high (I:A = 10:1).

2. The division of the total interceptor load, I, between the constituent subsystems, $I_1 : I_2$. While this division is immaterial for the parallel implementation, it might be a significant decision parameter for the interconnection in series. A reasonable range for $I_1 : I_2$ could be from 1:10 to 10:1. The former would heavily backload the passive defense, saving the heaviest bombardment for the second subsystem, while the latter would frontload the passive defense, with the brunt of the chore of dispatching the interceptive volley falling upon the first module.

3. The single shot kill probability, p, which we are constraining to be the same for both defense modules. This identity requirement is reasonable since the problem we are trying to resolve is whether a total defending interceptor contingent of I should be launched simultaneously at an invading force or should be split into two modules of interception strength I_1 and I_2, which launch their onslaught in succession. Thus there is no rationale for distinguishing with respect to p across the two subsystems. We shall consider the effects of p for two extreme values, p = 0.1 and p = 0.9. The smooth continuity of behavior displayed by the basic passive defense equation as revealed by Figures 2-1 and 2-2 of Part Two permits us to restrict our analysis to two limiting bounds for p; if our proposition holds for both extremes, we can be confident in asserting the truth of our theorem for all intermediate values of p as well.

4. The detection capability, D, of the surveillance network of the defense. In conformity with our assumptions regarding p, we constrain our analysis to two extreme values for D, namely D = 0.1 and D = 0.9.

The figures below plot the number of attackers that survive the parallel implementation, S, and each stage of the cascade interconnection, S_1 and S_2, as a function of the division ratio, $I_1:I_2$, in proportion to which the interceptor load is split between the two subsystems. The graphs are constructed for three distinct scenarios of total interception capacity: LO I:A = 1:10, MED I:A = 1:1 and HI I:A = 10:1. Each individual I:A scenario itself involves four possibilities for p and D: LO-LO p = 0.1 D = 0.1, LO-HI p = 0.1 D = 0.9, HI-LO p = 0.9 D = 0.1 and HI-HI p = 0.9 and D = 0.9. When constructing the curves the total number of attacking bodies, A, is normalized to 100 as before. Note the different scales and ranges used for the y-axis and the logarithmic scale employed for the x-axis.

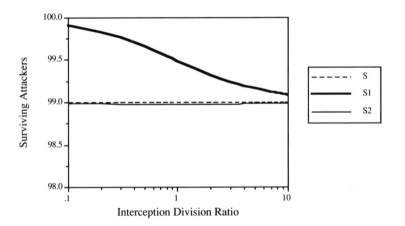

Figure 2A-1   LO-LO-LO I:A = 1:10 p = 0.1 D = 0.1

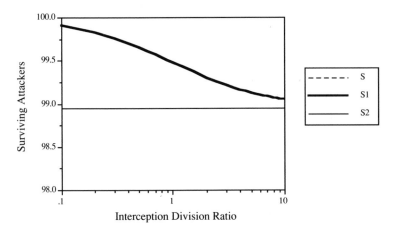

Figure 2A-2   LO-LO-HI I:A = 1:10 p = 0.1 D = 0.9

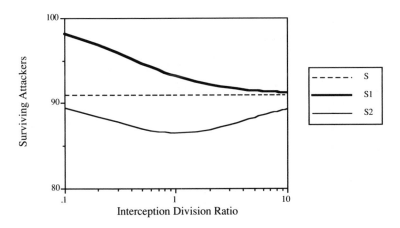

Figure 2A-3   LO-HI-LO I:A = 1:10 p = 0.9 D = 0.1

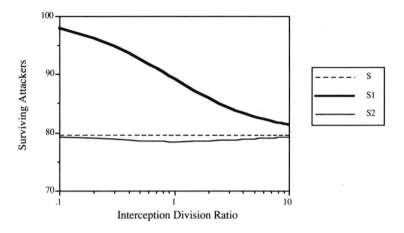

Figure 2A-4   LO-HI-HI I:A = 1:10 p = 0.9 D = 0.9

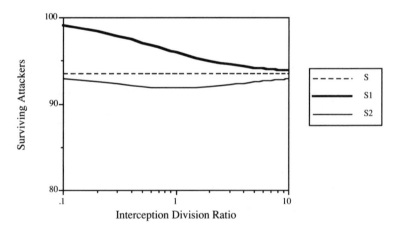

Figure 2A-5   MED-LO-LO I:A = 1:1 p = 0.1 D = 0.1

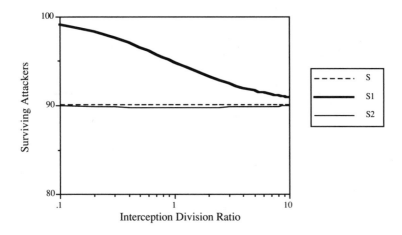

Figure 2A-6   MED-LO-HI I:A = 1:1 p = 0.1 D = 0.9

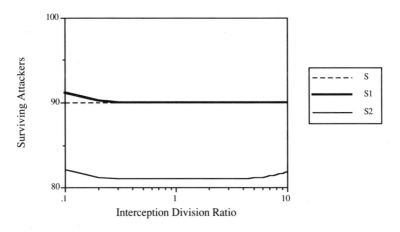

Figure 2A-7   MED-HI-LO I:A = 1:1 p = 0.9 D = 0.1

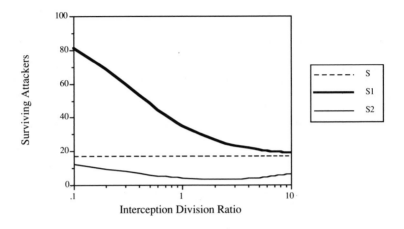

Figure 2A-8   MED-HI-HI I:A = 1:1 P = 0.9 D = 0.9

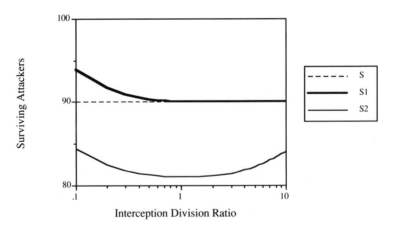

Figure 2A-9   HI-LO-LO- I:A = 10:1 P = 0.1 D = 0.1

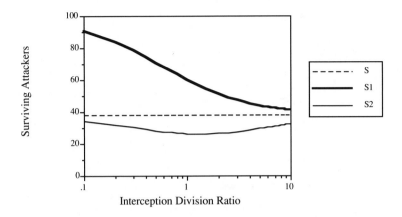

Figure 2A-10   HI-LO-HI I:A = 10:1 P = 0.1 D = 0.9

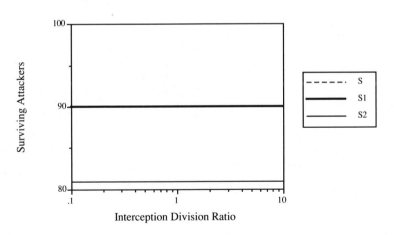

Figure 2A-11   HI-HI-LO I:A = 10:1 P = 0.9 D = 0.1

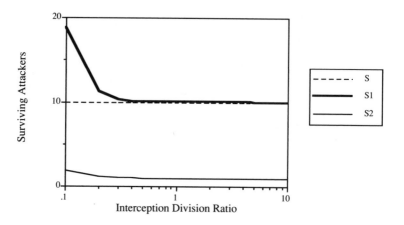

Figure 2A-12   HI-HI-HI I:A = 10:1 P = 0.9 D = 0.9

Our graphic analysis enables us to draw the following conclusions:

1. $S_2 \leq S$ $\forall$ $p, D, I:A$ and $I_1 : I_2$.

It is always preferable to interconnect passive defense systems in cascade. When compared to a parallel implementation, a cascade connection is at least equally efficient in destroying attackers and in most cases offers a higher attrition of the offensive force.

2. Let $S - S_2 = \Delta S$. Then ΔS increases with increasing I:A.

The benefits from a cascade configuration are greater for a larger overall interceptor-to-attacker ratio. Thus the onus on a defense designer confronted with a fixed number of attackers to adopt a cascade system increases with rising deployment levels of the interception vehicle.

3. Defense efficiency is maximized by choosing $I_1 : I_2 = 1$.

To maximize the percentage of intruders annihilated, it is optimal to split the interceptor load equally between the two cascaded passive defense systems.

Why Firepower-to-Space Should Replace Force-to-Space in the Jargon of Force Planning

The literature and discussion on conventional force planning and arms control makes ample use of the term force-to-space ratio or force-to-space density.[1] Historically force-to-space has been used to justify everything from the inescapability of the "Security Dilemma" to the inadvisability of seeking substantial force cuts in Central Europe through arms reduction agreements. Threshold force-to-space densities are used by the RAND Corporation to construct elaborate models of warfare and were invoked by military experts to vindicate NATO's force posture prior to the collapse of the Warsaw Pact. The extremely significant question of whether force-to-space ratios are indeed as intrinsic to the evaluation of conventional force structure as avid force-to-space enthusiasts would have one believe is addressed elsewhere in this study along with exposing what lies hidden behind the rubric of force-to-space. It is doubtful that there is any profundity or intuition buried in the concept of force-to-space, and it is inadvisable to base actual strategic decisions on any unproven and untested rules of thumb. However if writers and discussion groups will continue to treasure the concept of force-to-space, here is a sincere appeal that the term force-to-space be forever replaced by the phrase firepower-to-space.

The fundamental distinction between force-to-space and firepower-to-space can be made explicit through the consideration of a typical war scenario. Consider a concrete example in which Red attacks Blue's forces with 5 distinct units: R_1 and R_2 are forward-deployed short-range attack units, R_3 and R_4 are medium-range follow-on units and R_5 is a long-range combat unit armed with precision-guided missiles. Blue's forces are composed of 10 identical units, each with short-range defense capabilities. Finally, assume that all units, both Red and Blue, can bring to bear identical firepower at their respective range of operation. At the time of the onset of the attack, the forces are deployed as below.

---

[1] See the writings of Barry Posen, Jack Snyder, John J. Mearsheimer, Robert D. Blackwill, Jeffrey Record, and David B. Rivkin, Jr.

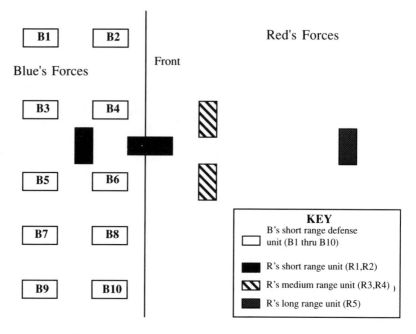

Figure 3A-1   An Example of a Simple Force-to-space Ratio Calculation

The usual aggregated method of calculation (for example using Armored Division Equivalents, ADEs) would credit the Blue defense with having 10 units of firepower x against 5 Red units, and the numbers that would enter an aggregated model framework would be $B_{t=0} = 10x$ and $R_{t=0} = 5x$. However since the Blue units are equipped with relatively short-range weapons, units B_1, B_2, B_7, B_8, B_9 and B_{10} might find themselves out of range of the battle zone. This reduces the effective Blue force to $B_{t=0} = 4x$. Similarly although R_5 ordinarily might not be included as part of the attacking force in this sector, given its large removal from the front, R_5 is the key element of Red's strike force since it is the only element that can strike without being counterattacked in retaliation. Thus though B has a greater physical force-to-space concentration (10x over the sector area), it is actually R who is achieving a higher firepower concentration per area under battle-field conditions. Nominally B has a 2-to-1 superiority over R in force-to-space ratios, but when the range of individual units is taken into consideration the defender's force-to-space advantage is transformed into a 4-to-5 disadvantage. Even if aggregation schemes take the range of individual combat units into account when assigning effectiveness scores, the heart of the issue is that the range and not simply the presence of a unit on the battlefield determines whether and how it can be used. It is not the physical force-to-space ratio that is of consequence in battle, rather it is the real force-to-space or actual firepower-to-space ratio achieved by all units firing within their ranges that is the

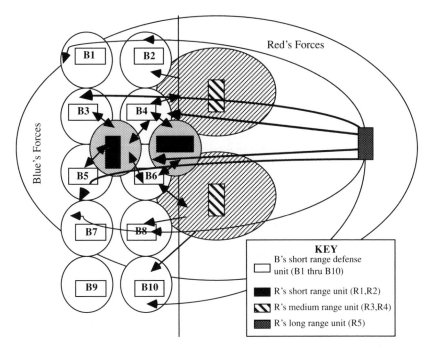

Figure 3A-2   Taking the Range of Individual Units into Consideration in the Calculation of Real Firepower-to-space Ratios. Arrows indicate axes of attack. Circles indicate the range of fire of each unit.

crucial determinant of the course of the conflict.[2] In the above example Blue is at the limit of saturating its physical force-to-space ratio, yet its inappropriate weapon range leaves vast room for improvement in terms of firepower-to-space quotients.

The units B_i and R_i were constituted under the requirement that the weapons composing each unit have a similar range. Thus Figure 3A-1 is transformed into the real force-to-space model depicted in Figure 3A-2 with the circles indicating the range of each

---

[2]The same point is made by Joshua M. Epstein in a slightly different manner in "Dynamic Analysis and the Conventional Balance in Europe," *International Security,* vol. 12 (Spring 1988), p. 161, and in "The 3:1 Rule, the Adaptive Dynamic Model, and the Future of Security Studies," *International Security,* vol. 13 (Spring 1989), p. 123. In the words of Epstein: "...when one posits a 'force-to-space' requirement or constraint, what is 'force'? Is it firing platforms (inputs), or is it delivered fire (output)? Force-to-space rules of thumb are generally insensitive to this distinction, but are usually stated in terms of platforms, or inputs. A rule stated in these (input) terms can be misleading. With long-range guns, precision-guided munitions, mines, and air power, it may be possible to concentrate fire on a given sector of the front while keeping fire sources (platforms) dispersed, producing a high 'force-to-space' ratio in delivered fire with a low 'force-to-space' ratio in firing platforms. One might care far more about the former ratio than the latter. Fortifications, terrain, and terrain enhancement can also affect 'force-to-space' requirements."

unit. Whenever a unit falls within the firing circle of an enemy unit, a barrage of fire might be initiated generating an actual firepower-to-space ratio.

If the practice of basing conventional force calculations and evaluations on measures of the density of firepower generated by either side in a given area of the battlefield is to be continued, it is crucial to consider the order of battle and the range limitations of specific force units on either side in determining real force-to-space ratios. As an example of this approach, it is misleading to assume, as is often done by some experts and modelers, that the maximum stretch of front that can be effectively defended by a division is unchanged since World War II. A myriad of technological revolutions since the late 1940s has radically transformed the machinery of war, and the division of today bears only a nominal resemblance to its counterpart of earlier days. A contemporary force unit is unmatched in range, firepower and precision by any of its predecessors and one has no choice but to recalculate the maximum holding area, if such a concept even exists or is practicable, for standing divisions in service. Hopefully the switch from force-to-space to firepower-to-space in the language of force planning will instill in the minds of defense analysts the critical difference between bean-counting calculations of force-to-space and the actual firepower-to-space ratios attained once combat begins.